RENAISSANCE THOUGHT AND THE ARTS

RENAISSANCE THOUGHT AND THE ARTS

Collected Essays

by

PAUL OSKAR KRISTELLER

An Expanded Edition, with a New Afterword

Princeton University Press

Princeton, New Jersey

To Hans Sarre, as a sign of our lifelong friendship

Published by Princeton University Press, 41 William Street, Princeton, New Jersey 08540
In the United Kingdom: Princeton University Press, Oxford

Library of Congress Cataloging-in-Publication Data

Kristeller, Paul Oskar, 1905–
Renaissance thought and the arts: collected essays/by Paul Oskar Kristeller.—
Expanded ed., with a new afterword. p. cm.
ISBN 0-691-07253-1. ISBN 0-691-02010-8 (pbk.)
1. Philosophy, Renaissance. 2. Philosophy, Italian. 3. Aesthetics, Italian.
4. Italy—Intellectual life—1268–1559. 5. Renaissance—Italy. I. Title.
B776.I8K72 1990   89-77969
945'.05—dc20

First printing of the expanded Princeton edition, 1990

"The Moral Thought of Renaissance Humanism" copyright © 1961 Columbia University Press.
"The Platonic Academy of Florence" copyrighted © 1961 by the Renaissance Society of America, Inc.
"Ficino and Pomponazzi on the Place of Man in the Universe" copyright 1944 and "The Modern System of the Arts" copyright 1951, 1952 Journal of the History of Ideas, Inc.
"Music and Learning in the Early Italian Renaissance," reprinted from *Journal of Renaissance and Baroque Music.* © Copyright 1946 by American Institute of Musicology/Hänssler-Verlag, Neuhausen-Stuttgart, West Germany.
" 'Creativity' and 'Tradition,' " is © 1983 by *The Journal of the History of Ideas.*
"Rhetoric in Medieval and Renaissance Culture," reprinted from *Renaissance Eloquence*, edited by James J. Murphy, © 1983 by the University of California Press.

10 9 8 7 6 5 4 3 2 1

10 9 8 7 6 5 4 3 2 1, pbk.

Printed in the United States of America by Princeton University Press, Princeton, New Jersey

Contents

Preface (1990)

Renaissance Thought and the Arts, published by Princeton University Press in 1980, has recently gone out of print, and I am grateful to the Press and to Miss Deborah Tegarden for their decision to reprint it, and also to add to it two more papers not included in the previous edition. The paper entitled "Rhetoric in Medieval and Renaissance Culture" was first published by the University of California Press in the volume *Renaissance Eloquence* (pp. 1–19), edited by James J. Murphy. The paper entitled " 'Creativity' and 'Tradition' " was published by the late Philip P. Wiener in the *Journal of the History of Ideas* (1983, 44:105–113). I wish to thank the University of California Press for its permission to reprint the first paper, and Professor Donald R. Kelley, editor of the *Journal of the History of Ideas*, for his permission to reprint the second paper.

The first paper touches on the relation of Renaissance thought to literature and thus is a suitable companion and supplement to chapter 7, an essay on the language of Italian prose. The importance of rhetoric in Renaissance culture has been emphasized in recent years by many scholars including myself, though the term *rhetoric* has lately become, as have many others, a magic and much misused word. In my opinion, rhetoric is not a substitute for philosophy, as it is for Valla and some of his recent admirers, but rather another genre and discipline whose importance, from classical antiquity to modern times, I learned long ago to appreciate from my teachers Werner Jaeger and Eduard Norden.

The second, rather short paper has been added to the volume as a kind of appendix. It is less scholarly and more polemical than the rest of the volume, but it is nevertheless pertinent to the relation that existed between thought and the arts not only during the Renaissance but also at other times, including our own. The paper discusses and criticizes the concept of creativity—a concept that is fairly recent in origin, but that has become a kind of sacred cow in contemporary discourse. The paper originally was commissioned and then rejected by a prestigious national institution that had organized a conference on the topic, but it was later approved by several of my colleagues and friends before being published in the *Journal of the History of Ideas.* It was subsequently translated into Italian and published in the periodical *Il Veltro* (1984, 28:17–29). This episode illustrates the fact, not widely admitted, that in a time and place where we do enjoy an almost unlimited freedom from political censorship, another kind of censorship—on ideological grounds or in the service of the goddess Fashion—is secretly being exercised against views that are contrary to prevalent opinions, whatever their validity or their factual or logical basis. I am glad I have this opportunity to make this paper available to the readers of this volume. I am sure that its ironic critique of fashionable views will be disparaged by many readers whose preconceived views it attempts to question, but I hope it will be appreciated by some other, though perhaps fewer, readers.

Although I do not wish to repeat here what I said in the preface to the 1980 edition about the current state of public and academic opinion and its more or less open hostility to all historical scholarship, especially to the study of intellectual history, I am afraid the climate of opinion has not changed for the better during the past ten years; indeed, it may have even changed for the worse. The kind of philosophical, historical, and literary scholarship that is based on the tested methods of philology and on the careful interpretation of original texts and documents—in my view, the only valid basis—is held in contempt and dismissed as "traditional," not only by journalists and popular writers but also by many members of the academic community. They prefer to work from translations and secondary literature, and to use approaches and methods that are reductionist, purely speculative, arbitrary, or even journalistic (but advertised as novel and superior to "traditional" methods) in the name of psychology, new historicism, social history, Marxism, literary criticism or theory, structuralism or deconstructionism, linguistics, analytical philosophy, or hermeneutics; and they often pretend to discover the secret thought of past thinkers and writers that is actually contrary to the straight meaning of their writings.

In a more recent paper ("Philosophy and Its Historiography," *The Journal of Philosophy* [1985, 82:618–625]), I called these methods "ventriloquistic," and I am amused to note that a recent practitioner of these methods has tried to give a positive twist to this term. I should also like to call them "extratextual," alluding to the fashionable use of *textuality* and *intertextuality*, artificial terms that add nothing except an aura of novelty to the well-known study of sources and influences. All these methods have in common a contempt for what the sources tell us, and a desperate wish to know what the sources do not and cannot tell us. The proponents of these approaches believe that they enrich history by imposing some present ideas on the past, but in fact they impoverish the present and the future by foregoing the chance of enriching modern readers with the additional or alternative ideas and insights that the literature of the past, much of it neglected or forgotten, can offer them. All this is defended with an uncritical kind of relativism that claims that all interpretations are equally valid, without any recognition of the fact that some are valid, some are uncertain or possible, and some are plainly wrong and in contrast with the ascertained facts and with the rules of logical discourse and consistency. Much use is made of what I like to call the *argumentum ex ignorantia*, that is, the naive or intentional disregard of well-established facts and the setting forth of ideas contrary to the author's opinions—all cheerfully presented under the (correct) assumption that the readers and critics, who are equally ignorant, will not know the difference. Yet I do not wish to exaggerate, and I gladly admit that many excellent studies have been published in recent years, by older and younger scholars alike, who have either ignored the fashionable errors to which I allude or made but minor concessions to them.

I may be too old to understand or appreciate these new trends and their purported value. But I know many younger scholars who share my views, who are hampered in their careers by the political and academic power of the modern charlatans, and cannot afford to say in public what they think about these methods and their proponents. Because I *can* afford to say what I think, I feel obliged to do so, and to speak on behalf of many younger scholars and of the continuing scholarly tradition, which I hope will survive the current fads and follies as it has survived so many earlier ones. I should like to conclude with this hope, although I see no signs that it will be fulfilled in the foreseeable future. Moreover, unlike many contemporary prophets of doom, who seem to enjoy their dire predictions,

I, like Cassandra, long to find out that my fears and predictions were groundless.

I should like to dedicate this volume to Hans Sarre in honor of our lifelong friendship, which has survived many good and bad events.

New York, Columbia University
September 21, 1989

PAUL OSKAR KRISTELLER

Preface (1980)

THE PRESENT VOLUME, *Renaissance Thought and the Arts*, is a new edition of the volume first published in 1965 as a Harper Torchbook under the title *Renaissance Thought II: Papers on Humanism and the Arts*, which has been out of print for some time. It is completely different from the volume recently published by the Columbia University Press under the title *Renaissance Thought and Its Sources*. This other volume includes, in addition to some new chapters, most of the contents of two other Harper Torchbooks, *Renaissance Thought* (1961) and *Renaissance Concepts of Man* (1972). The latter is also out of print, whereas the former is still available as a Harper Torchbook.

I am very glad to see the papers included in this volume made again available to scholars, students and other interested readers. In reprinting them in their original form after fifteen years, I realize they might be considered out of date by some critics. I have learned a good deal in these years, both from my own research and from the studies of other scholars, and might have added to my articles a number of details and references. On the other hand, I have not changed my basic views since the papers were first published, and I must cheerfully accept the fact that some of the opinions that appeared to be most heretical when first proposed may by now seem to be obvious or even trivial.

I am more seriously disturbed by the profound changes that have occurred in the general outlook and climate of opinion during these last fifteen years and that may make this volume, and the papers contained in it, less "relevant" than in 1965, let alone at the time when the individual papers were first published as articles between 1946 and 1962. I still believe that any responsible study of intellectual history should be based on a careful reading of the primary sources in their original language, but the fear expressed in the preface to the first edition of this volume that the increasing reliance on translations and secondary accounts may lead us into an age of scholastic pseudo–learning has largely come true, and the signs for a new humanistic reaction are hardly discernible. The disastrous decline in the study of history and of classical and other foreign languages on all levels of our educational system threatens the very foundations of historical scholarship, for it erodes the training of future scholars and it deprives the general reading public of that minimum of knowledge which is needed for a proper appreciation of historical scholarship.

No less serious is the decline of interest in historical studies, and especially in intellectual and cultural history, even within the academic world. The widespread obsession with the political and social problems of our time has led to an excessive growth of many subjects that have great practical and actual appeal and promise, but very dubious scientific or scholarly credentials, whereas an anti-historical and anti-intellectual bias has penetrated even subjects such as philosophy, literature and history that used to be the chief foundations of the study of intellectual history. The dominance of formal logic, linguistics and analytical philosophy among philosophers, of new criticism and structuralism among literary scholars, of political, economic and social history among historians has put the students of intellectual, literary and cultural history on the defensive and seriously diminished their opportunities for teaching positions, grants and fellowships, publication and recognition. We can only hope that the natural talent and curiosity of individual scholars cannot be completely suppressed by public and professional fashion or even discrimination.

We must hope for a gradual return of historical interest among philosophers, and even more among literary scholars whose very source materials call for a historical as well as philosophical interpretation. As to the historians proper, the emphasis on political history is as old as classical antiquity, the stress on economic history is a heritage of the nineteenth century and partly but not entirely due to the powerful impact of Marxism, whereas the emphasis on social history (a magic but rather vague term) reflects more recent populist and egalitarian trends. I do not deny the importance of political and economic history, or the light it may shed on cultural and intellectual history. I firmly deny that cultural, artistic, intellectual or philosophical developments are entirely reducible to political, economic or social factors. There is no philosophical or historical basis for such claims, and no actual attempt at such a reduction has ever been successful. There is a clear distinction, in history as in the sciences, between necessary and sufficient causes, a distinction that is too easily forgotten by historians and ideologists of many persuasions. Political, economic and social factors do account for certain features of cultural and intellectual history, but by no means for all. The philosopher, the scientist, the scholar and writer, the poet and artist are not only influenced and shaped by their political and social background, but also by their respective professional tradition and by their individual talents and spontaneous interests. A modern thinker or artist, however dependent on his time, its fashions and opportunities, is also original to a greater or lesser degree, and he is always dependent, with or without his knowledge, on the past traditions and masters of his craft.

We may go even further. Philosophical and other ideas are not only in part dependent on their contemporary political and economic background, but vice versa, they have always exercised an influence on the political and economic developments of their own time and of later times. The practicing statesman and politician, businessman and social reformer act according to their ideas and convictions, and these ideas are shaped by their readings, by the intellectual climate of their time, and ultimately by the thought of earlier philosophers, theologians, scientists, scholars and writers. The history of our civilization, in the present as in the past, is woven out of many threads, difficult but interesting to disentangle. The claim that only certain aspects of our civilization and its history are basic and worthy of investigation is wrong and must be rejected. All its aspects deserve investigation, and each scholar should be free to explore those problems that attract his curiosity and his talent. I do not intend to question the legitimate claims of systematic philosophy, of literary criticism or of social history. I merely want to insist that intellectual history is an independent and worthwhile subject that should continue to be cultivated by those philosophers, literary scholars and historians who are competent and inclined to pursue it.

I should like to thank the Princeton University Press, and especially Mr. Herbert Bailey and Mr. Loren Hoekzema, for their willingness to republish this volume. I am also grateful to

the editors and publishers of the articles included in this volume
for their permission to reprint them, and to Harper & Row, and
especially to Mr. Hugh Van Dusen, for their permission to have
the Harper Torchbook, now out of print, republished by the
Princeton University Press. The places where these papers had
been previously printed are indicated in the headnotes to each
chapter. All articles of this volume have also been published in
German in the volume *Humanismus und Renaissance II*, edited
by Eckhard Kessler and translated by Renate Schweyen-Ott
(Munich, Wilhelm Fink, 1976). Chapters 3 and 7-9 have also
appeared in Italian in the volume *Concetti rinascimentali dell'
uomo e altri saggi*, translated by Simonetta Salvestroni (Florence, La Nuova Italia, 1978). Chapter 9 alone was also reprinted
in *Problems in Aesthetics: An Introdutory Book of Readings*,
2nd ed., edited by Morris Weitz (New York, Macmillan, 1970,
108-163), and in an abridged version without footnotes in *Art
and Philosophy*, 2nd edition, ed. W. E. Kennick (New York,
St. Martin's Press, 1979, 7-33).

New York,
Columbia University
January 3, 1980

PAUL OSKAR KRISTELLER

I

Humanist Learning in the Italian Renaissance*

I

THE INTELLECTUAL MOVEMENT which I shall try to describe in this paper has been quite often ignored, minimized, or misunderstood in recent historical discussions. Yet the classical humanism of the Italian Renaissance can be shown to be a very significant phenomenon in the history of Western civilization. It represents a new and very important phase in the transmission, study, and interpretation of the heritage of classical antiquity, which has always played a unique role in Western cultural history. Under the influence of classical models, Renaissance humanism brought about a profound transformation of literature, first of Neo-Latin literature, and second of the various vernacular or national literatures, affecting their content as well as their literary form and style. In the area of philosophical thought, which happens to be my special field of interest, Renaissance humanism was less important for the originality of its ideas than for the fermenting effect it had upon older patterns of thought. It restated many ancient ideas that had not been seriously considered hitherto and brought to the fore a number of favorite and partly novel problems, and, in so doing, altered profoundly the form and style of philosophical thinking, teaching, and writing. Finally, although the movement was in its origin literary and scholarly, it came to affect, through the fashionable prestige that accompanied the claims as well as the achievements of its repre-

* Reprinted from *The Centennial Review*, Vol. IV, No. 2, Spring, 1960, 243–266. This paper is based on a lecture given at Syracuse University on March 18, 1959.

sentatives, all other areas of Renaissance civilization, in Italy as well as elsewhere: its art and music, its science and theology, and even its legal and political theory and practice.

Before entering further into this subject, it seems necessary to clear up some ambiguities in the terms which I am going to use, especially in the terms "Renaissance" and "Humanism." The term "Renaissance" has given rise to an unending debate among the historians of the last hundred years or so, and there has been a great variety of opinions concerning the significance and characteristics of this historical period, its relation to the periods preceding and following it, and the precise time of its beginning and of its end. Depending upon one's views, the Renaissance would seem to have lasted as much as four hundred years, or only 27 years, not counting the view of those scholars who think that the Renaissance did not exist at all. As we may see from Professor Ferguson's and Professor Weisinger's studies, attempts to define and to evaluate the meaning of the period have been so numerous and inconclusive that we might be tempted to fall back on the kind of definition that is sometimes offered in other fields as a sign of despair, and define the Renaissance as that historical period of which Renaissance historians are talking. I am not seriously satisfied with this definition, and rather prefer to define the Renaissance as that historical period which understood itself as a Renaissance or rebirth of letters and of learning, whether the reality conformed to this claim or not. Yet I think it is still safer to avoid even this questionable commitment, and to identify the Renaissance with the historical period that extends roughly from 1300 to 1600 A.D. and that has been conventionally designated by that name. This is at least the sense in which I shall employ the term.

The term "Italy," I am happy to say, is not subject to the same kind of ambiguity, yet the role of Italy during the Renaissance period has been the subject of a heated scholarly controversy which is closely connected with the problem of the Renaissance itself. According to Jacob Burckhardt's famous book, whose centenary we are going to celebrate this year, Italy occupied a special position of cultural leadership during the Renaissance period, and many characteristic features of Renaissance civilization appeared in the other European countries much later than in Italy, and as a direct result of Italian influence. This view has been challenged by many historians who are partial to one of the other countries, and they have succeeded in showing that the Renaissance assumed in each country a peculiar physiognomy that differentiates it from the Renaissance in Italy and that reflects the native background and traditions of each country concerned. Although I am quite prepared to grant that much, I am inclined to endorse the core of Burckhardt's view, and to defend the statement that a number of important cultural developments of the Renaissance originated in Italy and spread to the rest of Europe through Italian influence. The evidence for this statement is overwhelming in the visual arts, and it is equally striking in Renaissance humanism.

The term "humanism," however, is itself no less subject to ambiguities and controversies than the term "Renaissance." In present day discussions, the term "humanism" is widely and rather vaguely used to indicate some kind of emphasis on human values, whether this emphasis is said to be religious or antireligious, scientific or antiscientific. In this sense I suppose everybody likes to be a humanist, or to appear as one, and the term ceases to be very distinctive. In speaking of Renaissance humanism, however, I am not referring at all to humanism in the modern sense of an emphasis on human values; I am restricting the term to a meaning that seems to be much closer to what the Renaissance itself understood by a humanist. For although the word "humanism" as applied to the Renaissance emphasis on classical scholarship and on classical education originated among German scholars and educators early in the nineteenth century, it developed from the term "humanist," which had been used ever since the late fifteenth century in a specific sense and which originated probably in the slang of the Italian university students of that time: a humanist was a professor or student of the *studia humanitatis,* of the humanities—as distinct from a jurist, for example. And the *studia humanitatis,* although the term was borrowed from ancient authors and was consciously adopted for a programmatic stress on the human and educational values of the studies thus designated, had stood ever since the early 15th century for a well defined cycle of teaching subjects listed as grammar, rhetoric, poetry, history and moral philosophy, all of them to be based on the reading of the classical Greek and Latin authors.

To put it more broadly, even though the civilization of Renaissance Italy may show a unity of style in all its aspects, this civilization—like that of the later Middle Ages—is clearly articulated and compartmentalized in its various cultural and professional sectors. I do not believe that this rich structure is reducible to a few political or economic or religious factors, but, allowing for all kinds of personal combinations and mutual influences, there is within each cultural sector a core of autonomous tradition and development. It seems important to realize that Renaissance humanism is bound up with the professional tradition of one particular sector, namely the *studia humanitatis*. This is its center of operation, from which it was able to act upon the other areas of the intellectual life of the period. There is a touch of humanism in the modern sense also in Renaissance humanism, in so far as the term *studia humanitatis* indicates an emphasis on man and his values, and for this reason the dignity of man was a favorite theme with some, although by no means with all, Renaissance humanists. Yet we should always keep in mind that there was for all of them only one means through which these human values and ideals could be attained: through classical and literary—that is, through humanistic—studies.

This professional place of the *studia humanitatis* in Renaissance Italy helps us to understand their medieval antecedents. These are not to be found in the scholastic philosophy or theology of the 13th century, which continued to flourish through the Renaissance period, in Italy as elsewhere, but operated, as it were, in a different department of learning. So far as I can see, there were three medieval phenomena which contributed to the rise of Renaissance humanism, but which underwent a thorough transformation through their very combination, if for no other reason. One was the formal rhetoric or *ars dictaminis* which had flourished in medieval Italy as a technique of composing letters, documents, and public orations, and as a training for the class of chancellors and secretaries who composed such letters and documents for popes, emperors, bishops, princes, and city republics. The second medieval influence on Renaissance humanism was the study of Latin grammar as it had been cultivated in the medieval schools, and especially in the French schools, where this study had been combined with the reading of classical Latin poets and prose writers. This influence was felt in Italy towards the very end of the thirteenth century, when the study and imitation of classical Latin authors came to be considered as the prerequisite for the elegant composition of those letters and speeches which the professional rhetorician was supposed to write. The third medieval antecedent of Renaissance humanism leads us away from the traditions of the Latin West to those of the Byzantine

East. For the study of classical Greek literature, while practically unknown in Western Europe, with the possible exception of the Greek speaking sections of Southern Italy and Sicily, was more or less continuously pursued in medieval Constantinople. When the Italian humanists towards the very end of the 14th century began to add the study of classical Greek language and literature to that of Latin literature and of formal rhetoric, they became the pupils of Byzantine scholarship and traditions. This fact has been long recognized, but it still remains to be studied in some of its aspects.

When Italian humanism had developed from these contributing factors into its full stature, in the 15th and 16th centuries, we find it associated mainly with two professions. The humanists represent the class of professional teachers of the humanistic disciplines, at the universities as well as in the secondary schools; they represent also the class of the professional chancellors and secretaries who knew how to compose the documents, letters, and orations required by their posts. Although the humanists at the universities had to compete with teachers of philosophy, theology, jurisprudence, medicine, and mathematics, the humanists came to dominate the secondary schools because they supplied most of the subject matter. Hence they were able to exercise a formative influence on entire generations of educated people, some of whom took an active part in humanist learning and writing without ever becoming professional humanist teachers or chancellors. These included princes and statesmen, churchmen and businessmen, and even artists, poets, philosophers, theologians, jurists, and physicians. By the middle of the 15th century, the influence of humanism penetrated into all areas of Italian civilization; and during the 16th century it began to be felt in all other European countries.

II

If we want to get an idea of the achievement of Italian humanism, we must first try to survey its literary and scholarly contributions, a large mass of material still embodied in manuscripts and early editions that defies any attempt to describe it, not merely because one paper, or even one volume, would not be sufficient, but also because a large part of this material has been very imperfectly explored so far. Let me begin with the contributions of the humanists to classical scholarship. Whereas a sizable core of classical

Latin literature had been known to the Middle Ages, the Italian humanists extended the knowledge of this literature almost to its present limits by discovering manuscripts of a number of authors and works that had been almost forgotten during the preceding period. To emphasize the importance of this contribution, it is enough to refer to the manuscript discoveries of Poggio Bracciolini, and to mention some of the more important authors or texts thus rediscovered for the reading public: Lucretius, Tacitus, and some of the orations and dialogues of Cicero. No less important were the contributions of the humanists to the study and diffusion of those Latin authors and writings that had been available during the medieval centuries. The number of humanist copies of these Latin classical texts is very large indeed, and this in itself shows how the rise of classical studies during the Renaissance period helped to spread such texts. Not only were there numerous 15th-century copies of classical Latin authors; the average library in the Renaissance contained more classical Latin texts, in proportion to religious or medieval or even contemporary literature, than it had in previous centuries.

This wide diffusion of classical texts reached new proportions after the introduction of printing, when we find a very large number and proportion of editions of the classics, due to the efforts of humanist editors and sometimes of humanist printers. The work done by the humanists on these texts was not limited to mechanical copying. They developed a keen sense of the correctness of classical Latin grammar and style. They also developed a successful method of textual criticism: by comparing the texts of several old manuscripts and by emending the texts, they eliminated errors found in the manuscripts. Furthermore, the humanists were engaged in understanding and explaining the difficult passages of the classical authors. They produced a large literature of commentaries that grew out of their class lectures, and in doing so, they not only continued the work of the medieval grammarians, but also expanded and improved it very greatly. In all this, the humanists were the direct forerunners of modern classical scholarship. In their double concern with studying and imitating classical Latin literature, and in direct connection with their activity as teachers, the humanists were careful students of the classical Latin language and vocabulary, of its orthography, grammar, metrics, and prosody, as well as of its style and literary genres. In order to understand the content of ancient literature and to apply it for their own purposes, they investigated ancient history and mythology, ancient customs and institutions. And in their effort to take into account all evidence for the study of ancient civilization, they paid attention to inscriptions and coins, cameos and statues; they began to develop such auxiliary disciplines as epigraphy, numismatics, and archaeology.

The field of Greek scholarship required a still greater effort, since it had no antecedents to speak of in the Latin West, and since even during the Renaissance period the number of good Greek scholars was considerably smaller than that of Latin scholars. Here the Italian humanists share with their Byzantine teachers and contemporaries the merit of having brought to Western libraries the large body of Greek manuscripts in which the texts of ancient Greek literature were preserved, at the very time the Byzantine Empire was being threatened and finally destroyed by the Turkish conquest. Renaissance scholars did for classical Greek writers what they had done for the Roman writers: copying, printing, editing, and expounding them, and studying the grammar, style, and subject matter of those authors. They also did something that is not sufficiently well known or appreciated in its great historical importance, that is, they gradually translated into Latin the entire body of classical Greek literature. The task becomes even more impressive when we realize that Greek was understood or mastered by only a few scholars, whereas, throughout the Renaissance period, Latin remained the language commonly read and written by scholars all over Western Europe. By 1600 the humanist translators had given Western readers the entire range of ancient Greek literature.

The extent of Greek literature available in Latin to medieval Western readers was much more limited. It comprised a certain number of philosophical, theological, and scientific writings, but it failed to include any poetry, historiography, or oratory. As a result of the translating activity of the Renaissance humanists, a large body of ancient Greek writings became available in the West for the first time: all the poets, including Homer and the tragedians; all the historians, including Herodotus and Thucydides; and all the orators, including Isocrates and Demosthenes. Even in the areas where Greek texts had been available in the Middle Ages, many more were now made accessible: not only Aristotle and Proclus and a little Plato, but all of Plato and Plotinus and Epicurus and Epictetus and Sextus Empiricus; not only some, but all Greek writers on medicine, mathematics, and astronomy; and all Greek patristic writers. This was a thorough change in the reading material of the average scholar, and its effects were bound to be felt in literature as well as in philosophy, theology, and the sciences.

III

Let us pass from the scholarly work of the Italian humanists to their original literary productions, which were thoroughly influenced by their scholarship and by their endeavor to imitate the models of the classics in all types of writing. I should like to explain at this point that most of the original writing of the humanists was done in Latin, so that they were able to imitate classical Latin models in the same linguistic medium. However, many humanists also wrote part of their works in the Italian vernacular, and even those writers who used only the vernacular and could not be classified as humanist scholars were in many ways influenced by the humanist scholarship and writing of their time.

A very large portion of the literary production of the humanists consists in their letters. The composition of state letters was, of course, a part of their professional activity. As chancellors and secretaries, they were the paid ghost writers of princes and city governments, and the state letters, manifestoes, and other political documents then as now served to express and to spread the interests, ideology, and propaganda of each government, and sometimes to accompany the war of the swords with a war of the pens. Consequently, the state letters of the humanists are valuable documents for the political thought of the period, provided that we take into account the particular circumstances under which these documents were written, and do not take every statement at its face value as the expression of the personal convictions of the writer. The private letters of the humanists constitute an even larger body of material that has not yet been sufficiently explored. The private letter was not merely a vehicle of personal communication; it was intended from the beginning as a literary composition to be copied and read. The humanist letter-writers consciously imitated the classical example of Cicero or Seneca, and they wrote and collected and published their letters with the purpose of having them serve as models for their pupils and successors. Moreover, the letter served some of the functions of the newspaper at a time when there was no press and when communications were slow and uncertain. Finally, the letter was a favored substitute for a short treatise of scholarly or literary or philosophical content, favored because the humanists liked to speak of their experiences and opinions in a personal and subjective fashion, in the first person. In other words, the letter, being more personal than the treatise, performed the functions of the essay, and actually was its literary forerunner.

Another very large literary genre which was cultivated by the humanists and closely related to their professional activity was the speech or oration. It is true that the humanists in their speeches as in other compositions liked to imitate classical models. Yet we should add that Renaissance Italy inherited from medieval Italy a variety of occasions for speechmaking that were not at all comparable with the examples of ancient oratory but were rooted instead in medieval customs and institutions. Consequently, there is a real flood of humanist speeches, and although many of these ephemeral products must have perished with the occasion that gave rise to them, a surprisingly large number of such speeches has come down to us. Many of them were obviously composed with care and with the intention and ambition to serve as models for pupils and followers. The humanists evidently were commissioned to write the speeches demanded by the occasion. There were many funeral speeches which usually tell us more about the life and person of the deceased than any funeral sermon I have heard in my life. There were wedding speeches, apparently a literary development from the formula of contract demanded by Lombard law. A number of speeches grew out of the ceremonies of schools and universities: commencement speeches in praise of studies or of particular disciplines; opening speeches at the beginning of a course of lectures, or of a public dispute (Pico's famous oration belongs to this latter type); speeches given by both professors and students after an examination, and on many other academic occasions. Another large body of speeches was connected with the political life of the time, or at least with its ceremonial side: there were speeches made by ambassadors to the princes or governments to which they had been sent, and especially to a newly elected pope; speeches of welcome for a distinguished foreign visitor; and speeches addressed to newly elected bishops or governors or magistrates, with the appropriate replies. Much rarer, though not entirely lacking, are the speeches of the types to which belong the most famous masterpieces of ancient oratory: political speeches held during the deliberations of a council or public assembly, or forensic speeches given at a public trial or lawsuit before a law court. In other words, the humanist speech was seldom connected with occasions of political or legal importance but was more often composed for decorative purposes. It was clearly considered a kind of public entertainment, and it competed on many occasions with a musical or dramatic performance. Many humanist speeches were evidently much admired by their contemporaries, and though it is customary among historians to dismiss them as empty oratory, I must confess that I have read many of them with pleasure and found them to be well written, as well as interesting for their ideas and historical information.

Another large body of the writings of the humanists consists of their historiography. One might expect that this was largely due to their scholarly interest, and that they consequently concentrated their efforts on ancient history. However, this is true only for a small part of their historical production. In most instances, the historical works of the humanists were connected with their professional activity, in so far as the chancellor or secretary of a prince or of a city was expected to serve also as their historian. The type of the paid court or city historiographer whom we encounter occasionally also in medieval Italy becomes a common type during the Italian Renaissance. Consequently, most of the historical works of the humanists are histories of cities or countries or ruling families, and, for obvious reasons, they usually concentrated on the Middle Ages and their own times rather than on classical antiquity. Thus we find humanist histories of Florence and of Venice, of the Popes, of the Dukes of Milan, or of the Gonzaga family; and by the second half of the fifteenth century, Italian humanists began to be employed as official historiographers by the Kings of Hungary, Poland, Spain, England, and France, as well as by the German emperors.

The humanist works on history have a number of peculiarities, both good and bad. They are often written in a highly rhetorical Latin, and they show the influence of classical historiography in the use of fictitious speeches. Since they were usually commissioned by the very state or city whose history was to be written, there is an element of eulogy and of regional or dynastic bias, something which I understand is not entirely absent from the national histories of modern times. On the other hand, the humanists usually did not place much credence in miracles and avoided theological speculations, and they tend to account for historical events on a strictly rational basis. Moreover, they often had access to the archives and original documents illustrating the subject matter of their history, and employed more exacting standards of documentation and historical criticism than had been the custom during the preceding centuries. Valla's treatise on the Donation of Constantine is a famous example of historical criticism in the fifteenth century; in the sixteenth, we might single out humanists such as Sigonius, who must be considered in their erudition and critical acumen as the direct forerunners of the great historians of the seventeenth and eighteenth centuries.

Another branch of historical literature that was very much cultivated by the humanists was biography. There was the model of Plutarch and of other ancient writers, but there obviously was a great contemporary demand for biographies, not merely of princes or saints, but also of statesmen and distinguished citizens, of poets and artists, of scholars and businessmen. Like the portrait painting of the time, the biographical literature reflects the so-called individualism of the period, that is, the importance attached to personal experiences, opinions, and achievements, and the eagerness to see them perpetuated in a distinguished work of art or of literature.

There are other types of humanist prose composition which we might connect with their activity as orators rather than as historians, and which we can mention merely in passing, although they constitute a fairly large and famous part of their production. One task of the orator was traditionally defined as that of praising and blaming, and this task was taken rather literally in the Renaissance. There were many political invectives written in the name of a government against its enemies, and numerous personal invectives composed by humanists against their rivals. They are full of nasty remarks which were probably not taken as seriously by contemporary readers as they are sometimes by modern scholars, but which show the humanists' love of gossip. This is another aspect of Renaissance "individualism," and though the love of gossip is not peculiar to that period alone, the inclination to incorporate it in published and even in highbrow literature definitely is. At the other end stands the literature of praise, the numerous eulogies of princes and of cities, sometimes most useful for biographical or descriptive details, as well as the eulogies of various arts and sciences, usually comparing them favorably with some of their rival disciplines. Also the descriptions of festivals were quite in vogue, and we have charming descriptions of tournaments or of snowball fights in

Latin prose which seem to compete more or less purposely with similar descriptions written in verse or in Italian. Humanist prose literature also rivaled the vernacular by borrowing from it the narrative form of the short story, the Novella, sometimes translating such stories from Italian into Latin and sometimes composing original stories in Latin, some of which attained a tremendous popularity. Finally, humanist prose also assumed a lighter and more humorous garb in the collections of anecdotes and of facetious stories that have come down to us from the Renaissance period.

The humanists thought of themselves as orators and poets, and the crowning of poets was a favorite humanist ceremony and honor. Their notion of poetry was far removed from the modern romantic notion of the creative poet. For them, poetry was largely the ability to write verse, especially Latin verse. This was something that could be taught and learned, at least to some extent. They also were convinced that any literary form or subject could be treated in verse as well as in prose, in Latin as well as in the vernacular, and they tolerated as poetry a good deal that by more severe modern standards is rather mediocre. Moreover, the study and interpretation of ancient poets was considered as a part of the business of poetry, since the composing of verse depended on a knowledge and imitation of the classical poets. All this may explain why a very large proportion indeed of humanist literature belongs to the category of poetry broadly understood. In this vast body of material, dramatic pieces constitute a relatively small part, but this small group of material does have its historical importance. Some of the humanist plays were widely known, and in the fifteenth century, classical and humanist Latin plays were repeatedly performed in schools and courts. This was undoubtedly one of the factors leading to the rise of dramatic literature in the sixteenth century. Also the eclogue or pastoral poem had a number of cultivators, after the model of Vergil and other ancients, and when this type of poetry was transferred to the vernacular and given a more dramatic turn, the ground was laid for the tremendous vogue of pastoral poetry which lasted down to the eighteenth century. Humanist poetry includes specimens of the satire and of the ode, although the latter tended to be rare on account of its metrical difficulties which but a few consummate writers could master. Much larger is the volume of epical poetry. It includes verse translations of Homer and other Greek poets, and even of Dante's *Divine Comedy*. The bulk

of the compositions may be characterized as historical, mytho-
logical, and didactic, and this corresponded to the available
classical models. There are long poems on ancient history, such
as Petrarch's *Africa,* on contemporary wars, in praise of princes
and cities, and in praise of Columbus' discoveries. Various ancient myths were made the subject of long epical poems, and
some humanists even dared to write a supplement to Vergil's
Aeneid. An effort was also made to apply the form of classical
epics to Christian subjects, and there are a number of famous
poems dealing with the life of Christ or of the saints. Finally,
there are didactic poems on a variety of subjects such as astronomy or astrology, on poetics and natural history, on the silk
worm, and on the game of chess, to cite only a few of the better
known examples.

Yet by far the largest part of humanist poetry takes the form
of elegies and epigrams, two types of poetry which are closely
related to each other through their metrical form and which are
comparatively easy to handle. The elegy is the longer of the two
and is more serious in content; most frequently, it describes the
poet's love for a beautiful girl in a variety of its phases and
episodes. There are a number of scattered elegies which were
quite popular, but many of the greater and smaller humanist
poets tried to establish their fame by entire cycles of elegies
collected in books, after the model of Ovid, Propertius, or Tibul-
lus. Some elegies belong to the very best specimens of humanist
poetry, and famous poets such as Pontano or Poliziano excelled
especially in this genre.

Much more numerous and common than the elegy is the related form of the epigram. It was the favorite form of humanist
poetry, being shorter and less serious than the elegy, and allowing
a much greater variety of content and tone. A large number of
humanist writers have left us collections of epigrams. Some of
them are skillful in their formal elegance and in the variety of
the subjects treated. They include a good number of frivolous
and indecent pieces, for which the Greek Anthology and Martial
offered ample precedents. Aside from that, the chief attraction
of even the more modest collections is historical: many of them
are addressed to persons and contain historical, biographical, or
literary allusions that are often a welcome addition to the scanty
documentary evidence which we might otherwise possess. There
was a mass production of occasional epigrams, and especially of
epitaphs, which is likewise uneven in its literary merit, but again

usually of historical interest. There were also poetical contests on specific occasions such as tournaments, and especially on the death of a famous or of a beautiful young person, and the fifteenth century saw the rise of the poetical miscellany, a collection of verses by different poets on the wedding or death of a particular person, a type that was to continue for centuries in various countries. After their appearance in Petrarch's time, epigrams in praise of the works of a friend continued to be popular; these laudatory verses were added as a kind of preface to the friend's manuscripts or editions.

I hope this very short survey will give at least a glimpse of the amazing bulk and variety of humanist Latin poetry, and will thus make it clear that this production was bound to have its repercussions also in the vernacular literatures of the same period, in style and form as well as in subject matter, especially since many of the leading vernacular poets both in Italy and elsewhere had enjoyed a humanist training and sometimes even wrote and composed in both Latin and their native vernacular. The view that Latin and vernacular literature represented in the Renaissance two hostile and mutually exclusive camps has been much cherished by many literary historians since the times of Romanticism, and it has combined with the ignorance of Latin in causing much contempt for and neglect of humanist Latin literature, but this view does not correspond to the historical facts as they are now known to us.

IV

I now come to the last branch of humanist literature, which to the student of philosophy and of intellectual history is by far the most important, and which to be sure has much intrinsic significance, but which represents only a comparatively small sector of humanist writings: the dialogues and treatises dealing with moral and other philosophical subjects. Moral philosophy was clearly a part of the province of the humanists; Petrarch liked to be called a moral philosopher, and many humanist scholars taught the subject in various schools and universities. Actually, the moral treatises of the humanists are a very important source if we want to understand the interests, the taste, and sometimes the wisdom of the time. They also help us to know the opinions of particular humanists on particular questions. Yet I cannot agree with some of my fellow students of the history of philosophy who try to reconstruct from the humanist treatises a body of uniform philosophical opinion that would be common to all humanists and in this way to distinguish them from the philosophers of other times. I cannot help feeling that for every opinion that we find expressed by a humanist in one of his writings, we can find different or even opposite opinions on the same matter expressed by other humanists or even by the same humanist in another part of his work. In each instance, we must carefully consider the particular purpose for which a given work was written, the numerous citations taken from classical authors (citations that very often are not even explicitly identified), and, finally, the concern for formal literary elegance and the conscious avoidance of technical language, an avoidance that reflected the authors' imitation of Cicero. In many instances, although not in all, the humanists are more interested in airing and discussing several possible opinions on a given issue than in taking a firm stand on one side or the other. Yet despite all this, the humanists clearly show a marked interest in some special problems, and most of them show a preference for one rather than another of the possible views on that problem. The humanists wrote a number of treatises on happiness or the supreme good, the standard topic of ancient moral philosophy, and they would more frequently side with Aristotle's moderate view than with the extreme positions of the Stoics or Epicureans, although the latter also had their distinguished adherents. They would discuss particular virtues, or the power of fortune, usually insisting that human reason can overcome fortune, at least within certain limits. They wrote a good deal on education, and defended the reading of the classics on both moral and intellectual grounds. A favorite subject was nobility, and as its chief cause they would favor merit more often than birth. They would variously discuss the merits of the active and contemplative life, the married and the single life. They would discuss the duties of a particular profession, including that of the monk or cleric. They would write about the family and the state, adapting ancient precepts from various sources to the peculiar circumstances of their own time and country. They would discuss the relative merits of a republic and a monarchy, and many of them would praise the virtues of republican government, especially if they happened to write in Florence or Venice. They would discuss the merits of law and medicine, of literature and of military service, of ancient and modern times. Much of this is interesting, if not profound, and a good deal more could be learned by studying the unexplored and unpublished part of this literature. Yet at the present state of my knowledge, I should still maintain that the contribution of the Italian humanists does not lie in any particular opinions which all of them would have defended, or in any particularly strong arguments they might have offered for such opinions.

Their contribution is much more intangible and indirect. It lies in the educational program which they set forth and carried through, that is, in the thorough propagation of classical learning through the schools, and in the emphasis on man and his dignity which was implicit in the slogan of the *studia humanitatis,* and which was defended explicitly by many, if not all, of the humanists. It lies in the conviction, perhaps erroneous, that through this study and imitation of the classics they had brought about a renaissance, a rebirth, of learning and literature, of the arts and sciences, that led mankind back to the heights of classical antiquity after a long period of decay. This historical view has been much opposed by modern students of the Middle Ages, but it still underlies our customary division of the periods of history. It lies in the elegant and non-technical discussion of concrete human problems which were of general interest to the educated readers of the time but which were neglected by the technical philosophers, the scholastic logicians, and physicists. It lies, above all, in the vast amount of fresh ancient source material supplied to the students of philosophy; this made it possible for them to restate the ancient doctrines of Platonism, Stoicism, Epicureanism, and Scepticism, to restate even Aristotelianism on the basis of Greek rather than Arabic or medieval sources, and finally to attempt new philosophical solutions independent of any particular ancient sources. All this was to characterize the philosophical thought of the Renaissance period. I am not prepared to consider this as a part of humanism since this involved many traditions and problems of a different origin, but it surely was influenced by humanism, and would not have been possible without the work and the attitudes of the humanists.

What I said about the impact of Italian humanism upon philosophy may be said with the appropriate modifications for all other branches of Renaissance civilization. Most Italian humanists were not theologians (and some of them may have been indifferent Christians, although very few, if any, can be proven to have been pagans). Yet some of them preceded Erasmus and the Reformers in applying the tools of classical scholarship to Christian texts and in preparing the way for a kind of sacred philology. There were many new editions and translations of the Church Fathers, and even some of the Bible, and the methods of textual and historical criticism were consciously and conscientiously used for them. The humanist insistence on ancient primary sources and their distrust and critique of scholastic dialectic were to have their repercussions in theology no less than in philosophy. In the history of the sciences, the merits and achievements of the later Middle Ages have been rightly emphasized by recent historians. Yet, although the Middle Ages possessed a significant selection of Greek writings on mathematics, astronomy, and medicine, the humanist translators added important texts in these fields as well as in geography. Most of the humanists were not professional scientists, but many scientists of the fifteenth and sixteenth centuries had enjoyed a humanist education, and it was only at that time that the results of the Greeks were fully absorbed so that the road was cleared for entirely new discoveries. In jurisprudence, it was humanist scholarship that led to a historical understanding of the sources of Roman law during the sixteenth century, just as the humanist translations of ancient philosophical, historical, and rhetorical literature refreshed the discussion of political theory. In architecture and the decorative arts, the prevalent classicism of the age led to a revival of ancient forms and styles, while the revived interest in classical history, mythology, and allegory enriched the subject matter of painting and of sculpture for many centuries to come, down to the 19th. Even in music, where no ancient specimens had been preserved, the study and even the misinterpretation of classical theory had an important effect on its development during the later 16th century. In other words, Italian humanism was essentially at home in one particular compartment of Renaissance civilization, but its influence gradually spread from this center and affected all other areas.

Moreover, its influence was not limited to Italy alone, but its traces can be found all over Europe, for better or worse, at least after the middle of the fifteenth century. Students from all European countries attended the Italian universities, were exposed to the methods and sources of Italian humanism, and went home with many new ideas and tastes as well as with many books which they had copied or acquired and which are still to be found in Northern, Western, or Eastern libraries. These same texts were copied and read and later printed outside of Italy, some of them

more widely than at home. Many Italian humanists had occasion
to go abroad and to spread their interests through their personal
and professional associations, if not through their teaching; they
went as ambassadors of Italian governments, or as political and
later religious exiles, or as chancellors or professors in the service
of foreign governments. The exchange of books and of persons then as now was an important factor in cultural communication, and at that time, Italian humanism had much to offer
that was unknown and neglected in the other countries. In the
sixteenth century, humanism became less dependent on Italy and
put down native roots in the other countries. Scholars like Erasmus and More, Vives and Budé, were equal or superior to their
Italian contemporaries and were often unwilling to acknowledge
their debt to their Italian predecessors; but while they surely
owed a great deal to their native traditions as well as to their
own personal talent, yet from our perspective we cannot possibly
deny that they were continuing and developing the traditions of
Italian humanism, and that their work, novel and original as
it may be, would not have been possible without that of their
Italian predecessors.

I hope this very brief survey of a vast area of Renaissance
learning and literature may give at least a general idea of the
contributions and historical significance of Italian humanism.
Some of the works of the humanists may be of questionable
value, or of slight importance from the modern point of view.
But I should like to stress two points. First, as a result of Renaissance humanism, the intellectual climate had completely changed
between 1300 and 1600, as, for example, in philosophy, between
Aquinas and Descartes. Even where the humanists did not formulate any new ideas in philosophy or the sciences, they made them
possible by clearing the ground of some medieval traditions and
by making available a variety of ancient sources. In the 16th
century, humanism was not superseded by the Protestant and
Catholic Reformation, as many historians claim, for it was not
a theology, but a literary and scholarly tradition that survived
in both Catholic and Protestant countries. In philosophy and
the sciences, humanism was definitely superseded during the 17th
century by the new developments which started with Galileo
and Descartes, developments which had in part been prepared
by humanism itself. Yet the works of the humanists, and those
of the Renaissance thinkers influenced by humanism, were still
widely read down to the eighteenth and early nineteenth century,

and thus continued to nourish many secondary currents of thought and literature during that period. The ideal of humanist education dominated the secondary schools of the West at least to the beginning of this century, and it still survives in the term humanities as we use it, which denotes a residual of the *studia humanitatis*. Moreover, it is Renaissance humanism that is the ancestor of our philological, historical, and literary scholarship, just as medieval and Renaissance learning in logic, physics, mathematics, and medicine anticipates early and recent modern science.

The second and chief lesson which I should like to draw from the place of humanism in Renaissance civilization is this: in our time, the humanities are on the defensive everywhere, and we are, as it were, threatened by the bleak prospect of a world that consists only of practical life, of science, of religion, and of an art deprived of intellectual content. By contrast, we see in the Renaissance a vast body of the humanities, that is, secular learning which partially, at least, is independent of practical life, of science, of religion, and of the arts, and which occupies a large and important place in the attention and initiative of the time, and which is in turn capable of exerting a deep and fruitful influence on all other areas of human activity. Let us hope that the humanities as we know them may survive and fulfill again a similar productive function, either now or in a not too distant future.

II

The Moral Thought of
Renaissance Humanism *

IN THE WESTERN tradition that began with classical antiquity and continued through the Middle Ages down to modern times, the period commonly called the Renaissance occupies a place of its own and has its own peculiar characteristics. Historians have tried for a long time, and in various ways, to describe the civilization of the Renaissance. As a result, there has been so much controversy and difference of views that the so-called problem of the Renaissance has become the subject of an entire literature.

The traditional view of the Renaissance was formulated exactly 100 years ago by Jacob Burckhardt. In a most perceptive synthesis which focused on Italy in the fifteenth and early sixteenth century, he described the achievement of the period in the arts, literature, and scholarship, and stressed such general characteristics as individualism, the revival of antiquity, and the discovery of the world and of man. This picture was expanded and popularized by J. A. Symonds and others, among them those who stressed the pagan tendencies of the period more than Burckhardt had ever done. Other historians engaged in the task of analyzing the Renaissance as a broader European phenomenon, especially during the sixteenth century, and of exploring both the Italian influences and the national characteristics which the period assumed in each of the major European countries.

Burckhardt's views were challenged and criticized in a number of ways. Historians of the Middle Ages discovered that this

* Reprinted by permission from *Chapters in Western Civilization*, ed. by the Contemporary Civilization Staff of Columbia College, Vol. I, 3rd ed. (New York, Columbia University Press, 1961), 289–335.

period, especially in its later phases, had its own impressive achievements as a civilization, and was very far from a "dark age" that needed to make room for a period of "rebirth." In many instances, phenomena considered peculiar to the Renaissance were found to have had their counterparts or precedents in the Middle Ages. Historians of French literature, followed by those of other literatures, tended to minimize the Italian influences and to stress the independent contributions, during and before the Renaissance, of the other countries. Johan Huizinga, in his *Waning of the Middle Ages,* emphasized the thoroughly medieval features of so late a time as the fifteenth century, and his contribution is especially impressive since he focused on the Low Countries, an area that was at that time the chief artistic and economic center of Europe outside of Italy. While many historians, albeit with different evaluations, agreed that the Protestant and Catholic reformations of the sixteenth century put a sudden end to the secular and pagan culture radiating from Italy during the fifteenth century, others stressed the thoroughly religious character of the Renaissance in the northern countries, or even in Italy. One scholar, Giuseppe Toffanin, went so far as to suggest that Renaissance humanism was basically a Catholic reaction against the heretical tendencies inherent in the thought of the later Middle Ages. Continuity with the Middle Ages was the watchword of many historians who studied the economic and scientific development of the period—aspects that had been neglected by Burckhardt but have been particularly important in recent historical scholarship. Other historians speak of an actual economic and scientific decline during the fifteenth century, but this view is by no means shared by all specialists on the subject. These controversies are the more confusing since they affect even the chronological limits of the Renaissance period, whose beginning and end are subject to considerable fluctuation, depending on the persons or regions, developments or cultural aspects, on which the historian focuses his attention.

In the face of so much disagreement, one may only suggest that we apply the term Renaissance, which has by now become conventional, to the period in European history that goes at least from the middle of the fourteenth century to the beginning of the seventeenth. If we attach no value judgment to the term Renaissance, we shall not be surprised if we discover in the period many shortcomings as well as many achievements. If we grant that the Renaissance was a period of transition, we shal' not be surprised to find in it many medieval as well as modern traits, and also some that are peculiar only to the Renaissance. There is no need to emphasize one of these aspects over the others for we can accept continuity as basic to history, while also realizing that historical continuity involves change as well as stability, and that a gradual change taking place over a period of several centuries is bound to be not only cumulative, but also to become considerable in the end. Each European country, we can also agree, made its own contribution to the civilization of the Renaissance, and did so in part by drawing upon its native medieval traditions, but Italy, both by the excellence of her own contributions and by the influence she exercised upon all other countries, occupied a position of cultural predominance that she never possessed before or after.

If the claim made by some older historians that the Renaissance was a period of revival after many dark centuries must now be subjected to severe qualification, the fact remains that writers of the period thought of their age as one that witnessed the rebirth of arts, letters, and learning after a long decay. Finally, in a complex, but articulated, civilization each area of culture may have its own distinct line of development. We have no reason to assume that the Renaissance, or any other period, must show the same characteristics, the same "style," the same rate of development or regional diffusion in art and literature, in politics, economy, or religion, in philosophy, or in the sciences. The perception of such a common style may be the ultimate aim of the historian of a period, but he cannot take it for granted at the start. Many of the controversies about the Renaissance are due to the tendency of historians to focus exclusively on one aspect of the culture of the period, to make one-sided generalizations on the basis of their favorite subject matter, and to ignore the other relevant aspects of the era. To approach a more objective view of the Renaissance, it seems preferable to respect the independence of the various fields of human endeavor, without denying or neglecting their mutual relations.

I

Within the broader outlines of Renaissance civilization, humanism may be considered as one of the more important, but limited, aspects or movements. The interpretation of Renaissance humanism, like that of the Renaissance itself, has been subject to a great deal of controversy and disagreement among recent historians. Moreover, humanism is even more difficult to define than is the Renaissance, since it is not enough to indicate its chronological limits. We must also try to describe its intellectual content and the range of its activities. This task is further complicated since the word *humanism* has come to stand for any kind of emphasis on human values. Quite naturally, when we hear Renaissance humanism mentioned, we think of an emphasis on human values that was supposedly current in the Renaissance period, or even was characteristic of that period. Humanism in this sense may certainly be found in the Renaissance, yet it was not as widespread as is often assumed. When historians speak of Renaissance humanism, they use the word in a sense that is different from our contemporary meaning. They are referring to a broad class of Renaissance intellectuals who are traditionally called humanists and who were active as teachers and secretaries, writers, scholars and thinkers; who exercised a wide and deep influence on all aspects of Renaissance civilization; and who left to posterity, along with the record of their lives and activities, vast writings that may be roughly classified as literature, historical and philological scholarship, and moral thought, but which often deal with such diverse subjects as philosophy and the sciences, literary and art criticism, education, government, and religion. The revival of antiquity generally associated with the Renaissance period, the thoroughgoing classicism that we notice in all its literary and artistic manifestations, is surely the direct or indirect effect of Renaissance humanism. When Georg Voigt, in 1859, described the earlier phases of Italian humanism, he emphasized its contributions to classical scholarship. Burckhardt and Symonds, without neglecting the impact of the humanists on Renaissance thought and literature, gave due importance to their work as historians and classical scholars. In later German scholarship this emphasis continued and was facilitated by the nineteenth-century use of the word *humanism,* then almost exclusively associated with the humanistic disciplines, that is, history and philology, and with the humanistic schools in which these disciplines were cultivated. On the other hand, because humanism seemed to predominate in Italian literature and civilization during the fifteenth century but to lose some of its importance during the sixteenth, Italian scholars tended to use "humanism" as a name for a period—mainly the fifteenth century —a period which scholars in other countries have called the early

Renaissance. Recently, the tendency has been to shift emphasis from the scholarly and literary achievements of the humanists and to define the movement in terms of certain ideas or ideals. This tendency may be due to a declining respect for scholarship as such, and to the feeling that Renaissance humanism must be identified with a set of well-defined ideas if it is to be acceptable to contemporary opinion. The modern undertones of the word may also have played their part in the process. Konrad Burdach assigned to humanism a religious origin and considered its secular orientation a later development. Giuseppe Toffanin believed that Renaissance humanism was a Catholic reaction against certain heretical tendencies inherent in medieval thought. Douglas Bush, thinking of northern rather than Italian humanists, identifies the core of Renaissance humanism as Christian humanism, which shares with Thomas Aquinas the concern for harmony between ancient reason and Christian faith. On the other hand, Hans Baron placed in the center of his interpretation the civic humanism of fifteenth-century Florence, which was primarily concerned with the training of responsible citizens leading active lives in a republican community. Finally, Eugenio Garin, in a number of well-informed and influential studies, used the term humanism as a common denominator for what was best in the philosophical thought of the Renaissance, stressing its preoccupation with the human and moral problems of the layman and its contrast with the theological orientation of medieval scholasticism.

II

There is some truth in most of these views, but it is difficult to derive from them a clear and coherent picture of Renaissance humanism that would do justice to the movement as a whole. It is thus more useful perhaps to go back to the Renaissance meanings of the terms *humanist* and *humanities,* from which the modern term *humanism* is clearly derived. It seems that "humanist," probably coined in the slang of university students, designated a professional teacher of the humanities, and that "humanities," or *Studia humanitatis,* was understood to include such subjects as grammar, rhetoric, poetry, history, and moral philosophy. This well-defined cycle of studies consisted, in other words, of the subjects that would train a student to speak and write well, both in prose and in verse and primarily in Latin (which was still the accepted language of the schools and of the Church, of law, and of international diplomacy); it included the study and writing of history, and finally one of the philosophical disciplines—moral philosophy. Since the humanists were firmly convinced that it was necessary for each genre of writing to follow the models of ancient literature, the study of the Greek and Latin classics became a central and inseparable part of humanistic education: to study poetry meant to study the ancient poets as well as to learn how to write verse. In this way we can understand why Renaissance humanism was both literary and scholarly in its central concern, that classicism was at its heart, and why it spread through the influence of the humanists into all of Renaissance civilization. When the Renaissance scholars took over the classical term "humanities" for the studies in which they were interested, they meant to emphasize the human values inherent in these subjects, and the teaching of moral philosophy was an essential part of their program. In this way they were humanists also in the twentieth-century sense of the word. Yet Renaissance humanism, unlike its twentieth-century namesake, was strongly committed to a cultural program and ideal, and it is this ideal that all Renaissance humanists have in common. The particular philosophical, religious, or political ideas by which modern historians have tried to define Renaissance humanism are actually found in the writings of some humanists, and many of them are intrinsically quite significant. Yet since these ideas were not shared by all humanists, and since such a large part of the work of the humanists was not concerned with ideas at all, but was literary or scholarly in character, a proper definition or understanding of the movement as a whole cannot be based on them. On the other hand, since the main, and, as it were, professional concern of the humanists was limited to the humanities, we should not assume, as many scholars do, that humanism was identical with Renaissance civilization or Renaissance learning as a whole. Theology and law, medicine and mathematics, astronomy, astrology and alchemy, logic, natural philosophy and metaphysics, the vernacular literatures, the visual arts and music were all vigorously cultivated during the Renaissance but not primarily by the humanists. Each discipline had its own traditions and development, and was pursued by its own specialists. If all were strongly influenced by Renaissance humanism, this influence was largely external to the discipline itself and limited in its nature. It was owing to those humanists who had a personal interest or competence in one or more of these other disciplines, or to those specialists in the other disciplines who had enjoyed a humanist education in their youth, as became more and more the rule after the middle of the fifteenth century. The nature of this humanist influence is also characteristic: it consists primarily in the introduction of fresh classical sources and in the restatement of their ideas, in the vogue of classical quotations and allusions, in the use of the newly refined methods of historical and philological scholarship, and in an attempt to replace the specialized terminology of the medieval schools, their tight methods of arguing, their elaborate commentaries and disputed questions, by treatises, dialogues, and essays written in a smooth and elegant style.

Since moral philosophy, unlike the other philosophical disciplines, was considered a part of the humanities, we can easily understand that the moral thought of the Renaissance was closely associated with the humanist movement. A considerable part of the moral literature of the Renaissance was written by humanists, or by laymen with a humanist training, and practically all writers on moral subjects were influenced by humanism. The connection of this literature with humanism accounts for several of its peculiar features. Many, if not all, of the humanists were teachers, so that their moral thought was strongly centered on the education of the young. The humanists considered classical antiquity their major guide and model in thought and literature and their moral writings are accordingly studded with quotations from Greek and Roman authors, with episodes from classical history and mythology, with ideas and theories derived from ancient philosophers and writers. Finally, the humanists were professional rhetoricians, that is, writers and critics, who wished not only to say the truth, but to say it well, according to their literary taste and standards. They believed in the ancient rhetorical doctrine that a professional speaker and writer must acquire and show skill in making any idea that is related to his chosen topic plausible to his public. Consequently, a given idea is often expressed in phrases that aim at elegance rather than at precision, and many times, especially in a dialogue or in a speech, opinions may be defended with vigor and eloquence that are appropriate for the occasion, but do not express the author's final or considered view.

III

Moral teaching is often contained in literary genres cultivated by the humanists where a modern reader might not expect to find it. The humanists inherited from the ancient and medieval grammarians and literary critics the view that moral instruction is one of the main tasks of the poet. Hence there is a moral or even moralistic note in some of the poetry they wrote, and in the interpretation they gave of the ancient poets in the class-room and in their published commentaries. The humanists also followed ancient and medieval theory and practice in their belief that the orator and prose writer is a moral teacher and ought to adorn his compositions with pithy sentences quoted from the poets or coined by himself. To facilitate his task, a humanist would gather quotations and sentences in a commonplace book, and some writers would publish collections of sentences, proverbs, or historical anecdotes from which an author could freely quote on the appropriate occasion. Plutarch's *Apophthegmata,* in humanist translations, enjoyed great popularity for this reason, and Erasmus's *Adagia,* collected from many ancient sources and revised and enlarged several times by the author, was printed and used, though not always quoted, for several centuries.

Finally, another branch of study cultivated by the humanists, history, had moral significance for them. The humanists shared the view of many ancient and medieval authors that one of the tasks of historiography is to teach a moral lesson. Much Renaissance historiography is sustained by this belief. In the same way, the extensive biographical literature produced during the period is often animated by the desire to supply the reader with models worthy of imitation. The medieval lives of saints provided a precedent, since they too were written to provide the reader with models of pious conduct. But it makes a difference whether the persons whose lives are described as models of human conduct are Christian saints or ancient statesmen and generals, philosophers and poets, contemporary princes, citizens, or artists. The Renaissance continued to produce biographies of the saints, but it left a much larger number of secular biographies. The lives of famous ancients as written by Petrarch and other humanists were clearly intended to provide models for imitation, since classical antiquity was for the humanists the admired model in all fields of human endeavor. No wonder that in a famous hu-

manist controversy the relative superiority of the Romans Scipio
and Caesar served as a basis for discussing the merits of republican and monarchical government. When Machiavelli in his
Discourses on Livy holds out the institutions and actions of the
Roman republic as a model to his contemporaries, he follows
the practice of his humanist predecessors, and he states his underlying assumption more clearly than any of them had done:
human beings are fundamentally the same at all times, and
therefore it is possible to study the conduct of the ancients, to
learn from their mistakes and from their achievements, and to
follow their example where they were successful.

If we turn from these writings of the humanists in which a
moral or moralistic interest appeared to those works which deal
explicitly with moral philosophy, we may notice the favorite
genres used for this kind of literature. Most important are the
treatise and the dialogue, and later on, the essay. More marginal
forms are the oration and the letter, the most widespread forms
of humanist literature, which at times, serve to express moral
ideas. The letter was especially popular with the humanists, as
it allowed them to express their views in a personal and subjective fashion, although they considered letter-writing a branch
of literature, and gave the same polished elegance to their letters
as to their other literary compositions. To these we might add
the collections of sentences, proverbs, and commonplaces.

The language of these writings was usually Latin, but the use
of the vernacular appears especially in Tuscany, during the
fifteenth century, and becomes more widespread in the rest of
Italy and of Europe during the sixteenth. The choice of language
indicated the reading public to which an author wished to
address a given work. Latin writings were intended for an international audience of scholars and of educated alumni of humanist schools, while within a particular country or region works in
the vernacular were read chiefly by a middle class of ladies, businessmen, and artisans who were able to read and eager to be
entertained and instructed, but who usually knew no Latin and
lacked a humanist school education or a university training.

IV

The existence of this large body of moral literature written by
humanists and popularizers, and of the still larger body of humanist learning and literature, is in itself a significant historical

phenomenon. We are confronted with a vast body of secular learning, nourished from ancient sources and contemporary experience, and basically independent of, though not entirely unrelated to, the medieval traditions of scholastic philosophy and science, theology and law. As a part of this learning, or derived from it, we find a body of moral thought that is never opposed to religious doctrine—often explicitly harmonized with it—existing side by side with religious doctrine and claiming for its domain wider and wider areas of human life and experience. There are several medieval precedents for such secular moral thought, but these were different and more limited in scope. Certain moralists like Cicero, Seneca, and Boethius had enjoyed a continuous popularity throughout the Middle Ages, and medieval grammarians had tried to provide moral interpretations of ancient poets such as Ovid and Vergil. This tradition was apparently absorbed by Renaissance humanism in its beginnings in the fourteenth century. When Aristotle's writings were all translated into Latin and adopted as textbooks of philosophy at Paris and other universities during the thirteenth century, his *Ethics,* along with his *Politics,* his *Rhetoric,* and the *Economics* attributed to him, was expounded in the classroom, and a number of commentaries on these works owe their origin to this teaching tradition, although the course on ethics was an elective rather than a required course, and considered less important than logic or natural philosophy. Thus Aristotle's doctrines of the virtues and of the supreme good, and also his theory of the passions as presented in the *Rhetoric,* were well known to students of philosophy and to many others. When the humanists took over much of the teaching of ethics in the fifteenth century and wrote general treatises on moral subjects, they continued to use the Aristotelian writings, which recommended themselves by their topical completeness and the wealth of their detail, and the humanists often tended to follow his views though they might interpret them in a different way or combine them with theories derived from other sources. Finally, in the later Middle Ages there had developed a code of moral conduct for knights, that is, for a privileged class of laymen, and this code found its literary expression in lyrical poetry, in romances in verse and prose, and in a few theoretical treatises. The moral literature of the Renaissance was similarly intended for laymen rather than for clerics. Yet aside from its heavy classical equipment which had been lacking in the medieval literature of the knights, it was written by and for a different class of people: it had a different political, economic, and social foundation.

Renaissance humanism, which began in Italy toward the very end of the thirteenth century, at the earliest, cannot be explained as a delayed but direct result of the economic and political development of the city communities that began in the eleventh century. For even a theory of a "cultural lag," whatever that may mean, does not seem to supply the missing link, as there was, after all, a distinctive tradition of learning and literature in twelfth- and early thirteenth-century Italy that was not humanistic. On the other hand, an urban, not a feudal society provided at least the background of Renaissance civilization. The Renaissance humanists wrote their moral works for their fellow scholars, for their students, and for an elite of business-men and of urbanized noblemen who were willing to adopt their cultural and moral ideas. During the sixteenth century, ever wider circles of the middle class seem to have taken interest in this literature.

Political theory was traditionally a part of ethics or a supplement to it, and the Renaissance moralists took a strong and sometimes primary interest in political theory. The nature of their political ideas varied a good deal according to circumstances. There was a tradition of civic and republican humanism, especially in Florence, and to a lesser degree in Venice, whose historical significance has been recently emphasized by Hans Baron and other scholars. Yet much Renaissance political thinking developed also along monarchical lines, especially during the sixteenth century. Both Machiavelli and Thomas More were also linked to the humanist movement.

Aside from the political treatises, the moral literature of the Renaissance addressed itself mainly to the private individual. The political and economic realities of the day are taken more or less for granted, and the purpose of the moral treatise is to give theoretical or practical instruction to the individual, especially to the young. The lines between decency and success are not always as clearly drawn as we might wish, and as a result, the word virtue came to have a curious ambiguity. It meant moral virtue, to be sure, but Machiavelli's *virtù* stood more for the strong character that assured political success, and the "virtuoso" was distinguished by intellectual and social skill rather than by moral excellence.

At this point, we might very well stop to consider the variety of meanings of the term "moral thought," both for the Renaissance and in its wider applications. When we speak of the morals of a person or a period, we think primarily of actual behavior, and assume that this behavior expresses some conscious or unconscious convictions, although it may be quite contrary to the professed ideals of the person and of the time. In this respect, the Renaissance, and especially the Italian Renaissance, enjoys a dubious reputation. In the popular view, which seems to find support in Symonds and other historians, the Italian Renaissance was a period of political ruthlessness, of crimes of violence and of passion; and the glittering melodrama of dagger and poison seems to provide an appropriate foil for the admired beauty of Renaissance poetry and painting. Examples of crime and cruelty were numerous in the Renaissance, in Italy and elsewhere, as they are in other periods of history, including the Middle Ages and our century. However, not all the stories and anecdotes that found their way from the Renaissance chroniclers and gossip-writers into modern textbooks of history are well documented, and those that we can accept were probably disapproved of in their own time as much as in ours. Moreover, it would be quite wrong to assume that such misdeeds dominated the picture of public or private life during the Renaissance. There were a great many decent people whose conduct agreed with the highest moral standards.

Yet, ignoring the actual conduct of people during the Renaissance or whatever secret or unexpressed thought may have guided them, and examining those moral ideas that we find more or less explicitly stated in the literature of the period, we find that moral subjects were discussed in a variety of ways. An author may describe the actual moral customs and manners of his time, either through examples, as is often done in narrative literature, or through a discussion of their general traits, without explicitly setting forth any standards of how people should behave. He may also, however, try to guide the conduct of people, especially of his younger readers, by prescribing how they should behave. Description and prescription are often confused in our contemporary discussions of moral and social problems, and they cannot always be kept apart in Renaissance literature, but it would help proper understanding of such discussions if the distinction is clearly kept in mind. In the literature which emphasizes the prescriptive aspect and tends to set standards for the young, we must distinguish between those authors who are mainly concerned with rules of prudence and expediency, and teach their readers how to behave in order to get along with other people and to have a successful career, and those who emphasize honesty and moral decency regardless of their practical consequences. In works of the latter kind there is often a mixture of ethical theory, which properly belongs to philosophy, and of moral exhortation and persuasion, which belongs to oratory and tends toward edification. Finally, there is the literature of strictly philosophical ethics, which intends to set forth general principles of moral thought and which is prescriptive only in an implicit way or by deducing rules of conduct from those general principles. This literature may take the form of systematic handbooks of ethics or of monographic treatises dealing with specific topics in ethics.

All these types are present in the moral literature of the Renaissance, and it would be wrong to say that any of them is limited to a particular phase of the period. However, the literature of the fifteenth and early sixteenth century is more frequently concerned with moralistic prescription and edification. As the sixteenth century progresses, rules of expediency and descriptions of manners and customs tend to prevail. One gets the impression of a more settled society in which standards of conduct and manners are well established and the main task of the young man is not to acquire valid ethical principles through independent critical thinking but rather to assure his success by learning how to adjust to life—that is, to the accepted modes of moral thought and conduct. This literature gains in historical and psychological interest what it loses in ethical solidity, and it leads the way towards such famous examples of seventeenth-century literature as Gracian, La Bruyère, or La Rochefoucauld.

V

In contrast to the books of manners stand the philosophical treatises on ethics that supply whatever theoretical structure and systematic thinking on moral problems there was during the Renaissance. Because of the general direction of Renaissance humanism, most, though not all, of their subject matter is derived from classical sources. The authors known during the Middle Ages, especially Aristotle, Cicero, and Seneca, continue to be important and in some ways become even more important, as there is a greater effort to interpret and to utilize them in great detail. Equally important are some other sources of ancient moral philosophy made available for the first time by humanist scholarship. These new sources include most of the writings of Plato and of the Neoplatonists, Stoic authors such as Epictetus and Marcus Aurelius, Sceptics like Sextus Empiricus, and Epicureans like Lucretius. Diogenes Laertius supplied new information on several schools of ancient thought, especially on Epicurus. Of equal, if not even greater, importance were a number of popular ancient moralists not identified with any particular school of philosophy, such as Xenophon and Isocrates, Plutarch and Lucian. The number both of their translations and of the quotations taken from them shows that they were among the favorite sources of Renaissance humanists.

The impact of these various sources and schools on the moral thought of the Renaissance was varied and complex. Moreover, the history of moral thought during the Renaissance is related to, but not identical with, the history of philosophy. Only a part of the moral literature of the period came from philosophers in the technical sense of the word, or was systematic in content. On the other hand, some of the most important philosophers of the Renaissance, and even entire groups and schools of Renaissance philosophy, such as the Aristotelians, the Platonists, and the philosophers of nature, were not interested primarily in ethics but made their major contributions to other parts of philosophy, especially logic, metaphysics, and natural philosophy. With these qualifications, we may say that there was a solid body of Aristotelian ethics throughout the Renaissance period. Its most obvious expressions are the numerous editions, translations, commentaries, and summaries of the ethical writings of Aristotle, among which the *Eudemian Ethics* now takes its proper place for the first time, and of their ancient and medieval interpreters. This literature has not been sufficiently explored until recent times, and we are just beginning to learn more about it. However, we may safely say of the Aristotelian ethics what has become apparent about Renaissance Aristotelianism in general. It continues in many ways the traditions of medieval Aristotelianism, which were very much alive at the universities, in Italy as elsewhere. On the other hand, there was among the humanists a strong tendency to recapture the genuine thought of Aristotle apart from its supposed distortions by medieval translators and commentators. Finally, there were all kinds of combinations on the part of Aristotelian philosophers, who tried to reconcile and to synthesize what seemed to be valuable in the scholastic and humanistic interpretations of Aristotle. In the study of ethics, as in other disciplines, the main contribution of the humanists to Aristotelian studies was to supply new translations based on a better philological understanding of the Greek text. This is more important than one might suspect. For in an author as difficult and elusive as Aristotle, whose every word was (and still is) considered by many thinkers as the ultimate source and authority of philosophical truth, a different translation may be equivalent to a different philosophy. Moreover, whereas the medieval scholastics treated Aristotle pretty much in isolation, the humanist Aristotelians read and interpreted Aristotle in close conjunction with the other Greek philosophers and writers. On the whole, the humanist Aristotelians were primarily interested in Aristotle's ethical writings. Leonardo Bruni translated and summarized only Aristotle's *Ethics, Politics* and *Economics,* while Francesco Filelfo wrote a summary of ethics based on Aristotle. Ermolao Barbaro, though not limited to Aristotle's ethical writings, favored them in his lectures and in a summary of ethics. Philip Melanchthon, Luther's colleague, wrote several treatises on ethics, in which Aristotle's doctrine is preferred to that of other ancient philosophers, and it was due to Melanchthon's influence that the Reformed universities of Protestant Germany continued to base their teaching of philosophy on the works of Aristotle.

As a result of this widespread study of Aristotle, practically every writer of the period was acquainted with the main doctrines of Aristotelian ethics and was inclined to adopt them or to discuss them. Aristotle's views that the supreme good of man must include a minimum of external advantages and that the contemplative life is the highest goal of human existence are as familiar in the moral literature of the Renaissance as are his distinction between moral and intellectual virtues, his definition of the moral virtues as habits and as means between two opposite vices, and his detailed descriptions of individual virtues and vices.

Plato's influence on the moral thought of the Renaissance is much more limited than Aristotle's, in spite of the well-known role played generally by Platonism in Renaissance philosophy. Plato's early dialogues, to be sure, deal with moral topics, and were widely read in school, mainly in courses of Greek. Yet we do not find any system of ethics based primarily on Plato, as so many were on Aristotle. This is due partly to the unsystematic character of Plato's writings. More important, the leading Platonists of the Renaissance, like their late ancient and medieval predecessors, were interested in questions of metaphysics and cosmology rather than of ethics. They were not so much concerned with specific moral problems or theories but tended to reduce all ethical questions to the single task of attaining the contemplative life. Some of their specific theories that are relevant to moral thought we shall encounter later. The most important and widespread contribution of Platonism to the subject is the theory of love, based on the *Symposium* and *Phaedrus,* which was to constitute the subject matter of poems and lectures and of a special branch of prose literature. Among the moralists not committed to any special school of philosophy, quotations and borrowings from Plato were frequent, and became increasingly so after the rise of Florentine Platonism during the second half of the fifteenth century.

Stoic ethics as expressed in the writings of Seneca, and discussed in Cicero's philosophical works, had been a familiar ingredient of medieval moral thought, and continued to exercise a widespread influence during the Renaissance, when the writings of these Roman authors became even more popular than they had been before. The Stoic view that the supreme good of man consisted of virtue alone and that to secure virtue all passions must be thoroughly eradicated was generally known and often approved. Some Stoic theories appealed even to thinkers, such as Pomponazzi, who cannot be labeled as Stoic philosophers in their general orientation. Yet in contrast with this popular and eclectic Stoicism based on Cicero and Seneca, which permeated the moral thought of the fifteenth and early sixteenth century, it was only during the latter part of the sixteenth century that the Greek sources of ancient Stoicism became better known and that systematic attempts were made to restate Stoic philosophy (and especially Stoic ethics) in its original purity. The distinguished humanist, Justus Lipsius, compiled from the ancient sources a valuable handbook of Stoic ethics that was to enjoy great popularity during the seventeenth century, and the French writer, Guillaume Du Vair, gave a more literary expression to the same doctrine. Most Renaissance humanists found Stoic ethics uncongenial on account of its rigidity. The great vogue of pure Stoicism came only in the seventeenth century. In order to understand this later appeal, we must remember that the Stoics are rigorous only in their emphasis on the difference between virtue and vice, but reserve a very large area of human life to the things they call morally indifferent. Where questions of virtue and vice are not involved the Stoic sage is allowed and even encouraged to follow expediency. With virtue and vice often limited to a few ultimate decisions, the sway of expediency becomes very large indeed, and the Stoic moralist, while continuing to be rigorous in theory, may turn out to be lax, if not selfish, on most practical questions. The same may happen to the Platonist (and to the mystic), as soon as he has to act on matters unrelated to the life of contemplation.

The ethics of Epicurus, which proposed intellectual pleasure as the chief end of human life, was widely known in the Renaissance, and frequently discussed. Most humanists rejected Epicurean ethics and were more or less influenced by Cicero's unsympathetic account of that doctrine. Yet gradually the more favorable presentation of Epicurus in the works of Lucretius and Diogenes Laertius became better known, and Epicurus's emphasis on intellectual pleasure was more fully appreciated. Thus Epicurean ethics was endorsed by a few humanists, such as Lorenzo Valla and Cosimo Raimondi, and some of its tenets made an impression on thinkers whose general outlook was very different—for example, Marsilio Ficino.

Finally, ancient Scepticism had a number of followers in the Renaissance, especially in the sixteenth century, when the writings of Sextus became more widely known. The main appeal of Scepticism was in its claim that by abandoning all rigid doctrines and opinions we free ourselves from unnecessary worries and are left to face only the unavoidable necessities of life. If we wish to have a standard for our conduct, we should follow the customs of our country, at least in all matters that concern other people. In this way the boundaries between moral standards and established manners tend to be blurred, although there may remain a realm of personal and individual life in which we may think and do as we please. Scepticism in matters of reason is by no means incompatible with religious faith, as the example of Augustine may show; consequently this position had many more followers during the sixteenth century than is usually realized. The chief expression of this sceptical ethics is found in some of the essays of Montaigne, and in the writings of his pupil, Pierre Charron.

VI

The influence of ancient ethics on the Renaissance is not limited to an acceptance of the main systematic theories of antiquity by some Renaissance thinkers. The constant use of specific ancient ideas or sentences or examples in the discussion of moral topics is more widespread. This eclectic use of ancient material, for which some favorite author such as Cicero could serve as a classical model, is especially characteristic of the humanists and their popular followers. In this way, particular ideas or sentences taken from a given philosopher, such as Plato or Aristotle, were indiscriminately combined with those of other philosophers who held a very different position on major questions or with those of ancient moralists like Isocrates, Lucian, or Plutarch, who cannot even be credited with a coherent systematic position in philosophy. Thus the sharp boundaries between philosophical concepts or theories derived from different sources tend to vanish. Furthermore, Renaissance humanists were not so much interested as modern scholars are in emphasizing the distinctive traits of various periods, schools, and writers of antiquity or in playing up one against the other. They tended to admire ancient literature in all its periods and representatives (although some authors were more admired than others), and to be syncretistic as well as eclectic; that is, they liked to harmonize the views of various classical authors, and to extract from their writings a kind of common wisdom that could be learned, imitated, and utilized.

The numerous classical quotations that characterize most humanist treatises and even the essays of Montaigne, and which are apt to bore and annoy the modern reader, were not vain displays of empty erudition, although they might often serve this purpose. The quotations served as authorities—as confirmations of the validity of what the author was trying to say. Quotations from recognized authors were counted by ancient theorists of rhetoric among the forms of proof that an orator was supposed to produce. Augustine had emphasized the authority of Scripture as a chief source of theological discourse, and during the Middle Ages not only theology but each discipline of knowledge employed its standard authorities, along with rational arguments, in support of its theories. For a Renaissance humanist, a sentence from a classical writer served as such an authority, and if he added to his quotation what seems to us an arbitrary interpretation, he merely did what his predecessors and contemporaries also had done. In a period in which the emphasis is on authority and tradition, originality will assert itself in the adaptation and interpretation of the tradition. Moreover, there may be some originality even in the choice of one's quotations. It makes a difference whether an author keeps quoting the same passages that had been quoted by his predecessors or for the first time introduces new quotations, singling them out from their context and, as it were, discovering their significance.

The frequency of quotations and of commonplaces repeated in the moral literature of the Renaissance gives to all but its very best products an air of triviality that is often very boring to the modern critical reader, especially when he is acquainted with the ancient sources from which the quotations are drawn and in which they seem to have a much more subtle and precise meaning. If we want to do justice to these Renaissance writers we must try to understand the circumstances under which they wrote, and the purposes which they had in mind. Whenever many books of the same type are written, most of them are bound to be dull and mediocre, and only a few will stand out by reason of their authors' intellectual or literary merits. Human inventiveness seems limited, and repetition is the rule rather than the exception, even where no direct copying or plagiarism is involved. After all, no single reader was expected to read all the treatises on the same topic, just as a modern student will not read more than one or two textbooks on the same subject. Each treatise is addressed to its own readers, and must supply to them the same amount of general information that other readers may derive from other works on the same topic. This is even more the case with orations, which were delivered on only a single occasion and were published only incidentally when they happened to be very successful. An oration is composed to entertain and edify its audience by adapting general ideas to the occasion. While it was the custom in Florence to have each incoming group of magistrates treated to a speech in praise of justice, it was not so important that the orator should produce new or profound ideas about the meaning of justice—it was his job to impress his listeners with their duty to follow justice in the administration of their office. This was surely of great practical importance for the city as a whole. Since the oration was a principal form of humanist literature, the example might be applied to its other branches. Each moral treatise had to exhort and edify its readers by instructing them in matters of great practical and human importance, and this was in most instances more valuable than the presentation of novel or original thoughts. In other words, we should not approach the average moral literature of the Renaissance with excessive expectations as to its depth or originality, but with an awareness of its limited purposes, and a recognition that it was well suited to these objectives.

VII

The frequency of ancient ideas and quotations in the moral writings of the Renaissance humanists, and of humanist literature in general, raises another question that has been the subject of much debate: what was the attitude of the Renaissance humanists toward Christianity, and in what sense and to what extent were they inclined toward paganism? The charge of paganism was made against the humanists by some theologians of their own time, and it has been repeated by a number of modern historians, some of whom have turned the charge into praise. There were, however, very few attempts to revive the pagan religions of classical antiquity, although this has been charged by contemporaries and by modern scholars in a few instances. Although much was made of pagan mythology in the poetry and also in the prose treatises of the period, it was not intended to replace the use of Christian religious thought and imagery but to supplement it. In most instances it was no more than a literary ornament sanctioned by ancient precedent. Where it served a more serious intention, its use was justified by allegory —by attributing to the pagan stories a hidden meaning that was in accordance with Christian truth. This attitude culminates in Pico della Mirandola's notion of a poetic theology, that is, of a philosophical and theological truth that could be discovered through the allegorical interpretation of pagan poetry and mythology. Yet the main impact of "paganism" on the moral thought of the Renaissance consists in its heavy indebtedness to ancient philosophical ideas, which we have already noted. The task of assimilating the moral and philosophical thought of the ancients to Christianity presented itself to the Church Fathers and again to many medieval thinkers. From these earlier attempts, the Renaissance differed at least in degree, if not in

kind. The Church Fathers tended to fit Christianity into the
ancient modes of thought that had been previously familiar to
them and to their contemporaries. The humanists wanted to
adapt classical ideas to a previously accepted Christian view of
the world. Nevertheless, the affinity between the humanists and
the Church Fathers has been stressed with some justification by
modern historians like Toffanin, and the humanists themselves
were to some extent aware of this affinity. For when they defended "poetry," that is, humanist learning and the reading of
the pagan authors, against the theological critics of their own
time, they cited the precedent of the Church Fathers. No doubt
Bruni's translation of the letter in which Basil, one of the
Fathers, defended the reading of pagan poets by a Christian
youth owed its tremendous popularity to this issue. There were
many humanists who were not concerned with religious or theological problems, and did not touch on them in their writings.
Those who did, and they were important, never undertook a
general critique of the religious tradition such as appeared in
the eighteenth century. They usually praised the Bible and the
Church Fathers as the Christian classics, and attacked scholastic
theology as a barren distortion of original Christian doctrine
and piety. A few of them attacked the weaknesses they observed
in the Church of their time, and especially in monasticism. When
the humanists wrote about moral subjects, either they tried to
combine and to harmonize ancient and Christian ideas in the
manner of Erasmus, or they discussed moral topics on a purely
classical and secular basis—without however indicating any hostility toward Christianity, but rather taking for granted the
compatibility between the two, as was done by Alberti and many
other Italian humanists. In the sixteenth century, after the Protestant and Catholic reformations, we find humanist scholars and
moralists among the followers of both major camps, as well as
among those who favored some of the smaller heretical movements, or who tried hard to keep aloof from the religious struggle.
This shows once more, that Renaissance humanism as a whole
cannot be identified with a particular set of opinions or convictions, but is rather characterized by a cultural ideal and a range
of scholarly, literary, and intellectual interests that the individual
humanist was able to combine with a variety of professional,
philosophical, or theological convictions.

VIII

If we try to survey in more concrete detail the moral thought of the Renaissance period, it seems best to focus on the chief genres and themes of this literature, rather than on the ideas of individual writers and thinkers. The character of this literature, with its uncertain position between philosophical and popular thought, its dependence on classical sources, and its widespread eclecticism and triviality, seems to call for such an approach.

The most technical type of Renaissance literature on moral topics is the general treatise on ethics that was usually written for the use of students. Since Aristotle was and remained the chief basis of university instruction in the philosophical disciplines, many general treatises on ethics take the form of commentaries on Aristotle's *Nicomachean Ethics* and *Politics,* or of introductions, paraphrases, and summaries of those works. In the fifteenth century, the commentary of Donato Acciaiuoli and the *Compendium* of Ermolao Barbaro deserve mention; and in the sixteenth century there was Francesco Piccolomini, a Paduan, and a few other scholars such as Alessandro Piccolomini, who composed a handbook of Aristotelian ethics in Italian, indicating by this very fact that he was addressing himself to a broader educated public. Outside of Italy, the introductions of Jacques Lefèvre d'Etaples to Aristotle's writings on moral philosophy and Melanchthon's ethical writings represent the most influential attempts to restate Aristotle's ethics—especially his belief that the natural goods contribute to the supreme good of happiness and that the moral virtues are means between two opposite extremes —and to harmonize this natural ethics with the teachings of Scripture. John Case's moral questions on Aristotle, which originated in Oxford, are important as a rare example of a type of literature that must have flourished also at the English universities to a greater degree than is usually realized. More eclectic but still largely Aristotelian are the handbooks of Francesco Filelfo and of Sebastian Fox Morcillo. An early and very popular introduction to ethics, Leonardo Bruni's *Isagogicon Moralis Disciplinae,* follows Aristotle in the discussion of the moral and intellectual virtues, but advances a somewhat eclectic view on the supreme good. He bases the ultimate end of human life mainly on virtue but also grants some importance to external advantages and thus stays close enough to Aristotle's position, but at the same time he claims that this view is essentially identical with those of the Stoics and Epicureans. The most consistent attempt to present Stoic ethics in a systematic handbook was made by Justus Lipsius toward the end of the sixteenth century. Its major effects were to be felt only during the following century.

Aside from such handbooks of ethics, there are a number of more informal humanist treatises and dialogues in which the central topic of ancient ethics, that is, happiness or the supreme good, is discussed. Whereas Petrarch had blamed Aristotle for his belief that man may attain his ultimate end during the present life, an attitude echoed by Bartolommeo Fazio and others, many writers identified the goal of life with the knowledge and enjoyment of God but thought that this goal could be attained during the present life, at least by some people and for some time. This view was held especially by the leading Platonist, Marsilio Ficino, who wrote several short treatises on it. Bartolomeo Platina stresses endurance and wisdom in a Stoic sense, and Pietro Pomponazzi approaches Stoicism rather than the view of Aristotle when in his treatise on immortality he defines moral virtue as the task peculiar to human beings, and emphasizes that this virtue is its own reward, just as wickedness is its own punishment. Also the Epicurean view that pleasure is the supreme good found its defenders. The most famous of them, Lorenzo Valla, considers Epicureanism as the best among the pagan philosophies but endorses as his own view a kind of Christian Epicureanism in which the pleasures of the present life are abandoned for the sake of the pleasures, both physical and spiritual, which are promised in a future life to the faithful Christian.

A number of humanistic treatises deal with individual virtues, a subject that occupies a large part of Aristotle's *Ethics* and now is singled out for monographic treatment. Several of the virtues are discussed in the moral treatises of the Neapolitan humanist, Giovanni Pontano, such as courage, magnanimity, or prudence. Attempts to define the respective virtues are accompanied by a variety of moral rules and examples, and the concern is as much with stylistic elegance and moral edification, as with precise philosophical definitions or distinctions. Similar treatises were written by several Italian and other humanist writers.

A whole literature was dedicated to the highest virtue, wisdom, which was identified either with the attainment of pure knowledge, or with moral and practical ability in the affairs of life.

The latter tendency culminated in Pierre Charron, theologian and sceptical philosopher of the early seventeenth century. Analogous treatises were written on some specific vices such as ingratitude or avarice. There is a famous treatise on avarice by Poggio Bracciolini, in which some of the beneficial effects of this vice also are mentioned, in a way which some historians have tended to link with the spirit of modern capitalism.

IX

The humanist movement was closely identified with a reform of the program and curriculum of the secondary schools. Many of the humanists were professional tutors or school teachers, and it was through the training offered in the schools that most of the educated persons of the Renaissance period were influenced by humanist ideas, which they then carried into the larger spheres of public and professional life. Hence it was natural that the humanists would be very much concerned with the tasks and problems of education. The treatises on the education of the young form a large and important genre of humanist prose, and thanks to these treatises Renaissance humanism occupies as prominent a place in the history of educational theory as in that of educational practice.

The most influential early treatises were by Pier Paolo Vergerio the Elder and by Leonardo Bruni, to which we may add the treatise on education attributed to Plutarch that was translated by Guarino of Verona, who along with Vittorino da Feltre was the most famous and successful humanist teacher in fifteenth-century Italy. Other influential educational treatises were written by Maffeo Vegio and by Enea Silvio Piccolomini, a prominent humanist who entered the ecclesiastic career and finally became pope under the name of Pius II. Outside of Italy, educational treatises were written by many humanists such as Erasmus and Vives, by Wimpfeling and Camerarius in Germany, and by Ascham in England. These treatises were written either for the young students themselves or for the parents of prospective students to convince them of the value of a humanist education. A good deal of attention is paid to the praise of Greek and Latin literature, whose study formed the core of humanist instruction, and to the value of such an education for the future citizen or statesman. Often the author would offer actual reading lists, discussing the merits and educational value of specific classical

authors and their different works. Aside from the genuine concern for a ruling class thoroughly imbued with a cultural heritage of unquestioned intellectual importance, the humanist
educators laid much stress on the moral value inherent in the
study of ancient literature, history, and philosophy. Through
the reading of the classical authors, the student was to acquire
a fund of moral ideas, sentences, and examples that would give
him the necessary preparation to face the tasks of his own life.
In stressing the moral value of a classical education, the humanists effectively countered the charge made by some theologians
that the reading of the pagan poets and writers would corrupt
the morals of the young. The humanists knew, of course, that
there was much in ancient literature that could not stand muster
before a strict Christian censor, and many of them did not hesitate to emulate it in prose and verse, pleading with Martial
that their life was pure though their verse might be licentious.
Yet they knew how to distinguish between a literature written
by and for adults and the requirements of the education of the
young. In their treatises on education they would usually omit
from their reading list those ancient writings that gave rise to
moral criticism, and Erasmus added the pointed remark that we
should be careful not to imbibe the manners of the ancients
along with their literature. In this way, the humanists managed
to link their cultural ideals very closely with the moral aspirations of their time, and to make their educational program
acceptable to all but the most narrow-minded theologians.

The actual human ideal of the Renaissance has often been
characterized as that of the *uomo universale,* the universal man,
or to use a modern phrase, the well-rounded personality. We
rarely encounter this slogan in the literature of the period, but
the actual life of persons like Leon Battista Alberti or Leonardo
da Vinci seems to illustrate a quest for excellence in a great
variety of pursuits, and the educational treatises of the time
envisage a person who would achieve reasonable distinction in
physical and artistic, intellectual and practical activities. This
is also apparent in another large branch of literature that is
concerned, not with education in general, but with the training
of particular groups or classes of society.

A large number of treatises is dedicated to the education or
the description of the good prince, and this literature has
attracted a great deal of attention among historians of literature
and of political thought. The "mirror of princes" was an impor-

tant branch of literature during the later medieval centuries, and
it has been shown that the ideal of the Christian king, based on
Germanic customs and theological theories, was gradually transformed under the impact of the study of Roman law and of
Aristotle's *Politics*. In fifteenth-century Italy, monarchical states
were firmly established in Naples and Milan, and on a smaller
scale, in Piedmont, Ferrara, and Mantua, not to speak of the
numerous tiny and ephemeral principalities. It is against this
background that the treatises on the best prince by humanists
like Platina or Pontano and others must be understood. Important new sources for these treatises were several works of Isocrates
and Plutarch that were widely diffused in a number of different
translations. These humanist treatises were largely theoretical
and gave much space to a list of the virtues that the prince
should possess and to ancient examples of good conduct. It is
characteristic that the tone of these treatises is secular rather
than religious and that the reward promised to the good prince
is everlasting fame rather than blessedness in a future life. The
quest for fame was a central concern of the humanists and of
their contemporaries, and the power of its appeal may be discovered in many episodes and writings of the period.

Another topic discussed in these treatises was the relation between virtue and expediency, and the authors of these usually
concluded with Cicero that the most virtuous course of action
is also in the long run the most advantageous. It has been
pointed out by Allan Gilbert, Felix Gilbert, and other scholars
that Machiavelli's *Prince*, though original in its extreme realism
and its exclusive stress on expediency, is linked in its themes
and problems with the late medieval and early humanist literature on the best prince. In the sixteenth century, the establish-
ment of strong national monarchies outside of Italy forms the
background for an important series of humanist treatises by
Budé, Sepulveda, and others. The most famous is Erasmus's *Education of a Christian Prince*, which is explicitly introduced as a
counterpart of Isocrates' treatise *Ad Nicoclem*, which Erasmus
had translated. The prince is expected to read a number of
ancient writers, in addition to the Bible. Among his suggestions
for the administration of the state, Erasmus reminds the ruler
that he is merely a member of the state, that his rule rests basically on the consent of the people, and that the public welfare
is the only standard of the laws. Erasmus wants to limit the
death penalty to extreme cases and urges the rulers to submit

their quarrels to arbitration, advocating on religious grounds the ideal of universal peace, a subject which he also treated elsewhere.

X

In fifteenth-century Italy, the ideal of republican liberty was as much alive as that of the monarchical state, as many humanist writings show. The Roman republic was as much a model for imitation as the Roman Empire, and it was no coincidence that the superiority of Scipio interpreted as a symbol of republican virtue was defended by Poggio, a Florentine citizen, against the claims of Caesar that were supported by Guarino, a subject of the Marquess of Ferrara. The comparison between different con- stitutions in the works of Plato, Aristotle, and Polybius found parallels in the writings of Francesco Patrizi, Aurelio Brandolini, and Machiavelli—who in his actual political career and in his *Discourses on Livy* attested his preference for the republican form of government. When Florentine political liberty was being undermined by the Medici regime, Alamanno Rinuccini wrote, but probably did not publish, his *De libertate*. Historians often exaggerate the significance of the fact that many of the city republics of the twelfth and thirteenth century succumbed to various forms of despotism during the fourteenth and fifteenth. The Venetian republic, ruled by its tightly restricted but respon- sible and educated nobility, became more powerful than ever, and was considered, on account of its wealth and stability, as a model by many political writers. The Florentine republic, which showed much less stability and underwent a variety of changes and revolutions, maintained its power and independence against several attacks from the outside and acquired, especially in the fifteenth century, a cultural and artistic predominance that was recognized throughout Italy and Europe. When Florence was threatened during the late fourteenth and early fifteenth century by the repeated attacks of the Visconti princes of Milan, who were expanding their rule over large areas of northern and cen- tral Italy, Florence mobilized against them her intellectual as well as her material resources. In this political crisis, many Flor- entine humanists emphasized the ideals of the republican state and of the responsible citizen called to govern that state. Hans Baron in a series of studies has forcefully described this civic humanism which flourished in Florence during the first half of the fifteenth century, and it certainly deserves attention as one of the most impressive phases of Renaissance humanism, even though it would be quite mistaken to identify Renaissance humanism as a whole with this Florentine civic humanism. There was a good deal of "despotic humanism" even in fifteenth-century Italy, and it would be quite impossible to comprise under the heading of "civic humanism" the entire political literature of the Renaissance period, let alone the large body of humanist literature that was not concerned with political problems at all. Florentine civic humanism found its best expression in the writings of Leonardo Bruni, Leon Battista Alberti, and Matteo Palmieri. Humanist learning is presented by them as serving the active life of the citizen involved in the affairs of his business and of his republic. He will not only occupy his leisure with the reading of the best authors, but will follow in his own life and activities the examples and precepts offered in their writings. It was not always mentioned but evidently understood that the prominent citizen was often called upon to deliver speeches, or to compose letters, of public importance, and that his humanist training would give him the necessary literary ability to accomplish these tasks with sufficient distinction to earn a good reputation for himself and for his city. Florentine history between 1434 and 1537 was characterized by a gradual transition from a republican form of government to the monarchy of the Medici—a development which was slowed and sometimes interrupted by a strong resistance on the part of the followers of the republican tradition. The political strife between the various parties was accompanied by literary controversy, as often happens, and the decline and fall of the Florentine republic thus produced a long series of political treatises defending the republican form of government and expounding the best ways to give it stability and perfection.

All Italian cities, whether their government was republican or monarchical, had a class of noble families of feudal or commercial antecedents. Its political influence varies greatly from place to place. In Venice, the nobles were the ruling class which monopolized all public office. In Naples, the feudal nobility possessed large landed property and traditional privileges, but the kings tended to reduce these privileges and to build a modern monarchy and a bureaucracy of trained persons directly responsible to them, just as the kings of England, France, and Spain were to do in the sixteenth century. In Florence, the older families were divided into bitterly opposed factions, and depending upon the regime prevailing at a given time, some of them were excluded from office or even exiled, while others shared the administration of the republic with able persons of more modest origins. Everywhere, regardless of their political position, the families of the nobility managed to maintain a good deal of wealth and social prestige, and their style of life served as model for the newcomers who established themselves through business enterprises or political careers or even through professional success. However, with the exception of Naples and possibly Rome, this nobility was no longer feudal in character but thoroughly urbanized and hence may be called more appropriately a patriciate. The humanists succeeded in gaining this important class for their cause, educated their children, and impressed upon them the conviction that they needed a good education by humanist standards to be worthy of their social status. On the other hand, the humanists cherished the ambition of attaining for themselves a comparable social position, and at least some of them succeeded. For the trained humanist could have a career as chancellor or secretary of princes and republics, and thus was able to contribute his share, along with the much larger body of lawyers, to what was to be called in later centuries the *noblesse de robe*. Against this background, it is quite understandable why the humanists of the fifteenth century were interested in the problem of nobility and why they should focus on the question whether nobility is or should be based on birth or on personal merit. The question had been discussed by a few late medieval authors, and some of them had already emphasized the role of personal merit as a basis of nobility. In the fifteenth century, there was a whole series of treatises, *De Nobilitate*, in which this problem is investigated further. In the treatises by Poggio Bracciolini, Buonaccorso da Montemagno, Bartolomeo Platina, and the still unpublished but interesting dialogue of Cristoforo Landino, the thesis that nobility rests on virtue is strongly defended. The problem is treated in typically humanist fashion in the work of Buonaccorso da Montemagno, which enjoyed tremendous popularity. Two Romans compete for the hand of a noble woman, and support their claims in elaborate speeches, one of them praising his illustrious ancestry, the other his personal achievements. The author does not tell us which of the two married the girl, but the greater force seems to be in the second speech which defends the claims of merit. The tendency apparent in these treatises has led many scholars to consider the preference for personal merit as against inherited nobility as typical of Renaissance humanism. This is to some extent justified, but not entirely so. The authors of the treatises we have mentioned were for the most part Tuscans. We should not overlook the fact that the claims of the Neapolitan nobility were defended by one of its members who was himself a humanist, Tristano Caracciolo, and those of the Venetian nobility by Lauro Querini, another well-known humanist who happened to be a Venetian nobleman himself. It is apparent once more how difficult it is to identify humanism as a whole with any given set of opinions, although these opinions may be held by some of its representatives. The common denominator is always, not a set of opinions, but a cultural and educational ideal.

XI

Another group of significant Renaissance moral treatises tries to describe, and to propose for imitation, the human ideal of the perfect citizen, magistrate, courtier, or gentleman. It is the ideal of a member of the ruling class, apart from its political connotations, held out as a model for young and old people alike. This genre, represented in the fifteenth century by some treatises of Alberti, Platina, and others, became especially important in the sixteenth. The most famous work of the group, Baldassarre Castiglione's *Book of the Courtier,* was translated into several languages and found imitators all over Europe. This work, which has great stylistic merit and occupies an important place in the history of Italian prose literature, clearly envisages a member of the aristocracy, and reflects many personal traits of its author who was active as a diplomat for many years in the service of the princes of Mantua and of the papal Curia. Castiglione's *Courtier* represents a human ideal of great breadth; it might be said to reflect the concept of the *uomo universale,* and it clearly exercised a civilizing influence upon the ruling classes of Renaissance Europe. Aside from the traditional knightly virtues of courage and physical prowess, the courtier is expected to have polished manners, to be an able participant in elegant conversation, to have a good literary education, and to be moderately accomplished in the arts of painting, music, and dance. An English counterpart is Sir Thomas Elyot's *Boke of the Governour,* in which moral and religious considerations play a some-

what larger role. Later in the century, the emphasis shifts more
and more to a description of manners practiced in good society
and to the requirements of polite conversation. Giovanni della
Casa's *Galateo,* and Stefano Guazzo's book *On Civil Conversation* were widely read, translated, and imitated, and form
the core of a large literature in all languages, usually described
as books of courtesy, of conduct, or of manners. Louis Wright
has shown that for England this literature more and more addressed itself not only to the members of the aristocracy, but also
to the middle class of merchants and professionals who were
eager to strengthen their social position by imitating the manners
of the older ruling class. This literature prepares the way for the
treatises on the perfect gentleman that were to be composed in
the seventeenth century. Yet it also contains a good many prudential rules and seems to be intended partly for the young man
of talent and modest means who is trying to get ahead in life
and make a career. The straight preaching of moral virtues, so
prominent in the early humanist treatises, now occupies less and
less space, although the possession of these virtues is taken more
or less for granted.

XII

Aside from the generalized ideal of the courtier or gentleman,
many treatises were written on the duties of persons who occupied a particular status, or practiced a particular profession.
There were books on the duties of a magistrate or ambassador,
or even on the duties of a bishop, in which moral prescriptions
were combined with advice concerning the practical conduct of
affairs. In the extensive literature of treatises on art that was
written during the Renaissance period, the technical rules of
the craft were embellished with moral advice for the artist. What
Cicero and Quintilian had required of the orator, namely that
he should combine moral stature and a general education with
the technical competence appropriate for his profession, was
now applied to all other professions, and especially to that of
the artist. The painter, the sculptor, and the architect not only
acquired a higher social status and prestige than they ever possessed before or afterwards, they also tended to combine artistic
skill with literary, scholarly, and scientific interests and competence—as we may see in the writings of Alberti, Piero della
Francesca, Leonardo, Dürer, Michelangelo, and Rubens—and

hence to appropriate for their profession the moral claims advanced originally by the humanist scholars.

One of the chief innovations brought about by the Protestant Reformation was the abolition of the monastic orders, which had played such an important role during the Middle Ages and which retained and even increased their importance in the modern Catholic world. The radical move of the Reformers was preceded, as is well known, by centuries of medieval attacks on the vices and shortcomings of the monks and friars, charges that were at least in part justified and that the Catholic Reformation of the sixteenth century tended to obviate. The humanists contributed their share to the critique of monasticism. Valla and others wrote against the monks, and Erasmus in his *Praise of Folly* poured a good deal of ridicule upon them. Yet it should be noted that Erasmus in this work did not spare any class of contemporary society, not even his own, the grammarians and rhetoricians; elsewhere he insists that the pious life was not a monopoly of the monastic orders, asserting an ideal of lay piety which he inherited from the "Modern Devotion," the Dutch mystic movement in whose schools he had received his first education. Yet he nowhere advocates the abolition of the orders. Among the earlier Italian humanists, we find several writers and scholars of distinction, such as Petrarch, Salutati, and Ermolao Barbaro, who actually came out in praise of the monastic life, and there were many learned monks, such as Ambrogio Traversari, who took a significant part in the humanist movement. Again it would be wrong to identify humanism as a whole with one or the other opinion on this important question.

A good deal has been written by Burckhardt and others about the place of women in Renaissance society. Women had not yet acquired an important place in professional life, and their activities were still largely confined to the house and the family. Yet within this limited range they were respected, and at least a few of them, especially the daughters of princes, noblemen, and scholars, received a literary and scholarly education and distinguished themselves as patrons of learning, or even as scholars and writers in their own right. Thus it is significant that one of the most important humanist treatises on education, Leonardo Bruni's *De studiis et litteris,* was dedicated to a woman. A series of treatises by fifteenth-century humanists deal with the family and with marriage, and hence have a good deal to say about the moral and practical duties of the housewife and mother. Famous and influential specimens of this literature are Francesco Barbaro's *De re uxoria*, and Alberti's treatise *Della famiglia*. The former emphasizes moral advice, and the latter contains charming pages on the way the wife of a wealthy citizen is supposed to assist her husband and to govern the household, servants, and children. In the sixteenth century, Castiglione in his *Courtier* devotes a special section of his work to the court lady, the female counterpart of his male subject, and Vives composed a significant treatise *On the Education of a Christian Woman*. Later in the century, in Italy as elsewhere, a whole series of treatises was written on the conduct of women, in which prudential rules played a large part and some advice was even offered on how to dress and how to use cosmetics.

XIII

A large segment of literature extending from the end of the fifteenth to the end of the sixteenth century deals with the subject of love. A famous medieval example had been Andreas Capellanus's book on courtly love, in which the customs of French chivalry received a more theoretical, though not a more philosophical, expression than in the lyric and epic poetry of the period. More philosophical was the lyric poetry of Cavalcanti, Dante, and their contemporaries in Italy, and the prose speculation on love began with Dante's *Vita Nuova* and *Convivio* as well as with the commentaries on Cavalcanti's obscure poem. This whole literature was given a new impulse and direction by Marsilio Ficino, the head of the Platonic Academy of Florence, and one of the leading Platonists of the Renaissance. He supplied to Western readers the first complete translations of Plato's *Symposium* and *Phaedrus* (parts of which had already been translated by Leonardo Bruni), and also published important commentaries on these two dialogues. In particular, the commentary on the *Symposium* became very famous. Basing himself primarily on Plato but transforming his doctrine under the influence of other philosophical, theological, and literary traditions, Ficino understood the love for another human being as a preliminary form and disguise of the basic love that each human being has for God and that finds its fulfillment only in the direct enjoyment and knowledge of God—a goal that is reached during the present life by only a few persons and for a short time, but will be attained forever in the future life by those who have aspired to it while on earth. Without rejecting sexual and earthly love, Ficino praises above all the pure and celestial love, that is, the mutual affection and friendship between two persons who are dedicated to the contemplative life and hence recognize that their mutual relationship is founded upon the love each of them has for God. This divine love Ficino claimed to define according to the teachings of Plato, and hence coining a term that was to become famous as well as ridiculous, he called it "Platonic" or "Socratic love." The doctrine of Platonic love constitutes only a small, though important, part of Ficino's philosophical system, but it enjoyed a wide popularity apart from the rest of his work, especially among poets and moralists. The notion of Platonic love was taken over and adapted by many poets, including Lorenzo de' Medici and Michelangelo. Moreover, Ficino's commentary on Plato's *Symposium* became the fountainhead of a whole literature of love treatises, in Italy and elsewhere, in which the philosophical notion of Platonic love was repeated, developed, and sometimes distorted. The authors of these treatises include distinguished philosophers, such as Pico della Mirandola, Leone Ebreo (from whom Spinoza seems to have borrowed his notion of the intellectual love of God), Francesco Patrizi, and Giordano Bruno, as well as famous writers like Bembo and Castiglione. For the last book of Castiglione's *Courtier* deals precisely with Platonic love along the lines defined by Ficino, and through this work the theory attained a very wide diffusion indeed. In the later treatises, the original link between Platonic love and the contemplative life was gradually lost, and the cult of Platonic love came to be a hypocritical disguise for refined sexual passion, or an empty game fashionable in good society. However, we should try to understand that originally it had a serious philosophical meaning, and that a good deal of serious talk and writing on love in the sixteenth century was shaped by the Platonist "philosophy of love."

XIV

Another typically humanist fashion in which the various forms of human life were discussed during the fifteenth and sixteenth century was the so-called comparison (*paragone*). Ancient rhetoric had insisted that it was the task of the orator to praise and to blame, and the praise of some virtue or quality was often combined with the blame of its contrary. To show their skill, orators even composed mock praises of bad or ridiculous things such as tyranny or baldness, and it was against this literary background and upon such models that Erasmus wrote his admirable *Praise of Folly*. Rhetorical contests left their traces in medieval Latin and vernacular poetry where the contrast between winter and spring, youth and old age are common themes. In humanistic literature, the rhetorical contest between two contrasts or rivals was a favorite sport, and we have encountered several examples already: the comparison between Scipio and Caesar, between republic and monarchy, and Buonaccorso's comparison between nobility by birth and by merit. In the same way, the merits and relative superiority of various arts, professions, or ways of life were frequently discussed. There are treatises on "arms and letters," debating the advantages of the military and the literary life. Leonardo da Vinci seriously argued that painting was superior to the other arts and sciences, and Michelangelo was consulted on the question of whether painting or sculpture was superior. The humanist defense of poetry, of which we have spoken before, took the form of attacking other learned disciplines, as in Petrarch's invectives against a physician. There was a whole literature on the relative merits of medicine and of law that had its roots in the rivalry of the university faculties and in which distinguished humanists such as Salutati and Poggio took an active part. Salutati sided with the jurists because the law had a greater significance for the life of the citizen and of the state. Several historians would like to consider this as the typically humanist position, but it happens that Poggio, no less a humanist than Salutati, voted in this contest in favor of medicine.

The argument used by Salutati in this discussion and on other occasions touches upon another more serious issue, the relative merits of the contemplative and of the active life. The distinction occurs already in Aristotle, who tends, along with most ancient philosophers, to consider the life of contemplation, rather than that of action, to be most perfect and desirable. A notable exception was Cicero, the Roman statesman, who insisted upon the political duties of the responsible citizen. During the Middle Ages, the life of contemplation was usually associated with the monastic ideal and was more or less persistently praised. In the Renaissance, we hear again several voices in praise of the active life, such as those of Salutati, Bruni, Alberti, and Palmieri, and these views have been emphasized by Hans Baron and other scholars as an important aspect of their civic humanism. Eugene Rice goes even further and treats the emphasis on the active life in these humanists, in some sixteenth-century writers and in Pierre Charron, as an important development leading away from the monastic ideal of the Middle Ages to the this-worldly and practical orientation of the modern age. Although it is significant that, from the fifteenth century on, the active life was finding more partisans among the writers of the age, the monastic life also had its defenders among the humanists, as we have seen, and even Salutati, one of the chief protagonists of the active life, wrote a whole treatise in praise of the monastic life, a fact that has puzzled several of his interpreters. Moreover, the ideal of the theoretical or contemplative life became dissociated during the Renaissance from the specific ideal of monasticism, and rather identified with the private existence of the scholar, writer, and scientist, no doubt under the influence of ancient philosophy, and this secularization of the contemplative life seems to me no less characteristic of the Renaissance (and of modern times) than the simultaneous emphasis on the claims of the active life. This tendency appears already in Petrarch's praise of solitude, and it is in this sense that the Platonists of the Florentine Academy praised the life of contemplation which occupied a central place in their philosophy. The most famous document in which the question is debated is Cristoforo Landino's *Camaldulensian Disputations,* a dialogue in which the active life is defended by Lorenzo de' Medici and the contemplative life by Leon Battista Alberti—and the victory seems to go to the latter. In the sixteenth century, Pomponazzi considers the theoretical life as superior but uses the practical life to define the end of man, as this life is peculiar to man and all human beings are able to have a part in it. In Montaigne there is a strong, though by no means exclusive, emphasis on the solitary life of contemplation, and most other philosophers take its superiority for granted, whereas the popular moralists insist on the needs and claims of the active life. Far from being resolved in the sixteenth century, the question is still with us. Whereas many writers decry the "ivory tower" of the intellectual, others would still insist on the right of the scholar, artist, or scientist to concentrate on his peculiar task. The rival claims of the active and contemplative life seem to illustrate a perennial human problem, and there seems to be no permanent answer to it, but each time, each profession, and each person will have to find a viable compromise.

Another similar question that was widely debated in Renaissance thought was the relation between the intellect and the will, or between knowledge and love. This question overlaps that of the contemplative and active life, but is not entirely identical with it. For some partisans of the contemplative life, for example, Petrarch, would still place will and love above intellect and knowledge, since they consider the willing of the good and the love of God as a part, and even as the most important part, of the contemplative life. The problem occupies a very important place in the history of Western thought. It has been rightly asserted that the concept of will is absent from ancient Greek philosophy. Plato, Aristotle, and other Greek thinkers know a conflict between reason and desire, but they inherited from Socrates the conviction that reason is capable by its own power to know the good, to put it into practice, and to overcome the resistance of any contrary desire. In the Christian view, this Greek belief in the independent power of reason was far too optimistic. In order to overcome his native propensity to evil brought about by Adam's fall, man needed the grace of God. On the basis of this Christian conception, Augustine formulated his notion of the will. Aside from his faculty of knowing, man has an independent faculty of willing. It is the will that was corrupted by Adam's fall, and that must be purified by divine grace if we are to attain the good. Medieval thought inherited from Augustine this distinction between will and intellect, and the relative merits of these two faculties became the subject of important discussions, with Thomas Aquinas, among others, emphasizing the superiority of the intellect, whereas Duns Scotus and other "voluntarists" insisted, in accordance with Augustine, on the superiority of the will. This question, in spite of its scholastic origin, continued to occupy the humanists. Both Petrarch and Salutati favored the superiority of the will. In the Platonic Academy of Florence, the problem was evidently a favorite topic of debate, as we may learn from Ficino's correspondence, and from the treatise of one of his pupils, Alamanno Donati. Ficino himself apparently changed his view on the matter in the course of his life, favoring at first the superiority of the intellect but insisting in his later writings on the importance of the will and of love for the ascent of the soul to God. His arguments show that the concept of will could be associated with the life of contemplation no less than with that of action.

XV

Renaissance thought was interested not merely in moral rules of conduct or in the specific ways of life that an individual might choose according to his status or profession, but also in the general situation in which human beings find themselves on earth, in the chief forces determining this situation, and in the place man and his world occupy within the larger universe. There has been a widespread belief that Renaissance humanists held an optimistic view of life and were prone to enjoy this earth without caring as much for the future life after death as their medieval predecessors had. It is true that the concern with earthly life and its problems tended to increase from medieval to modern times. Nevertheless we must try to avoid exaggerated opinions. Even in Lorenzo de' Medici's famous lines, "Let him be happy who so desires, for we are not sure of the next day," which used to be quoted as the quintessence of the Renaissance view of life as frivolous and superficial, we have learned to hear melancholy undertones. Historians like Walser and Trinkaus have shown that the writers of the period were keenly aware of the miseries and ills of our earthly existence. Sickness and poverty, exile and imprisonment, the loss of friends and relatives were a common experience, and when Poggio and other humanists wrote about the misery of the human condition, they had no difficulty collecting ancient and modern examples to illustrate the frail and transitory state of earthly happiness. Lest we think that some classes of men are untouched by the miseries that befall the common lot, the humanists wrote special treatises about the unhappiness of scholars and of courtiers, and especially of princes. These treatises were full of examples from history, and they were intended to warn their readers not to trust their happiness, and to comfort the unhappy with the record of the ills suffered by others that were worse than their own. This chorus of lament may seem to be out of tune with many real and imagined traits of the period, but it is nearly universal. The Platonic philosopher Ficino invokes the shade of Heraclitus to weep at the misery of men, as he would laugh with Democritus at their folly.

This feeling that man has to suffer many vicissitudes and that the events of his life, whether good or bad, are largely beyond his control was interpreted by the writers and thinkers of the period in a variety of ways that were not always consistent with each other, but that lend a common note to the literature of the Renaissance. Divine providence was stressed by the theologians and never denied by any other thinkers, but popular and philosophical writers frequently played with the notions of fortune and fate.

The concept of chance was repeatedly discussed by ancient philosophers and played a role in the thought of Aristotle, and especially in that of Epicurus. In the moral thought of late antiquity, chance was given an important part in human affairs, and its power was even personified and worshiped as the goddess Tyche or Fortuna. During the Christian Middle Ages, Fortuna remained pretty much alive, not as a goddess, to be sure, but as an allegory and as an instrument of God. In the Renaissance the power of Fortuna is again very often mentioned. She appears in emblems and allegorical pictures as well as in the writings of the period. Statesmen and businessmen hoped that this blind and arbitrary power would bring them success, and Machiavelli devoted some striking pages to the description of its role in history and politics.

Many thoughtful persons were not satisfied with this whimsical rule of Fortuna over human affairs, but believed instead, or additionally, in the power of an inexorable fate. The view that all earthly events were rigidly determined by an unbroken chain of antecedent causes had been held by the ancient Stoics, and it was revived in a more or less modified form by Pomponazzi and other thinkers. Still more widespread was the belief in astrology, an elaborate system that presented itself as a science and tried to tie all earthly events, with the help of detailed but flexible rules, to the influence of the stars. This system, which had passed from the Babylonians into late antiquity and was transmitted through the Arabs to medieval Europe, was usually opposed by the theologians but was supported by the philosophers and scientists. During the Renaissance, astrology had a few opponents, such as Petrarch and Pico, but on the whole its prestige rose higher than ever before, both among scholars and laymen. The belief that all human affairs were governed by the motions of the stars was satisfactory to many people because it seemed to give some significance and regularity to the vicissitudes of life. The astrologers claimed to be able to predict the future of persons and countries, and in their passionate desire to know and to control their future, people were as little disturbed as in other times by the inherent contradiction in prophecy (for how can I change the future to my advantage if it is dependent on unchangeable laws, and how can I predict the future if I or others can do anything about it?) and as willing to forget the numerous predictions that were not confirmed by the outcome.

Different from the belief in fate is the theological doctrine of predestination, which also played an important part in the discussions of the period. Augustine had emphasized against the Pelagians that not only all earthly events but even our own moral choices and actions were foreordained by divine forethought and will, and the problem of how predestination can be reconciled with human free will gave rise to many difficulties in medieval theology and philosophy. The problem came to the fore with the Protestant Reformers, Luther and Calvin, who completely denied free will, something neither Augustine nor his medieval successors had clearly done. The question was of importance also to secular thinkers before the Reformation, as the example of Valla and Pomponazzi shows. Valla argued that it was easy to reconcile divine foreknowledge with human free will but considered the relationship between God's will and human freedom as a mystery of faith. Pomponazzi gave an intricate defense of predestination as well as of fate, but his attempt to make free will appear compatible with both of them seems neither clear nor convincing.

The concepts of fortune, of fate, and of predestination express in different ways and on different levels the feeling that human life is governed by divine and natural powers over which we have no control and to which we must submit more or less helplessly. Yet most Renaissance thinkers did not stop with the assertion of these superhuman powers, but tried in some way to uphold and defend the power of man over his own destiny, in the face of fortune and fate. The attempt is in itself significant even where it seems to be inconsistent or unsuccessful. Already the ancient Stoics, the most outspoken proponents of rigid fate, had struggled to assert the role of human freedom within a system of complete determinism. The later Stoics found their solution in the view that the wise man, while enduring patiently the external circumstances of his life which he is unable to change, is entirely free in his thought and in his moral attitude. In a more popular fashion, they opposed the power of reason and virtue to that of fortune and claimed for the wise man an inner victory even when he may seem to be outwardly defeated.

This is the keynote also of much humanist thinking and writing on the subject. In his extremely influential treatise on the remedies of good and bad fortune Petrarch opposes reason to the passions in good Stoic manner and exhorts his readers to overcome through virtue the hold that good and bad fortune alike have on our minds. Salutati also opposes virtue and wisdom to fate and fortune. The recurrent theme in Alberti's moral writings is the victory of virtue over fortune, and Ficino restates the same view, adding a Neoplatonic note by basing moral virtue on the life of contemplation. After having described the power of fortune, Machiavelli also insists that the prudent statesman is able to overcome, or at least to modify, the power of fortune. Guillaume Budé teaches his readers to despise the external circumstances of life, which fortune may give or take away. Just as these thinkers wish to oppose the power of fortune, Pico della Mirandola made a strenuous effort to oppose the power of fate. His elaborate attack against astrology was actually a defense of human freedom, and the arguments that he uses show very clearly that his attitude was prompted by moral and religious as well as by scientific considerations. This same concern for man's moral autonomy was to prompt such humanist thinkers as Erasmus and Sepulveda to defend free will against Luther's exclusive doctrine of predestination.

XVI

The themes and ideas that we have briefly discussed may illustrate the way in which Renaissance thinkers were preoccupied with moral and human problems. It has often been asserted that Renaissance thought, in contrast with medieval thought, was man-centered, not God-centered, or—to quote a rather unfriendly remark of Gilson—that the Renaissance was the Middle Ages minus God. Such statements are obviously exaggerated, since Renaissance thought as a whole was anything but indifferent to God, and since hardly any thinker of the period denied the existence of God, however his conception of God may have differed from various forms of religious orthodoxy. Yet the humanists who have attracted most of the attention of Renaissance historians were interested primarily in moral problems, frequently to the exclusion of theology and metaphysics, of natural philosophy and other learned disciplines. The very name "humanities," which they adopted for their studies, emphasized their concern with man in a programmatic fashion. No wonder that they were inclined to stress the importance of human problems and to extol the place of man in the universe. Already Petrarch argues in his treatise *On His Own and Other People's Ignorance* that it does not help us to know the nature of animals unless we also know the nature of man, and in his famous letter describing his ascent of Mont Ventoux he opposes his admiration for the human soul to the impression made upon him by mountains and the sea. It is significant that the latter passage is woven out of quotations from Seneca and Augustine, for the Renaissance doctrine of the dignity of man was nourished in many ways by classical and Christian sources. In the fifteenth century, the excellence of man was the theme of special treatises by Giannozzo Manetti and others. Especially in Manetti's treatise, the dignity of man is based not only on his biblical similarity to God, but above all on his varied achievements in the arts and sciences, which are described at great length. This favorite humanist theme then received a more metaphysical treatment at the hands of the Platonic philosophers. Marsilio Ficino dedicated several books of his chief work, the *Platonic Theology,* to man's achievements in the sciences and in government, emphasizing the universality of his knowledge and of his aspirations. When he restates the Neoplatonic conception that the universe is made of several degrees of being that extend from God at the summit to the corporeal world at the bottom, he intentionally revises the scheme in order to assign a privileged place in its center to the rational soul of man, thus making it the bond and knot of the universe, second in dignity only to God Himself. Pico della Mirandola went even further. In the famous *Oration,* which deals only in its first half with the dignity of man, and in other writings, he states that man does not occupy any fixed place in the universal hierarchy, but can freely choose his place in it. For he has no fixed nature but possesses all the gifts that had been distributed singly among the other creatures. Thus man is capable of leading many forms of life from the lowest to the highest. Pico's view is echoed in Vives's *Fable on Man;* man is introduced here as an actor capable of playing the roles of all other creatures. The central position of man in the universe, half way between animals and angels, is accepted also by Pomponazzi as a sign of man's excellence. Thus we may say that under the impact of a humanist tradition, systematic philosophers as different from each other as the Florentine Platonists and Pomponazzi assigned to man a privileged position in their conception of the universe. The emphasis on man's universal skill in the arts and sciences will recur in Francis Bacon's notion of the reign of man over nature, and thus there is an echo of the Renaissance glorification of man in the ideology that still underlies the technological aspect of modern natural science.

However, even on this issue that seems to be so close to the heart of Renaissance humanism, the period does not speak to us with a single voice. Even in the fifteenth century, Pope Innocent III's treatise *On Contempt for the World,* which constituted the foil and starting point of Manetti's work, was widely read and had its imitators. In the sixteenth century, a strong reaction against the excessive glorification of man may be noted. In the Protestant Reformers there was a tremendous emphasis on the depraved nature of man, and this view was probably expressed in conscious protest against the current stress on his dignity. Also Montaigne, otherwise so far removed from the theology of the Reformers and so close to humanist thought, goes a long way in his *Apology of Raymond de Sebond* to criticize the unfounded opinions on man's privileged place in the universe, and to insist on his humble position and on the vanity of his aspirations.

This Renaissance concern for man and his place in the universe may also account for the great prominence given during that period to the question of the immortality of the soul. The notion that the individual human soul is immortal had been strongly defended by Plato and the Neoplatonists, whereas Aristotle and other ancient philosophers held ambiguous or contrary opinions. Augustine had adopted the Neoplatonic view, and he was followed by all medieval Christian thinkers. With Renaissance Platonism, the question assumed a central importance that it had never before. Ficino actually designed his *Platonic Theology* around this problem and tried to demonstrate the immortality of the soul against the Aristotelians by a variety of arguments. This emphasis on immortality appealed to a large number of poets, philosophers, and theologians, and it is tempting to assume that it was under Platonist influence that the immortality of the soul was adopted at the Lateran Council of 1513 as an official dogma of the Catholic Church. When the leading Aristotelian philosopher, Pietro Pomponazzi, set out to show that personal immortality cannot be demonstrated by reason, he not only accepted it as an article of faith, but also stressed that the human soul, even according to reason, is immortal at least in some respect (*secundum quid*), on account of its high place among the material forms. Moreover, by returning to the problem many times in published treatises and unpublished questions and lectures, Pomponazzi showed how much he was puzzled by the question and how great an importance he attributed to it. On the other hand, his treatise of 1516 gave rise to a large number of written attacks upon his position by philosophers and theologians, and the question continued to be debated beyond the end of the sixteenth century. The statement that Renaissance students were interested in problems of the soul rather than of nature, often repeated after the nineteenth century French scholar Renan, is based upon the misinterpretation of an episode in which a group of students wanted to hear a course on Aristotle's *On the Soul* rather than on his *Meteorology*, but it contains a grain of truth that may well be based on better evidence.

It might be in order to indicate very briefly at this point in what ways the moral thought of the humanists, even though it was primarily concerned with individual conduct, also led to broader social, political, and humanitarian ideals. The theory of friendship occupied an important place in the ethics of Aristotle, Epicurus and Cicero, and its value is very often stressed in the letters and other writings of the humanists. In the Florentine Academy, the concept of friendship is closely associated with those of Christian and Platonic love, and Ficino liked to think that the members of his Academy were bound to one another and to himself, their common master, by a tie of Platonic friendship, thus forming a close community after the model of the ancient schools of philosophy.

In political thought, not only were the humanists concerned with the education of princes and magistrates, or with the relative merits of republican and monarchical government, but some of the Renaissance thinkers began to reflect on ideal commonwealths more perfect than the ones in existence. Thomas More's *Utopia*, a highly original work in spite of its obvious indebtedness to Plato's *Republic*, was the first of an important genre that was to flourish down to the eighteenth century. Its example was followed by Campanella, Bacon, and many lesser writers. The influence of this utopian literature on social and political reforms in modern times has been generally recognized. Another contribution to social reform was Vive's treatise on assistance to the poor, written at a time when the responsibility for public relief was taken over by the cities in the Low Countries.

No less important was the contribution of Renaissance thought to the development of the ideal of religious toleration. This ideal arose first in the fifteenth century against the background of medieval controversy with Judaism and Islam and of the echoes of the polemics of the Church Fathers against ancient paganism. In the sixteenth century, the problem acquired a new poignancy in the face of religious dissent, persecution, and war within Western Christendom. Without abandoning a belief in the superiority of his own religion, Nicolaus Cusanus advocated perpetual peace and toleration between the different creeds dividing mankind. Ficino praised the solidarity and fellowship of all human beings, and insisted that religion was natural to man, and that all religions, though different in their practices and in the degree of their perfection, contained a common core of truth and expressed in some way the worship of the one true God. Moreover, Ficino maintained that there was a basic harmony between the true, Christian religion and the true, Platonic philosophy; and he accepted the apocryphal writings attributed to Zoroaster, Hermes Trismegistus, Orpheus, and Pythagoras as witnesses of an early pagan theology and philosophy that prepared the way for Plato and his followers, similarly as the Old Testament foreshadowed the New. These notions added a new and explicit force to the general humanist belief in the wisdom of the ancients and its compatibility with Christian religious teaching, and they exercised an enormous influence during the sixteenth century. Equally important were the ideas of Pico della Mirandola, who went even further. According to him, all known philosophies and religions contained some elements of truth, and he proposed to defend in a public disputation nine hundred theses taken principally from ancient and medieval, Arabic and Jewish, philosophers and theologians. In particular, he maintained that the writings of the Jewish Cabalists represented an ancient oral tradition, and were in agreement with the teachings of Christianity. In the second part of his famous oration, which was actually composed as an introductory speech for his projected disputation, Pico eloquently expresses his belief in the universality of truth in which every philosopher and theologian participates to a greater or lesser degree. A hundred years later, in his famous *Sevenfold Conversation*, which was widely circulated in manuscript but not printed until recent times, Jean Bodin defends the claims of all the different religions. In the seventeenth century, Herbert of Cherbury laid the ground for deism by describing a natural religion consisting of the common core of all the various human creeds.

XVII

In spite of these broad and interesting ramifications, the moral thought of the Renaissance was fundamentally individualistic in its outlook. Of course, the term individualism has several meanings, and its applications to the Renaissance have aroused a good deal of controversy among historians. It cannot be denied that outstanding human individuals are found in other periods of history, including the Middle Ages, or that medieval nominalism emphasized the reality of the individual physical thing. When we speak of Renaissance individualism, the term should be understood in a different way. Above all, Renaissance thought and literature are extremely individualistic in that they aim, to a degree unknown to the Middle Ages and to most of ancient and modern times, at the expression of individual, subjective opinions, feelings, and experiences. Every humanist takes himself very seriously and thinks that everything he has heard and seen is eminently worth recording. Treatises on highly abstract subjects are intermixed with personal stories, gossip, flattery, and invective to a degree and in a manner of which a modern scholar, like his ancient or medieval predecessors, would be thoroughly ashamed. Hence the widespread Renaissance preference for the letter as a form of literary expression in which the author may speak in the first person, for the biography in which another person is vividly delineated in all his concrete qualities, and for the diary and autobiography in which both these traits are in a way combined. The rise of portrait painting in the visual arts seems to indicate the same general tendency. In a curious way, this individualism is blended in both art and literature with a strong classicism and formalism that might seem to be incompatible with it, but actually contributes to it a special color and physiognomy. Where moral precepts are involved, the literature is of course full of the most general rules, but these rules are addressed to the effort of the individual person, just as they are based on individual historical examples. This subjective and personal trait pervades most humanist literature, and it is apparent already in its first great representative, Petrarch. He vents his opinions, his likes and dislikes, his scruples and preoccupations, whereas objective statements on general problems are rather rare and incidental even in his philosophical writings. When we come to the end of the Renaissance, this subjective and personal character of humanist thought finds its most conscious and consummate philosophical expression in the *Essais* of Michel de Montaigne. Montaigne had received a humanist education, he knew Latin before he knew French, and his quotations from ancient authors, especially Plutarch and Seneca, fill many pages of his writings. The essay, in the form which he created and bequeathed to later centuries, is written in the first person, like the humanist letter, and is equally free in its style and structure: we might call the essay a letter written by the author to himself. Montaigne shares with the humanist his exclusive preoccupation with moral questions, his lack of interest in logic and metaphysics and the other learned disciplines, as well as his dislike for the scholastic type of learning. His philosophical position, though flexible, shows the impact of ancient skepticism, and to a lesser extent, of Stoicism. He writes on a variety of moral topics, often starting from classical examples or sentences. He would always refer to his personal experience, and draw the lesson for himself. His skepticism, from which he excepts only his religious faith, is prompted by observation and experience. He knows how complex and changeable all human affairs are. Circumstances alter all the time, and so do our moods. Most of his thoughts are prompted by introspection. What all humanists actually felt but did not express in so many words, he states most bluntly and clearly, namely, that he intends to talk primarily about himself and that his own individual self is the chief subject matter of his philosophizing. "Authors communicate themselves to the public by some peculiar and strange quality; I, for the first time, through my entire self, as Michel de Montaigne, not as grammarian or poet or lawyer. If the world complains that I speak too much of myself, I complain that the world does not think only of itself." (*Essais,* III, 2) Yet by making of his personal way of talking a philosophical program, by elevating introspection and the observation of actual human conduct to the rank of a conscious method, Montaigne already passes beyond the boundaries of humanist thought and literature, and leads the way toward the psychological study of moods and manners that was to characterize the moral literature of the seventeenth century.

XVIII

While a scholar may be concerned with the complexities of a historical period which he is trying to understand, the layman and the student look for a broad synthesis that selects and emphasizes those aspects of the past that are significant for them and for their time, and constitute, as it were, a contribution to contemporary civilization. Such a view seemed easy when there was an unquestioned faith in the present and future status of our civilization, and in its steady and almost inevitable progress. In our own time, this faith has been shattered in many ways. There is no doubt notable progress in technology and in the natural sciences, and there is a good deal of hope for social and political progress, as there should be, since such progress depends at least in part on our efforts, and hence is our own responsibility. Yet the future is not completely under our control and is, at least to that extent, uncertain. There is constant change but no steady progress in a variety of fields, and a growing awareness that every gain, though necessary and desirable, may have to be paid for by some loss. The present—shifting, complex, and inconsistent—ceases to be a firm measure for selecting what is significant in the past. Concentration on the present and rejection of the past are actually widespread at this moment, but such attitudes are lacking in wisdom and are not likely to last very long. Philosophers, linguists, critics of the arts and of literature, and practitioners of the social sciences often treat present realities as if they were absolutes, valid for all times and places, and as if there were no alternatives. This outlook is narrow and provincial, and one of the tasks of historical scholarship, so widely ignored, is to broaden our outlook, to open our eyes to the achievements of the past, even where they differ from our own. In historical recollection, we may vicariously relive what is gone because it is intrinsically significant, and hence we can understand it. And by thus preserving it, we keep it available for the future that may still make a use of it which we cannot now foresee. The study of history is highly important in any living tradition, and we like to think of ourselves as heirs of such a tradition, which we call Western civilization. If the future belongs to a broader world culture, which will contain many strands other than those of the Western tradition, we still think and hope that it will include what we consider to be the best in the heritage of Western civilization.

If we look back upon the moral thought of Renaissance humanism for part of this heritage some of its most general traits will become apparent. Many of them are related to the social and professional situation in which most of the humanist writers found themselves. As scholars and writers professionally concerned with the study of history and of the classics, as well as with moral problems, they were thoroughly influenced by the form and ideas of ancient literature and philosophy, but at the same time eager to give expression to their personal feelings and experiences. As a result of their work and efforts through several centuries, the subject matter of the humanities was established as a branch of secular learning that included moral philosophy as distinct from, but not necessarily opposed to, theology and the natural sciences. It represented a peculiar combination of literature and scholarship that tended to disintegrate in the following centuries, but it left a double heritage that has more or less survived to the present day and that seems very much worth preserving. On the one hand, there are the historical and philological branches of knowledge that have greatly extended the range of their subject matter and refined the instruments of their research (as an echo of their origin in Renaissance humanism they are still called, in old-fashioned French and Italian, the moral sciences). On the other hand, there is a Renaissance tradition of literary culture that is not limited to formal techniques but is concerned with broad human and philosophical problems, without accepting the limitations (and responsibilities) of professional philosophy. This latter tradition was revived by nineteenth-century Romanticism and has recently found an influential representative in George Santayana, the American philosopher. After having surveyed the contributions made by Renaissance humanism to moral thought, some of them modest and trivial, we cannot help concluding with the hope that its double heritage, scholarly and literary, though now threatened by the onslaught of several competing forces may survive in the future.

III

The European Diffusion of
Italian Humanism *

The eminent position of Italy during the Renaissance, and the importance of Italian influences on the civilization of the other European countries during the fifteenth and sixteenth centuries are generally known, and hardly require an elaborate discussion. This Italian influence is evident in the visual arts and in music, in poetry and literature, in political and economic theory and practice, as well as in the sciences and in philosophy. Within this general framework, Italian humanism and its influence occupies a rather central place, and this fact, though quite well known in

* Reprinted from *Italica*, Vol. XXXIX (1962), 1–20. This article is based on a paper read before the Modern Language Association of America in Philadelphia on December 27, 1960, and on a somewhat longer lecture delivered at the Casa Italiana of Columbia University on February 23, 1961. In trying to annotate this lecture, I cannot hope to give anything like a full documentation. For recent treatments of our subject, see: R. Weiss, "Italian Humanism in Western Europe," in *Italian Renaissance Studies, A tribute to the late Cecilia M. Ady*, ed. E. F. Jacob (London, 1960), 69–93; Denys Hay, *The Italian Renaissance in Its Historical Background* (Cambridge, 1961), ch. 7 (p. 179–203): "The Reception of the Renaissance in the North." For England, see especially R. Weiss, *Humanism in England during the Fifteenth Century* (Oxford, 1941 and 1957). For France, A. Renaudet, *Préréforme et Humanisme à Paris pendant les premières guerres d' Italie* (Paris, 1916 and 1953); F. Simone, *Il rinascimento francese* (Turin, 1961). My purpose in this short paper is merely to point out a few general perspectives, summing up the results of recent studies, as far as they are known to me, adding a few details from my own research on Renaissance manuscripts, and indicating a few problems that would deserve further investigation. I shall not cite standard monographs on well known figures who are briefly mentioned in the text of the paper. For information on the manuscript collections cited in the text, I may be allowed once and for all to refer to my bibliography (*Latin Manuscript Books before 1600*, New York, 1960) where the printed catalogues are listed for each library.

a general way, has perhaps not been sufficiently appreciated or emphasized by the majority of recent scholars. Their lack of interest is due to a variety of preconceptions and misconceptions which we cannot discuss or criticize in this paper. To mention but the most important of them, there is still a widespread contempt, inherited from Romanticism, for the rhetoric and the Latin literature of the humanists. The recent decline in the public prestige of classical, and especially of Greek studies has diminished the interest in this aspect of the humanist contribution. The increased knowledge and appreciation of medieval civilization has made the Renaissance appear less novel and less original than it was thought to be. Finally, the students of the literatures and civilizations other than Italian have tended to emphasize the native traditions and contributions of the other European countries, and to minimize their indebtedness to Italian influences.

In order to give a more precise meaning to our further discussion, I should like to define first of all the place of humanism in the civilization of Renaissance Italy. The term humanism, as many other terms of a similarly general scope, has come to mean many things to many people. When we hear or read of humanism, or even of Renaissance humanism, we are apt to think primarily of some vaguely conceived emphasis on human values that is supposed to be characteristic of the Renaissance. Whether this kind of humanism was present in the Italian Renaissance, and how widespread or important it was, I do not plan to discuss in this paper. I rather shall discuss humanism in a much more specific sense, and understand by humanists those scholars who by profession or vocation were concerned with the *studia humanitatis*, the humanities, and by humanism, the body of literature, scholarship and thought represented by the writings of the humanists.[1] The *studia humanitatis* which we thus take as the basis for the definition of Renaissance humanism, comprised a well defined cycle of disciplines, as we may learn from a number of contemporary documents: grammar, rhetoric, poetry, history, and moral philosophy. To this list, we may add, as implied, the

[1] A. Campana, "The Origin of the Word 'Humanist,'" *Journal of the Warburg and Courtauld Institutes,"* IX (1946), 60–73, P. O. Kristeller, "Humanism and Scholasticism in the Italian Renaissance," *Byzantion* XVII (1944–45), 346–375 (reprinted in my *Studies in Renaissance Thought and Letters,* Rome, 1956, and in my *Renaissance Thought,* New York, 1961). I cannot discuss here the different interpretations of humanism offered by other scholars such as Baron, Garin or Toffanin.

study of the Greek and Roman authors of classical antiquity. This group of disciplines came to occupy in the Italian Renaissance a very central place, and to be in many ways connected with, and influential in, many other areas of Renaissance civilization. Yet in spite of these connections, Renaissance humanism was basically distinct from vernacular literature, from technical philosophy as cultivated by the Aristotelians, the Platonists and the philosophers of nature, and from the university disciplines of mathematics, medicine, law, and theology. Humanism represented a body of scholarship and literature that was secular, without being scientific, and that occupied a place of its own, independent of, though not opposed to, both theology and the sciences. Those of us who are literary scholars and historians have every reason to consider the humanists as our professional predecessors, and to do justice to their achievements.

In attempting to survey the European diffusion of Italian humanism, I shall discuss the various channels through which this diffusion was effected, but shall stop short of the actual manifestation of the influence of Italian humanism in the native literatures of the various other countries. I shall concentrate on the period between 1350 and 1600, and on the countries of Western and Central Europe, excluding the Byzantine Empire, Turkey and Russia.

The first important channel through which Italian humanism spread abroad was what we now like to call the exchange of persons. Many foreigners had occasion to visit Italy and to get acquainted with humanist learning, depending on the length of their stay, and on the range of their intellectual interests. There were tourists in the sixteenth century, as there are now; there were pilgrims as in the Middle Ages; and there were merchants who went for business reasons, clergymen who went to Rome on various church affairs, and political envoys who represented their governments at various Italian centers for a shorter or longer period.[2] In all these groups, we find also scholars who went to Italy on some business and took this opportunity to satisfy their intellectual or artistic curiosity. Others went on their own, as Erasmus or Montaigne, or in the company of traveling princes, as was the case with Reuchlin. Many foreign scholars came to settle permanently in Rome as employees of the papal curia or of a cardinal, as did Guillaume Fichet, John Free, or Jacob Questen-

[2] George Parks, *The English Traveler to Italy*, vol. I (Stanford, 1954). G. Mattingly, *Renaissance Diplomacy* (London, 1955).

berg.[3] During the fifteenth century, a large number of professional copyists from Flanders and Germany were active in Italy,[4] and later in the century, an even larger group of German printers came to settle in Rome, Venice and other centers.

Yet by far the most important group for our purpose are the foreign students who stayed in Italy for several years and then returned to their home countries to occupy more or less important places in the government or in the professions. The Italian universities were especially famous for the instruction they gave in medicine and in law, a tradition that went back to the early days of Salerno and Bologna. Most foreign students came to Italy to obtain degrees in one of these disciplines, before exercising their respective professions at home. During their stay in Italy, quite a few of these foreign students of law and medicine became interested in the humanities. Among the physicians we may mention Thomas Linacre, Hartmann Schedel and Georgius Agricola. Copernicus went to Italy to study both law and medicine, and on the side he seems to have cultivated the humanities as well as astronomy. The list of foreign students of law is probably even larger. It includes such leading German humanists as Wilibald Pirckheimer and Konrad Peutinger. Of special importance was the Spanish College in Bologna which counts among its alumni such leading humanists as Antonius Nebrissensis and Johannes Sepúlveda.[5] Less numerous, but no less important, were the foreigners who came to Italy for the sole purpose of studying the

[3] F. Simone, "Guillaume Fichet, retore ed umanista," *Memorie della Reale Accademia delle Scienze di Torino*, Ser. II, vol. 69, pt. 2 (Classe di Scienze Morali, Storiche e Filologiche) 1939, 103–144; R. J. Mitchell, *John Free* (London, 1955); G. card. Mercati, *Opere minori* IV (Vatican City, 1937), 437–461: "Questenbergiana." An oration on St. Stephen, composed by Fichet during his later years in Rome has remained unknown to his biographers (ms. Vat Chigi J VI 235). For a letter of John Colet from Rome, see W. K. Ferguson, "An Unpublished Letter of John Colet, Dean of St. Paul's," *American Historical Review* XXXIX (1933–34), 696–699 (I am indebted for this reference to Prof. Sears Jayne). The manuscript is now in the Princeton University Library (ms. 89).

[4] The evidence for this statement will be contained in my forthcoming *Iter Italicum*. For a French copyist trained by Poggio, see B. L. Ullman, *The Origin and Development of Humanistic Script* (Rome, 1960), p. 87.

[5] For the foreign students at Italian universities, see the bibliography in P. Kibre, *The Nations in the Mediaeval Universities* (Cambridge, Mass., 1948), 189–208. For Bologna, see S. Stelling-Michaud. *L' Université de Bologne et la pénétration des droits romain et canonique en Suisse aux XIIIe et XIVe siècles* (Geneva, 1955), 280–281. For Padua, see A. Favaro, *Saggio di Bibliografia dello Studio di Padova* (2 vols., Venice, 1922), for the references listed in the index (vol. II, p. 410).

humanities. Among the students of Guarino at Ferrara we find Janus Pannonius, later bishop of Pecs, and one of the most famous Hungarian humanists, and John Tiptoft who later translated humanist writings into English and collected an important library.[6] We may also mention Nicolaus Cusanus who spent the latter part of his life in Italy as a cardinal, after having studied for a while at Padua, the Dutch humanist Rodulphus Agricola who studied and taught at Pavia and Ferrara, and later at Heidelberg, and the Portuguese Hermicus Caiadus who was a pupil of Politian and Beroaldus. The reception of the Roman law in the German Empire and at the German universities took place during our period, and it seems still to be an open question whether and to what extent this important development was due to the legal and humanistic training which many German jurists and public officials had received in Italy.[7]

No less important for the diffusion of humanism were the Italians who lived in other countries for periods of varying length. Italian bankers and businessmen were active all over Europe, and especially in France, England and the Low Countries. A few of them such as Francesco Tedaldi even tried their hand in writing,[8] whereas many more had scholarly interests and contacts at home and in their places of residence. Italian princesses such as Beatrice of Aragon, queen of Hungary, or Bianca Maria Sforza, second consort of Maximilian I, and later Bona Sforza, queen of Poland,[9] were followed by Italian scholars as well as artists, and the same was true of Italian bishops appointed to foreign sees.[10] The political envoys sent abroad by the various Italian states included men of humanist training and

[6] For Guarino's students, see C. de' Rosmini, *Vita e disciplina di Guarino Veronese e de' suoi discepoli*, vol. III (Brescia, 1806). See also Vespasiano da Bisticci, *Vite di uomini illustri del secolo XV* (ed. P. D'Ancona and E. Aeschlimann, Milan, 1951). R. J. Mitchell, *John Tiptoft* (London, 1938). Charles G. Nauert, Jr., "Agrippa in Renaissance Italy," *Studies in the Renaissance* VI (1959), 195–222.

[7] R. Stintzing, *Geschichte der deutschen Rechtswissenschaft*, vol. I (Munich, 1880). Stelling-Michaud, *l. c.*

[8] P. O. Kristeller, "Una novella latina e il suo autore Francesco Tedaldi, mercante fiorentino del Quattrocento," in: *Studi letterari, Miscellanea in onore di Emilio Santini* (Palermo, 1956), 159–180.

[9] A. Berzeviczy, *Beatrice d'Aragon, Reine de Hongrie* (2 vols., Paris, 1911–12); *Maximilian I* (exhibition catalogue, Vienna, 1959), p. 13–16; W. Pociecha, *Królowa Bona* (4 vols., Poznan, 1949–58).

[10] Julius Caesar Scaliger came to France as the physician of Antonio della Rovere, bishop of Agen (V. Hall, "Life of Julius Caesar Scaliger," *Transactions of the American Philosophical Society*, N. S. 40, pt. 2, 1950, 85–170).

interests. When Ermolao Barbaro went as Venetian ambassador to Bruges to address Frederick III and Maximilian, his speech became an important local event, was printed in the Low Countries, and brought him into contact with Arnold Bostius.[11] The reputation which Ermolao was to enjoy with Erasmus and other Northern scholars seems to have owed much to this episode in his life.

Many Italian scholars entered the service of foreign princes or dignitaries, as tutors or secretaries, as librarians, as court poets or court historians. The list is long and distinguished, and it includes Aeneas Sylvius in Germany, Antonius Bonfinius in Hungary, Philippus Callimachus in Poland, Poggio, Titus Livius Frulovisius and Polydore Vergil in England, Paulus Aemilius in France, Lucius Marineus Siculus and Petrus Martyr Anglariensis in Spain.[12]

Italian students who wanted to obtain advanced training in theology usually went to Paris or to the English universities since the Italian universities had no comparable tradition in this field.[13] Among these students, we sometimes encounter persons who had strong humanist interests and spread them abroad, such as Lorenzo Guglielmo Traversagni, a Franciscan friar from Savona who was active in Vienna, Paris and Cambridge, and who has recently received some scholarly attention, both as an author and as a copyist.[14]

[11] Ermolao Barbaro, *Epistolae Orationes et Carmina*, ed. V. Branca, 2 vols., Florence, 1943. For the edition printed in Alost in 1486, see *Gesamtkatalog der Wiegendrucke*, no. 3343. Petrus de Monte went as a papal nuntius to England.

[12] Antonius de Bonfinis, *Rerum Ungaricarum Decades*, ed. J. Fogel and others, 4 vols., Leipzig, 1936–41. T. Livius de Frulovisiis de Ferraria, *Opera hactenus inedita*, ed. C. Previté-Orton, Cambridge, 1932. R. Weiss, "Humphrey Duke of Gloucester and Tito Livio Frulovisi," in *Fritz Saxl 1890–1948, A volume of Memorial Essays from his friends in England*, ed. D. J. Gordon (London, 1957), 218–227. Denys Hay, *Polydore Vergil*, Oxford, 1952. Katharine Davies, *Late XVth Century French historiography, as exemplified in the Compendium of Robert Gaguin and the De rebus gestis of Paulus Aemilius* (unpublished thesis, University of Edinburgh, 1954), Caro Lynn, *A college professor of the renaissance: Lucio Marineo Siculo among the Spanish Humanists* (Chicago, 1937).

[13] G. Dalla Santa, "Uomini e fatti dell'ultimo Trecento e del primo Quattrocento, Da lettere a Giovanni Contarini, patrizio veneziano, studente ad Oxford e a Parigi, poi Patriarca di Costantinopoli," *Nuovo Archivio Veneto*, N. S. Anno 16, Tomo 32, pt. 1 (1916) 5–105.

[14] J. Ruysschaert, "Lorenzo Guglielmo Traversagni de Savone." *Archivum Franciscanum Historicum* 46 (1953) 195-210. A manuscript of his *De arte*

A number of Italian humanists, or other scholars trained in Italy, were called to teach at foreign universities, and thus had occasion to exercise a more or less significant scholarly influence. In Paris, we find Gregorius Tiphernas and Philippus Beroaldus the Elder, and later Faustus Andrelinus and many others, in Basel, Petrus Antonius Finariensis.[15] We may add those modest wandering adventurers who offered their services as teachers or poets, such as Stephanus Surigonius or Johannes Michael Nagonius.[16] A characteristic case is Jacobus Publicius who taught at a number of German universities, and composed a number of influential textbooks. I have reason to believe that he was actually a Spaniard or Portuguese, but in Germany he passed himself for a Florentine, and apparently got away with it successfully.[17] For a humanist, it was obviously a good advertisement to be from Italy, and especially from Florence.

A last important group of Italian scholars abroad is constituted by the political and later by the religious exiles. A famous early example is Cola di Rienzo whose short stay in Bohemia left some significant traces. In the late fifteenth century, Philippus Callimachus came to Poland as a political exile, and gradually attained

metrica (wrongly attributed to Lorenzo Valla) was recently acquired by the Indiana University Library (ms. Poole 118). I am indebted to Miss Doris Reed for a partial photostat of the ms.

[15] For Paris, see Renaudet, 1. c. G. Busino, "Italiani all'Università di Basilea dal 1460 al 1601," *Bibliothèque d'Humanisme et Renaissance* XX (1958) 497-526. An oration in praise of Basel by Finariensis is being edited by Prof. Guido Kisch.

[16] For Surigonius, see William Nelson, *A Fifteenth Century Schoolbook* (Oxford, 1956), p. XVI. For Nagonius, see F. Wormald, "An Italian poet at the Court of Henry VII," *Journal of the Warburg and Courtauld Institutes* 14 (1951) 118-119. The poems composed by Nagonius for Henry VII of England are extant in a manuscript in York Minster Library (ms. XVI N. 2).

[17] For Publicius, see G. Bauch, *Die Universitaet Erfurt im Zeitalter des Fruehhumanismus* (Breslau, 1904), 53-55 (where it is reported that Publicius was called Hispanus by an opponent, Johann Riedner); L. Bertalot, "Humanistische Vorlesungsankuendigungen in Deutschland im 15. Jahrhundert," *Zeitschrift fuer Geschichte der Erziehung und des Unterrichts* 5 (1915), 1-24; E. P. Goldschmidt, *Hieronymus Muenzer und seine Bibliothek* (London, 1938). There is a notable lack of biographical and literary documents linking Publicius with Italy or especially with Florence, and the name is not Florentine. This was noted already by F. Fossius (*Catalogus codicum Saeculo XV. impressorum qui in publica Bibliotheca Magliabechiana adservantur,* II, Florence, 1794, col. 420-422) who considers Publicius as an Academic name. I consider as decisive the testimony of a ms. in Brno (A 100) written in Toulouse where Publicius is called a Spaniard.

a position of great cultural and political importance at the court of Cracow. In the sixteenth century, the Protestant exiles from Italy who went especially to Switzerland, England and Poland included many highly educated scholars. Pellegrino Morato and his daughter Olimpia went from Ferrara to Germany. In Basel, Italian Protestant scholars worked as authors and editors in close connection with the flourishing book trade. The most famous of the group was Celio Secundo Curione from Venice.[18]

Another important channel of humanist influence was the foreign correspondence of the humanists, which in most, though not in all, instances grew out of their personal contacts. We find a number of foreign addressees in the letter collections of all Italian humanists, beginning with Petrarch who spent a great part of his life in France, and a certain number of Italian addressees in the correspondence of Reuchlin, Erasmus and other foreign scholars.[19] This is a rich source of information which has not yet been properly explored, in spite of a stillborn international project to collect the foreign correspondence of all the humanists. It would not only be necessary to edit the letters, but also to study the biographies and the literary and other activities of the persons involved.

A related phenomenon is the dedication of Italian humanist writings to foreigners, and the patronage that usually went with such dedications. An Italian humanist in the service of a foreign prince would obviously dedicate some of his works to the latter. Yet these are by no means the only cases. Several Italian humanists who never went to Hungary dedicated some of their writings to Matthias Corvinus or to persons of his court.[20] Poliziano

[18] Frederic C. Church, *The Italian Reformers* (New York, 1932); D. Cantimori and E. Feist, *Per la storia degli eretici italiani del secolo XVI in Europa*, Rome, 1937; D. Cantimori, *Eretici italiani del cinquecento*, Florence, 1939; P. Bietenholz, *Der italienische Humanismus und die Bluetezeit des Buchdrucks in Basel* (Basel, 1959); M. Kutter, *Celio Secondo Curione* (Basel, 1955). O. Guenther, "Der Neapolitaner Johannes Bernardinus Bonifacius, Marchese von Oria, und die Anfaenge der Danziger Stadtbibliothek," in *Beitraege zur Buecherkunde und Philologie August Wilmanns . . . gewidmet* (Leipzig, 1903), 107–128.

[19] For a letter of an Italian scholar to Erasmus, not included in P. S. Allen's monumental *Opus Epistolarum Desiderii Erasmi*, see P. O. Kristeller, "Two Unpublished Letters to Erasmus," *Renaissance News* XIV (1961), 6–14.

[20] E. Abel and S. Hegedüs, *Analecta Nova ad historiam renascentium in Hungaria litterarum spectantia* (Budapest, 1903). P. O. Kristeller, "Sebastiano Salvini, a Florentine Humanist and Theologian, and a Member of Marsilio Ficino's Academy," in *Didascaliae: Studies in Honor of Anselm M. Albareda* (New York, 1961), 207–243.

planned to write for John of Portugal a history of his reign.[21] Alfonso of Aragon became for all practical purposes an Italian prince,[22] but it could be shown that the humanist writings dedicated to him and to his successors enjoyed a special popularity and diffusion in his native Spain, and many Spanish members of his court and administration became patrons of Italian scholars and acted as transmitters of Italian humanist learning in their country of birth.[23]

One field in which the influence of Italian humanism was very apparent, especially in the sixteenth century, is that of instruction. Many schools were founded or reorganized to center their teaching on the humanities, including the Greek and Roman authors,[24] and this pattern is quite evident in the schools of the Protestant reformers as well as in those of the Jesuits. On the university level, chairs of the humanistic disciplines were newly founded, or the older chairs of grammar and rhetoric acquired a new importance and direction. This new trend found expression in the persons of the teachers who were often trained in Italy, or imitated Italian methods, as well as in the texts and textbooks adopted for instruction. This subject has not yet been sufficiently studied, but some relevant information may be derived from the educational treatises of the period, from the statutes of schools and universities, and from the manuscripts and printed editions that were used by teachers and students. The University of Basel became a center of humanistic studies, and the new university of Wittenberg cultivated the humanities in addition to theology. Louvain received, under the influence of Erasmus, its *Collegium trilingue,* and Vienna, under that of Celtes, its *Collegium poetarum.* In Paris, Francis I founded the *Collège de France* for the pursuit of those humanistic and mathematical studies that were

[21] G. Battelli, "La corrispondenza del Poliziano col re Don Giovanni II di Portogallo," *Rinascita* II (1939) 280–298.

[22] A. Soria, *Los humanistas de la Corte de Alfonso el Magnánimo* (Granada, 1956).

[23] Among other Spanish patrons of Italian humanism, we may mention Iñigo López de Mendoza, marqués de Santillana, who owned many writings of the Italian humanists in Italian and Spanish translations (M. Schiff, *La Bibliothèque du Marquis de Santillane,* Paris, 1905), and Nuño de Guzmán who had Bruni's *Cicero Novus* translated into Italian (Milan, Biblioteca Nazionale Braidense, ms. A C IX 33) and who was in contact with Giannozzo Manetti (cf. Vat. Pal. lat. 1601 and 1606).

[24] W. H. Woodward, *Studies in Education during the Age of the Renaissance* (Cambridge, 1906); E. Garin, *L'educazione in Europa, 1400–1600* (Bari, 1957); D. L. Clark, *John Milton at St. Paul's School* (New York, 1948).

neglected by the university, and Henry VIII founded for the same purpose the Regius professorships at Oxford and Cambridge.[25] It appears that along with the classical authors, the compositions of the Italian humanists and of their foreign followers acquired an increasingly important place in the curriculum: their treatises on grammar and rhetoric, their letters, orations and poems, their commentaries on Latin authors, and their Latin translations of Greek authors were especially popular. Bruni's version of St. Basil's letter on the reading of the pagan poets was used as a textbook in England and elsewhere,[26] and his translations of Aristotle were copied all over Europe. The glossed manuscripts of Vergerius' *De ingenuis moribus*, of Agostino Dati's *Isagoge*, of the letters of Filelfo and of others, of Baptista Mantuanus' poems, of Stephanus Fliscus' *Synonyma*, of Hieronymus de Vallibus' *Jesuida* that we find in German and other libraries reflect the reading of these texts in the schools. The fact that in some instances authors and writings acquired a greater popularity abroad in proportion to others than they had possessed at home is a phenomenon which we may observe throughout the history of foreign literary and intellectual influences, and the particular reasons for it vary from case to case and should be investigated in each instance, as far as this is possible. In the case of Aristotle, the adoption of humanist translations in the place of the medieval ones was to have an impact on the history of philosophy that is not sufficiently appreciated.[27] We may even say in our own day that a different English translation of Aristotle produces a different philosophy, and the same was true, of course, during the Renaissance.

Aside from personal contacts of which we have spoken so far almost exclusively, the most important channel of diffusion were books, that is, both manuscript books and printed editions. The enormous number of Italian humanist manuscripts preserved in

[25] H. de Vocht, *History of the Foundation and the Rise of the Collegium trilingue Lovaniense* (Louvain, 1951): J. Ritter von Aschbach, *Geschichte der Wiener Universitaet*, vol. 2 (Vienna, 1887); G. Bauch, *Die Rezeption des Humanismus in Wien* (Breslau, 1903): A. Lefranc, *Histoire du Collège de France* (Paris, 1893); J. B. Mullinger, *The University of Cambridge*, vol. II (Cambridge, 1884), p. 52.

[26] R. Bolgar, *The Classical Review* 71 (N. S. 7, 1957), 158.

[27] At Wittenberg, Aristotle's logic, physics and metaphysics had to be taught *secundum novam translationem* in 1517–18 (*Urkundenbuch der Universitaet Wittenberg* I, ed. W. Friedensburg, Magdeburg, 1926, p. 85–86, no. 64).

libraries outside of Italy is hardly realized by most historians, and it tells an extremely interesting story that has not yet been fully explored by Renaissance scholars. If we wish to interpret the Italian humanist books in foreign libraries as evidence for the diffusion of Italian humanism during the Renaissance period, we must of course exclude from consideration the numerous instances in which the books reached their present locations as a result of more recent acquisitions. This is true of all Renaissance books now preserved in this country or in Russia. Also many books now found in English or German collections were purchased in the eighteenth century or later, just as the Cathedral Library in Toledo owes its splendid collection of Italian humanist manuscripts to the bequest of Cardinal Zelada. Interesting as these collections and their history are for other reasons, we must limit our discussion to those manuscripts and books that have been preserved abroad ever since the period of the Renaissance itself.

Their number is very large and impressive indeed. In some instances, the dedication copy sent or given by an Italian scholar to a foreign patron is still extant, as the manuscript which contains the poems written by Johannes Michael Nagonius for Henry VII of England.[28] Several copies of humanist texts in Spanish libraries seem to be derived from the manuscripts sent by the Italian humanist authors to Spanish princes or scholars. We find individual books and even entire libraries in other countries that were originally received as gifts, or purchased, or stolen from Italy.[29] Some of them are still preserved as collections, others were subsequently dispersed and have been reconstructed by modern scholars with the help of old inventories, ownership notes, or coats of arms. A notable example is the library of King Matthias Corvinus of Hungary, which was scattered in the sixteenth century and whose remnants have been traced everywhere from Poland to the United States.[30] The personal library of Duke Humphrey of Gloucester has been reconstructed, and many of its books have been identi-

[28] See above, note 16.

[29] A manuscript of Laurentius Lippius which evidently was owned by the Catalan humanist, Petrus Michael Carbonellus, was unfortunately destroyed during the last war (P. Faider and P. Van Sint Jan, *Catalogue des manuscrits conservés à Tournai*, Gembloux, 1950, p. 73–79, where the correspondence between Lippius and Carbonellus is printed).

[30] A. de Hevesy, *La Bibliothèque du roi Matthias Corvin* (Paris, 1923); V. Fraknoi and others, *Bibliotheca Corvina* (Budapest, 1927).

fied in England and elsewhere.[31] The important collections of the
Visconti and Sforza in Milan and of the Aragon princes in Naples
were taken away shortly before or after 1500, and their holdings
have been reconstructed and located.[32] Most of the Sforza manuscripts are still in Paris, whereas the Aragon books are scattered
from Liverpool and Stockholm to the Vatican, although most of
the holdings have remained, since the sixteenth century, in Paris
and in Valencia. The manuscripts of Bruni and others copied for
Cardinal Fillastre are preserved in Rheims.[33] Toward the end of
the fifteenth century, Raphael de Marcatel, an abbot of Ghent
and a bastard of the house of Burgundy, had a large collection
of manuscripts copied, partly from printed editions, which includes many writings of Italian humanists. The manuscripts are
now found, not only in Ghent, but also in Holkham Hall, Haar-
lem and Seville. Fernando Colombo, the son of the great dis-
coverer, was an ardent bibliophile, and his personal library remains almost intact in Seville. From the purchase entries found
in many of his manuscripts, we learn that he bought his books all
over Europe, and that many of them came from Italy, some of
them quite rare or even unique.[34] The famous collection of the
Escorial includes many manuscripts that were purchased by
Philip II in Italy.

Aside from these collections brought together by wealthy amateurs who preferred de luxe manuscripts written on parchment
and decorated with initials and illuminations, we should not forget the more modest books and libraries copied or bought by foreign scholars during their students' days in Italy. A well known
example is the library of Hartmann Schedel most of whose manuscripts are now in Munich.[35] The manuscripts collected by the

---

[31] Kenneth H. Vickers, *Humphrey, Duke of Gloucester* (London, 1907);
B. L. Ullman, "Manuscripts of Duke Humphrey of Gloucester," in his *Studies
in the Italian Renaissance* (Rome, 1955), 345–355.

[32] E. Pellegrin, *La Bibliothèque des Visconti et des Sforza* (Paris, 1955);
T. De Marinis, *La biblioteca napoletana dei re d'Aragona* (4 vols., Milan,
1947–52).

[33] *Catalogue général des Manuscrits des Bibliothèques Publiques de France,
Départements*, vol. 39, pt. 2 (1905), p. 170–171, no. 862; p. 208, no. 893, and
others (see the index, p. 1189).

[34] Cf. *Catalogue of the Library of Ferdinand Columbus*, ed. Archer M.
Huntington (New York, 1905); Dennis E. Rhodes, "Don Fernando Colón and
his London Purchases," *Papers of the Bibliographical Society of America* 52
(1958) 231–248. These two publications deal only with printed books.

[35] R. Stauber, *Die Schedelsche Bibliothek* (Freiburg, 1908).

humanist Augustinus Moravus still constitute an important nucleus of the Chapter Library of Olomouc, now owned by the local state archive. Most of the small collection of manuscripts preserved in the Cathedral of Strängnäs comes from the personal library of Conrad Rogge who studied at Perugia around the middle of the fifteenth century and died as bishop of Strängnäs. The abbey library of Fiecht in Austria owns a group of manuscripts copied for its abbot in Northern Italy during the fifteenth century, including some very rare texts of Petrarch.[36] Some of the books of Albrecht von Eyb are still in the library in Eichstaett where he was a canon, and his popular *Margarita poetica*, extant in both manuscript and printed copies, was largely compiled from Italian humanist sources.[37] More numerous than entire libraries are the individual manuscripts copied by or for foreign students in Italy.[38] There are many miscellaneous manuscripts written by Northern hands but containing collections of Italian humanist texts, often along with legal or theological writings, and now preserved in Vienna, Melk or St. Paul, Eichstaett, Pommersfelden or Brussels.[39] A similar collection put together by a Bohemian student was until recently in the Dietrichstein collection in Nikolsburg, and is now in a private collection in New York. Some time, the obscure copyist or owner would sign his name in the book, and thus allow us to draw more specific inferences concerning his origin, interests and later life.[40]

Connected with the diffusion of the humanist manuscripts is the spread of the Italian humanist script over the rest of Europe, a very important subject which has not yet been fully explored. The Roman characters which we use as a matter of course, though based on Carolingian models, were generally adopted during the fifteenth and sixteenth centuries in the place of the Gothic script,

[36] Ms. 183 copied in Pavia in 1466 contains the same epigrams of Petrarch which had been known only from a ms. in Olomouc (K. Burdach, *Aus Petrarcas aeltestem deutschen Schuelerkreis*, Berlin, 1929, 3–75; 195–238).

[37] Max Herrmann, *Albrecht von Eyb und die Fruehzeit des deutschen Humanismus* (Berlin, 1893).

[38] L. Bertalot, *Eine humanistische Anthologie* (Berlin, 1908); The same, *Humanistisches Studienheft eines Nuernberger Scholaren aus Pavia* (Berlin, 1910).

[39] These manuscripts will be described in my forthcoming *Iter Italicum*.

[40] A manuscript in St. Gall, containing Seneca's tragedies, was copied near the end of the fourteenth century by "Georgius Niciensis dum discit iura Papie" (G. Scherer, *Verzeichniss der Manuscripte und Incunabeln der Vadianischen Bibliothek in St. Gallen*, St. Gall, 1864, p. 79–80, no. 303).

as a result of a conscious reform of handwriting carried out by the Italian humanists of the early fifteenth century, and especially by Poggio. The humanist cursive known as Italic was also created by Italian humanists before the middle of the fifteenth century, probably by Niccoli. The origin and early diffusion of these two scripts has been recently studied by B. L. Ullman,[41] but their later diffusion and their partial or complete adoption on the part of non-Italian scribes is still an open field for further study.

When the printed book began to replace the manuscript book, its role in the diffusion of Italian humanism was no less impressive than that of the manuscript book had been before. The numerous books issued by the Italian presses were sold all over Europe and found their way into all public and private libraries, as we may learn from the correspondence and from the inventories of the period. For the fifteenth century at least, we have a statistical analysis of the books printed in Italy, which shows that the writings of the humanists, and the classical texts edited by them, had a considerable share in this production.[42] Valuable as the *Short-Title Catalogue of Books Printed in England* is for the sixteenth century,[43] it does not give us a complete picture of the reading material available to English scholars during that period. For the English libraries included numerous books printed on the continent and imported from there,[44] and especially the printing of Latin texts seems to have been as difficult and expensive in England in the sixteenth century, as it is now in the United States. As a result, even English scholars had some of their Latin works printed on the continent.[45] Moreover, the diffusion of Italian humanist writings was not limited to the editions printed in Italy or sold from Italy. During the sixteenth century, these works were frequently reprinted by foreign presses, especially in Switzerland, Germany, France and the Low Countries. There are

[41] See above, note 4.

[42] V. Scholderer, "Introduction," in: *Catalogue of Books Printed in the XVth Century now in the British Museum*, pt. 5 (London, 1924), p. IX–LV.

[43] *A Short-Title Catalogue of Books printed in England, Scotland and Ireland and of English Books printed abroad, 1475–1640*, by A. W. Pollard and G. R. Redgrave (London, 1926).

[44] *The Lumley Library, the catalogue of 1609*, ed. Sears Jayne and Francis R. Johnson (London, 1956). A bibliographical identification of the numerous references given in Robert Burton's *The Anatomy of Melancholy* (Oxford, 1621) would also be instructive.

[45] For example, Thomas More's *Utopia* was printed in Paris (1517) and Basel (1518), his *Epigrammata* in Basel (1520).

recent studies covering the works of Italian scholars published in Basel during the sixteenth century,[46] and similar impressive results might be expected from an investigation of other printing centers, especially Lyons, Strasbourg, and Antwerp.[47]

If we ask which works of the Italian humanists enjoyed the greatest vogue abroad, the answer cannot be simple or uniform. A large number of the extant manuscript and printed copies belong to the category of textbooks, of which we have spoken already, and this is not surprising since textbooks, just as now, were needed in many copies. The interests of the educated reader, on the other hand, extended well beyond the needs of the school, and covered practically all branches of literature cultivated by the humanists: their copies, editions, translations and commentaries of the ancient classics as well as their treatises on grammar and rhetoric, their letters, orations and poems that were often used as models of stylistic imitation, their works of historiography, and finally their moral treatises and dialogues. The reasons why foreign publishers and readers preferred certain authors or works over others varied from case to case, as we said before. Of special interest for the student of Italian humanism are those instances where entire works by Italian humanists have been preserved for us by foreign copyists, printers or owners. For example, the only complete manuscript of the correspondence of Bartholomaeus Facius, which contains many letters not known from other sources, has been located in a Spanish library, as has been the vernacular translation of Isocrates made by the same humanist.[48] The humanist work by the Pavia jurist, Cato Saccus, which is entitled *Semideus*, exists only in libraries outside of Italy, and two of the three manuscripts were clearly by non-Italian hands.[49] A

[46] F. Luchsinger, *Der Basler Buchdruck als Vermittler italienischen Geistes 1470–1529* (Basel, 1953); Bietenholz, *l. c.*

[47] For Lyons, see, Baudrier, *Bibliographie Lyonnaise* (12 vols., Lyon, 1895–1921, and index by G. Tricou, Geneva, 1950–52). For the numerous foreign reprints of a typical Italian humanist product, see F. Babinger, "Laudivius Zacchia, der Erdichter der 'Epistolae Magni Turci,'" *Bayerische Akademie der Wissenschaften, Philosophisch-Historische Klasse, Sitzungsberichte*, 1960, no. 13, p. 40–42.

[48] For the latter, see Valencia, Biblioteca Universitaria, ms. 727. Of the ms. of his letters, I hope to speak on some other occasion.

[49] Only one of these manuscripts, written in Italy, probably for the Visconti library, and now in Leningrad (ms. Lat. Q v XVII 2), has been studied so far. See V. Lublinsky, *Analecta Medi Aevi* II (1927), 95–118. E. Pellegrin, *l. c.*, p. 317, no. 599, with the shelf mark Lat. Q v XIV 2.

whole group of Petrarch's Latin poems has been preserved almost entirely in manuscripts that have been in Moravia and in Austria for many centuries.[50] Enea Silvio's *Chrysis* survives in a single manuscript in Prague that was presumably copied by one of his Bohemian colleagues in the imperial chancery.[51] As Ludwig Bertalot has shown, one redaction of Gasparino Barzizza's form letters has been preserved exclusively in a manuscript which has been in Cracow ever since the fifteenth century,[52] and an interesting work by Laurus Quirinus that has some connection with the famous *Certame Coronario* in Florence, survives exclusively through manuscripts written by Northern scribes and preserved in foreign libraries.[53] Tito Livio Frulovisi's poem in praise of Duke Humphrey of Gloucester has been discovered in Seville where it has safely rested ever since the time of Fernando Colombo.[54]

Another type of diffusion which I should like to mention is represented by the vernacular translations and imitations of Italian humanist writings that were made in other countries during the Renaissance period. To my knowledge, this aspect has not yet been sufficiently explored or appreciated. In several instances, a single edition or manuscript is involved, and it might be argued that rare documents of this kind are unimportant when seen within the overall picture of the life and literature of the period. I am inclined to attribute greater significance to such cases. A single manuscript, if written on parchment, was destined for a library where it might have been read by many people, and even a paper copy of a text that carries a preface or dedication proves that the text was at least intended for diffusion and publication. The best known case is the library of the Marques de Santillana, which has been studied by Mario Schiff from the manuscripts

---

[50] See above, note 36.

[51] Aeneas Silvius Piccolomini, *Chrysis*, ed. A. Boutemy (Brussels, 1939); Enea Silvio Piccolomini, *Chrysis*, ed. I. Sanesi (Florence, 1941).

[52] L. Bertalot, "Die aelteste Briefsammlung des Gasparinus Barzizza," in *Beitraege zur Forschung, Studien aus dem Antiquariat Jacques Rosenthal* N. F. II (Munich, 1929), 39–84, at p. 40–41. For Lod. Lazzarelli's *Bucolicum Carmen*, preserved until the last war in a ms. in Goerlitz, see P. O. Kristeller, "Lodovico Lazzarelli e Giovanni da Correggio," in: Biblioteca degli Ardenti della Città di Viterbo, *Studi e Ricerche nel 150° della fondazione* (Viterbo, 1960), 13–47.

[53] L. Bertalot, "Lauri Quirini dialogus in gymnasiis florentinis," *Archivum Romanicum*, 7 (1923), 478–509.

[54] See the article by R. Weiss, cited above, note 12.

that once belonged to the Duque de Osuna and are now preserved in the Biblioteca Nacional in Madrid.[55] A notable feature
of this library is its wealth in Italian and Spanish translations,
some of them rare or unique, of Latin writings by the Italian
humanists. In view of the tendency prevalent among students of
Spanish literature to minimize the importance of Spanish humanism, the very existence of this library should be properly emphasized. I should like to add the Spanish translations of the Phalaris
letters and of the Hermetic writings, which I found in Spanish
collections, and which are clearly derived from the Latin translations of the Greek texts made by Italian scholars, since the
Spanish translators include the prefaces added by the Italian
scholars to their Latin translations.[56] In a manuscript in the
Hispanic Society of America, I found a Catalan translation of
one of the historical works of Leonardo Bruni, which is actually
a free adaptation of a Greek work by Polybius.[57] In another instance, we learn that an Italian translation of a Latin work was
made for a Spanish patron who evidently read Italian more easily
than Latin.[58] There are also sumptuous parchment manuscripts
now preserved in Leningrad and in the Hague which contain
French translations of the Latin compositions or versions due to
such Italian humanists as Aurispa, Decembrio, Donato Acciaiuoli
or Andrelini.[59] Bonaccursius' now forgotten but once extremely
popular *De nobilitate* was translated into English by Tiptoft and
printed by Caxton,[60] and it also supplied the plot for the earliest
secular play in the English language, Henry Medwall's *Fulgens*

[55] See above, note 23.

[56] The Phalaris translation is found in ms. S. Cruz 378 of the Biblioteca
Universitaria in Valladolid. The Hermetica translation is in ms. Escorial
b IV 29 (see my *Studies in Renaissance Thought and Letters*, Rome, 1956,
p. 174, where I published the Spanish preface).

[57] ms. H C 387/4327. The name of the translator is Francesch Alegra.
I am indebted to Miss Clara Penney for having called my attention to the
manuscript.

[58] See above, note 23.

[59] ms. Leningrad Franc. F v XIV 8 contains French versions of Latin poems
of Andrelini and others, ms. Hague 76 F 26 contains French versions of
Decembrio and Aurispa, and ms. Hague 134 F 19, of Donato Acciaiuoli and
Leonardo Bruni. I am indebted for information on the last 2 ms. to Miss A. F.
Dekker.

[60] Rosamond J. Mitchell (*John Tiptoft*, London, 1938, p. 213–241) republished Tiptoft's English translation from the edition of 1481. For the diffusion
of the Latin text, see L. Bertalot, "Forschungen ueber Leonardo Bruni
Aretino" (*Archivum Romanicum* 15, 1931, 284–323) at p. 306–309.

and Lucres.[61] I am sure it would be quite easy to extend this list much further.[62]

Other documents that have not yet been sufficiently explored are the covering letters added by foreign copyists, editors or printers to foreign manuscripts and editions which contain writings of Italian humanists. A copy of Aeneas Silvius and Leonardo Bruni, now in Princeton, contains a letter of transmission from John Colet to an English friend, written in Rome, which constitutes the only direct evidence we have of Colet's journey to Italy.[63] All Souls College in Oxford has a printed copy of Ficino's letters once owned and annotated by Colet, which preserves a few letters exchanged between Colet and Ficino that had been completely unknown until a few years ago.[64] A copy of Cincius' translation of the pseudo-Platonic *Axiochus,* written by an English hand and now preserved in Aberystwyth, is preceded by a letter, probably from the scribe, to an English bishop.[65] A copy of a translation of John Chrysostom, now in Bruges, contains a preface by the Flemish scribe in which he compares the merits of the earlier and of the new humanistic translations of that church father.[66] In a manuscript now preserved in Stockholm but formerly in Frombork (Frauenburg), Petrarch's *De vita solitaria* is preceded by a preface from the scribe, a German friar, to the bishop of Varmia.[67] The prefaces of editors and printers should yield many more data on the fortuna of the Italian scholars, but they have been hardly studied or even considered. A few remarks found in

[61] Henry Medwall, *Fulgens & Lucres,* ed. F. S. Boas and A. W. Reed (Oxford, 1926).

[62] Heinrich Steinhoewel translated into German Aesop's life and fables from the Latin version of Rinucius (ed. H. Oesterley, Tuebingen, 1873), and Boccaccio's *De claris mulieribus* (ed. K. Drescher, Tuebingen, 1895). German translations by the same Steinhoewel (Petrarch, Griseldis), Niclas von Wyle (Aeneas Silvius, *De duobus amantibus*), Johann Gottfried (Aeneas Silvius, Bruni, Franciscus Aretinus, Rinucius Aretinus, Aurispa) are preserved in Berlin manuscripts (*Mitteilungen aus der Koeniglichen Bibliothek* II 1914, 86–87; III 1917, 71–77; VIII 1926, 135; 242).

[63] See above, note 3.

[64] R. Marcel, "Les découvertes d'Erasme en Angleterre," *Bibliothèque d'Humanisme et Renaissance* XIV (1952) 117–123. The volume will be fully studied in a forthcoming book by Prof. Sears Jayne.

[65] National Library of Wales, ms. Peniarth 336. I am indebted for a photostat to Mr. E. D. Jones.

[66] Bruges, Grand Séminaire, ms. 15/76, f. l. I am indebted for a photostat to the Rev. B. Janssens de Bisthoven.

[67] ms. V u 3. Cracow ms. 515 contains Poggio's *De miseria conditionis humanae* with a letter of transmission from N. Merboth Canonicus Wratislaviensis to Wladislaus of Poland.

two recent dissertations on the Basel press of the sixteenth century show what might be expected from a further pursuit of this subject.[68] A special case, somewhat different from the ones we mentioned, is a manuscript now preserved in Dublin in which an English scribe added King Henry V to the comparison between Alexander, Hannibal and Scipio in an extremely popular work composed by Aurispa after Lucian.[69] All these documents not only show the interest and respect which foreign scholars had for the Italian humanists in general, but also indicate in many instances the reasons why they favored a particular author or work.

This respect may best be summed up in the words in which the German humanist and jurist Martin Brenninger praised the Italian humanists, and which I chanced upon in a manuscript preserved in Austria: "Petrarch, Bruni, Guarino, Valla and Poggio have recently flourished among the Italians, and have through their efforts revived the Latin language which had almost perished. It would be a crime to depart from the practice of such eminent and famous men."[70] The wording is of exceptional interest, for we see that the slogan of the rebirth of learning, which the Italian humanists had used to underscore their own achievements,[71] was fully endorsed by one of their German pupils and admirers.

[68] See notes 18 (Bietenholz) and 46.

[69] Trinity College, ms. D 4. 24, f. 41. Cf. M. Esposito ("Classical Manuscripts in Irish Libraries," *Hermathena* XIX 42, 1920, 123–140), p. 137, note with the self mark D 4. 26.

[70] "Franciscus Petrarcha, Leonardus Arretinus, Guarinus Forenensis (sic), Lau. Vallensis, Poigius (sic) Florentinus qui iam noviter apud Ytaros (sic) claruerunt et latinam linguam que pene interierat sua opera studio industria reviviscere fecerunt. Nephas igitur putandum est discedere ab usu virorum tam insignium tamque preclarorum." Martinus Brenninger, de conficiendis epistolis, Seitenstetten, cod. 178, f. 23v–24 (I cite from a microfilm kindly supplied by the library). On the author, see my *Supplementum Ficinianum*, vol. I (Florence, 1937), p. 130–131. We may also compare the treatise on education composed by an anonymous Polish humanist after Enea Silvio: "Si quis Leonardum Arethinum, Guarinum et alios plures legerit qui quamvis mortui tamen apud prudentes et doctos vivunt et florent" (Berlin, cod. lat. oct. 3). V. Rose, *Verzeichnis der lateinischen Handschriften der kgl. Bibliothek zu Berlin*, vol. II, pt. 3 (Berlin, 1905), p. 1313–1315, no. 1022. Cf. I. Zarebski, "Najwcześnejszy Humanistyczny Polski Traktat Pedagogiczny," in: *Dziesieciolecie wyszej szkloy pedagogicznej w Krakowie 1946–1956* (Cracow, 1957), 151–178. I am indebted to Dr. J. Zathey for the latter reference, and to Dr. W. Gebhardt for having verified the ms. for me in Tuebingen.

[71] Wallace K. Ferguson, *The Renaissance in Historical Thought* (Boston, 1948); H. Weisinger, "Renaissance Accounts of the Revival of Learning," *Studies in Philology* 45 (1948) 105–118; E. Panofsky, *Renaissance and Renascences in Western Art* (Stockholm, 1960).

I have tried to describe some of the main channels through which Italian humanism spread to the other countries of Western and Central Europe. I must refrain from describing the actual manifestations of this influence, that is, the rise of a local humanism in the various countries, its characteristics and achievements, and its impact on the literature and civilization of the different nations. The general pattern seems to be one of adaptation rather than of mere imitation, and this would explain why humanism assumed in each country a somewhat different form. I must leave it to the historians of the different literatures to study these developments, and can merely suggest that this should be done with some consideration for the available sources and influences of Italian humanism, in addition to those of Italian vernacular literature. Conversely, it is important for the student of Italian humanism to know which of its many aspects were influential in other European countries. The historians of Italian literature who usually follow a scholarly tradition established in nineteenth-century Italy might do well to pay greater attention to certain aspects of Italian literature that seem to be peripheral from that traditional point of view, but that were extremely important for the international diffusion of Italian civilization. For Italian humanism and the Italian Renaissance represent beyond any doubt that period of Italian literature and civilization in which its international influence and prestige were greater than at any other time before or afterwards.

IV

The Platonic Academy of Florence *

SINCE THE BEGINNINGS of its greatness, Florence was a town of merchants and of craftsmen where the arts, literature, and religious devotion were highly cultivated and where the vernacular tongue, probably after the French and Provençal model, was used as a literary language much earlier than in the rest of Italy, not only in lyrical poetry but also in all other branches of literature. The example of Dante alone is sufficient to show that the interest in philosophy and theology was very much alive in early Florence. Yet the university which was founded during the fourteenth century never occupied a predominant place in the intellectual life of the city, and hence the learned disciplines characteristic of the medieval universities were less strongly represented in Florence than in the old university centers. Yet for this very reason, Florence was more open and more accessible to intellectual currents of a different kind. In the period between Dante and Ficino, the intellectual life of Florence was dominated by the civic humanism of such writers as Boccaccio, Salutati, Bruni, Marsuppini, and Alberti, that is, by a literary culture which had its centers in the chancery of the republic and in the private circles of the leading

* Reprinted from *Renaissance News*, Vol. XIV (1961), 147–159. This paper was read before the Middle Atlantic Renaissance Conference in Philadelphia on October 29, 1960. A somewhat different version of it appeared in German in the series *Agora* (no. 12, Darmstadt, 1959, pp. 35–47). For more detailed data on the subject, see: A. Della Torre, *Storia dell'Accademia Platonica di Firenze* (Florence, 1902); G. Saitta, *La filosofia di Marsilio Ficino* (Messina, 1923, and later editions); P. O. Kristeller, *The Philosophy of Marsilio Ficino* (New York, 1943), and *Studies in Renaissance Thought and Letters* (Rome, 1956); *Supplementum Ficinianum*, ed. P. O. Kristeller (2 vols., Florence, 1937); R. Marcel, *Marsile Ficin* (Paris, 1958); A. Chastel, *Marsile Ficin et l'Art* (Geneva, 1954); M. Schiavone, *Problemi filosofici in Marsilio Ficino* (Milan, 1957); Marsilius Ficinus, *Opera Omnia* (Basel, 1576, and Turin, 1959).

families rather than in the university, although the latter also played at times its part. This was a literary culture, or to use the terms of the period, a rhetorical and poetical culture, as well as a classical culture nourished by the study of the ancient Greek and Latin authors. It included, to be sure, a good deal of thought on problems of the state, of education, and of moral conduct, but it lacked a specific interest in metaphysical speculations.[1] It was only around the middle of the fifteenth century, with the arrival of Johannes Argyropulus, that this defect began to be felt and at the same time to be corrected.

It seems significant that it was Alamanno Rinuccini, a pupil of Argyropulus, who stated in a treatise on education dedicated to his son that we must proceed from grammar and rhetoric, where our ancestors stopped, towards philosophy.[2] More effectively than by Argyropulus, this gap in traditional Florentine culture was filled by Marsilio Ficino and his Platonic Academy. We should not interpret this development merely as the result of a Medici policy to distract the attention of the citizens from the affairs of the state towards metaphysical speculation, as has been said a number of times; for Ficino's influence affected the enemies as well as the friends of the Medici. His Platonism, as a metaphysics based on reason and on the Platonic tradition, was able to satisfy the spiritual needs of those who were accustomed and inclined to hold on to Christianity and to the study of the ancients at the same time, and who were looking for a new historical and philosophical justification of their twofold commitment. This seems to be the reason for Ficino's astonishing success and for the profound change he brought about in the general climate and direction of Florentine culture.

The broader role played by Florentine Platonism in the development of European thought as a whole is more difficult to explain. Fashion was no doubt a factor. In a period when everybody was disposed to follow Florentine models in the arts, in literature, and in scholarship, a philosophical movement which originated in Florence and was in a way linked with Florentine humanism could not fail to hold a good deal of attraction for educated persons all over Europe. Yet there was more to it than fashion. There was at the time a profound intellectual gap between dogmatic theology which had its basis in faith, and Aris-

[1] H. Baron, *The Crisis of the Early Italian Renaissance* (2 vols., Princeton, 1955); E. Garin, *Der italienische Humanismus* (Bern, 1947).

[2] A. Rinuccini, *Lettere ed Orazioni,* ed. V. R. Giustiniani (Florence, 1953), 97.

totelian scholasticism which was then largely limited to logic and physics. This gap could not be bridged by a purely literary or scholarly humanism but rather by a metaphysical Platonism based on reason and on the most respected ancient authorities besides Aristotle. This Platonism did not oppose the Christian religion or the Aristotelian science of the time, and it did not attempt to replace them. It rather tended to supplement them in an area of thought that had been neglected up to that moment but now had become increasingly important for a large number of writers, scholars, and thinkers. To this we may add the appeal of a doctrine that advocated harmony and tolerance in a period torn by the theological conflicts preceding and following the Reformation.

Marsilio Ficino, the leader of the Florentine Academy, was born in 1433, the eldest son of a physician. We know little about his youth and early studies and have just begun to substitute for the unreliable reports of his first biographers the surer testimony of his early writings; we may expect further information from a study of the manuscripts copied or owned by him during that period.[3] He acquired a good knowledge of Latin grammar and rhetoric and of the standard Latin authors such as Cicero and Vergil. He probably attended courses on Aristotelian physics and on medicine at the University of Florence, but we do not know whether he obtained a medical degree. He later practised medicine and also wrote several works on this subject. His interest in astrology was probably linked with his medical training. Those writings of his youth that have been preserved disclose a great variety of interests. They include treatises on natural philosophy in the scholastic vein, moral treatises and personal letters in the style of the humanists, and letters and sermons in the Tuscan vernacular that seem to be related to the traditions of popular religious literature. They all show a marked, though by no means exclusive, preference for Platonism, but as yet no direct acquaintance with its Greek sources. The young author is also familiar with St. Augustine and even with Lucretius and with the medieval Aristotle and his Arabic commentators. These traits are quite significant for a proper understanding of Florentine Platonism. In 1456, at the age of twenty-three, Ficino had already composed a lengthy work on Platonic philosophy that has not been preserved, and at that time he began to study Greek. His first translations from Greek into Latin date from the following years. In

[3] H. D. Saffrey, 'Notes platoniciennes de Marsile Ficin dans un manuscrit de Proclus', *Bibliothèque d'Humanisme et Renaissance*, XXI (1959), 161–184.

1462 Cosimo de' Medici gave him a house in Careggi and commissioned him to translate Plato and the other sources of Platonist thought. In 1463 Ficino finished his first translation intended for publication, that of the Hermetic Corpus, and it had a tremendous success. He then proceeded to translate Plato, beginning with ten dialogues which he thought had not been translated before. His translation of all dialogues of Plato was finished around 1468. In 1469 Ficino wrote his famous commentary on Plato's *Symposium,* and during the following years, his main philosophical work, the *Platonic Theology.* In 1473 he became a priest, and on that occasion he composed his apologetic treatise on the Christian religion. He also began to collect his letters, which include many philosophical treatises, and revised his *Platonic Theology* and his translation of Plato, printed, respectively, in 1482 and 1484. He then attended to the translation of and commentary on Plotinus, printed in 1492, wrote his influential treatise on medicine and astrology, *De Vita Libri Tres* (1489), and finally published his other commentaries on Plato (1496), his translations of Jamblichus and other Neoplatonic writings (1497), and that of Dionysius the Areopagite (ca. 1497). He died in 1499.

He spent the better part of his life under the personal patronage of the Medici family, and his political sympathies evidently went with them. Yet he was not a man of strong political interests, and since the Valori and Soderini were no less his friends and pupils than the Del Nero, he did not suffer any personal troubles after the revolution of 1494. He admired Savonarola for a short while but had good reasons for deploring his political activities after 1494. In his writings, Ficino shows remarkable gifts: a thorough knowledge of the Greek language and of ancient philosophical literature give to his translations a merit that is still recognized today. His own philosophical works are also distinguished for the clarity and consistency of his basic ideas. His learning included theology, medicine, and astrology. He was a practising musician and an expert on musical theory, and he knew and loved both Latin and Tuscan poetry and literature. He was of small stature and of a melancholy temper, full of hypochondria and of superstition. His features are known from a medal and a posthumous monument and perhaps best from several illuminated manuscripts. He liked intelligent company and was agreeable in his conversation, gaining the friendship and admiration not only of princes and scholars but also of many businessmen, writers, and artists. Thus he became the leader and center of the Platonic Academy.

The Platonic Academy of Florence was not, as historians formerly thought, an organized institution like the academies of the sixteenth century, but merely a circle around Ficino, with no common doctrine except that of Ficino, and closely linked, but not identical with, the circle or court of the Medici. The name 'Academy' was merely adopted in imitation of Plato's Academy. The circle included scholars and writers who had ideas and interests of their own, sometimes quite different from those of Ficino, as in the case of Pico or Poliziano. Politian, though a personal friend of Ficino, was primarily interested in poetry and in philology, and his philosophical orientation was Aristotelian rather than Platonic. Pico della Mirandola was influenced by Ficino in a number of ways, but his background and thought were independent and so was his influence. He had a direct contact with the scholastic traditions of Padua and Paris, learned Hebrew and Arabic, and studied philosophical and cabalistic sources in these languages. He was a bitter opponent of astrology and deeply influenced by Savonarola. Among the members of the Academy, Francesco da Diacceto was Ficino's chief pupil, and later he became his successor and formulated his own philosophical doctrine. The others did not write much about philosophical topics; most of them were poets and men of letters who tended to repeat Ficino's ideas, such as Girolamo Benivieni, Lorenzo de' Medici, and Cristoforo Landino.

The chief activities of the Academy were closely linked with Ficino himself: improvised conversations with friends or visitors; organized banquets and discussions such as the famous celebrations on Plato's birthday; speeches or declamations delivered by Ficino; public courses given by Ficino in the church of S. Maria degli Angeli on Plato, on Plotinus, on St. Paul; also a certain amount of private instruction, based on the reading of Plato and perhaps of other authors. These activities of the Academy must be added to the writings and correspondence of Ficino and his friends if we wish to understand the vogue and prestige attained by the Academy during the more than thirty years of its life and in the course of the subsequent centuries.

In the light of these remarks, we can easily understand that the Platonism of Ficino and of his friends was a highly complex and unique system of thought that cannot be taken as a mere repetition of the thought of Plato or of the ancient Neoplatonists. The

basic influence of these ancient sources must be supplemented by
many ingredients of later origin and by the original interests and
ideas of Ficino and of Pico. We must take into account the
Platonism and Augustinianism of the Middle Ages and even
more the tradition of scholastic Aristotelianism that was known
to Ficino through many channels and left many traces in his
terminology and in his method of reasoning. To the humanists
of the preceding generations Ficino is linked through his Latin
style, through the tone and purpose of his learned correspondence, through his work as a translator and commentator, and even
through his tendency to worship ancient authorities and to bring
about a rebirth of the ancient wisdom of Platonism. He is influenced by the Byzantine Platonism of Gemistus Pletho and his
school, and I recently came across a translation of Pletho's commentary on the *Chaldaic Oracles* which I should like to attribute
to Ficino.[4] Certain other features of Ficino's thought and writings
are best explained by an influence of the popular literature that
originated in the lay religious guilds. As to the mystical elements
of Ficino's thought, I am inclined to attribute them to Ficino's
personal experience and to his reading of the Neoplatonic authors. I see no direct evidence for his dependence on medieval
mysticism or on Nicolaus Cusanus.

For a brief discussion of Ficino's philosophical ideas, it seems
best to begin with his fundamental concept of contemplation.
Contemplation represents for Ficino a direct spiritual experience
to which he refers everywhere in his writings. In contemplation,
the soul withdraws from the body and from all external things
into its own self, that is, into its own substance, and there it dis-
covers not only its own divinity, but in a gradual ascent, the
intelligible world, the transcendent ideas, and God Himself, their
common source and essence. The tone of the numerous passages
in which Ficino speaks about contemplation shows very clearly
that it is for him a direct and personal experience. Yet his language and terminology also show that he avails himself, with
certain Christian and personal modifications, of Neoplatonic
theories for the interpretation of this experience. The withdrawal
of consciousness into itself becomes a separation of the soul from
the body, and the higher vision disclosed to the soul in the experience of meditation becomes a knowledge of the intelligible
world. Yet since Ficino puts the Christian God in the place of

---

[4] I hope to deal with this translation in a forthcoming article. On Pletho,
see F. Masai, *Pléthon et le platonisme de Mistra* (Paris, 1956).

Plotinus' One and Nous, he must depart from Plotinus by identifying the ideas with the essence of God. Moreover, following Plotinus and Plato's *Phaedo*, Ficino treats the contemplative experience not only as the basis of metaphysical speculation since it makes us certain of God's existence and of His attributes, of the intelligible world, and of the soul, but he also considers it as the only source of a true moral life. Everything Ficino says about the virtues and other moral phenomena is basically a reduction of moral theory to the life of contemplation. Inasmuch as we withdraw into the inner and spiritual life, we escape from vices and from the blows of chance, and our actions from there on are dictated by a purified knowledge and conscience. Thus the life of contemplation is the goal all human beings must aim at in order to attain not only true knowledge but also moral perfection. Hence Ficino's letters are full of declamations and exhortations in favor of the inner and contemplative life. He assumes the role of the spiritual guide who leads his friends and pupils through his Platonist preaching towards the true life, that is, to the life of the spirit and of contemplation.

This central concept of contemplation is also the key to a proper understanding of two other theories of Ficino that are probably the most famous among his contributions to Renaissance thought: the theory of the immortality of the soul and the theory of Platonic love. The personal immortality of the soul had been accepted and taught by nearly all thinkers of the Platonist and Christian traditions, and hence it is not surprising to encounter it in the thought of Florentine Platonism. What remains to be explained is the predominant and exceptional role played by the doctrine of immortality in this philosophical system. For Ficino, immortality is the central dogma of Platonism, and hence it constitutes the chief theme of his main work, the *Platonic Theology*, which has the subtitle 'On the Immortality of the Souls'. In my opinion, the problem of immortality became of such pressing importance within the framework of Renaissance theology and metaphysics as a result of the individualism of the period, that is, of its tendency to attach very great importance to the concrete and individual qualities and experiences of each human being, a tendency which we encounter in all humanists of the period and which finds its culminating expression in Montaigne. Only in the sixteenth century, and precisely at the Lateran Council of 1513, was the immortality of the soul (as distinct from the resurrection of the body) officially proclaimed as a Catholic dogma, and around the same time the discussion of this problem that centered around the famous treatise of Pomponazzi attracted general attention. All this we must take into account if we wish to understand the importance of the problem of immortality in Ficino's thought. Yet there are also deeper reasons for this importance that are directly related to his basic concept of contemplation. Inner experience or contemplation is for him a gradual ascent of the soul towards a highest goal, the direct knowledge of God. In accordance with the Neoplatonic tradition, Ficino admits that this highest goal may be attained for a short while by a few wise men during their earthly life. Yet since this direct knowledge of God is proposed as the highest goal for all human beings and since it is the goal of all our spiritual efforts, it is not sufficient to think that this goal may be attained by a few persons for a few rare and fleeting moments. If the ideal of the contemplative life is to be recognized as a valid ideal for all men, we must postulate a future life in which the vision and enjoyment of God, that is, the highest goal of contemplation, will actually be attained by a large number of persons and in a continuous and permanent fashion. This is exactly one of the most frequent and most forceful arguments proposed by Ficino for the immortality of the soul Since this argument is closely related to the center of his philo sophical thought, I am inclined to consider it as decisive.

The theory of Platonic love to which I should now like to turn our attention has a famous and at the same time a ridiculous ring, as happens when an idea becomes fashionable and finally through constant repetition empty and superficial. In this case, the original idea is far more serious. Ficino was the first to use the terms 'Platonic' or 'Socratic' love, and in doing so, he merely thought of the love theory found in Plato's *Symposium* and *Phaedrus* as he understood it. More frequently Ficino speaks of divine love, which he tends to identify with Christian *charitas* and with friendship. For him, this divine love is not a sublimated form of sexual love (although he is very far from condemning sexual love as such). It is rather a spiritual bond between two persons who both participate in the contemplative life. For each of them, this life is a personal and individual experience, yet there is a natural community and friendship between those who pursue this ideal. Thus Ficino could say that friendship was the bond that linked the members of his Academy with each other, or that a true friendship always required three partners, two friends and God, the common ground of their friendship. It is necessary

to remember the notion of the contemplative life in order to understand this interpretation of love and friendship. On the other
hand, the solitary experience of the contemplative life acquires
for Ficino and his friends, through the theory of divine love, a
human and social significance which it would otherwise have
lacked.

Having spoken of Ficino's metaphysics and of his ethics, we
may turn to his cosmology. Here we must limit ourselves to a
brief mention of what seems to be the most interesting and original aspect of it, his concept of the unity of the world. Ficino inherited from Neoplatonic and medieval thought a hierarchical
view of the universe in which each being occupies a determined
place and degree. Yet. the view that all things coexist, as it were,
in a universal hierarchy does not seem to satisfy him. He demands
that they should also be connected by mutual links. Hence he
emphasizes the principle of continuity and postulates everywhere
the existence of intermediary beings which will bridge the gaps
in the ladder of things. Yet in order to give the world a more
intimate unity, he also postulates a more active and dynamic
kind of relationship. Thus he assigns a special role in the world
to knowledge and love and to the soul that possesses them. By
thinking and loving an object, the soul establishes a kind of unity
with it, and in a sense acts upon it and transforms it. In his commentary on the *Symposium,* following Plato and the pseudo-
Dionysius, Ficino treats love as a cosmological principle of the
unity of things, as a *vinculum mundi,* and in the *Platonic Theology* the same role is assigned to the rational soul. Through its
intermediary qualities, the soul is the link between the intelligible and the corporeal world, and through its ability to think
and to love all things the soul is also the active center, the link
and bond of the universe. In this manner Ficino gives a metaphysical basis to the doctrine of the excellence and dignity of man
that had been dear to the earlier humanists and was so close to
their cultural and educational program, the *studia humanitatis.*
For Ficino, man is identical with his rational soul, and his excellence consists in the role played by this soul as the center and
bond of the universe, in its infinite capacity of thinking and willing, knowing and loving, of identifying itself with all other
things. This important idea received a further development by
Pico in his famous oration. For him, man and his soul are no
longer a part, even a privileged central part, of the universal
hierarchy; man is now outside the hierarchy, he is a world for

himself and has no fixed place in the order of things but rather determines his place and nature through his own individual choice, since he is able to live all lives, those of the animals as well as those of the angels and even of God.

Another characteristic trait of Florentine Platonism seems to be its historical view of philosophy and religion. For Ficino, his work as a translator and commentator of Plato and Plotinus, and even as a Platonist philosopher, was justified by his conception of the history of human thought. On the one hand, there was the Hebrew and Christian religious tradition which had its basis in Scripture and faith and which for him was true beyond any shadow of doubt. On the other hand, there was the tradition of Platonic philosophy, which was equally true and in basic agreement with faith but had its basis in reason and in the authority of the ancient philosophers. In Ficino's view, this latter tradition did not merely begin with Plato or Socrates, from whom the thought of all Platonist philosophers down to himself was derived. There also existed, long before Plato, an ancient pagan philosophy and theology represented by the teachings and writings of Hermes Trismegistus, Zoroaster, Orpheus, and Pythagoras. The Hermetic writings, the *Chaldaic Oracles,* the Orphic hymns, the golden words and symbols of Pythagoras, writings which modern scholars consider as apocryphal products of late antiquity, were for Ficino, for his contemporaries and successors the authentic witnesses of an ancient wisdom that was prior to Plato himself, though in basic agreement with him. Thus there was a pagan tradition that was as old as the Hebrew Scripture. Ficino had borrowed elements of this notion of a pagan theological tradition from Proclus and from Pletho. Yet whereas Proclus had ignored the Biblical tradition and Pletho kept the two traditions apart, if he had not actually opposed them to each other, Ficino insisted on their basic harmony. Thus it was easy to arrive at the notion of a *philosophia perennis,* a concept actually formulated by a Platonizing Catholic theologian of the sixteenth century, Augustinus Steuchus. Against the background of this doctrine, we can better understand the frequent and almost excessive use of quotations and of allegories in the writings of Ficino and of his school. The quotations represent the authorities, the testimonies from tradition that serve to confirm a proposed opinion, and it is often necessary to interpret them in a tendentious and arbitrary fashion in order to discover in them the meaning that one wishes to derive from them. In his use of allegories, Ficino followed the model of the Neoplatonists and of other ancient authors when he attributed to the classical myths some deep philosophical or theological meaning. In this view, the myths when properly interpreted form a part of pagan theology and hence add their support to philosophical truth. Thus Pico della Mirandola could formulate the program of a poetic theology, although he was prevented by his early death from carrying it out. In the writings of Ficino, the quotations and allegories are an impressive ornament, and they contribute much to the lively style and color of his pages, yet I do not think that they constitute the substance or structure of his thought. We should not detach them from their context, or try to read and interpret them for their own sake, as several scholars have recently tried to do, but rather in terms of those abstract propositions which they are intended to sustain or to illustrate, frequently in a quite complicated and unconvincing manner.

The agreement between religion and philosophy, that is, between Christian religion and Platonic philosophy, passes in Ficino's thought into a more general concept of natural religion. There are certain elements of religion which each human being knows and accepts through natural reason and which are common to all peoples and to all particular religions. Ficino evidently thinks of the existence of God and of the divinity and immortality of the soul, and he asserts that this religion is natural for man and that it is found in varied and often distorted forms in the beliefs of all men. Pico went again one step further than his older friend. For him, truth is not found only in the Christian religion and in Platonic philosophy. When he proposed his 900 theses, the theses themselves and the speech that was to precede the disputation express the idea that there are particular truths in all religions and in all philosophies, also in the Greek, Arabic, and Latin Aristotelians, and in the Jewish Cabala. Thanks to Pico's influence, the Cabala was often added to Platonic, Pythagorean, Chaldaic, and Egyptian sources in a kind of universal syncretism. In spite of its fantastic aspects, this Platonist or pseudo-Platonist syncretism represented in the sixteenth century the most important and substantial body of philosophical sources and ideas other than those of Aristotelianism, and it has been shown that this syncretism had its share in preparing the way for later deism and for the modern idea of religious tolerance.

After having mentioned a few of the leading ideas of Ficino and Pico, we may try to describe the historical position of the Platonic Academy of Florence. It is no exaggeration to state that

Ficino and his circle dominated Florentine intellectual life during those decades that go from the death of Cosimo de' Medici in 1464 to the revolution of 1494, although some important figures such as Alamanno Rinuccini managed to evade their influence or even tried to oppose it, as was the case with the poet Pulci. Yet the role of the Academy was not limited to Florence. Through visits and through correspondence and through the numerous copies and printed editions of Ficino's writings, these ideas spread rather rapidly through the rest of Italy and of Europe. Ficino had his friends and correspondents in Rome and Venice, in Bologna and Ferrara, in France and Germany, in Poland and Hungary, and the traces of his influence appear also in the Low Countries, in Spain, in England, and in Bohemia.

Florentine Platonism was thus a considerable intellectual force, and its influence continued to be strong throughout the sixteenth century. This influence was not as broad as is often believed nor linked with the institutional traditions of schools or universities as was the influence of Aristotelianism or of literary humanism. Yet the influence of Platonism was based on individual appeal, and it was thus even deeper, especially since it affected a number of the most important thinkers and writers, including some that are not usually labeled as Platonists, such as Bruno, Galileo, Kepler, and Descartes.

With the seventeenth century, after Galileo and Descartes, a new epoch began for European philosophy and science. The speculative cosmology of the Renaissance was no longer possible within the framework of a natural science based on experiments and on mathematics. The influence of Platonism persisted, however, in metaphysics and in epistemology, and it even came to new life in the Cambridge Platonists. Moreover, the authority of Plato remained great, and as late as the eighteenth century we find many theories associated with the name and prestige of Plato that actually belong to his Florentine translator and commentator. With the nineteenth century, Renaissance Platonism loses even this anonymous or pseudonymous influence, after historical and philological criticism had begun to make a rigorous (and sometimes too rigorous) distinction between the genuine thought of Plato and that of his successors and commentators in late antiquity and during the Renaissance. Thus the direct role of Florentine Platonism as a spiritual force had come to an end.

Yet at the same time when the ideas of Florentine Platonism have ceased to influence us in their original and literal form, we have begun to understand and appreciate them in their true historical significance. If we wish to understand the notable difference which separates the philosophical and scientific thought of Bacon, Galileo, and Descartes from that of St. Thomas Aquinas or of Duns Scotus, we must study the thought of the two or three intervening centuries, and Florentine Platonism will occupy an important place alongside the other philosophical and intellectual currents of its time. If we wish to describe the complicated physiognomy of the Renaissance period in all of its facets, we must study not only its political and economic history, its theology, its literature and art but also its philosophical and scientific thought and try to find in it the counterparts, sources, or repercussions of those traits which we notice in the other aspects of this period, and Platonism will again occupy a rather significant place. If we try to trace the cultural history of Florence, the capital of the Renaissance, we shall recognize that besides the great Florentine thinkers who were poets or statesmen, artists or scientists, Ficino must be considered the greatest Florentine philosopher and metaphysician in the narrow and proper sense of the word and that he was worthy of his great and beautiful city through the richness and depth of his thought as well as through the vast extent of his influence in space and in time. Finally, if we are inclined to consider the history of Platonism in the West as a kind of *philosophia perennis* (and I must confess that I share this inclination), we shall have to admit that the Florentine Platonism of the Renaissance, with all its defects and weaknesses, represents one of the most important and most interesting phases in the history of this philosophical tradition.

V

Ficino and Pomponazzi on the
Place of Man in the Universe *

IN ATTEMPTING TO understand a given body of ideas, the student
of intellectual history will not only seek to determine its truth
or its philosophical and historical significance; he will also inquire how far these ideas were old or novel at the time a writer
first expressed them. To be sure, the history of thought has shifted
back and forth between an emphasis on originality and on adher-
ence to permanent principles, and the emphasis prevailing at a
given period has often guided the efforts of authors. Yet neither
extreme has ever at any time been realized. What we actually
find everywhere is a mixture of old and new elements, in varying
proportions to be sure.

There are several reasons for the acceptance and repetition of
old ideas. One factor is certainly the intellectual inertia which
leads a man to receive without question what he has been taught,
or to reject without proper examination other proposed ideas
which would conflict with his familiar views. More important, in
the case of a moderately independent mind, is the impossibility
of any indivdual's constructing a new system of the universe from
the ground up without the use of borrowed materials. This fact
makes clear the importance of investigating the sources and background of a philosopher, provided we do not stop with noting
that certain ideas have been taken from certain sources, but proceed to inquire why they have been borrowed and how they have
been transformed to become part of the new synthesis. Another

* Reprinted from *Studies in Renaissance Thought and Letters* (Rome,
Edizioni di Storia e Letteratura, 1956), 279–286. Originally published in
Journal of the History of Ideas, Vol. V (1944), 220–226.

factor which definitely makes for continuity, though this may sound like a paradox, is polemic and discussion. The current views against which a thinker reacts mark also the starting-point for his own thought, determine the range and direction of his ideas, and often constitute the necessary complement to his own system. This is one of the reasons why pupils seldom succeed in maintaining intact the system of their masters. Ideas lose their force when the conditions in opposition to which they were conceived disappear, just as a man leaning with all his force against a wall will collapse when the wall is suddenly taken away. Moreover, every philosophical thought is a response to a common world. There are certain basic facts which no thinker can disregard, and certain enduring problems which give continuity to their varying solutions. Finally, certain problems admit of only a limited number of basic solutions, which recur more or less regularly in the history of ideas, though the details may vary. This accounts for the fact that there are a few persistent trends which may be traced through the entire history of thought.

On the other hand, there are no less powerful factors contributing to a continual change and variety of ideas. Most thinkers derive some degree of novelty from their own personal outlook, or even from a conscious endeavor to be original or "up-to-date". Favorable circumstances may help them to reach conclusions for which the premises have been prepared by their predecessors. Intellectual, political, or social conditions prevailing at the time may force them to modify ideas they would prefer to restate, which were conceived under different circumstances. More important is the basic fact that each individual and each age starts life anew, has a new approach to truth, and may hence make a specifically new contribution to the realm of ideas. Even in the extreme case in which a thinker is merely copying or summarizing the work of previous writers, his selection and emphasis will depend on his preferences, if not on specific ideas. In view of this necessary combination of old and new elements, the history of ideas will often appear like the variations on a musical theme.

This point of view is particularly helpful in understanding the history of a specific trend or tradition which may be traced over a longer period, such as Platonism or Aristotelianism. Such a tradition is held together by a common orientation toward a great thinker of the past and toward some of his basic ideas. But it is by no means a succession of simple repetitions of theories established once and for all at the beginning. Otherwise it would have no interest whatsoever. What actually takes place is a process of continual adaptation, in which the basic ideas are gradually transformed and readjusted to the ever-changing historical and intellectual situation and to the specific interests and problems of individual thinkers. A later thinker who tries to interpret or to restate the ideas of an earlier thinker will always translate old concepts into new terms and will reconstruct the old system according to his own views. He will select and emphasize some elements of the previous tradition and omit or disregard others. He will also combine them with ideas borrowed from outside sources or added by himself.

It is obvious that the historian of philosophy must adjust his method to this state of affairs. For a long time the entire study of past philosophies had been limited to stating and criticizing "opinions", and this still remains the necessary basis or the final goal of any interpretation. But more recently the history of philosophy has come to be a special discipline aiming at a philosophical understanding of past thinkers through the resources of historical and philological scholarship. In pursuing this task, some students have been inclined to treat the great thinkers as isolated figures and to emphasize only the novel and original aspects of their thought. Others, on the contrary, have been more interested in the continuing tradition of certain ideas and tendencies, and have emphasized the permanent and recurring factors at the expense of the changing and varying details. I should think that a combination of both methods is needed. The historian should recognize the recurring basic ideas and attitudes in their various appearances, but he should also describe and explain what is specific in the different appearances and its relation to the basic principles. The method should be flexible, of course, according to the number and significance of the novel elements found in each representative of a given tradition. In this way the historian of philosophy will do justice to the fact that an intellectual tradition consists in the varying manifestations of permanent, basic principles.

When we apply this method to the history of Platonism or Aristotelianism, we are confronted with the additional difficulty that Platonism and Aristotelianism are, so to speak, complementary to each other. Closely related from the beginning, their very relation has been subject to a continually changing interpretation. The reason is to be found in the relation between Plato and Aristotle themselves. Modern historical research has led to the conclusion that the philosophies of Plato and Aristotle were not simply two opposite or merely different systems of thought, but rather stages in a gradual development which led from the mature works of Plato through the dialogues of his old age and through the early works of Aristotle (as reconstructed out of preserved fragments) to the treatises of Aristotle's mature period. But this historical insight cannot prevent us from recognizing that there really is a basic difference between the philosophies of Plato and Aristotle.

This ambiguous relation has determined the history of Platonism and Aristotelianism ever since. There were periods in which the contrast between the two traditions was strongly emphasized, but even then the followers of Plato could not help borrowing problems and concepts of Aristotelian origin, nor could the Aristotelians eliminate the Platonic elements contained in the system of their master. At other times a so-called eclectic tendency held that Plato and Aristotle "disagreed in words, but agreed in their doctrines"; but the disagreement in words still remained quite puzzling for the interpreters, and they were obliged in their attempted synthesis to subordinate the views of one master to those of the other. Thus the two currents represent two different poles of philosophical orientation, without being entirely exclusive of each other. On the contrary, we might say that each belongs to the history of the other, and that just in those times when one of the two traditions definitely prevails over the other, it is also bound to continue and to represent the heritage of that other tradition.

In medieval Europe, Platonism as modified by Augustine was the prevailing trend in philosophy and theology up to the twelfth century, and remained an important secondary current long thereafter. Aristotelianism on the other hand became predominant in the thirteenth century, and retained much of its hold up to the sixteenth century and even afterwards. Yet from the fifteenth century on both Platonism and Aristotelianism entered a novel phase under the influence of the new humanistic movement. Both currents, to be sure, continued the preceding traditions of the Middle Ages, but at the same time they formulated the traditional problems and doctrines in novel terms and thus represent new stages in the history of those traditions. Let us consider each of them in one of their chief representatives, that is, in Ficino and in Pomponazzi.

Ficino's main work, the *Theologia Platonica,* is an attempt to prove the immortality of the soul by rational arguments. The problem of immortality acquires this importance for him for the following reasons. Ficino argues that we are taught by a basic experience that contemplation of the invisible and of God is the major activity of human life and constitutes the very goal of our existence. But at the same time we find that in our present life this goal is attained only in an imperfect fashion, that is, by very few persons, and by them only for a brief time. Hence we must assume that there will be a future life in which the highest aim of our existence, the immediate knowledge and enjoyment of God, will be attained by a large number of human beings and in a permanent fashion. The immortality of the soul thus appears as a necessary postulate for maintaining that contemplation is the goal of human life.[1]

Pomponazzi also dedicates one of his most important works to the problem of immortality, but his solution is just the opposite from Ficino's. There are no rational proofs for the immortality of the soul; and since the doctrine of immortality must be upheld as a religious truth, it can be based only on the authority of the Bible and of the Church, but not on philosophical arguments. This denial of immortality, at least in the sphere of reason, is based on a characteristic premise which again is just the opposite of Ficino's emphasis on contemplation. The human intellect always depends on corporeal, empirical objects, and there is no reason to assume any higher activity of the human mind which would bring it into contact with purely intelligible entities. But Pomponazzi is no materialist. Although the intellect is corporeal with regard to its objects, as a subject of thought it is immaterial, and in this sense it may be said that the human soul, though mortal in its essence, does at least participate in immortality. Pomponazzi thus replaces the concept of immortality as a perfect life after death with that of a participation in immortality during the present life. The meaning of this change becomes apparent in his conception of virtue. Whereas Ficino still accepted the conventional opinion that immortality is a moral postulate in order that virtue and vice may be properly rewarded after death, Pomponazzi emphatically denies the moral value of such recompense. The essential reward of virtue is virtue itself, the essential punishment of vice, vice itself. Thus moral doctrine is freed of all metaphysical premises, and at the same time the goal of human

[1] See: P. O. Kristeller, *The Philosophy of Marsilio Ficino*, New York, 1943, 324; *Il pensiero filosofico di Marsilio Ficino* (Florence, 1953), p. 350.

existence is conceived as something attainable during our present life, and not to be expected in another, future life.[2]

Ficino and Pomponazzi thus represent two philosophical attitudes basically different from, if not opposed to each other, which may be roughly identified with the general trend of the Platonic and Aristotelian traditions respectively. It is hence all the more significant that in spite of this contrast they have something in common which seems to be characteristic of Renaissance thought. The very fact that such basic importance is attached to the problem of immortality shows a predominant interest in man and his metaphysical position, not nearly so marked in the previous period.[3] Moreover, the contrasting ideas of future contemplation and of self-contained virtuous conduct are but alternative solutions to the same basic problem, that is, to the question: what is the ultimate aim of human life? Finally, in the passages which illustrate Ficino's and Pomponazzi's doctrine of the place of man in the universe, both of them make very similar statements, emphasizing that man is the center of the universe and is related to all other parts of the world. Even if Pomponazzi borrowed the idea from Ficino, the fact that these statements are found in entirely different and even opposed contexts makes the coincidence all the more interesting. The passages acquire additional significance from their similarity to Pico's famous *Oration* on the Dignity of Man.[4]

It would be entirely wrong to claim that the glorification of man was a new discovery of the Renaissance. The praise of man because of his invention of the arts is quite familiar in Greek literature and thought, and so is the simile of man as microcosm. The intermediate position of the soul between the corporeal and the intelligible world is definitely suggested by Plato and further developed by the Neoplatonists and Hermetics. On the other hand, the superiority of man over other creatures is definitely indicated in *Genesis* and in several other passages of the Old Testa-

[2] Petrus Pomponatius, *Tractatus De Immortalitate Animae*, translated by William Henry Hay, II (Haverford, 1940). *The Renaissance Philosophy of Man*, ed. É. Cassirer, P. O. Kristeller, and J. H. Randall, Jr. (Chicago, 1948), pp. 280–381.

[3] G. Gentile, "Il concetto dell'uomo nel Rinascimento" in his *Il pensiero italiano del Rinascimento*, Florence, 1940, 47–113.

[4] «Of the Dignity of Man», translated by Elizabeth L. Forbes, *Journal of the History of Ideas*, III, 1942, 347–54; E. Cassirer, "Giovanni Pico della Mirandola," *ibid.*, 123–44, 319–46. *The Renaissance Philosophy of Man*, 223–54. Ioannes Picus, *Oratio de dignitate hominis*, Lexington, 1953.

ment. Early Christian emphasis on the salvation of mankind and on the incarnation of Christ implied a conception of the dignity of man which was further developed by some of the Church Fathers, Lactantius and Augustine for example.[5]

These ideas were never entirely forgotten during the Middle Ages. But I am under the impression that since the beginning of Renaissance humanism the emphasis on man becomes more persistent, more systematic, and more exclusive. Petrarch, who in his unsystematic way often expresses ideas which were to be elaborated in the succeeding period, insists that nothing is admirable but the soul, and that there is only one important subject of human thought, man himself.[6] Before the middle of the fifteenth century Giannozzo Manetti, the Florentine humanist, composed a treatise *On the Excellency and Dignity of Man* as a counterpart to Innocent III's work *On the Misery of Man*.[7] With Ficino the glorification of man assumes a more definite philosophical significance. He emphasizes mainly two aspects: man's universality and his central position. Man's universality is reflected in his relation to all parts of the universe and in his unlimited aspirations. His position in the center of the universe, moreover, gives man an importance unrivaled by any other being except God Himself. Pico, obviously following Ficino, modifies his theory on one characteristic point. Man is no longer the center of the universe, but he is detached from the entire series of existing things and free to choose his own form of life. Thus the dignity of man is no longer conceived in terms of his universality, but in terms of his liberty.[8] These ideas of Ficino and Pico exercised a wide influence in the later Renaissance. A good example of this influence is Vives' *Fable on Man*, based entirely on Pico's conception.[9]

The passages from Ficino about the universal rule of man over the elements seem also to have something in common with the Baconian program of the dominion of man over nature. His conclusion that man is endowed with an almost god-like mind be-

[5] G. Garin, «La 'dignitas hominis' e la letteratura pastristica», *Rinascita*, I, no. 4, 1938, 102–46.

[6] Francesco Petrarca, *Le Familiari*, bk. IV, no. 1, ed. V. Rossi, v. I, Florence, 1933, 159. Id., *Le traité De sui ipsius et multorum ignorantia*, ed. L. M. Capelli, Paris, 1906, 24–25. *The Renaissance Philosophy of Man*, 36–133.

[7] See Gentile, *op cit.*, 90 ff.

[8] See Kristeller, *op. cit.*, 117–120, 407–410.

[9] Joannes Ludovicus Vives, «Fabula de homine», in *Opera Omnia*, IV, Valencia, 1783, 3–8. *The Renaissance Philosophy of Man*, 387–93.

cause Archimedes was able to construct a model of the heavenly spheres, may even suggest Galileo's assertion that God's knowledge of mathematics is different in quantity but not in kind from our own mathematical knowledge.[10] Of course in the latter two cases no direct influence is likely, and the emphasis and context are entirely different; but the comparison may help to clarify some implications on both sides.

The position of man in the universe has a bearing not only on man, but also on the universe. Hence the statements of Ficino, Pico, and Pomponazzi have a definite significance not only in the history of the conception of man, but also in the history of cosmology. The medieval conception of the universe was dominated by the idea of a hierarchy of substances, which goes back to Neoplatonic sources. Whereas in the field of biology this idea of hierarchy survived up to fairly recent times, in the field of cosmology it was definitely abandoned by early modern science. In the astronomy of Kepler and Galileo there is no room for differences of rank and perfection between heaven and earth, or between the various stars or the various elements. But even before the new astronomy was definitely established a gradual disintegration of the old idea of hierarchy took place, most definitely in Nicholas of Cusa and later in Giordano Bruno.

It would seem that the conceptions of Ficino and Pico played their more modest part in this disintegration. To be sure, Ficino takes a hierarchy of five principles as the very starting-point of his metaphysical system. But he immediately asks how the various levels of that hierarchy are related to each other; and he seeks a central link which through its attributes could mediate between the opposite extremes of the universe, and through its manifold aspirations and movements could transmit forces and qualities from one end of the universe to the other. This question actually transcends the limits of the traditional notion of hierarchy, and implies a dynamic conception of the universe such as was developed by the natural philosophers of the sixteenth century. Whereas on this point Pomponazzi merely follows Ficino, Pico goes one step farther. He also maintains the notion of a hierarchy; but for him man is no longer a definite element in the hierarchial series, not even its privileged center: he is entirely detached from the hierarchy and can move upward and downward

[10] Galileo Galilei, *Dialogo sopra i due massimi sistemi del mondo, giornata prima,* in *Edizione Nazionale,* VII, Florence, 1897, 128 f.

according to his free will. Thus the hierarchy is no longer all-inclusive, while man, because of his possession or freedom, seems to be set entirely apart from the order of objective reality.

The last observation points to a more general characteristic of Renaissance thought: it is a period of transition, in a specific sense which does not apply to most other periods of thought. To be sure there are always varieties of opinion and orientation. But the philosophies of the thirteenth or of the seventeenth century were based on common principles. Renaissance thought has common problems and common aspirations, but no common principles or solutions. The disintegration of old principles that appears during the Renaissance has not only a negative value in clearing the way for the formulation of new principles that was bound to come. It has also a positive significance, because it is generated by new forms of experience and new problems which were destined to be absorbed in the succeeding synthesis of the seventeenth century.

VI

Paduan Averroism and Alexandrism
in the Light of Recent Studies *

THE RENAISSANCE PERIOD has been comparatively neglected by most historians of philosophy. However, a better knowledge of fifteenth and sixteenth century thought seems to be needed if we want to understand the transition from Aquinas or Ockham to Bacon or Descartes, to trace the sources of many side currents of the seventeenth and eighteenth century, or to identify the place in philosophy of a period as distinguished as the Renaissance in art and literature, in science and scholarship, in political and theological thought. The task is difficult, for Renaissance thought does not represent a unified picture, but is broken up into several schools and currents. The Aristotelian tradition which was inherited from the later Middle Ages continued to dominate the professional teaching of logic and natural philosophy at the universities and other schools. The broad current of classical humanism, largely rooted in literary and scholarly rather than in strictly philosophical interests, developed a strong concern with moral problems, attempted a reform of traditional logic, and brought about a wider and deeper acquaintance with ancient thought including Aristotle himself and his Greek commentators. The Platonic movement was centered in metaphysical and religious concerns, but also influenced cosmology as well as poetry and literature. In the sixteenth century, the philosophers of nature tried to replace the traditional Aristotelian cosmology with new specu-

* Reprinted from *Atti del XII Congresso Internazionale di Filosofia*, Venice and Padua, 12–18 September 1958, Vol. IX (Florence, 1960), 147–155.

I am indebted to my colleague, Prof. John H. Randall, Jr., for a number of valuable suggestions and references.

lations of their own. Finally, there was a steady progress in the
sciences, especially in medicine, mathematics and astronomy,
leading up to Galileo whose new conception of mathematical
physics marks the beginning of modern science and philosophy.

When confronted with this complex panorama, most modern
historians have displayed strong preferences and taken sides, in-
terpreting the controversies of the past in terms of those of their
own time. Many of them have favored the humanists, the Platonists, the philosophers of nature, or the early scientists, and
disparaged the Aristotelians whom they considered defenders of an
antiquated way of thinking because of intellectual inertia. When
the revival of Thomism in 1879 brought about an increased study
and appreciation of medieval Aristotelianism, interest usually
stopped with the thirteenth century, and the Aristotelians after
Thomas Aquinas were more or less gleefully abandoned to the
scorn of their contemporary and modern critics. More recently,
historians of science have discovered the contributions of fourteenth century Aristotelianism to physics and to logic, but most
of them have failed to appreciate the work of its pupils and successors in the fifteenth and sixteenth century who must have been,
if nothing else, the transmitters of fourteenth-century thought to
the early scientists who supposedly learned from it. It is only
recently that scholars such as Nardi or Randall have begun to see
Renaissance Aristotelianism in its proper perspective, and this
view is still very far from being generally accepted.

Renaissance Aristotelianism is by no means a uniform phenomenon, but it shows a great variety, especially along national
and regional lines. Its history in France and England has not yet
been studied, but for Germany its metaphysical teaching has been
explored as a background for Leibniz and Kant whereas in Spain
it forms an important aspect of her great age of Catholic theology.
In Italy to which I shall confine most of my remarks, Renaissance
Aristotelianism shows very different traits: due to the organization
of the Italian universities, it has very slight connections with theology, but is closely linked with medicine, and its emphasis is on
logic and physics rather than on ethics or metaphysics. This
Italian Aristotelianism has found favor with at least one group
of historians which begins with Ernest Renan. His famous book,
Averroès et l'Averroïsme, now slightly over one hundred years old
(1852), was a remarkable scholarly achievement for its time, and
its influence has been quite persistent up to the present day, especially in French and Italian scholarship. Whereas Renan's views

on Averroes and on the Latin Averroists of the thirteenth century have been thoroughly revised by more recent scholars, his
notions concerning the Averroism of the fourteenth, fifteenth and
sixteenth centuries are still generally repeated though they can
no longer stand scrutiny in the light of recent investigations. I
should like to sum up Renan's views as follows: there was in
Italy a continuous tradition of Aristotelian philosophy from the
early fourteenth to the early seventeenth century which may be
called Averroism because it derived its basic inspiration from the
Arabic commentator; in the sixteenth century, this school had a
more radical rival in another current called Alexandrism after
Alexander of Aphrodisias; both currents had their chief center at
the University of Padua, and hence Italian Aristotelianism may
be referred to as «the school of Padua»; this Paduan Averroism,
though antiquated in most of its specific doctrines, derives its
interest from its tendency to emphasize the contrast rather than
the harmony betweeny philosophy and theology; it thus barely
conceals its disbelief in religious truth, and must be considered
as the direct predecessor of later libertinism and free thought.

These views were expressed by Renan with many subtle qualifications, and subsequently repeated in a more or less crude
fashion. I should like to show briefly that these views should be
abandoned or at least considerably modified if we want to do justice to the facts as they are known at present.

Let me begin with the concept of Averroism. Labels of this
type enjoy some popularity with historians and are easily repeated, but they become more or less meaningless unless one
defines very clearly which set of philosophical opinions, or which
precise group of individual thinkers is intended by the general
term. In the case of Averroism, the ambiguity of the term is considerable, and Renan himself is largely responsible for it. He
often takes Averroism in the broadest possible sense, so as to cover
any thinker who made some use of Averroes' commentary on
Aristotle. By this definition, any Aristotelian philosopher after
the middle of the thirteenth century, including Thomas Aquinas,
would be an Averroist, and the term ceases to be distinctive. On
the other hand, the task of the Aristotelian philosopher was
largely to expound and correlate the various passages of Aristotle's writings, and also to resolve on Aristotelian principles all
those problems which were important to the expositors but on
which Aristotle had expressed no opinion, or on which his opinion was ambiguous. Aristotelian philosophy during the later Mid-

dle Ages and Renaissance was not a body of common doctrines, but rather a group of thinkers with many diversified opinions on many different issues who merely shared a common terminology, a common method of argument, and the reference to a common body of authoritative texts, especially Aristotle. Any particular text could be interpreted in several different ways, and the choice which a given thinker made on one particular issue did not necessarily commit him to a definite choice on other issues. Thus many combinations and alignments were possible and actually appeared, and there hardly ever occurs the case where a thinker adopts the views of one single commentator, such as Averroes, on all problems. If we call Averroists only those Aristotelians who agree with Averroes on the interpretation of every single passage in Aristotle, there hardly ever was a single Averroist. If we call Averroist any thinker who took any views from Averroes' commentaries, there hardly was a single Aristotelian who could not be thus called an Averroist. If the term Averroist is to have any meaning at all, it must be defined in a more specific way, that is, in terms of some particular philosophical theory. Mainly two such theories have been singled out as characteristically Averroistic: the unity of the intellect, and the double truth. The view that the intellect is only one for all human beings is in fact formulated by Averroes, and it was apparently adopted by some medieval and Renaissance Aristotelians. Yet their number is not large, and it has been recently shown that such prominent «Averroists» as Peter Abano[1] and Alessandro Achillini did not accept the unity of the intellect. If we take the unity of the intellect as a criterion of Averroism, the term is clearly defined, but no longer applicable to many thinkers traditionally labeled with it. As to the theory of the double truth for which Averroism has been quite famous and which seems to define it as a more or less avowed variety of free thought, it has been shown that the theory is not found in Averroes, and Averroists would thus be characterized by a view which was not derived from their supposed master. Moreover, the theory itself must be interpreted more carefully. The

---

[1] For Peter of Abano, see B. Nardi, "La teoria dell'anima e la generazione delle forme secondo Pietro d'Abano," *Rivista di filosofia Neo-scolastica* IV (1912), 723–737. The same, "Intorno alle dottrine filosofiche di Pietro d'Abano," *Nuova Rivista Storica* IV (1920), 81–97, 464–481; V (1921), 300–313. C. Giacon, "Pietro d'Abano e l'Averroismo Padovano," *Società Italiana per il Progresso delle Scienze, Atti della XXVI Riunione*, III, Rome, 1938, 334–339.

crude view that there are two contradictory, but equally true opinions was not expressed by any thinker. They usually said that theological doctrine is true since it is based on faith and divine authority, whereas some other doctrine not compatible with it may seem probable on purely rational or Aristotelian grounds. This position was held by many Aristotelian philosophers between the fourteenth and seventeenth centuries, and it was never condemned by the church authorities. It has been often argued by modern historians that this position implies a secret disbelief in theological truth, yet the evidence for this disbelief is slender, and largely based on innuendo, polemical charges, anecdotes, or on the traditions of a later age.[2] I am not convinced that this is good evidence, or that we have reliable methods for ascertaining what a philosopher says «between the lines». The so-called doctrine of double truth seems to indicate another position: those who propound it insist that philosophy is separate from, and independent of, theology, and that it should pursue its enquiry within its own field unhampered by the doctrines of theology which are valid in the realm of faith. The doctrine does not necessarily indicate secret disbelief (although it may have done so in some cases), but rather the ideal of philosophical and scientific liberty, and in this sense those who advocated it, the teachers of philosophy in the faculties of art, prepared the way for later rationalism and free thought, without necessarily sharing all the convictions of their later successors. Whether this doctrine really concealed secret disbelief in theological doctrines, and in which doctrines, is a question which differs in the case of each thinker, and one which we shall in many cases be quite unable to answer. In any case, this doctrine is not only alien to Averroes himself, but it is shared by many Aristotelians not normally classified as Averroists, such as Albertus Magnus, Buridan and Pomponazzi. Hence we are forced either to abandon the term Averroism altogether, or to limit it to those few thinkers who accepted the unity of the intellect, or finally to use it arbitrarily for that broad group of thinkers who pursued Aristotelian philosophy apart from theology and whom we might better describe as secular Aristotelians.

The case for Alexandrism is even weaker than that for Averro-

---

[2] Cfr. P. O. Kristeller, "El mito del ateísmo renacentista y la tradición francesa del libre pensamiento" *Notas y Estudios de Filosofia*, IV, 13 (1953), 1–14. S. MacClintock, *Perversity and Error: Studies on the «Averroist» John of Jandun,* Bloomington, Ind. 1956.

ism, and Renan himself was quite aware of this. There is practically no evidence that such a thing as Alexandrism ever existed. If we understand by an Alexandrist a thinker who follows Alexander on all issues, I doubt whether there ever was such a thinker in the sixteenth century, or at any other time. Certainly it was not Pomponazzi who is usually cited as the chief representative of Alexandrism, and who devoted a long section of his important *De fato* to a defense of the Stoic concept of fate against Alexander. Moreover, terms such as «Alexandrist» or «follower of Alexander» (unlike the term «Averroist») are extremely rare in Renaissance sources, and they usually refer to thinkers who adopt Alexander's view on one particular issue, the mortality of the soul.[3] The key passage on which historians usually rely does not prove what they infer from it. It is found in a letter and preface of Ficino written around 1480, that is, when Pomponazzi, the supposed initiator of Alexandrism was 18 years old, and it certainly does not prove anything for the sixteenth century, unless we make of Ficino a prophet, a role which would undoubtedly have pleased him. What Ficino had in mind was much more specific:[4] an Alexandrist was for him a thinker who accepted Alexander's view that according to Aristotle the soul is mortal. This specific doctrine was actually defended by Pomponazzi in 1516, and we now know that he was moving towards that position as early as 1504, and was aware of its derivation from Alexander.[5] If we re-

[3] Jac. Zabarella, *In tres Aristotelis libros de anima Commentarii*, Venetiis, 1605, l. III, 3, f. 10: «sectatorum Alexandri»; f. 10 v: «Alexandrei»; 5, f. 21: «sectatores Alexandri». Id., *De rebus naturalibus*, Frankfurt, 1617, 'De mente humana', ch. 9, col. 954: «sectatores Alexandri . . . alii posteriores Alexandraei»; ch. 14, col. 974-975: «sectatorum Alexandri». Cf. J. H. Randall, Jr., in *The Renaissance Philosophy of Man*, ed. E. Cassirer and others, Chicago, 1948, p. 266. Yet Simon Portius (*De humana mente disputatio*, Florentiae, 1551, preface) gives another classification of Aristotelian philosophers on the same issue («Averroicos, Simplicianos et Themistianos»). Prof. Edward Cranz in a forthcoming article will publish the prefaces of all Latin translations of Alexander printed in the fifteenth and sixteenth centuries. They contain no reference whatsoever to a compact school of Alexandrism, nor any attack on Averroes and his school. G. Contarini (*De immortalitate animae*, Opera, Parisiis, 1571, p. 179) merely discusses Alexander's opinion on immortality (cf. Randall, *op. cit.*, p. 265).

[4] Marsilius Ficinus, *Opera*, Basel, 1576, p. 871-872 and 1537: «Totus enim terrarum orbis a Peripateticis occupatus in duas plurimum divisus est sectas, Alexandrinam et Averroicam».

[5] P. O. Kristeller, "Two Unpublished Questions on the Soul of Pietro Pomponazzi," *Medievalia et Humanistica*, VIII (1955), 76-101.

strict the term Alexandrism to this specific meaning, it will apply
to a rather small group of thinkers which includes, oddly enough,
besides Pomponazzi the leading Thomist of his time, Cardinal
Caietanus. If we wish to take Alexandrism more broadly, and in
a sense not sanctioned by Renaissance usage, we may understand
by it the increasing use made of the Greek text of Aristotle and
of his Greek commentators, as against the medieval Latin translations and commentaries. Yet if a philosopher like Pomponazzi
follows Alexander on such a specific issue as the immortality of
the soul, this does not mean that he stops using Averroes on numerous other problems. Thus «Alexandrism», if taken in the most
specific sense of the term, is not exclusive of «Averroism», as the
traditional formula would make us believe.

Let me finally comment on Renan's rather loose use of the
term «the school of Padua». He did add a few qualifications, but
the actual situation is much more complicated than he could
know. In the light of documents not available to him, it can be
shown that many thinkers claimed by Renan for the «school of
Padua» had no connection with that university. Moreover, it is
true that Padua was the most important center of Italian Aristotelianism during the fifteenth and sixteenth centuries, but it
did not have a philosophical tradition distinct from that of its
sister universities, as the term «school of Padua» might suggest.
Finally, it has become increasingly clear that in the thirteenth
and fourteenth centuries, Padua had not yet attained its later
position as the chief Italian center of Aristotelian studies, in spite
of its distinction in other branches of learning, and of the important role of Peter of Abano. Petrarch's «Averroists» have no connection with Padua, and at present there is scanty evidence of
Aristotelian studies at Padua before Peter, or between his time
and the last decades of the fourteenth century.[6] On the other
hand, a whole group of secular Aristotelians or «Averroists» has
been discovered at Bologna during the last quarter of the thirteenth and the first half of the fourteenth century whereas in
other centers such as Siena, Naples and Salerno this trend may
be traced back even earlier. Hence I think that it will be more
appropriate to speak henceforth not of «Paduan Averroism», but
rather of Italian secular Aristotelianism, recognizing the great
importance of Padua during the later period, but giving their

[6] P. O. Kristeller, "Petrarch's 'Averroists,'" *Bibliothèque d' Humanisme et
Renaissance*, XIV (1952), 59–65.

due share, especially for the earlier period, to Bologna and the other universities.[7]

I hope the proposed views are supported by the results of recent scholarship, and may be confirmed by future research. If the proposed views happen to be slightly more correct than the traditional ones, I shall not be impressed by the objection that they concern minutiae, or that they are contrary to the cherished preferences of some distinguished scholar, or that the traditional notions, though perhaps incorrect in some detail, are still «true in a higher sense». The history of philosophy, no less than other branches of knowledge, is based on «scientific and empirical evidence», which in this case consists of the testimony of texts and documents. A historical view is valid to the extent to which it can be supported by such evidence. Within the realm of ascertained truth there is no room for preferences or "higher truths," and if its present boundaries are small, it will be our task and that of our successors to expand them. In this effort we should never falter although it is probably quite true that there are important problems in the history of philosophy, as in other branches of inquiry, that cannot be solved through our ordinary methods of factual research and rational interpretation.

[7] For Bologna, see M. Grabmann, *Mittelalterliches Geistesleben*, II, Munich, 1936, 239–71. Id., "Gentile da Cingoli," *Sitzungsberichte der Bayerischen Akademie der Wissenschaften, Philosophisch-Historische Abteilung*, 1941, n. 9. Anneliese Maier, *Die Vorlaeufer Galileis im 14. Jahrhundert*, Rome, 1949, pp. 251–78. B. Nardi, "L'averroismo bolognese nel secolo XIII e Taddeo Alderotto," *Rivista di Storia della Filosofia*, IV (1949), 11–22. P. O. Kristeller, "A Philosophical Treatise from Bologna dedicated to Guido Cavalcanti," in *Medio Evo e Rinascimento, Studi in onore di Bruno Nardi*, Florence, 1955, vol. I, pp. 425–63. For Salerno, cf. P. O. Kristeller, *Studies in Renaissance Thought and Letters*, Rome, 1956, pp. 495–551 (*La Scuola di Salerno*, trad. di A. Cassese, Salerno, 1955).

VII

The Origin and Development
of the Language of Italian Prose [*]

DURING THE EARLIER phases of modern linguistics, literary languages were commonly used as points of departure for the comparative study of the various languages. More recently the interest
of most linguists has shifted to the spoken languages and dialects
and accordingly the relationship between the written or literary
languages and the spoken dialects has become a problem of increasing importance. Although a literary language may serve for
the territory of many different dialects, it is usually taken to originate in one or two particular dialects. In this sense, the problem
of the Italian literary language is quite familiar to modern linguists. They have debated the question whether it is based on the
Tuscan dialect or not, and they have studied the historical antecedents of this controversy which can be traced back to the fourteenth century and which assumed especial importance in the
sixteenth.[1] This problem of the relationship between literary

[*] Reprinted from *Studies in Renaissance Thought and Letters* (Rome,
Edizioni di Storia e Letteratura, 1956), 473–493. Originally published, in a
somewhat shorter form, in *Word*, II (1946), 50–65. Based on a paper read
before the Linguistic Circle of New York on April 13, 1946. An Italian version
of this paper appeared in *Cultura Neolatina*, X (1950), 137–56.

[1] For a bibliography of the subject, see Robert A. Hall, Jr., *Bibliography of
Italian Linguistics*, Baltimore, 1941, especially pp. 30 ff., 53 ff., 425 ff. For the
history of the "Questione della lingua," see Thérèse Labande-Jeanroy, *La
Question de la langue en Italie*, Strasbourg, 1925; V. Vivaldi, *Storia delle con-
troversie linguistiche in Italia da Dante ai nostri giorni*, I, Catanzaro, 1925;
Robert A. Hall, Jr., *The Italian Questione della Lingua: An Interpretative
Essay*, Chapel Hill, 1942; B. Migliorini, "Storia della lingua italiana . . , in *Un
Cinquantenario di studi sulla letteratura italiana* (1886–1936): *Saggi raccolti
dalla Società Filologica Romana e dedicati a Vittorio Rossi*, II, Florence, 1937,
3–27; Id., "Storia della lingua italiana," in *Problemi ed orientamenti critici*

Italian and the various dialects of Italy will not be the major subject of the following consideration although we shall have to mention it at several points.[2] Instead we shall try to concentrate on another related problem which has also been discussed by many historians of Italian language and literature, although in a rather subordinate and almost reluctant manner: the relation of the Italian literary language to Latin. I am not referring to classical Latin, or to its late ancient successor, vulgar Latin, which was the basis of all Italian dialects, as of all other Romance languages. I am speaking of the Latin of the Middle Ages and the Renaissance, which in Italy, as in all other countries of Western Europe, served as a written literary language for many centuries after the commonly spoken language had changed from vulgar Latin to the vernacular Italian dialects. The Italian literary language hence did not grow in a vacuum, but it had to conquer its territory from medieval Latin. During the period that goes at least from the tenth to the end of the twelfth century, when Italian dialects were commonly spoken throughout the peninsula, Latin continued to serve almost exclusively as a vehicle of literary expression. Long after literary Italian had made its appearance, from the thirteenth century to the end of the eighteenth, Latin survived as an alternate literary language.[3] The gradual rise and expansion of the Italian literary language at the expense of its Latin rival will be the major subject of this paper.[4]

---

di lingua e di letteratura italiana, ed. A. Momigliano, vol. II: *Tecnica e teoria letteraria*, Milan, 1948, pp. 57–104; Id., "La questione dell a lingua," *ibid.*, vol. III: *Questioni e correnti di storia letteraria*, Milan, 1949, pp. 1–75.

[2] For the various Italian dialects and their literary documents, see Mario E. Pei, *The Italian Language*, New York, 1941. Several early examples are given in E. Monaci's *Crestomazia italiana dei primi secoli*, Città di Castello, 1912.

[3] The medieval term *per lettera* or *literaliter* for Latin as opposed to *volgare* or *vulgariter* reflects the earlier stage in which Latin was the written language in contrast to the spoken vernacular. The term *grammatica* for Latin reflects the later situation in which the vernacular, although used for writing, had no fixed grammatical rules.

[4] There are no bibliographies illustrating the respective use of Latin and vernacular in Italian literature. The major data can be derived from Bertoni's *Il Duecento* and the other volumes of the *Storia letteraria d'Italia*, see below. For a bibliography of the vernacular works alone, see G. Fontanini, *Biblioteca dell'Eloquenza Italiana* (with the annotations of Apostolo Zeno), 2 vols., Venice, 1753; B. Gamba, *Serie dei testi di lingua e di altre opere importanti nella italiana letteratura scritte dal secolo XIV al XIX*, 4th ed., Venice, 1839; F. Zambrini, *Le opere volgari a stampa dei secoli XIII e XIV*, 4th ed., Bologna, 1878, and several supplements. Zambrini's work stops with the fourteenth century, is dominated by purist prejudices, and often fails to indicate the dialect, place and date of origin.

Let us begin with the familiar view of the matter. As it is well known, vernacular literature began in Italy much later than in France, Germany, or England, that is, toward the end of the twelfth century. The thirteenth century witnessed a rapid development of lyrical poetry in the three schools of Sicily, Bologna, and Tuscany, which all left the impact of their dialects upon the resulting literary language. The influence of Tuscany finally prevailed because it dominated the last phase of this development and produced the greatest poets.[5] The Tuscan school culminated in Dante who also gave the language its final form, and thus Italy attained around 1300 a common literary language. This language made further progress during the fourteenth century which produced a large amount of vernacular literature, and at least two great writers, Petrarch and Boccaccio. This promising development was suddenly stopped around 1400 when the humanists attempted their artificial revival of classical Latin. Vernacular literature was thus doomed to decline, and almost threatened with extinction. Yet it began to rise again toward the end of the fifteenth century, and in spite of continuing humanist opposition, the vernacular asserted itself against Latin and achieved a complete and permanent victory after the beginning of the sixteenth century.[6]

This general view seems to find its confirmation in the theoretical treatises of the sixteenth century, and also in the general history of Italian literature as represented by its greatest writers. However, it has never been made the subject of a thorough and accurate examination that would take into account the full range of available textual and documentary material. Several scholars who came across certain facts that did not fit the general conception have questioned or corrected it in various points, but even these scholars usually failed to draw all the conclusions suggested by their own findings, and certainly their criticism did not influence common opinion. The latter is often presented in quite suggestive fashion and with colorful oratory that tends to fill the gaps left by textual evidence. The rise of the vernacular against Latin is pictured as a fight of the lay spirit against Church authority, of

[5] The development of the poetical language in the thirteenth century has been the subject of a lengthy discussion that does not directly concern our problem.

[6] For this common view, see Robert A. Hall, Jr., *The Italian Questione della lingua, l. c.*, 3 f., 12 ff., 51 f.; Vernon Hall, Jr., *Renaissance Literary Criticism*, New York, 1945, 16 ff. The common view is assumed by most general historians of Italian literature, and by many students of Italian humanism, although some of the details are differently presented by different scholars.

democracy against the forces of feudalism and absolutism, of pa-
triotism against foreign or international influences, or of the
open-minded plain citizen against the narrow professional interests of Academic cliques. Such statements which are scattered
with more or less emphasis in the scholarly literature on the subject may contain a nucleus of truth, yet on the whole they are
difficult to reconcile with each other, or with the historical development which they intend to explain. They reflect ideas that have
been prominent in the nineteenth and twentieth centuries and
that may in part be traced back to the late sixteenth century,[7]
but that should be applied to earlier periods only with the greatest possible caution. The vigorous and extensive religious literature in the vernacular produced during the fourteenth and
fifteenth centuries shows that religious and ecclesiastic interests
were not identified with the use of Latin or opposed to the vernacular. Since the vernacular was cultivated at many feudal and
monarchical courts whereas Latin literature was often promoted
in the free republics, the rivalry between the two languages can
hardly be reduced to a political issue. The active part taken by
learned circles and even by many humanists in the development
of vernacular literature shows that the latter was not merely the
concern of the plain citizen, whereas the Latin literature of the
Renaissance, which includes descriptions of tournaments, and of
snowball fights as well as translations from the vernacular of son-
nets and *novelle* cannot be labeled as "academic". In Italy where
the heritage of ancient Rome was always considered as a national
glory Latin could not easily be discarded as a "foreign" language.

There thus arises considerable doubt concerning many general
notions associated with the language question, and this doubt also
seems to affect the current view of the question and to call for a
careful reexamination of its various elements. For this purpose, it
is not sufficient to accept the statements made in various theoretical treatises of the distant or recent past, or to base generalizations upon narrowly selected material. It is rather necessary to
study the actual use of Latin and literary Italian through the
course of the centuries as they were employed by great and by
small poets, by poets and by prose writers, by popular and by

---

[7] Lionardo Salviati expresses the view that the Italian language declined in
the fifteenth century as a result of the excessive study of Latin, and that among
the writers of the "buon secolo" the unlearned authors must be preferred to
the learned ones (*Degli Avvertimenti della lingua sopra'l Decamerone*,
Venice, 1584, pp. 87 ff., 93 f., 100).

learned writers, in literary and in documentary material, in Tuscany and in the rest of Italy. The task has been recognized by a few scholars, but so far very little has been done for an actual investigation of the problems involved.[8] To attain a satisfactory solution, the work of many scholars will be required. I do not claim to offer any definite solution of these problems, but shall merely try, in a tentative and hypothetical manner, to propose a revision of the current opinion.

This current opinion would seem to be largely correct as far as the history of poetry is concerned. There was around 1300 a common poetical language for all of Italy, which has maintained itself up to the present day.[9] However, although the fifteenth century, especially in its earlier part, failed to produce any major poet, the tradition of vernacular poetry was by no means interrupted during that period.[10] On the other hand, Latin poetry did by no means disappear after the beginning of the sixteenth century, but continued to flourish in respectable quantity and quality long after that period.[11] Moreover, the fact that throughout the sixteenth century, as in earlier times, many authors wrote verses in both languages,[12] and that the collections of occasional poetry often would include compositions in both Latin

[8] Jacob Burckhardt formulated the problem as early as 1860: "Das allmaehliche Vordringen derselben (that is, of the ideal or literary language) in Literatur und Leben koennte ein einheimischer Kenner leicht tabellarisch darstellen. Es muesste konstatiert werden, wie lange sich waehrend des 14. und 15. Jahrhunderts die einzelnen Dialekte in der taeglichen Korrespondenz, in den Regierungsschriften und Gerichtsprotokollen, endlich in den Chroniken und in der freien Literatur ganz oder gemischt behauptet haben. Auch das Fortleben der italienischen Dialekte neben einem reinern oder geringeren Latein, welches dann als offizielle Sprache diente, kaeme dabei in Betracht" (*Die Kultur der Renaissance in Italien*, 13th ed., Stuttgart, 1921, p. 418). In 1937, Migliorini had to admit that such a study is still lacking: "Manca una storia esterna della lingua la quale tracci la storia dell'espansione dell'italiano normale. Essa dovrebbe anzitutto mostrarci in che tempi, in che luoghi, in che circostanze l'italiano scritto si sostituì al latino nella scuola, nel foro, nelle scienze, . . ." (*l. c.*, p. 6).

[9] This common poetical language is called Tuscan by two non-Tuscan authors of the fourteenth century, Antonio da Tempo of Padua and Gidino da Sommacampagna of Verona (O. Bacci, *La Critica Letteraria*, Milan, 1910, 169 ff.).

[10] V. Rossi, *Il Quattrocento*, 2nd ed., Milan, 1933; F. Flamini, *La Lirica Toscana del Rinascimento anteriore ai tempi del Magnifico*, Pisa, 1891.

[11] Some of the most famous Latin poets belong to the sixteenth century, such as Bembo, Fracastoro, Navagero, Vida, Flaminio.

[12] Ariosto, Bembo, Castiglione, Fracastoro, and many others. They were preceded by Dante, Petrarch, and Poliziano.

and Italian [13] shows that the rivalry between Latin and literary Italian even in the field of poetry was not always a struggle for existence or a matter of deep convictions, but rather a peaceful competition between two alternative modes of literary expression.

On the other hand, the development of literary Italian seems to have been different as far as prose is concerned, and it is in this point that the traditional view is especially subject to criticism.[14] If we want to understand the development of literary prose in Italy, we must take for our basis primarily the extant material and refrain from postulating the existence of earlier or more numerous vernacular works than have actually been preserved. This is often done by scholars who argue that there are analogous vernacular works in French, or that an extant Latin work must have been based on a vernacular original since Latin could not have been understood by the people. These arguments do not carry much weight. The fact that a certain type of vernacular literature existed in French does not prove that it must have existed at the same time also in Italian. The opinion that Latin could not be understood by the people is hardly convincing for a period in which any person who could read and write acquired some elements of Latin, and in a country where Latin is to some extent understood even nowadays, let alone medieval Latin which was pronounced in the Italian manner and which became so non-classical and "barbarous" just because it was adapted to the spoken vernacular language.

The use of vernacular prose for literary purposes began in Italy during the thirteenth century. Attempts to link the early phases of its development with Bologna and its university are suggestive, but not entirely convincing.[15] Whereas examples of

[13] The titles of some such collections are given by F. S. Quadrio (*Della Storia e della Ragione d'ogni poesia*, II, Milan, 1741, 516, 519, 525, 529 f., 676, 763 ff.) who analyzes, however, only the vernacular contents.

[14] The difference between the development of the prose language and of the poetical language was clearly seen as early as 1869 by Gino Capponi in an excellent article which has attracted too little attention ("Fatti relativi alla storia della nostra lingua," *Nuova Antologia*, XI, 665–82, especially p. 673).

[15] The theory that Bologna was the cradle of the Italian literary prose language is held by E. Monaci, "Su la Gemma purpurea e altri scritti volgari di Guido Fava o Faba, maestro di grammatica in Bologna nella prima metà del secolo XIII," in *Atti della Reale Accademia dei Lincei, Rendiconti*, Series IV, vol. IV, 1888, pt. II, pp. 399–405; A. Gaudenzi, *I Suoni, le forme e le parole dell'odierno dialetto della Città di Bologna*, Turin, 1889; G. Bertoni, *La Prosa della Vita Nuova di Dante*, Genoa, 1914; G. Zaccagnini, "I grammatici e l'uso del volgare eloquio a Bologna nel secolo XIII," in *Studi e Memorie per la*

Storia dell'Università di Bologna, XII, 1935, 177–91, and others. However, the number of vernacular prose texts and documents from Bologna remained scarce throughout the fourteenth century, and the examples cited for the earlier period present several difficulties. The statute for the notaries published in 1246 proves only that they had to be able to translate documents from or into the vernacular for the benefit of their clients, but not that they had to compose the documents in the vernacular. The decree of Oct. 14, 1321, appointing Bartholinus filius Benincaxe de Canullo to teach rhetoric on the basis of Cicero, "et artem dictandi domini Johannis Bonandree bis in anno incipiendo in quadragessima et in eodem tempore dando epistolas et formando themata quelibet dicendorum . . . ita quod ab eo discere possunt tam vulgares quam licterati et quelibet alia persona" (E. Orioli, *La cancelleria pepolesca*, Bologna, 1910, pp. 65–67) does indicate the use of the vernacular in the instruction of the *ars dictaminis* at that time, whereas the statutes of 1335 merely say that the city chancellor must open all incoming letters in the presence of the city fathers "ac legere literaliter vel vulgariter ad volumptatem eorum" (*ibid.*, pp. 67–70). The vernacular forms included in the works of Fava and other "dictatores" served in most cases as helps for drawing up Latin models, not as vernacular models. Fava's *Parlamenti ed epistole* contain references to Siena and may have been written in that city. Fra Guidotto's *Fiore di Rettorica* survives only in several more or less Tuscanized versions, some of which are attributed to the Florentine, Bono Giamboni, and Guidotto himself is known to have lived and taught in Siena. A parchment manuscript of the thirteenth or fourteenth century in the Biblioteca Comunale of Siena (cod. JII 7) would seem to deserve further study. The description in the inventory lists on f. 73 "avvertimenti per saviamente parlare (doctrina loquendi)" and on f. 94 "esposizione d'una ambasceria di Bologna al Papa, alla quale segue una lunga allocuzione fatta dinanzi al consiglio di Bologna, nella quale si rende conto della detta ambasciata ed ove si fa menzione di un Pietro de Boatieri come uno degli ambasciatori . . . tutti questi opuscoli sono scritti d'una mano, e con dialetto semibarbaro." This shows the use of the vernacular in Bologna, but in the form of the local dialect rather than of Tuscan or standardized language. For Pietro de' Boattieri who appears in documents from 1285 to 1334, see G. Zaccagnini, "Le epistole in latino e in volgare di Pietro de'Boattieri," *Studi e Memorie per la Storia dell'Università di Bologna*, VIII, 1924, 211–48. The Siena ms. which I have consulted since consists of 106 fols. and contains a collection of texts in vernacular prose in dialect which is probably Bolognese. The text on f. 73–82 begins: "Dise lo maestro guardate da tuti superbi," and ends: "explicit doctrina loquendi." The late table of contents identifies it as the work of Albertano da Brescia. f. 95–96v contain an oration of Bolognese ambassadors to the pope, inc. Quisti signuri ambasaduri et eo cum loro si vignimo seguramente denanzi da voi sancto padre. f. 96v–106 contain various other pieces in dialect referring to Bologna, inc. Eo fazo prego alabona cavalaria e al franco povolo. The last piece is a marriage contract. The mention of Pedro deliboateri occurs on f. 99v. Fra Tommaso Gozzadini's *Fior di Virtù* was written in dialect and later Tuscanized. Giovanni di Bonandrea's treatise on rhetoric, Pier de' Crescenzi's book on agriculture, and Graziolo Bambagliuoli's commentary on Dante were written in Latin and later Tuscanized. The same probably happened with Matteo de' Libri's *Dicerie* which survive only in Tuscan translations. Kristeller, "Matteo de' Libri . . . and his *Artes dictaminis*," in *Miscellanea Giovanni Galbiati* II (Milan, 1951) 283–320. I hope to discuss the problem of his vernacular prose from earlier periods and from other parts of Italy are comparatively rare, a rich and diversified prose literature appeared in Tuscany during the second half of the thirteenth century and continued to develop vigorously during the fourteenth century. This literature included fiction and chronicles, sermons and ascetic works, letters and speeches, business and family records, a large number of translations from the French, from classical and medieval Latin, and even a number of learned treatises.[16] Dante contributed to this prose literature his *Vita Nuova* and *Convivio,* but his place in the history of Italian prose literature was not as original or influential as it was in poetry. The language of this Tuscan prose was often free from the colloquial elements of local dialects, but it was undoubtedly based on the speech of Tuscany as compared with that of other Italian provinces. These texts provide the great mass of the *Testi di lingua* and of the *Testi del buon secolo della lingua,* which have been the delight of purists even since and actually display all the charm and attractiveness of which Tuscan prose is capable. The quality, variety and quantity of this literature easily explains why it could become the linguistic basis and model for later Italian prose. For this literature gave to the Tuscan dialect such an advantage in comparison with other dialects that its adoption was practically inevitable when the question of a literary prose for all of Italy became a burning problem, that is, in the sixteenth century.

Most scholars seem to assume that this Tuscan prose was actually an Italian prose, used and understood as a literary language of all Italy, as early as the time of Dante. They take it for granted that since there was a common poetical language the same must also be true for prose literature. Some of them also cite the testimony of Dante who in his *De vulgari eloquentia* seems to prove that there was at his time a *volgare illustre,* a common

---

Dicerie in a future study. Jacopo della Lana's commentary on Dante most probably was written in Bolognese dialect and Tuscanized to a varying degree by the copyists. Armannino Giudice's *Fiorita d'Italia* which may be the most serious exception was written in Fabriano, and has never been published or thoroughly studied.

[16] G. Bertoni, *Il Duecento,* Milan, 1939; N. Sapegno, *Il Trecento,* Milan, 1934; A. Schiaffini, *Testi Fiorentini del Dugento e dei primi del Trecento,* Florence, 1926. Especially striking is the Tuscan origin of most vernacular translations whose authors are known. An example of an early doctrinal treatise in Tuscan is Ristoro d'Arezzo's *Composizione del mondo.*

literary language actually used in poetry, in prose, and in conversation.[17] Yet there are many reasons for assuming that Dante
was speaking of an ideal rather than of an accomplished fact,
at least in the case of prose language.[18] Moreover, his testimony
is contradicted by that of a contemporary, and by the evidence
of the extant literary and documentary sources. About 1290, an
anonymous copyist of the *Fior di Virtù* confesses his ignorance
of the vernacular, stresses the poverty of abstract terms in the
vernacular as compared with Latin, and adds that the vernacular
differs in every town and region whereas Latin is the same everywhere.[19] He thus implies that it was for him more difficult to
understand a vernacular dialect different from his own than it

[17] See *De vulg. eloq.* I 13 ff., II 1. Recently, the *volgare illustre* has been
assumed as a historical fact by A. Ewert, "Dante's Theory of Language,"
Modern Language Review, XXXV, 1940, 355–66. He bases his statement on
Dante's testimony, and on general considerations about the possibility of such
a development. He does not even ask whether the numerous literary and
documentary sources of the time confirm such an assumption.

[18] The ideal character of the *volgare illustre* in Dante is suggested by the
political consideration that it is the language of an imperial court which
actually did not exist, in contrast to the "municipal" dialects (G. Bertoni, "Il
De Vulgari Eloquentia," *Archivum Romanicum*, XX, 1936, 91–102, especially
pp. 100 f.), and by the philosophical consideration that it is the most perfect
of its kind, in which the dialects participate to a higher or lesser degree
(A. Gaspary, *Storia della letteratura italiana*, tr. by N. Zingarelli, I, 2nd ed.,
Turin, 1914, p. 247).

[19] "Poichè de' vocaboli volgari son molto ignoranti (ignorante?), però (che)
io gli ho poco usati. Anche perchè le cose spirituali, oltre non si possono sì
propriamente esprimere per paravole volgari, come si esprimono per latino e
per grammatica, per la penuria dei vocaboli volgari; e perciò che ogni con-
trada et ogni terra ha i suoi propri vocaboli volgari, diversi da quelli de l'altre
terre et contrade; ma la grammatica et latino non è così, perchè è uno appo
tutti e latini" (quoted from O. Bacci, *La Critica letteraria, l. c.*, p. 80). For
another similar case in the fourteenth century, I quote the colophon of cod.
Barb. lat. 4037, written on parchment in 1399: "Explicit comentus comedie
Dantis . . . compositus per magistrum Jacobum de la Lana . . . et fecit in
sermone vulgari tusco, et quia tale ydioma non est omnibus notum ideo ad
utilitatem volencium studere in ipsa comedia transtuli de vulgari tusco in
gramaticali scientia literarum ego Albericus de Rox (i. e., de Roxate) dictus
in utroque iure peritus Pergamensis et si quis defectus foret in translatione
maxime in astrologicis theologicis et algorismo veniam peto et me excuset
aliqualiter defectus exempli et ignorantia dictarum scientiarum . . ." Albericus
de Rosate of Bergamo died in 1354. See K. Burdach, *Rienzo und die geistige
Wandlung seiner Zeit*, Berlin, 1913–28, p. 415, who speaks, however, errone-
ously of his "italienische Bearbeitung des lateinischen Kommentars von Jacopo
della Lana zur 'Komoedie.'" This error is derived from F. C. von Savigny,
Geschichte des Roemischen Rechts im Mittelalter, VI, 2nd ed., Heidelberg
1850, 133.

was to understand Latin, and that he was not aware of any common literary language other than Latin. This statement is confirmed by a number of additional facts. Above all, Latin remained the language of the great majority of documents far beyond the end of the fourteenth century.[20] After the middle of the fourteenth century, the various local dialects were used with increasing frequency for internal communications between officials of the same city, whereas the diplomatic correspondence between various Italian cities or states continued in Latin.[21] Moreover, although there was certainly no lack of a prose literature in the other, non-Tuscan dialects during the thirteenth and fourteenth centuries, a literature that has deserved the interest of linguistic and literary historians,[22] it is by no means comparable in quantity or quality to the Tuscan prose literature of the same period. Finally, even if it were more extensive or more important than it actually is, its existence would not decide the question which we are considering. If there had been a common Italian prose language during the fourteenth century, there should be abundant evidence that the prose language which we call Tuscan was used and written by non-Tuscan writers, as it certainly was the case for poetry. However, examples of that kind are very rare, and they are all of a peculiar character. That is, either there is reason to believe that the author lived in Tuscany

[20] The number of vernacular documents which Gaudenzi and others were able to publish from the Bologna archives is exceedingly small in proportion to the wealth of printed and unprinted Latin documents preserved in those archives. The same holds true for Florence.

[21] For example, in 1401, the republic of Florence wrote to its ambassadors to Bologna in the vernacular, but to Giovanni Bentivoglio in Latin (F. Bosdari, "Giovanni I Bentivoglio Signore di Bologna," in *Atti e Memorie della R. Deputazione di Storia Patria per le provincie di Romagna*, Ser. IV, vol. V, 1915, 275 ff.). The same picture is found in most publications of documents from the same period.

[22] Notable is the version into Mantuan dialect of Bartholomaeus Anglicus by Vivaldo Belcalzer who appears in documents between 1279 and 1308 (V. Cian, *Vivaldo Belcalzer e l'enciclopedismo italiano delle origini, Giornale Storico della letteratura italiana*, Supplement V, Turin, 1902). The *Diurnali* of Matteo Spinelli da Giovenazzo, long considered as a thirteenth century chronicle in Neapolitan dialect, is now generally recognized as a forgery of the sixteenth century (R. Morghen, in *Enciclopedia Italiana*, XXXII, 1936, 376 f.). Tiraboschi who accepts it as authentic adds the following comment (*Storia della letteratura italiana* IV, Naples, 1777, 266 f.): "è questa la prima opera, che noi troviamo scritta in prosa volgare, mentre finora essa non erasi usata che verseggiando; e tutti gli scrittori di prosa si eran serviti della lingua latina." See also: *Testi non toscani del Trecento*, ed. B. Migliorini and G. Folena, Modena, 1952.

and adopted the language of his residence, or there are indica-
tions that the extant work was revised or translated by a native
Tuscan from another dialect or even from Latin.[23] The conclusion seems to be inevitable that there was a Tuscan, but no
common Italian prose language during the thirteenth and fourteenth century, and that it is an anachronism to speak of an
"Italian" prose for that period. However, the fact that Tuscany
was ahead of the other regions in the production of literary
vernacular prose does not mean that Tuscany had a kind of
monopoly in the intellectual life of Italy. Many branches of
literature were cultivated in the other provinces as much as, or
even more than, in Tuscany. Yet their linguistic vehicle was
mostly Latin, and in some cases French,[24] whereas Tuscany had
already begun to use its own vernacular. Accordingly, many
prose works were composed in Latin by non-Tuscan writers and
soon translated into the Tuscan vernacular by native Tuscans.[25]
However, the rapid rise of vernacular prose in Tuscany did not
mean that Latin was abandoned as a literary language even in
Tuscany. Dante and Boccaccio wrote in Latin as well as in Italian
and the same was done by a host of other writers and scholars.

We might very well ask why the trend to shift from the literary
use of Latin prose to the vernacular was so much earlier and
more outspoken in Tuscany than in the other Italian provinces.
As for all such questions about the causes of certain historical
phenomena, it is difficult to give a simple and clear-cut answer.
The Tuscan dialect certainly possesses some inherent advantages
in its clarity, beauty and in its proximity to Latin. Moreover,
Tuscany had many political and commercial links with France
and may have been stimulated to imitate the example given by
the French and Provençal literatures. The most important element probably was the fact that Tuscany after the middle of the
thirteenth century developed a kind of "business civilization,"
whose literary expression was determined by the intellectual interests of a large class of merchants and craftsmen, and not

[23] For the prose texts from Bologna, see above, note 15. The *Avventuroso
Ciciliano* in Tuscan prose was supposedly written by Bosone da Gubbio in
1311, but the date has been disputed, and hence the authorship questioned
(G. Mazzatinti, "Bosone da Gubbio e le sue opere," *Studi di Filologia
Romanza*, I, 1885, 324 f.). Albertano da Brescia's moral treatises and Guido
delle Colonne's *Excidium Troiae* were written in Latin and then translated
into Tuscan by anonymous Tuscans.
[24] Marco Polo offers an example of the literary use of French.
[25] See above, notes 15 and 23.

directed by the traditions of any old native center of higher learning such as Bologna, Padua or Naples.

The situation thus described persisted without any major changes down to the end of the fourteenth century. During that century, Tuscany produced an increasing amount of prose literature, and also its first major prose classic, Giovanni Boccaccio. At the same time, prose literature in the other provinces of Italy was written either in Latin, or less often in the local dialects.[26] Only toward the end of the century, some of these dialect writers seem to have modified their local vernacular under the influence of Tuscan, and especially of Boccaccio.[27]

The fifteenth century in which classical humanism first attained a dominating influence is usually considered as a period of decline for vernacular literature. The humanists who tried to revive the use of classical Latin in writing and in speaking supposedly held a strong prejudice against the use of the vernacular and thus delayed and even threatened the further development of vernacular literature, according to the prevailing opinion.[28] Since the second half of the century produced a number of distinguished vernacular writers, the decline is attributed more specifically to the first four decades of the century. This judgment is based on the absence of great writers during that period, and on a group of polemical treatises in which certain humanists were charged by their opponents with a strong hostility against the vernacular and against its great fourteenth-century writers.[29]

[26] Examples of learned prose in non-Tuscan dialects are offered by the treatises of Fra Paolino Minorita of Venice and of Gidino da Sommacampagna of Verona. Petrarch who was of Florentine descent but never lived in Tuscany wrote nothing in vernacular prose; the only apparent exception, one of his orations, is hence considered as an anonymous translation of a Latin original. See above, notes 22 and 23. For Vivaldo Belcalzer, see above, note 22.

[27] This claim is made for the Paduan chronists Gatari by A. Medin, "La Coltura toscana nel Veneto durante il Medio Evo," *Atti del Reale Istituto Veneto*, LXXXII, pt. I, 1922–23, 83–154. The vernacular chronicles printed by Muratori were all modernized in their language by the editors.

[28] V. Rossi, *Il Quattrocento*, Milan, 1933; R. Sabbadini, *Storia del Ciceronianismo*, Turin, 1885, 127 ff.; G. Fioretto, *Gli Umanisti*, Verona, 1881, 121 ff.

[29] See the polemical treatises of Domenico da Prato and of Cino Rinuccini published by A. Wesselofsky, *Il Paradiso degli Alberti*, in *Scelta di Curiosità letterarie*, LXXXVI, pt. II, Bologna, 1867, 321 ff. and 303 ff. To these documents may be added the anonymous Florentine protest against the decision of the papal secretaries at the poetical contest of 1441 (G. Mancini, "Un nuovo documento sul certame coronario di Firenze del 1441," *Archivio Storico Italiano*, Ser. V, vol. IX, 1892, 326–46), and the first book of Bruni's *Dialogi ad Petrum Histrum*. Yet the statements of Wesselofsky and Mancini based on

However, such charges made for polemical purposes and in a highly rhetorical manner should not be accepted without qualifications. Direct statements of fifteenth-century humanists against the use of the vernacular are not entirely lacking, to be sure, but they are not sufficiently emphatic, consistent, or frequent to reflect a generally hostile attitude. The only major humanist who was insistently charged with such hostility, Niccolò Niccoli, did not write anything either in the vernacular or in Latin, and his attitude apparently was not entirely consistent.[30] However, more important than the theory is the actual practice of the humanists and their contemporaries, and this presents an entirely different picture. The fifteenth century, including its earlier phases, shows no interruption or decline in the development of vernacular prose literature, but rather an advance and expansion, and the humanists took an active part in this literature.[31] In order to realize these facts, it is necessary to study the much neglected source materials, and to compare the fifteenth century not with the fourteenth century as it has been imagined in the light of much later developments, but as it actually was. Above all, the sharp distinction in the development of vernacular prose literature which existed throughout the fourteenth century between Tuscany and the other Italian provinces continued to persist during the greater part of the fifteenth century. In Tuscany, the prose literature of the fourteenth century was eagerly copied and read, the various branches of that literature continued to flourish, and even new areas of expression were conquered for the vernacular.[32] The fact that none of these authors reached literary

---

these documents are greatly exaggerated. Charges made in polemical treatises are always a precarious basis of historical interpretation. Moreover, the criticism of the volgare language is not even a major issue in these treatises, and the first book of Bruni's dialogue is refuted by the content of the second book.

[30] G. Zippel, *Niccolò Niccoli*, Florence, 1890, 14 ff.

[31] G. Capponi, *l. c.;* O. Bacci, "Della prosa volgare del Quattrocento," in his *Prosa e Prosatori*, Milan, c. 1906, 41–93; D. Gravino, *Saggio d'una storia dei volgarizzamenti d'opere greche nel secolo XV*, Naples, 1896, 7 ff.; A. Galletti, *L'Eloquenza*, Milan, 1904–38; E. Santini, *Firenze e i suoi "oratori" nel Quattrocento*, Palermo, 1922; Id., "La produzione volgare di Leonardo Bruni Aretino," *Giornale Storico della letteratura italiana*, LX, 1912, 289–339. See also V. Rossi, *Il Quattrocento, l. c.* R. Spongano, *Un capitolo di storia della nostra prosa d'arte, La prosa letteraria del Quattrocento*, Florence, 1941.

[32] The Florentine manuscripts containing "dicerie" of the fourteenth and fifteenth centuries are numerous. Some are indicated by Rossi, *l. c.*, p. 166 and by I. Del Lungo, *Dino Compagni e la sua Cronica*, vol. I, pt. II, Florence, 1879, p. 1037 ff. See also Galletti, *l. c.*

distinction of the first order certainly must be noted, but the quantity and variety of this literature testifies to the actual increase in the literary use of the Tuscan vernacular. It has been a dogma of the purists ever since the sixteenth century that the language and style of this fifteenth-century Tuscan literature is inferior in quality to that of the "golden" fourteenth century, and the neglect of its documents is largely due to this prejudice. The validity of this judgment may reasonably be doubted until it has been confirmed by a more accurate examination of the texts many of which are still unpublished.[33] The production of vernacular sermons and of devotional treatises continued and even increased during the fifteenth century. The artful composition of letters and of speeches of which there had been a few earlier examples was cultivated on a larger scale than ever before. Many works of classical authors and of contemporary humanists were translated from Latin into the vernacular, frequently by writers who possessed themselves a considerable humanistic training.[34] Tuscan humanists often made vernacular versions of their own Latin writings, or composed original works in Tuscan prose.[35] Leonardo Bruni who is often presented as one of the opponents of the vernacular, wrote several works in Tuscan prose,[36] and in his comparison of Dante and Petrarch, he clearly treats Latin and Tuscan as two alternate instruments of literary expression.[37] Fifteenth-century Tuscany produced many *Novelle* and chronicles, and its personal records and private letters are probably more numerous than those of the preceding centuries. They include such works as the Vespasiano Memoirs which are an important source for the humanists of the period. The fif-

[33] Capponi, *l. c.;* Bacci, *l. c.* The judgment that fifteenth-century Tuscan is inferior to that of the fourteenth or sixteenth centuries rests upon the acceptance of the language of the fourteenth century as a standard of "purity." The writers of the fourteenth century used the language that was natural in their time, and so did those of the fifteenth after that language had undergone certain changes. In neither case can there be a question of greater or lesser "care" since there was no intent of imitation. Writing became "careful" only in the sixteenth century when the language of the fourteenth had been accepted as a model of purity. For the linguistic changes in the popular Florentine prose of the fifteenth century, see K. Huber, "Notizen zur Sprache des Quattrocento," *Vox Romanica* XII 1951, 1–20. G. Nencioni, *Fra grammatica e Retorica,* Florence, 1953.

[34] Gravino, *l. c.;* Rossi, *l. c.* Bruni's History of Florence was translated by Donato Acciaiuoli.

[35] Alberti, Palmieri, Manetti, Landino, Ficino, and many others.

[36] See the article of Santini, quoted above, note 31.

[37] *Le Vite di Dante, Petrarca e Boccaccio scritte fino al secolo XVI,* ed. A. Solerti, Milan, 1904, p. 293.

teenth century also shows a marked increase in the use of the vernacular in public documents of a domestic nature, and this development ought to be studied in detail.[38] That the use of the vernacular for foreign correspondence was unusual even among the Tuscan cities themselves is shown by an interesting letter sent in 1453 by the government of Florence to that of Siena. The Florentines begin their letter with a lengthy explanation of the reasons which induced them to reply in the vernacular to the Latin letters they had received. They say that they want to express their thoughts and intentions with complete frankness and to have them understood in their proper meaning without the need of interpretation.[39]

That this vernacular prose language was still considered as a specialty of Tuscany and not as the common property of all Italy seems to result from several facts. Famous Tuscan preachers such as S. Bernardino of Siena seem to have delivered their sermons in the vernacular in Tuscan cities only, but in Latin when they went to the cities of Northern Italy.[40] The language is called Tuscan by Filelfo and by other contemporary sources.[41] More-

[38] The use of the vernacular was made mandatory for the courts of trades and crafts in Florence through a decree of 1414 (G. Mancini, *l. c.*, p. 334). In the *Priorista di Palazzo* and the other lists of Florentine officials, the names are entered in Latin down to 1530 (Florence, Archivio di Stato). The instructions for ambassadors in the fifteenth century were given partly in Latin and partly in volgare.

[39] "E perchè noi crediamo che sia utilissimo a voi e a noi dichiarare bene e apertamente senza punto di simulazione ovvero di dissimulazione qual sia la vera intenzione e il puro e sincero proposito di ciascuno di noi, abbiamo deliberato di farvi questa risposta più tosto in volgare che in latino, sì e per sodisfar meglio e più agli animi nostri, sì etiamdio perchè la S. V. non abbia di bisogno nell'intendere di questo nostro così sincero proposito d'altra interpretazione che della nostra propria, nè in altro sentimento si possa interpetrare che in quello che è il naturale e il vero intelletto delle parole volgari" (*Anecdota litteraria ex manusciptis codicibus eruta,* ed. Jo. Christ. Amadutius, I, Rome, 1773, p. 378).

[40] Of S. Bernardino's sermons, only those delivered in Florence and in Siena are extant in a vernacular text (Galletti, *l. c.,* 212).

[41] Filelfo, in a letter to Marcus Aurelius of Venice, dated Milan, January 30, 1477, writes as follows: "Sed tu eum sermonem vernaculum vocas quo nos interdum ethrusce scribentes utimur. At ex universa Italia ethrusca lingua maxime laudatur. Hoc autem scribendi more utimur iis in rebus quarum memoriam nolumus transferre ad posteros. Et ethrusca quidem lingua vix toti Italiae nota est, et latina oratio longe ac late per universum orbem est diffusa" (C. de' Rosmini, *Vita di Francesco Filelfo da Tolentino,* Milan, 1808, II, 282). The second part of the passage, with its negative attitude toward the Tuscan vernacular, is usually quoted without the more positive first part. In 1496, the envoys of the emperor Maximilian to Florence delivered their address "aetrusca lingua" (Galletti, *l. c.,* p. 575).

over, during the greater part of the century at least, Tuscan prose was hardly written by any non-Tuscan author. The few apparent exceptions, such as the vernacular orations of Filelfo and Porcari, are linked with the residence of these authors in Florence, and in the latter case, many scholars assume that a Tuscan, Buonaccorso da Montemagno, had acted as a reviser or ghost writer.[42]

Outside of Tuscany, the fifteenth century witnessed a very important new development, that is, a considerable rise of a vernacular prose literature in the various local dialects. It included not only religious works, chronicles, and *Novelle*, but also learned treatises and translations of Latin classics.[43] The language of these writers has often been criticized by the purists on account of its non-Tuscan character, and they certainly cannot serve as models of correct language according to the prevailing standards. Yet it seems unfair to blame them for not complying with an ideal that was neither attained nor even recognized in their own time. It would be much more important to analyze the actual characteristics of their language and style and thus to determine whether they merely intended to write in their local dialects, or whether and to what extent they tried to modify those dialects under the influence of the Tuscan model.

During the second half of the fifteenth century, and especially during the last decades, we seem to notice a tendency among non-Tuscan prose writers to approach or even to adopt the literary language of Tuscany. Filelfo wrote many private letters in "Tuscan" long after his departure from Florence,[44] and a

[42] For the orations delivered by Filelfo in Florence, see *Prose e poesie volgari di Francesco Filelfo*, ed. G. Benadduci, *Atti e Memorie della R. Deputazione di Storia patria per le province delle Marche*, V, 1901, 1–262. For the speeches held in Florence by Porcari, see Galletti, *l. c.*, p. 576.

[43] For a group of translators at Ferrara, see G. Fatini, "Il volgare preariosteo a Ferrara," in his "Le Rime di Ludovico Ariosto," *Giornale Storico della letteratura italiana*, Supplement no. 25, 1934, 3–41. The vernacular works in prose produced in Milan include Corio's chronicle, and several translations of the classics by the humanist Pier Candido Decembrio. Bologna had Giovanni Sabadino degli Arienti, Venice Marin Sanudo, and Naples Diomede Carafa. In the Milanese chancery, the local dialect began to be used in 1426, see M. Vitale, "Il volgare nella cancelleria milanese del s. XV," *Paideia III*, 1948, 322–29. There are vernacular texts by the humanist Mario Filelfo in cod. V u 9 of the Royal Library in Stockholm, a vernacular version of Isocrates by Bartolommeo Fazio of Genoa in cod. 727 of the Biblioteca Universitaria in Valencia, and a vernacular version of Buonaccorso's *De nobilitate* by Aurispa in cod. Magl. VII 956. See also: *Testi non toscani del Quattrocento*, ed. B. Migliorini and G. Folena, Modena, 1953.

[44] They are printed by Benadduci, *l. c.*

number of other writers such as Collenuccio, Masuccio, and San-
nazaro are praised for their comparatively or completely "pure"
language.[45] The chronology and language of these writings
should be carefully reexamined, for they represent the first traces
of an important new development that reached its climax with
the beginning of the sixteenth century, I mean the emergence of
a common literary prose language for all of Italy on the basis
of Tuscan. So far, scholars have taken these facts too much for
granted, since they were under the wrong impression that such
a language had already existed ever since the early fourteenth
century.

The rise of non-Tuscan prose in the fifteenth century might
have led to the formation of other literary languages based on
the various dialects. This did not materialize, since Tuscan
literature had too great an advantage and began to act as a
model during the same period. However, the existence of this
non-Tuscan prose goes a long way to explain the resistance with
which the Tuscan movement was received during the sixteenth
century especially in Northern Italy, and the modifications that
were finally imposed upon the older Tuscan language after it
had been generally adopted by the rest of Italy.

Another fact should be noticed which distinguished the Tuscan
prose language of the fifteenth and earlier centuries from the
standard Italian prose of the sixteenth century: it had not yet
any fixed rules of spelling or of grammar. The old Tuscan prose
texts, not regulated by the requirements of verse and rhyme,
show in the manuscripts a confusing variety and fluidity of
spelling and of grammatical structure, of which the normalized
and simplified modern text editions rarely give us an adequate
impression. Grammatical regularity long was considered a privilege of Latin, and the attempt to establish the rules of Tuscan
grammar was not made before the second half of the fifteenth
century.[46]

---

[45] Rossi, *l. c.* It would be important to examine the language of Roberto
da Lecce's *Specchio della fede cristiana*, Venice, 1495, a work which is based
on sermons delivered in Naples and said to be the only vernacular work of
the kind edited by any fifteenth-century author (Galletti, *l. c.,* p. 276 f.). The
author was a pupil of S. Bernardino of Siena. Savonarola's sermons in
Florence were probably delivered in the vernacular (*ibid.,* p. 335). For San-
nazaro's language and his gradual progress towards a purer Tuscan prose,
see G. Folena, *La crisi linguistica del Quattrocento e l'Arcadia di I. San-
nazaro,* Florence, 1952.

[46] C. Trabalza, *Storia della grammatica italiana,* Milan, 1908.

The decisive period in the development of the Italian literary prose language was the sixteenth century. It faced and solved, after the tentative efforts of the late fifteenth century, the problem of a common literary prose language for all of Italy. In the field of prose literature, this was not the return to a situation which had supposedly existed in the fourteenth century, but an entirely new achievement. The first authoritative representative, if not the initiator, of this movement was Pietro Bembo, a non-Tuscan, and a humanist. In his *Asolani* (1505) he gave the first outstanding example of a pure Tuscan prose written by a non-Tuscan, and in his *Prose della volgar lingua,* published in 1525, but composed soon after 1500, he defended this practice with theoretical arguments. Throughout this work, Bembo prescribed the use of Tuscan both for poetry and for prose. Curiously enough, the fact that he was thus making an important innovation with regard to prose escaped his own attention and hence most later writers and scholars. Bembo did notice that practically all older prose writers that could serve as literary and linguistic models were Tuscans,[47] but he believed that Pietro de' Crescenzi of Bologna and Guido delle Colonne of Messina had written their works in Tuscan prose,[48] and thus he could consider himself as their successor. Actually, their works were composed in Latin and translated into the vernacular by anonymous Tuscan authors.

That the problem of a common literary language for Italy was forcefully posed, but not yet definitely settled by Bembo, appears from an interesting remark of the Neapolitan Benedetto di Falco,[49] as well as from the famous language controversy which was carried on after the publication of Bembo's treatise, and which continued until the nineteenth century. The discussion between the Tuscans and the anti-Tuscans can be easily understood in the light of the preceding development. There was the large store of old Tuscan prose of the thirteenth and fourteenth centuries, and there was the spoken Tuscan language of more

[47] "Di prosa non pare già che ancor si veggano, oltra i Toscani, molti scrittori" (Bembo, *Opere,* 1810, vol. X, p. 62).

[48] *L. c.,* p. 275. Bembo's error was corrected by Lodovico Castelvetro in his *Giunte* (*l. c.,* p. 348 ff.).

[49] In his *Rimario* (1535), he expresses the hope that the Signoria of Venice would reform "l'idioma italiano, componendo una sola lingua comune a tutti, che generalmente si potesse usare senza biasimo, come n'era una latina per tutto il mondo" (quoted from Vivaldi, *l. c.,* 49 f.).

recent times, which had become different from the language of
the earlier prose literature and had found its way into the literature of the fifteenth century. When the question of adopting a
common literary language for Italy was ripe in the sixteenth
century, there were obviously three possibilities: either to imitate
the language of the old Tuscan literature of the "golden century", or to follow the usage of contemporary spoken Tuscan, or
to free either form of Tuscan of its too local or antiquated flavor
and thus to transform it into a more neutral language that could
be easily learned and used by non-Tuscans.[50] All these possibilities had their advocates in the sixteenth century and afterwards, and all of these schools of thought had some influence on
the later history of Italian language and literature. On the whole,
the tendency to develop a more neutral standard language free
of local flavor seems to have prevailed. However, this does not
alter the basic fact that Tuscan was the only dialect which was
accepted as the foundation of this common literary language.
There was never a choice between the use of Tuscan or of any
other dialect, but between an orthodox, imitative Tuscan, the
contemporary Tuscan, and a modified, standardized Tuscan.
This general adoption of Tuscan was accompanied by efforts to
normalize its spelling and grammar, and it thus acquired all the
characteristics of a fully developed literary language.

This emergence of a common Italian language in prose as well
as in poetry gave a strong new impulse to the tendency of expanding its use in the areas hitherto dominated by Latin. Many
Italian writers of the sixteenth century took the universal use
of the vernacular for granted, whereas others, such as Muzio and
Varchi, advocated such a general use against the defenders of
Latin. The issue was especially important in the field of learned
and scientific literature where the prevalence of Latin remained
most notable. The Florentine Academy was founded in 1540
with the express purpose of translating all the sciences into the
Tuscan vernacular,[51] and Sperone Speroni in his dialogue on the
languages demanded that all the sciences should henceforth be

[50] The issue is presented in a similar fashion by Mme. Labande-Jeanroy
and by Robert A. Hall.
[51] "interpetrando, componendo e da ogni altra lingua ogni bella scienza in
questa nostra riducendo" (decree of Cosimo I, dated Feb. 23, 1541, published
in *Notizie letterarie ed istoriche intorno agli uomini illustri dell'Accademia
Fiorentina*, ed. J. Rilli, Florence, 1700, p. XXI f.).

treated in the vernacular alone.[52] Throughout the latter part of
the sixteenth century and thereafter, comedians and satirists ridiculed the type of the pedant and made his obstinate use of Latin
one of the points of their attacks.[53] Scholars have hence spoken
of a fight against Latin that characterized the later Renaissance
and led to the eventual disappearance of that language. This
view calls for a few qualifications. The satire directed against
the pedant and his Latin was merely one of the many cases in
which certain professions were exposed to public laughter and
did not necessarily imply that the writers or their audience intended to abolish that profession or any of its particular aspects.
Moreover, the statutes of the Florentine Academy, as well as
Speroni's dialogue, show that the universal use of the vernacular
for scientific treatises at that time was not an accomplished fact,
but an ideal to be realized in the future. Even some representatives of this movement were ready to admit that their aim could
be better attained by utilizing the achievements of Latin learning
rather than by making a completely new start.[54]

Yet the advocates of the vernacular were challenged in their
own time by a numerous group of defenders of Latin, and most
of these defenders belonged to the class of the humanists, that is,
of the professional students and teachers of Latin. Modern
scholars have often asserted that the humanists as a class were
opposed to the vernacular and even tried to abolish its literary
use altogether. This view is certainly exaggerated. Many humanists, beginning with Bembo himself, were among the founders
and leaders of the vernacular movement. Those sixteenth-century
humanists who did attack the vernacular hardly meant to abolish
its use in daily life or even in literature. They were led by the
heat of the argument and by the rhetorical habits of the time
to certain exaggerated statements against the vernacular, but

[52] Sperone Speroni, *Dialogo delle lingue*, ed. in his *Opere*, I, Venice, 1740,
166–201. Cf. L. Olschki, *Bildung und Wissenschaft im Zeitalter der Renaissance in Italien* (*Geschichte der neusprachlichen wissenschaftlichen Literatur*
II, Leipzig, 1922) p. 165 ff.

[53] A. Graf, "I Pedanti," in his *Attraverso il Cinquecento*, Turin, 1888, 169–
213. Olschki, *l. c.*, p. 147 ff.

[54] Gelli attributed the recent progress of the vernacular language to the
great number of people learned in Latin and Greek: "la moltitudine grande
di coloro che oggi si dànno in Firenze a la lingua latina e greca; i quali, im-
parando quelle con regola, favellano dipoi ancora regolatamente la nostra e
con leggiadria." He adds that important state documents are now composed
in the vernacular, "che da non molto in dietro si scrivevano tutti in lingua
latina" (quoted from Vernon Hall, *l. c.*, p. 35).

their major concern was defensive, and some of their arguments were far from superficial. Most famous is the case of Romolo Amaseo who in 1529 gave two public lectures at Bologna in which he advocated the continued study and literary use of Latin and rejected the rising claims of the vernacular.[55] Even Varchi who criticizes Amaseo suggests that the latter may not have been quite serious in his slighting remarks about the vernacular.[56] In their original context, Amaseo's orations give the impression that his major concern was to defend the use of Latin as a learned and international language, and to stress the great wealth of intellectual traditions embodied in Latin, of which the exclusive advocates of the vernacular would deprive themselves and their pupils.[57] Similar arguments were used about the same time by Francesco Bellafini [58] and by Francesco Florido Sabino,[59] and several decades later by Bartolommeo Ricci,[60] Carlo Sigonio [61] and Uberto Foglietta.[62] The controversy obviously was not dead in the later sixteenth century, and it was kept alive by the tendency of the humanists to exalt the value of their professional field in comparison with others.[63] Yet even Amaseo who is so often described as an obstinate enemy of the vernacular praised a contemporary attempt to teach Latin grammar in Italian, and composed a number of letters in the vernacular which are quite

[55] *De latinae linguae usu retinendo schola I–II* (in Romuli Amasei *Orationum Volumen*, Bologna, 1564, p. 101–46. I used the copy kindly made available to me by the Trustees of the Boston Athenaeum).

[56] *L'Ercolano*, in his *Opere*, ed. A. Racheli, Trieste, 1859, II, p. 160.

[57] See especially Amaseo, *l. c.*, p. 104, 127 f., 132. The best information on Amaseo's orations is given by P. Rajna, "La data di una lettera di Claudio Tolomei ad Agnolo Firenzuola," *La Rassegna*, Ser. III, vol. I, 1916, p. 7 ff. Other scholars who mention the orations know them only through Varchi or Muzio.

[58] V. Cian, "Contro il volgare," in *Studi Letterari e linguistici dedicati a Pio Rajna*, Milan, 1911, 251–97. This article contains much information on the whole question. Bellafini's letter is reproduced on p. 287–91.

[59] R. Sabbadini, *Storia del Ciceronianismo*, Turin, 1885, 127–36.

[60] *De imitatione*, Paris, 1557, f. 35 f. and 37 verso f.

[61] *De latinae linguae usu retinendo oratio quinta* (1556), in his *Opera Omnia*, ed. Ph. Argelatus, VI, Milan, 1737, col. 521–28.

[62] *De linguae latinae usu et praestantia libri tres*, Rome, 1574, and Hamburg, 1723. Cf. E. Norden, *Die antike Kunstprosa*, II, 4th ed., Leipzig, 1923, 771 f.

[63] Varchi lists as further opponents of the vernacular Pier Angelio Bargeo, Celio Calcagnini, and G. B. Goineo (*l. c.*, p. 160 f.). Fontanini and Zeno add Lazaro Buonamico, Quinto Mario Corrado, Raffaele Cillenio, Gabriele Barrio, Girolamo Rorario, Lodovico Nogarola, and Anastasio Germonio (*l. c.*, I, p. 35).

an impressive document of his personal feelings and intellectual interests.[64]

If the humanists of the sixteenth century really meant to stop or delay the development of vernacular literature their efforts certainly were entirely in vain. However, in so far as they tried to defend the use of Latin as a learned and literary language they were by no means defeated. Latin continued to be used, long after the middle of the sixteenth century, in poetry as well as in prose literature, and especially in university teaching and in learned treatises. This fact is abundantly confirmed by documentary and bibliographical evidence.[65] As late as 1640, a North Italian physician trained at Padua could blame a sixteenth-century Tuscan writer for having treated philosophical subjects in the vernacular rather than in Latin.[66] An eighteenth-century treatise instructing prospective authors how to write a book recommends the use of Latin for works that should be read by an international audience of scholars, and praises a contemporary author for his elegant Latin.[67] The progress of the vernacular at the expense of Latin was hence much slower than it is usually presented. Moreover, the continued practice on the part of the same authors to employ both languages alternatively shows that their rivalry was not always considered as a matter of philosophical or literary convictions. On the other hand, where the vernacular succeeded in taking over completely the literary function of Latin, it inherited a good deal from preceding and contem-

[64] Many of these letters are published in Flaminio Scarselli's *Vita Romuli Amasaei*, Bologna, 1769. A letter of Bembo refers to Amaseo's careful study of the Tuscan language and its grammar (Cian, "Contro il volgare," p. 281 f.). See also V. Cian, "Per la storia dello Studio bolognese nel Rinascimento: Pro e contro l'Amaseo," in *Miscellanea di Studi critici edita in onore di Arturo Graf*, Bergamo, 1903, 201–22.

[65] Fontanini and Zeno's bibliography of vernacular literature, which is quite comprehensive for the sixteenth century, lists few titles of learned works as compared with the great number of Latin works of the same period, known from other sources.

[66] ". . . latinae locutionis maiestatem ac studium abdicare, qua ultro utilissima quaeque comprehensa et consignata esse palam est. Hac de causa perpauci eius vestigia secuti, Tuscum sermonem in doctrinarum traditione probarunt, caeteris abunde omnibus Romani decus acriter venustatemque tuentibus" (Joannes Vincentius Imperialis, *Musaeum Historicum et Physicum*, pt. I, Venice, 1640, p. 81, in his biography of Alessandro Piccolomini).

[67] "Scrivendo unicamente per le persone dotte, e di materie assolutamente non popolari, dovrebbero usare piuttosto la lingua latina" (C. Denina, *Bibliopea o sia l'arte di compor libri*, Turin, 1776, p. 53). Facciolati is called "sì rinomato a' tempi nostri per l'eleganza del suo latino" (*ibid.* p. 55).

porary Latin traditions. This applied to vocabulary and syntax as well as to subject matter and literary forms. The Latin titles found in so many fifteenth-century manuscripts of vernacular poetry or attached to the chapters of Machiavelli's *Prince* are a symbol of this process through which the vernacular gradually occupied the forms and patterns prepared and developed in the literary traditions of medieval and Renaissance Latin. The final disappearance of Latin from learned and literary usage did not occur before the end of the eighteenth century, and some traces of its use have persisted to the present day.[68]

Let us briefly summarize some of our basic conclusions. The fourteenth century did not create a common literary prose language for Italy, but that was left to the sixteenth century. The sixteenth century did not abolish the literary and learned use of Latin, but that was left to the nineteenth century. The fifteenth century did not interrupt the development of vernacular literature, but marks a definite advance in a slow process that extends from the thirteenth to the nineteenth century and that leads the language of Italian literary prose from its modest beginnings in Tuscany to its present role as the exclusive linguistic medium of a highly developed national civilization. This slow rise of Italian has its counterpart in an equally slow decline of literary Latin. This Latin literary language had its merits and its definite historical importance, and even if we dislike it, we are not entitled to ignore its existence or to antedate its disappearance.

The details of this outline are rather tentative, and it was merely my intention to formulate the problem and to indicate the direction in which its solution might be sought. The actual study of the problem in all its aspects is still to be undertaken. It is a task in which linguistic and literary historians should join forces. For the subject itself is of a nature to illustrate the link that exists between linguistics and intellectual history. Word and language are not merely phonetic phenomena, but also carriers of thought. Inasmuch as ideas are subject to a historical process of origin and development, the words and languages that serve as media of such ideas also contain a historical element and may hence be subjected to historical analysis and interpretation.

---

[68] Especially in ecclesiastic documents and treatises, and in works of classical scholars. The poet Pascoli also published Latin verses. See now the periodical *Latinitas* (vol. I, 1953) which publishes all kinds of material in Latin prose and verse.

VIII

Music and Learning
in the Early Italian Renaissance*

ALTHOUGH RECENT TRENDS in music have been more favorable to
the preservation of some intellectual and literary content than
they were in the visual arts, the modern cult of genius has tended
to isolate the composer, if not the performer, from his social
environment and from the learning of his time. This situation
quite understandably has affected also the study of the history of
music, in a way that was further encouraged by the necessities
of increasing scholarly specialization. Consequently, the history
of music in the Middle Ages and the Renaissance has often been
presented as a completely separate development, and only quite
recently attempts have been made to consider it within the
framework of a more general cultural and intellectual situation.[1]
The following pages, written without any claim to competence
in music or its history, are meant as a contribution to the general
"background" of Renaissance music, and might encourage more
qualified scholars to investigate in greater detail the pertinent
facts and problems.

In the history of music, as well as in many other branches of
cultural history, medieval Italy occupies a somewhat peculiar
position.[2] Whereas there is every reason to believe that the tradition of Gregorian chant was preserved and cultivated in the

---

* Reprinted from *Studies in Renaissance Thought and Letters* (Rome,
Edizioni di Storia e Letteratura, 1956), 451–469. Originally published in
Journal of Renaissance and Baroque Music, I (1947), 255–274.

[1] A. Pirro, *Histoire de la Musique de la fin du XIVe siècle à la fin du XVIe*,
Paris, 1940. P. H. Lang, *Music in Western Civilization*, New York, 1941.

[2] For this historical position of medieval Italy, see Kristeller, *Renaissance
Thought* [vol. I], New York, Harper Torchbooks, 1961, 93–95.

more important monasteries, cathedrals, and other ecclesiastic centers, Italy apparently had no part in the early development of polyphony which had its center in France.[3] Prior to the end of the thirteenth century, musical compositions and treatises of Italian origin are extremely rare, and the records of musical activity and teaching are amazingly scanty. The figure of Guido of Arezzo in the eleventh century is so much of an exception that the hypothesis of his French origin deserves some consideration.[4] The treatise on arithmetic, geometry, and music written toward the end of the twelfth century by William, canon and bishop of Lucca, discussed by local scholars,[5] but apparently neglected by general historians of music, does not change the comprehensive picture, which is not likely to be affected by similar discoveries that may be made in the future in libraries or archives. During the thirteenth century, popular religious movements created the type of the *Laudi* which from the very beginning must have been accompanied by music, although the extant examples of such music are of a later date.[6] Among the early members of the Franciscan Order we find at least two musicians, Henry of Pisa and Vita of Lucca, who achieved a reputation both as singers and composers and gave at least some private instruction in music. They composed music for one, two, and three voices, and they used texts that were either written by themselves or by such famous authors as Philip the Chancelor

[3] I should like to refer, once and for all, to the following general works which I have consulted for this paper: A. W. Ambros, *Geschichte der Musik* II, 2nd ed., Leipzig, 1880; III, 2nd ed., 1881; IV, 3rd ed. by H. Leichtentritt, 1909. Guido Adler, *Handbuch der Musikgeschichte*, Berlin, 1930. H. Riemann, *Handbuch der Musikgeschichte*, 2nd ed., Leipzig, 1920. J. Wolf, *Geschichte der Mensural-Notation von 1250–1460*, I, Leipzig, 1904. Th. Gérold, *Histoire de la Musique des origines à la fin du XIVe siècle*, Paris, 1936. A. Pirro, *op. cit.* G. Reese, *Music in the Middle Ages*, New York, 1940. Id., *Music in the Renaissance*, New York, 1954. P. H. Lang. *op. cit.* H. Riemann, *Geschichte der Musiktheorie im IX.–XIX. Jahrhundert*, 2nd ed., Berlin, 1920. *The Oxford History of Music*, 2nd ed., Oxford, 1929–32. R. Eitner, *Biographisch-Bibliographisches Quellen-Lexikon der Musiker*, Leipzig, n. d. Grove's *Dictionary of Music and Musicians*, 3rd ed., New York, 1938. F. J. Fétis, *Biographie Universelle des Musiciens*, Paris, 1870. H. Besseler, *Die Musik des Mittelalters und der Renaissance*, Potsdam, 1931–35.

[4] Lang, *op. cit.*, 84.

[5] L. Nerici, "Storia della musica in Lucca," *Memorie e documenti per servire alla storia di Lucca*, XII, Lucca, 1880, p. 16 and 90 f. The work is preserved in cod. 614 of the Biblioteca Capitolare in Lucca.

[6] I am indebted for this information to Prof. Manfred Bukofzer. F. Liuzzi, *La laude e i primordi della melodia italiana*, Rome, 1935.

and Richard of St. Victor.[7] Also the practice of secular music must have been stimulated by the fashionable recital and imitation of French and Provençal poetry, but very little seems to be known about it.[8] The traditional place of music among the seven liberal arts may have led many students to give some time to musical theory, but the extant records of the schools and early universities in Italy show no evidence that music held a definite place in their curriculum, either as a separate field or even as an annex to the study of mathematics and astronomy.[9]

It is only with the fourteenth century that Italy began to play a major role in the history of music. The Italian *Ars Nova* which had its center in Florence and in Lombardy produced a large number of secular compositions and held an important place in contemporary society, as is shown by several literary testimonies. This music, as that of the troubadours, developed in close connection with vernacular poetry. The composers set to music either their own verses or those of contemporary poets with whom they often maintained personal relations. Whereas religious music was cultivated in monasteries and cathedrals,[10] this secular music was fostered not only by the courts of the princes and nobles, but also by the republican governments of the various cities and communities. The published records on the musical culture and activities in numerous Italian cities begin to become more frequent and more detailed with the fourteenth century, but apparently they have been very little utilized by general historians of music.[11] It appears that the authorities of

---

[7] "Cronica Fratris Salimbene de Adam Ordinis Minorum," ed. O. Holder-Egger, *Monumenta Germaniae Historica, Scriptores,* XXXII, Hannover, 1905–13, pp. 181 ff. I am indebted for this and several other references to Prof. Leo Schrade.

[8] Such a recital by a noble party in Pisa is described by Salimbene, *op. cit.,* 44 f.

[9] G. Manacorda, *Storia della Scuola in Italia, Milan,* n. d., is completely silent on the place of music in the medieval Italian schools and lists only one work on music among the textbooks that were in use: Librum artis musicae (in the Library of S. Vito e Gorgona, 1379, pt. II, p. 357).

[10] The chronicle of the Dominican monastery of S. Caterina in Pisa praises several friars for their accomplishments in music, especially in singing and teaching, cf. "Chronica Antiqua Conventus Sanctae Catharinae de Pisis," *Archivo Storico Italiano,* VI, pt. II, 1845, pp. 522, 547, 549, 555.

[11] The numerous periodicals on local history as well as the proceedings of the provincial historical societies and of the academies include several articles and documents illustrating the history of music. Since they are seldom mentioned by general historians of music it might be worth while to utilize this material, beginning with a bibliography.

such cities as Florence, Lucca, and Perugia quite regularly employed groups of musicians to entertain them during hours of rest from business and to play in public on special occasions.[12] The teaching of music must have been primarily of a practical nature. There is almost no trace of musical instruction at the universities.[13] The chief theorist of the period, Marchettus of Padua, whose works are now commonly dated after 1309, was active in Cesena, Verona, and perhaps in Naples, and had no connection with the university of his home town.[14] The combination of music and learning appears especially in the most famous composer of the period, Francesco Landini of Florence.[15] He was not only a distinguished musician, but also a poet, both in the vernacular and in Latin. He was praised for his knowledge

[12] For Florence, see L. Cellesi, "Documenti per la storia musicale di Firenze," *Rivista Musicale Italiana*, XXXIV, 1927, 579–602; XXV, 1928, 553–82. For Lucca see Nerici, *op cit.*, who also quotes documents for Perugia from an article of A. Rossi, published in the *Giornale di Erudizione Artistica*.

[13] This is the one exception which I have been able to find: A criminal record of February, 1308, in Bologna, mentions «. . . magistrum Iohannem domini Guillelmi teotonicum de Valegio dictum alias magistrum Johannem della Luna, astrologhum, professorem et doctorem in scientiis medicine et in artibus, sive gramatica, dialectica, rethorica, aritmetica, geometria, musica et astrologia de motibus et astrologia de effectibus sive operibus que est ipsa phylosofia . . . qui quidem magister Johannes est de universitate scolarium studentium Bononie . . .». From another document it results that in 1298 he received his degree and license "in scientia medicine et in supradictis artibus. . . ." G. Zaccagnini, "Giovanni di Bonandrea dettatore e rimatore ed altri grammatici e dottori in arti dello Studio Bolognese," *Studi e Memorie per la Storia dell'Università di Bologna*, V, 1920, pp. 167 f. and. 200. Johannes de Luna apparently was chiefly active as an astrologer. The document does not prove that there was a chair of music, but it shows that the concept of the seven liberal arts was still alive at Bologna around 1300.

[14] For the correct date of Marchettus's treatises, see F. Ludwig, "Die Quellen der Motetten aeltesten Stils," *Archiv für Musikwissenschaft*, V, 1923, 289, and H. Besseler, "Studien zur Musik des Mittelalters," I, *ibid.*, VII, 1925, 177. His works were published by M. Gerbert, *Scriptores ecclesiastici de musica*, III, St. Blasien, 1784, 64 ff. and by E. de Coussemaker, *Scriptorum de musica medii aevi nova series*, III, Paris, 1869, 1 ff. Coussemaker also published the following treatises that were presumably written in fourteenth-century Italy: *Phillipoti Andrea de contrapuncto* (III, 116 ff.); *Philippi de Caserta de diversis figuris* (ibid., 118 ff.); *fratris Johannis Veruli de Anagnia de musica* (ibid., 129 ff.); *Guillelmi monachi de praeceptis artis musicae* (ibid., 273 ff.). Nothing specific seems to be known about the life and precise dates of these authors. To this may be added *L'arte del biscanto misurato secondo el maestro Jacopo da Bologna*, published by J. Wolf in *Theodor Kroyer-Festschrift*, Regensburg, 1933, 17–39.

[15] *The Works of Francesco Landini*, ed. Leonard Ellinwood, Cambridge, Mass., 1939, with a biographical introduction and documents.

of grammar, astronomy, and the other liberal arts, and in one of his extant Latin poems he defends the logic of Ockham against its humanist critics. This poem is an interesting document for the controversy between the humanist rhetoricians and the scholastic logicians in its earlier phase.[16] Landini was also crowned with the laurel by the King of Cyprus in Venice, and this episode which apparently makes him the only "musician laureate" in Western history illustrates his fame as well as his ambitions. The statement made by several scholars that Landini must have been crowned as a poet and not as a musician has no documentary foundation.[17] In all probability, he was crowned as a musician. On the other hand, since there were no precedents for the coronation of musicians, but several for that of poets, of which Landini, being himself a poet, must have known, he obviously wanted to emulate Petrarch and other crowned poets and to have music share in the honor previously bestowed upon poetry.

With the fifteenth century began for Italy the culminating period of the Renaissance which was to continue through the greater part of the sixteenth century. In the field of music the earlier part of this period was characterized by strong foreign influences originating in France and especially in the Low Countries. In dealing with fifteenth-century Italy, musical historians have studied not only the extant compositions, but especially the theoretical literature and the institutions and centers at which musical theory and practice was cultivated. The links that connect especially the musical theorists with the various centers of teaching and learning and with the main intellectual currents

[16] This poem was published by A. Wesselofsky, *Il Paradiso degli Alberti*, in *Scelta di Curiosità Letterarie*, vol. 86, pt. 2, Bologna, 1867, 295 ff., and by Ph. Boehner, O.F.M., "Ein Gedicht auf die Logik Ockhams," *Franziskanische Studien*, XXVI, 1938, 81 ff. C. Vasoli, "Polemiche occamiste," *Rinascimento* III 1952, 119–41.

[17] The only testimony of the coronation is the following sentence of Filippo Villani: "ut Venetiis ab illustrissimo ac nobilissimo Cyprorum rege publice ut poetis et Caesaribus mos est laurea donaretur." *Philippi Villani Liber de Civitatis Florentiae famosis civibus*, ed. G. C. Galletti, Florence, 1847, 35; the passage has been reprinted by Ellinwood, *op. cit.*, 301 ff. All other details were added, without documentary basis, by F. Caffi, *Storia della Musica Sacra nella già Cappella Ducale di San Marco in Venezia dal 1318 al 1797*, I, Venice, 1854, 62 f., who postulated Landini's coronation as a poet since he would not admit the possibility of his triumph over the local musicians of Venice. This version was then repeated and further embellished, without criticism or new documents, by Ch. Van den Borren, *Les Débuts de la musique à Venise*, Brussels, 1914, 12 f. The wording and context in Villani definitely suggest that Landini was crowned as a musician.

of the period will also be the subject of this paper. Its major purpose will be to coordinate a few facts well known to musical historians with a few others that are primarily known to students of the history of literature, philosophy, and education.

The history of musical education, and especially the teaching of music at the schools and universities of the Middle Ages and of the Renaissance, is a subject worthy of much further investigation.[18] Although Johannes de Muris, the influential musical theorist and mathematician of the early fourteenth century, was connected with the Collegium Sorbonicum, the evidence for musical teaching at Paris and the other French Universities is very slight.[19] During the fifteenth and sixteenth centuries, music was taught at Salamanca, Oxford, and Cambridge as well as at many German and other Central European universities. This teaching was based on Boethius, on Muris, or on the textbooks produced by the various professors of music, and in many places it can be traced far into the seventeenth and eighteenth centuries.[20] Those who expect or postulate a similar development at the Italian universities will be greatly disappointed. The documents which indicate the teaching of music at the Italian universities are nearly all limited to the fifteenth century, and they are scanty and even elusive. There is a decree of the year 1450 by pope Nicolas V which provided for a chair of music at the University of Bologna, but there is no evidence that this chair was ever occupied during the following years.[21] When the

[18] The chapter in Gérold (op. cit., 384 ff.) is rather superficial. The most substantial contribution was published by P. Wagner, "Zur Musikgeschichte der Universität," Archiv für Musikwissenschaft, III, 1921, 1–16. This study is well documented, especially for the German and other Central European universities. See also: D. Iselin, "Die Musikwissenschaft an den schweizerischen Universitäten," Mitteilungen der Internationalen Gesellschaft für Musikwissenschaft, I, 1928–29, 27–32; 39–46. C. A. Moberg, "Musik und Musikwissenschaft an den schwedischen Universitäten," ibid., 54–70; II, 1930, 10–26; 34–44. A. Pirro, "L'enseignement de la musique aux universités françaises," ibid., 26–32; 45–56 (which contains many interesting facts, but hardly anything pertinent to the subject). Edward J. Dent, "The Scientific Study of Music in England," ibid., 83–92.

[19] See Pirro, op. cit. It should be added that in the Middle Ages the Sorbonne was not identical with the University of Paris. This example suggests that the records of the colleges of students might yield more for the history of music than do the records of the universities proper.

[20] See the literature cited above (note 18).

[21] The decree was published by Ph. C. Saccus, Statuta Civilia et criminalia civitatis Bononiae, II, Bologna, 1737, 283 ff. It lists, among the other lecturers in the Faculty of Arts: ad lecturam musicae unum. The Faculty list for

Spaniard Bartolomeo Ramis de Pareja, who had previously lectured on Boethius at Salamanca, published his musical Treatise in Bologna in 1482, he was called in the colophon a public professor of music.[22] Yet his pupil, Giovanni Spataro, reports in a letter that this chair had merely been promised to Ramis by the city authorities, and that he left Bologna in the same year because the promise was not fulfilled.[23] This testimony can hardly be contradicted, and the university records contain no evidence that Ramis ever was on its staff either in that year or in the preceding period. One of the most important musical theorists of the early fifteenth century, Prosdocimus de Beldemandis, was a professor of astronomy at the University of Padua. Yet there is no evidence that he ever taught music at the university, and his extant musical treatises show no trace of such a teaching.[24] Of course the

---

the year 1450–51 is lost. That for 1451–52 has the entry: Ad lecturam Musicae D. M., yet the name is erased. The lists for the successive years contain no entry for music at all (U. Dallari, *I Rotuli dei lettori legisti e artisti dello Studio Bolognese dal 1384 al 1799*, I, Bologna, 1888, p. 32). Hence the chair was either occupied for one year only, or not at all.

[22] *Musica Practica Bartolomei Rami de Pareia*, ed. J. Wolf (*Publikationen der Internationalen Musikgesellschaft, Beihefte*, II, Leipzig, 1901). The two editions, both published in Bologna in 1482, have in the colophon: almae urbis Bononiae dum eam (sc. musicam) ibidem publice legeret, and, respectively: dum publice musicam Bononiae legeret (*ibid.*, 104).

[23] ". . . perchè lui (Ramis) fece stampare a Bologna tale particole perchè el se credeva de legerla (sc. music) con stipendio in publico. Ma in quello tempo acade che per certe cause lui non hebe la lectura publica, et lui quasi sdegnato andò a Roma. . . ." (G. Gaspari, "Ricerche, documenti e memorie riguardanti la storia dell'arte musicale in Bologna," *Atti e Memorie della R. Deputazione de storia patria per le provincie di Romagna*, VI, 1868, 24 f.). This invalidates an earlier statement of Gaspari (*La musica in Bologna*, Milan, 1858, 6) and a remark of Gafori (dum Bononiae illitteratus tamen publice legeret, Wolf, *op. cit.*, 110) that was probably based on the colophon of Ramis's treatise. Strangely enough, Wolf who quotes Spataro's letter yet maintains that Ramis was connected with the university (*op. cit.*, XIII). The whole matter has been clarified by L. Torri, *Rivista Musicale Italiana*, XX, 1913, 711 f. Of course, there is no doubt that Ramis taught music in the city of Bologna.

[24] For his biography and works, see A. Favaro, "Intorno alla vita ed alle opere di Prosdocimo de' Beldomandi matematico padovano del secolo XV," *Bullettino di Bibliografia e di Storia delle Scienze Matematiche e Fisiche*, XII, 1879, 1–74; 115–251. Id., "Appendice agli Studi intorno alla vita ed alle opere di Prosdocimo de' Beldomandi, matematico padovano del secolo XV," *ibid.*, XVIII, 1885, 405–23. See also, A. Gloria, *Monumenti della Università di Padova (1381–1405)*, Padua, 1888, I, 399 ff. and 514 f. *Acta Graduum Academicorum Gymnasii Patavini ab anno MCCCCVI ad annum MCCCCL*, ed. C. Zonta et J. Brotto, Padua, 1922, 4; 153; 156 Several of Prosdocimus' treatises were published by Coussemaker III, 193 ff. Further texts were pub-

fact that in his writings he covered musical theory as well as mathematics and astronomy is an interesting proof, as is the earlier case of Muris, that the tradition of the Quadrivium was still alive in the fifteenth century. The only certain example of a chair of music at any Italian university is that held by Francesco Gafori at Pavia between 1494 and 1499. The founding of that chair is praised by contemporary poets as a great innovation, and Gafori does appear on the payroll of the University, with the additional statement that he is actually lecturing at Milan, as was the case with several lecturers in other fields.[25] However, since Gafori's university connection is attested only for a comparatively short period, whereas the position of a choirmaster at Milan Cathedral which he held over many years also included the duty of teaching, I am inclined to believe that his appointment as a university professor was nothing but a special favor granted him by Lodovico Sforza to provide him with a higher standing and an additional salary. Yet even if we accept his university appointment without qualifications, it remains for Italy an entirely unique case. The statements often repeated about chairs of music at Bologna and Padua have no foundation except the above mentioned facts, and the similar statements about Naples or other universities have no foundation at all.[26] The assumption that music in many cases must have been taught as a part of, or annex to, mathematics, according to the tradition

lished by L. Torri, "Il trattato di Prosdocimo de' Beldomandi contro il Lucidario di Marchetto da Padova," *Rivista Musicale Italiana*, XX, 1913, 707–62 and by Cl. Sartori, *La notazione italiana del Trecento in una redazione inedita del "Tractatus practice cantus mensurabilis ad modum Ytalicorum" di Prosdocimo de Beldemandis*, Florence, 1938.

[25] The faculty list for Pavia of 1498 contains the entry: ad lecturam musices D. Presb. Franchinus Gaffurus Mediol. legens (G. Porro, "Pianta delle spese per l'università di Pavia nel 1498," *Archivio Storico Lombardo*, V, 1878, p. 511). *See* also E. Motta, "Musici alla Corte degli Sforza," *ibid.*, XIV, 1887, 547 ff. Apparently Gaffori was also listed in a similar document of 1499 (Porro, *op. cit.*, 514 ff.). Another list of Pavia professors, compiled from documents, has "Francisco Gaffuro, ad lect. Musices a Milano, stipendiato dello Studio pavese, leggente a Milano," for the period between 1494 and 1499 (*Memorie e documenti per la storia dell'Università di Pavia*, pt. I, Pavia, 1878, 166). Another testimony of 1497, and a poem by Lancinus Curtius, with the title "laudat duces instituta musicae lectione" are quoted by G. Cesari, "Musica e Musicisti alla Corte Sforzesca," *Rivista Musicale Italiana*, XXIX 1922, 24 f. *Franchino Gaffurio*, Lodi, 1951, p. 89 ff.

[26] Some scholars assert that Johannes Tinctoris taught at the university of Naples, but the university records of the period are silent about him, and about a chair of music in general (E. Cannavale, *Lo Studio di Napoli nel Rinascimento*, Naples, 1895).

of the Quadrivium, is in need of further documentary evidence. As to the teaching of music in the secondary schools, both secular and ecclesiastic, a good deal of evidence may be brought to light by a further examination of the published and unpublished local records.

Thus, since the universities had, if any, only a modest part in the teaching of music during the Italian Renaissance, we may very well ask whether there were any other centers of musical teaching—a question which might also throw some light on the relationship of music with the other arts and sciences. There must have been, of course, a good deal of private instruction—in chant and instrumental playing as well as in theory—which was not linked to any institution, and the title of a "professor" of music was apparently assumed by any more or less successful teacher. Of this type seems to have been the teaching of Ramis in Bologna as well as that of his opponent, Nicolas Burcius, who was at the same time a university student of canon law.[27] Yet the main centers of musical teaching were the cathedrals and the courts.

The cathedrals and other important churches needed not only an organist and a choir for their services, but also a choirmaster who often had the task of composing music for various occasions and of training and teaching the singers of the choir. In Italy this system was not merely a heritage of earlier mediaeval centuries, but in many important cases the church service and the cathedral school were organized or reorganized during the fourteenth, fifteenth, and even sixteenth centuries. As we follow the careers of many Renaissance theorists, we find that they often held the position of choirmasters at various churches or were in other ways connected with cathedral chapters. Gafori was for many years choirmaster at Milan Cathedral, after having served in a similar function in other places.[28] Giovanni Spataro was choirmaster at S. Petronio in Bologna,[29] Giuseppe Zarlino at St.

[27] On the title page of his *Musices opusculum* (1487), he is called "musices professoris ac iuris pontificii studiosissimi" (Ramis, ed. Wolf, 105).

[28] D. Muoni, "Maestri di Cappella del Duomo di Milano," *Archivio Storico Lombardo*, X, 1883, 211 ff. An important source for Gafori's career is the contemporary biography by Pantaleo Malegulus, reprinted by Sassi in Ph. Argelati, *Biblotheca Scriptorum Mediolanensium*, I, pt. I, Milan 1745, col CCCXLVI f. See also G. Cesari, *l. c.*, and id., in F. Malaguzzi Valeri, *La Corte di Lodovico il Moro*, IV, Milan, 1923, 206 ff. *Franchino Gaffurio*, Lodi, 1951.

[29] Gaspari, "Ricerche" etc. L. Frati, "Per la storia della musica in Bologna dal secolo XV al XVI," *Rivista Musicale Italiana*, XXIV, 1917, 456 ff. Spataro's *Dilucide et probatissime demonstrationi* were reprinted by J. Wolf, *Veroeffentlichungen der Musik-Bibliothek Paul Hirsch*, VII, Berlin, 1925.

Mark's in Venice,[30] the English Carmelite, John Hothby, at the Cathedral of Lucca.[31] Pietro Aron served at the church of Imola.[32] Earlier in the fifteenth century, Johannes Ciconia of Liège was a canon of Padua,[33] and Ugolino of Orvieto who was probably born in Forlì, was a canon of Ferrara.[34] The treatises as well as the compositions of all these masters are most probably connected with these positions and activities.[35]

The importance of the Renaissance courts as centers of musical life is so well known that it does not need further emphasis. The popes as well as the rulers of Naples, Milan, Florence, Mantua, Ferrara, and Urbino had their choirs, players, and court composers who made their regular contributions to daily entertainment as well as to special festivals and celebrations. Yet musical

[30] Caffi, op. cit., I, 127 ff.

[31] The documents for his career in Lucca are all quoted by Nerici, op cit., 43; 80; 92 ff.; 113 f. See also, U. Kornmueller, "Johann Hothby," Kirchenmusikalisches Jahrbuch, VIII, 1893, 1–23. Some of his shorter treatises were published in Coussemaker, III, 328 ff., and his main work, entitled Calliopea legale, was also edited by Coussemaker, Histoire de l'harmonie au Moyen Age, Paris, 1852, 295–349. On the latter work, see A. W. Schmidt, Die Calliopea Legale des Johannes Hothby, diss., Leipzig, 1897. For the title, I like to quote the following sentence from Ficino's De rationibus musicae: ". . . proportio dupla que diapason scilicet octave vocis perfectam procreat consonantiam Calliopeo apud poetas nomine designatam" (Supplementum Ficinianum, Florence, 1937, I, 51). A pupil of Hothby, a certain Matheus de Testadraconibus Florentinus O. Serv. (Coussemaker, III, p. XXXI f.), was the author of another treatise on music (A. De La Fage, Essais de diphthérographie musicale I, Paris, 1864, 375 ff.).

[32] Fétis, op. cit., I, 1 ff.

[33] On his life and compositions, see Ambros, op. cit. III, 146; W. Korte, "Contributi alla storia della musica in Italia", Rivista Musicale Italiana, XXXIX, 1932, 516 ff. For his inedited treatises one of which is dedicated "presbytero Johanni Gasparo canonico Vicentino" and dated Padua 1411, see A. De La Fage, op. cit., 387 ff.; G. Gaspari, Catalogo della Biblioteca del Liceo Musicale di Bologna, I, Bologna, 1890, 203 f. and 347 f.

[34] On his life and inedited treatise, see A. De La Fage, op. cit., 116 ff., U. Kornmüller, "Musiklehre des Ugolino von Orvieto", Kirchenmusikalisches Jahrbuch, X, 1895, 19–40; F. X. Haberl, "Bio-bibliographische Notizen über Ugolino von Orvieto", ibid., 40–49; G. Pietzsch, Die Klassification der Musik von Boethius bis Ugolino von Orvieto, diss. Freiburg, Halle, 1929.

[35] Two other treatises of the fifteenth century apparently stem from this ecclesiastic tradition: the Ars cantus figurati Antonii de Luca (ed. Coussemaker, IV, 421 ff.) whose author mentions his teacher ("quam michi Antonio de Luca Ordinis Servorum declaravit legit perfecteque aperuit Magister meus dominus Laurentius de Urbe Veteri... canonicus ecclesie Sancte Marie Majoris...", op. cit., 421); and the Compendium Musicale, "a multis doctoribus editum et compositum et per presbyterum Nicolaum de Capua ordinatum sub anno 1415", published by De La Fage (op. cit., 308 ff.). For Johannes Bonadies and Johannes Gallicus, see below.

instruction also played a part in the education of the princes
and their courtiers as it had in the chivaleresque period. In
Castiglione's *Courtier* musical accomplishments are discussed at
length.[36] At the court of Ferrante of Aragon in Naples, Johannes
Tinctoris of Nivelles who was a learned man and held a law
degree from the University of Louvain, acted not only as royal
choirmaster, but also as a musical teacher of Princess Beatrice
and of various young noblemen to whom he dedicated his treatises.[37] In Vittorino da Feltre's school in Mantua, which was con-
ducted primarily for the Gonzaga princes and their noble
companions, music was one of the required subjects of study.[38]
Also Cardinals and private noblemen kept musicians as players
or teachers in their retinue, and thus we find Nicola Vicentino
in the train of Cardinal Ippolito d'Este,[39] and Pietro Aron in
that of Sebastiano Michiel in Venice.[40] The remaining republics
also played their part in the cultivation and patronage of music.
The Florentine government had its salaried musicians throughout the fifteenth century, and the republic of Lucca organized
its palace choir, after the model of princely courts, during the
sixteenth century.[41] Sometimes the republican governments con-
curred in the maintenance of music at the local churches. The
musicians at St. Mark's in Venice received their appointments,
salaries, and regulations from the civil government,[42] and we
know in the case of John Hothby in Lucca that his salary was
paid in part by the cathedral chapter and in part by the city
authorities.[43] When we reach the later Renaissance, a new kind
of institution begins to take its place in musical activities and

[36] Bianca Becherini, "Il 'Cortegiano' e la musica", *La Bibliofilia*, XLV,
1943, 84–96. I am indebted for this reference to Prof. Leonardo Olschki.

[37] Most of his treatises were published by Coussemaker, *op. cit.*, IV, 1 ff.
The author calls himself regis Siciliae Capellanus. For his connection with
Princess Beatrice, see especially p. 41, 177, 191. See also: K. Weinmann,
Johannes Tinctoris..., Regensburg, 1917. Ch. Van den Borren in *Biographie
Nationale* XXIV, Brussels, 1930–32, coll. 288–316. Lucie Balmer, *Tonsystem
und Kirchentöne bei Johannes Tinctoris*, Bern-Leipzig, 1935.

[38] William H. Woodward, *Vittorino da Feltre and other Humanist Educators*, Cambridge, 1897, 43; Id., *Studies in Education during the Age of the
Renaissance*, Cambridge, 1924, 19 f.

[39] Fétis, *op. cit.*, VIII, 338 ff.

[40] *Ibid.*, I, 1 ff. Nothing is known about the background of Antonius de
Leno, author of a treatise on counterpoint in Italian (ed. Coussemaker, III,
307 ff.).

[41] See above, note 12.

[42] Caffi, *op. cit.*

[43] Nerici, *op. cit.*, 92 ff. and 113 f.

instruction: the Academies. Earlier in the sixteenth century, musical performances appear among the miscellaneous activities of these well organized clubs, and toward the end of the century we encounter the first examples of Academies devoted exclusively to music, the forerunners of our modern conservatories and schools of music. One of the theorists of the period, Ercole Bottrigari in Bologna, seems to have founded such an academy in his own home, and the Florentine Camerata has many characteristics of an Academy.[44]

After having discussed the institutional background of early Renaissance music it might be well to examine the influences it received from the two major intellectual currents of the period, that is, humanism and Platonism. Early Italian humanism was in its origin a literary and rhetorical movement. Its major concern was the study and imitation of classical literature, and its major claim was to have revived ancient eloquence and learning after a long period of decay. In the other learned disciplines that had a solid and substantial medieval tradition the influence of humanism was necessarily belated and somewhat external, but often quite significant. The humanist contribution consisted mostly in greater elegance of style, in a new emphasis on ancient source materials, in the claim of a rebirth of the subject after a time of decline, and finally in various attempts to restore certain forms of ancient doctrine or practice. All this had to be done with a certain regard for professional traditions which remained basically medieval, and hence led to different forms of compromise and adjustment. This development which characterizes the history of philosophy, theology, law, medicine, and the other sciences and arts in the Renaissance may also be observed in the field of music and especially of musical theory.[45]

One significant example is the relationship between Johannes Gallicus and Vittorino da Feltre. Johannes Gallicus, a musician from Namur who later entered the Carmelite order and spent most of his life in Italy, composed an important treatise on music in which he emphasizes twice that he had attended the school of Vittorino da Feltre in Mantua and owed to him his right

[44] Count Pietro de' Bardi, in his letter to G. B. Doni (1634), says of his father: "Formava quasi una dilettevole e continua accademia" (A. Solerti, *Le origini del Melodramma*, Turin, 1903, 143 f.).

[45] The statements of Renaissance musical theorists on ancient music have been studied in an interesting article by D. P. Walker, "Musical Humanism in the 16th and early 17th centuries", *The Music Review* II, 1941, and III, 1942.

understanding of Boethius and of musical theory.[46] Literary
students of Vittorino who was one of the most influential educators of the early Italian Renaissance know that he was interested in music and gave a certain place to it in his scheme of
education, but they ignore the fact that he had a pupil who
became a professional musician and who attributed part of his
musical learning to Vittorino's interpretation of Boethius.[47] On
the other hand, musical historians who mention the fact of
Johannes Gallicus' training do not seem to realize the central
position which Vittorino and his school occupied in the humanistic movement. Certainly the rich content of Gallicus' treatise
cannot be credited to Vittorino, but he probably owed to him
not only his Latin style, but also the enthusiasm with which he
emphasized the study of Boethius, the classical theorist of music.
Curiously enough, this Belgian musician reciprocated the influence which he had received from Italian humanism. We learn
from the colophon of the manuscript copy of Gallicus' treatise
that he was the teacher of Nicolaus Burcius of Parma who is
known as an author of several Latin poems and also of a treatise
on music in which he defends the old doctrines of Boethius and
of Guido of Arezzo against the innovations of the Spaniard
Ramis de Pareja. Burcius, who lived for many years in Bologna
as a student of canon law and as a courtier of the Bentivoglio,
was a priest and later became choirmaster at a church in Parma.
Musical historians who know his connection with Gallicus and
his treatise against Ramis are not interested in his literary activities as a humanist whereas students of literature who know his
biography and his various works are unaware of the fact that he
was in music a pupil of Gallicus and thus indirectly of Vittorino
da Feltre.[48]

A similar combination of Burgundian traditions of music and
of Italian literary influences is apparent in the career of Francesco Gafori who was not merely the only Italian professor of

[46] Coussemaker IV, 299, and 345.

[47] Woodward, *op. cit.* The long list of Vittorino's pupils given by C. de'
Rosmini (*Idea dell'ottimo precettore nella vita e disciplina di Vittorino da
Feltre e de' suoi discrepoli*, Bassano, 1801, 249 ff.) does not include Johannes
Gallicus.

[48] For the life and writings of Burcius, see G. M. Mazzuchelli, *Gli Scrittori
d'Italia*, II, pt. IV, Brescia, 1763, col. 2449. I. Affò, *Memorie degli Scrittori e
Letterati Parmigiani*, III, Parma, 1791, 151 ff. A. Pezzana, *Continuazione delle
Memorie degli Scrittori Parmigiani*, VI, pt. II, Parma, 1827, 403 ff. For his
connection with Johannes Gallicus, see Coussemaker, IV, 421.

music, but also one of the outstanding representatives of musical humanism. We know that he was a pupil of the Flemish Carmelite Johannes Bonadies or Godendach, and he may also have been influenced by Tinctoris with whom he came into contact during his stay in Naples.[49] Very little is known about the life of Godendach except that he copied a number of musical treatises composed by Italians or by foreigners living in Italy.[50] He thus must have transmitted to Gafori a good deal of musical theory, and a detailed comparison between the works of Gafori and the treatises copied by Godendach may lead to some further conclusions. Whether Gafori owed his humanistic inclinations to Godendach we do not know; nor do we know who were his teachers in the humanistic fields. Yet the fact that Gafori had much in common with the attitudes of contemporary humanists has been noticed by many scholars and is confirmed by his writings. He is proud of his elegant Latin, criticizes the style of his "illiterate" opponents, Ramis and Spataro, and apologizes for writing one of his treatises in the vernacular for the instruction of uneducated readers. He claims to raise music to its ancient dignity. He had several ancient Greek treatises on music translated into Latin, and one of these translations, made for Gafori by Johannes Baptista Burana of Verona, survives in a manuscript

---

[49] For Gafori, see notes 25 and 28. See also: G. S. Mayr, *Biografie di scrittori e artisti musicali Bergamaschi* (ed. A. Alessandri), Bergamo, 1875, 59–85. E. Praetorius, *Die Mensuraltheorie des Franchinus Gafurius und der folgenden Zeit bis zur Mitte des 16. Jahrhunderts* (Publikationen der Internationalen Musikgesellschaft, Beihefte, Zweite Folge, II), Leipzig, 1905. P. Hirsch, "Bibliographie der musiktheoretischen Drucke des Franchino Gafori", *Festschrift fuer Johannes Wolf*, Berlin, 1929, 65–72. K. Jeppesen, "Die drei Gafurius-Kodizes der Fabbrica del Duomo, Milano", *Acta Musicologica* III, 1931, 14–28. *Franchino Gaffurio*, Lodi, 1951.

[50] Bonadies copied: Philippi de Caserta tractatus de diversis figuris (Reggio, 1474, Coussemaker, III, 124); Johannis Hothby de cantu figurato (Reggio, 1474, *ibid.*, 332); Johannis Ciconia de proportionibus (Mantua, 1473, G. Gaspari, *Catalogo*, p. 348); Jacobi de Regio de proportionibus (Reggio, 1474, *ibid.*, 227). The ms. of Bonadies, cod. 117 of the Biblioteca Comunale of Faenza, has been described by G. Roncaglia, "Intorno ad un codice di Johannes Bonadies", *Reale Accademia di Scienze, Lettere ed Arti, Modena, Atti e Memorie*, Ser. V, vol. IV, 1939, 31–43. In listing the treatises contained in the manuscript, Roncaglia omits Philip of Caserta, but adds several pieces by Jo. de Muris, Hothby, Nicasius Weyts, Pater Bartholomaeus, Guilelmus monachus and by anonymous authors. See also Ch. Van den Borren, "Le Codex de Johannes Bonadies...", *Revue Belge d'Archéologie et d'Historie de l'Art* X, 1940, 251–61, who rightly notes that the name Godendach goes back to Malegulus (see above, note 28).

of Lodi.[51] This humanist tendency of Gafori is of some importance since he was a great authority during the sixteenth century, and since he was in no way isolated in this respect. The claim that music was being restored to its ancient dignity, so commonly repeated during the sixteenth century down to the Camerata Fiorentina, can be traced back to the fifteenth century.[52] Nicola Vicentino's attempt to revive the enharmonic and chromatic genera of ancient music was inspired by the same humanistic slogan, as the very title of his treatise indicates.[53] Also the musical reform propagated by Vincenzo Galilei and the other members of the Florentine Camerata was first presented as a revival of ancient music, although eventually it developed into something quite different.[54]

The influence of the other great movement of the early Renaissance, Platonism, on the history of music is even less known than that of humanism. Among the historians of music, Ambros alone stresses the fact that the theorists of the Camerata quote Plato as an authority and were to some extent influenced by his doctrine.[55] This fact has remained unknown to historians of philosophy and science although it is of some significance for their studies. For it shows that as late as the end of the sixteenth cen-

[51] The authors translated for Gafori were Manuel Bryennios, Bakchios, Aristides Quintilianos, and Ptolemy (see the facsimile given by Cesari in F. Malaguzzi Valeri, *op. cit.*, 217). The manuscript version of Manuel Bryennios made by Burana for Gafori is mentioned by Mayr (*op. cit.*, 76). It is dated 1497. See the ms. XXVIII A 8 of the Biblioteca Communale in Lodi, cf. *Franchino Gaffurio*, Lodi, 1951, pp. 101 f. and 171.

[52] The history of this concept will be treated by Prof. Leo Schrade in a forthcoming article. See now L. Schrade, *Monteverdi: Creator of Modern Music*, New York, 1950, ch. 1, p. 17 ff., esp. p. 36 ff., where the concept of the renaissance of music in Vincenzo Galilei is discussed. Some material is given for the sixteenth century by F. Fano (*La Camerata Fiorentina: Vicenzo Galilei*, ed. F. Fano, in *Istituzioni e Monumenti dell'Arte Musicale Italiana*, IV, Milan, 1934, p. XVI ff. Yet Ficino as early as 1492 includes music among the arts and sciences that had been revived in his time (*Opera*, Basileae, 1576, I, 944: letter to Paul of Middleburg).

[53] *L'antica musica ridotta alla moderna pratica*, Rome, 1555. See Fétis, *op. cit.*, VIII, 338 ff.

[54] Fano, *op. cit.* I am indebted for this reference to Prof. Leo Schrade. An inedited treatise *De musica et poetica* by the humanist, Raphael Brandolinus, is discussed by De La Fage, *op. cit.*, 61 ff. The ms. is not in Padua, as he asserts, but it is cod. 805 of the Biblioteca Casanatense in Rome.

[55] *Geschichte...* IV, 2nd ed., Leipzig, 1881, 156 ff. It should be noted, however, that Vincenzo Galilei in his *Dialogo della musica antica et moderna* (ed. F. Fano, Rome, 1934) also quotes Aristotle quite frequently. For the other documents concerning the Camerata and the early opera, see Solerti, *op. cit.*

tury Platonism was in Florence still of sufficient strength to exercise an influence upon such a comparatively remote field as music.
On the other hand, the fact that Vincenzo Galilei was affected by
this current adds a new element to the disputed question whether
Platonism was a major influence upon the thought of his great
son, Galileo Galilei.

Musical historians seem to be entirely unaware of the fact that
music played a major role in the life and thought of Marsilio
Ficino, founder and leader of the Florentine Academy, with
whom the tradition of Florentine Platonism began over a hundred years before Vincenzo Galilei.[56] We know from Ficino's
letters and from contemporary testimonies that he played the
lyre not only for his own relaxation, but also performed music at
his home and in the palaces of the Medici before an admiring
audience.[57] He even liked to be compared to the ancient mythical
singer Orpheus whose supposed hymns and poems he eagerly
studied and translated.[58] His interest extended also to musical
theory, and his letters and other writings contain a number of
interesting remarks on the subject, which are closely connected
with his philosophical opinions and those of his favorite ancient
authors. In a letter to Franciscus Musanus, Ficino justifies his
combination of medicine, music, and theology with the statement
that music is as important for the intermediary "spirit" as medicine is for the body, and theology for the soul.[59] In his treatise on
divine madness, he states that the human soul acquires through
the ears a memory of that divine music which is found first in the
eternal mind of God, and second in the order and movements of

[56] The only exception is a forthcoming article by Prof. E. Lowinsky, "The
Concept of Physical and Musical Space in the Renaissance". See now *Papers of
the American Musicological Society*, Annual Meeting 1941, published 1946, pp.
57–84, esp. pp. 78–80. See also the article by Kinkeldey, cited below, note 71.
Reese, *Music in the Renaissance*, 182. D. P. Walker, "Ficino's 'Spiritus' and
Music", *Annales Musicologiques* I 1935, 131–50. Id., "Orpheus the Theologian
and Renaissance Platonists", *Journal of the Warburg and Courtauld Institutes*
XVI 1953, 100–120. Much material on the rôle of music in Ficino's life and
circle was collected by A. Della Torre, *Storia dell'Accademia Platonica di
Firenze*, Florence, 1902, 788 f. I have briefly discussed Ficino's theory of music
(*The Philosophy of Marsilio Ficino*, New York, 1943, 307 f. *Il pensiero filosofico
di Marsilio Ficino*, Florence, 1953, p. 331 ff.).

[57] *Opera, loc. cit.*, 608, 609, 651, 725, 788, 822 f. *Supplementum, Ficinianum*,
Florence, 1937, II, 87 f., 89, 230, 262 f. See also Lorenzo de' Medici's poem
I'Altercazione, ed. A. Simioni, II, Bari, 1914, 41.

[58] Della Torre, *op. cit.*, 789 ff. See also Kristeller, *Studies*, p. 52 f. and 96 f.

[59] *Opera, loc. cit.*, 609.

the heavens. There is also a twofold imitation of that divine music among men, a lower one through voices and instruments, and a higher one through verse and metre. The former kind is called vulgar music, whereas the latter is called by Plato serious music and poetry.[60] In another letter to Antonio Canigiani, Ficino again compares music with medicine. The sound of voices and instruments affects the listener's spirit and, through the latter, his body and soul. For Ficino himself, music is a means for expelling the disturbances of body and soul, and for lifting his mind toward God and things intelligible.[61] In his commentary on Plato's *Symposium*, Ficino distinguishes a threefold beauty and proportion which consists, respectively, in thoughts, shapes, and sounds.[62] In the twelfth book of his chief philosophical work, the *Platonic Theology*, he discusses the relation between the senses, phantasy, reason and God in terms of hearing and of rhythmical proportions, following almost verbatim the sixth book of Augustine's *De Musica*.[63] A more extensive treatment of music is found in a short treatise *De Rationibus Musicae* which I published from the only surviving manuscript and which has not yet attracted the attention of musical historians.[64] The treatise was composed about 1484 and originally destined for the collection of Ficino's letters. Quoting Plato, Trismegistus, and Pythagoras, Ficino distinguishes between music of the soul and that of the ears. He then discusses the proportions underlying the musical intervals. He recognizes not only the soft harmony of the third, but also compares the third, fifth, and octave to the three Graces.[65] Discussing once more the eight tones of the scale, Ficino compares their sequence to an oval figure, and the chord of the first tone and the octave to a pyramid. He then examines the common causes of consonance and concludes that the degrees of consonance and dissonance are determined by the extent to which the corresponding proportions approach unity or plurality, respectively. As physi-

[60] *Ibid.*, 614.
[61] *Ibid.*, 650 f. See also p. 502.
[62] *Ibid.*, 1322 f. See also pp. 631 f.
[63] *Ibid.*, 278 ff. Cf. *De Musica* VI, 2; 7–10; 12.
[64] *Supplementum Ficinianum* I, 51–56. A manuscript copy of this treatise was in Pico's library (P. Kibre, *The Library of Pico della Mirandola*, New York, 1936, p. 215, no. 706). See now the article of Lowinsky, cited above, note 56. A tract *De laudibus. musicae* found in the Turin ms. Pas. lat. 603 among the letters of Ficino is of uncertain authenticity.
[65] "vocis tertie lenis... harmonia...". "Precipue vero tertia, quinta, octava ceteris gratiores tris nobis Gratias referunt" (*op. cit.*, 51).

cal causes of consonance Ficino considers the proportions between the four elements which supposedly correspond to the proportions determining the consonant intervals. Finally, in discussing the astronomical or astrological causes of consonance, Ficino not only refers to the Pythagorean harmony of the spheres, but also relates the signs of the zodiac to the tones of the scale and compares the favorable and harmful "aspects" of the twelve signs to the consonant and dissonant intervals. Another lengthy discussion of music is found in Ficino's commentary on Plato's Timaeus.[66] Trying to explain the use Plato makes of musical proportions in the composition of the soul, Ficino emphasizes the effect of music upon the soul of the listener. He then discusses the various sounds and intervals, the ancient instrument[67] of the tetrachord, and the correspondence between mathematical proportions and musical consonance. Comparing the mixture of sounds to the mixture of drugs made by the physician, he emphasizes that the combination of several sounds produced at the same time results in some new characteristic phenomenon which is perceived as consonance when the two composing sounds attain a kind of union.[68] This composed sound is compared to a mixed flavor. Ficino adds that according to the physicists a sound reaches our ears through circles in the air that are comparable to the circles produced by a stone thrown into water. Consonance between a low and a high sound is compared to an oval figure, and this is used to explain the oval shape of our ear, tongue and many musical instruments.[69] Discussing the proportions that correspond to the musical intervals, Ficino admits that the fourth is in itself dissonant,[70] and finally compares the tones of the scale to the planets.

Ficino never quotes any recent authors on music, but his treatment of the third and fourth certainly shows that he did not merely repeat ancient theories but was familiar with contemporary taste and theory. On the other hand, his complete neglect

[66] *Opera, loc. cit.*, 1453 ff.

[67] It should be: concept of the tetrachord, as I am informed by Mr. D. P. Walker.

[68] "...ex acuta gravique voce tertiam fieri communemque vocalem formam... voces plures rite commixtae unum quendam invicem resonant reboatum virtutis novae atque mirabilis fundamentum... Reliquum est ut sola (sc. unio) placeat quae nova et efficax ex moderata quadam conflatione resultat. Hinc igitur consonantia definitur soni gravis et acuti mixtura uniformiter ad aures suaviterque accedens" (*ibid.*, 1455 f.).

[69] *Ibid.*, 1456.

[70] *Ibid.*, 1457 ("diatessaron... per se quidem auditam non approbari").

of polyphony and his emphasis on harmony as produced by simultaneous chords might have had some influence on the theories of the Camerata. Otherwise, his remarks are not so much a contribution to musical theory as an attempt to relate music to his favorite conceptions in metaphysics, medicine, and astrology. Whether Ficino's doctrines had any tangible influence on contemporary or successive theory and practice would have to be established by further investigations.[71] In any case, Ficino as a player was highly praised by members of his circle, and he counted several musicians among his most intimate friends and pupils.

I should like to conclude this paper with a few suggestions concerning the relations of music with poetry and with rhetoric. The link between musical composition and vernacular poetry, which was a heritage of the troubadour period and had been continued in the Ars Nova of the fourteenth century, had its counterpart in the Strambotti of the late fifteenth century, and again in the madrigals of the sixteenth century. Whereas the extant musical compositions have been widely studied it seems to be less well known that there are several printed and manuscript collections of Strambotti which show no trace of musical notation, but apparently were composed for a recital with musical accompaniment.[72] Moreover, we hear of the Improvvisatori who were highly esteemed at the Italian courts of the late fifteenth and early sixteenth century, and who in part achieved real literary fame.[73] When they recited their own verses they may have improvised the poem together with the music. Yet often they also recited verses composed by others, and in such cases they probably improvised the music.[74] This would explain why the text of many Strambotti has been transmitted without any music, and why some of them seem to be older than most of those that have been preserved with their music.[75]

[71] The influence of Ficino on Gafori has recently been established by O. Kinkeldey, "Franchino Gafori and Marsilio Ficino", *Harvard Library Bulletin* I, 1947, 379–82. Gafori owned and annotated a copy of Ficino's translation of Plato, now at the Harvard Library, and he also quoted Ficino in one of his works.

[72] A good example is the cod. Urbinas lat. 729, possibly written for the Duchess Elisabetta Gonzaga.

[73] Cf. Della Torre, *op. cit.*, 796 ff.

[74] This is what Baccio Ugolini seems to have done when he played the role of Poliziano's Orfeo in Mantua.

[75] The poetry of the earlier fifteenth century has been discussed, without any reference to music, by F. Flamini, *La Lirica Toscana del Rinascimento anteriore ai tempi del Magnifico*, Pisa, 1891.

As to the Latin poetry of the humanists, their connection with music is less certain. On the other hand, we know in the case of Ficino that he used to improvise a musical setting for the Latin verses sent to him by his humanist friends.[76] More light on this subject might be expected if musical scholars would examine some of the numerous printed and manuscript collections of Latin poetry that date from the fifteenth and sixteenth centuries. Such a study may also yield new information on musical history in another respect, since some of these collections include epigrams dealing with music and musicians. The collection of epitaphs for Antonio Squarcialupi that was attached to the famous codex in the time of Lorenzo de' Medici is certainly not the only example of this kind.[77]

Whereas music and poetry often appeared in close alliance, the relation between music and oratory seems to have been rather that of rivals. In Italy the use of oratory at weddings, funerals, and all kinds of public celebrations can be traced back at least to the thirteenth century. It had originally a legal significance, but under the influence of humanism it developed more and more into a form of public entertainment that seems to have reached its climax in the fifteenth century. Now the use of music at celebrations of the very same character is attested at least since the fourteenth century, although it may have been limited to a few trumpet sounds that marked the beginning of the festival. However, as early as the beginning of the fifteenth century we encounter substantial musical compositions such as masses or motets written for public celebrations, especially in Venice and her subject cities.[78] During the sixteenth century when court celebrations became more elaborate and their descriptions in literature more frequent, stage plays, eclogues, masques, and similar poems were the center of the celebration and of public attention, and most of these performances were accompanied by music. A study of the specific types of occasions for which orations or musical poetry or both were composed in the various periods and places might be of some interest for the student of Renaissance civilization. Apparently, when the legal significance of oratory had faded into the background, and when it was considered merely as a piece of

[76] *Opera, loc. cit.,* 651 and 673.

[77] These epitaphs have been published by J. Wolf, *Geschichte der Mensural-Notation von 1250–1460,* I, Leipzig, 1904, 229 ff. They are also found in the Cod. Vaticanus lat. 7192.

[78] Ambros, *op. cit.,* III (2nd ed.), 1881, 509 ff.

entertainment, poetry and music became its successful rivals and finally replaced it entirely during the sixteenth century. Such a change of taste has again occurred in recent years, and nowadays at public celebrations musical performances are better liked by most people than ceremonious oratory. This change seems to reflect a transformation that is taking place in the habits and ideas of a society or culture. Bored and dissatisfied with the traditional formulas that no longer evoke strong convictions, and unable to produce new ideas that have a common appeal, people are more at ease in the neutral atmosphere of play and of music where the underlying ideas are disguised in an imaginative language that need not be translated into the prose of reason and of every day life.

The history of music, like every branch of intellectual history, is confronted with two different tasks: it has to trace the development of music as an autonomous process, based on professional and technical traditions and changes that have no counterpart in any other field of civilization; and it also has to consider the place which music occupies at any given time within the general framework of culture, its relations to other arts and sciences, the influences it receives from them or exercises upon them. The relative importance of either task may vary according to the period under consideration; and on the whole, the former task may be the more important one for the musical historian who certainly is alone equipped to accomplish it. The second task, however, is not without its value, and it is here that a non-specialist may hope to be able to contribute to musical history and that the collaboration between the history of music and the histories of literature and of thought may be expected to bear some fruit.

IX

The Modern System of the Arts*

Dedicated to Professor Hans Tietze on his 70th birthday

I

THE FUNDAMENTAL IMPORTANCE of the eighteenth century in the history of aesthetics and of art criticism is generally recognized. To be sure, there has been a great variety of theories and currents within the last two hundred years that cannot be easily brought under one common demnominator. Yet all the changes and controversies of the more recent past presuppose certain fundamental notions which go back to that classical century of modern aesthetics. It is known that the very term "Aesthetics" was coined at that time, and, at least in the opinion of some historians, the subject matter itself, the "philosophy of art," was invented in that comparatively recent period and can be applied to earlier phases of Western thought only with reservations.[1] It is also generally

* Reprinted by permission from the *Journal of the History of Ideas*, Vol. XII (1951), No. 4, 496–527 and Vol. XIII (1952) No. 1, 17–46. Also published in *Ideas in Cultural Perspective*, ed. Philip P. Wiener and A. Noland (New Brunswick, Rutgers University Press, 1962), 145–206. I am indebted for several suggestions and references to Professors Julius S. Held, Rensselaer Lee, Philip Merlan, Ernest Moody, Erwin Panofsky, Meyer Schapiro, and Norman Torrey.

[1] B. Croce, *Estetica come scienza dell'espressione e linguistica generale: Teoria e storia*, 5th ed. (Bari, 1922; first ed., 1901); *Problemi di estetica*, 2nd ed. (Bari, 1923); *Storia dell'estetica per saggi* (Bari, 1942). Katharine E. Gilbert and Helmut Kuhn, *A History of Esthetics* (New York, 1939). See also: J. Koller, *Entwurf zur Geschichte und Literatur der Aesthetik von Baumgarten bis auf die neueste Zeit* (Regensburg, 1799). R. Zimmermann, *Aesthetik*, pt. I: *Geschichte der Aesthetik als philosophischer Wissenschaft* (Vienna, 1858). M. Schasler, *Kritische Geschichte der Aesthetik* (Berlin, 1872). K. Heinrich von Stein, Die *Entstehung der neueren Aesthetik* (Stuttgart, 1886). William

agreed that such dominating concepts of modern aesthetics as taste and sentiment, genius, originality and creative imagination did not assume their definite modern meaning before the eighteenth century. Some scholars have rightly noticed that only the eighteenth century produced a type of literature in which the various arts were compared with each other and discussed on the basis of common principles, whereas up to that period treatises on poetics and rhetoric, on painting and architecture, and on music had represented quite distinct branches of writing and were primarily concerned with technical precepts rather than with general ideas.[2] Finally, at least a few scholars have noticed that the term "Art," with a capital A and in its modern sense, and the related term "Fine Arts" (Beaux Arts) originated in all probability in the eighteenth century.[3]

In this paper, I shall take all these facts for granted, and shall concentrate instead on a much simpler and in a sense more fundamental point that is closely related to the problems so far mentioned, but does not seem to have received sufficient attention in its own right. Although the terms "Art," "Fine Arts" or "Beaux Arts" are often identified with the visual arts alone, they are also quite commonly understood in a broader sense. In this broader meaning, the term "Art" comprises above all the five major arts

Knight, *The Philosophy of the Beautiful*, vol. I (*Being Outlines of the History of Aesthetics*) (London, 1891). B. Bosanquet, *A History of Aesthetic*, 3rd ed. (London, 1910). Max Dessoir, *Aesthetik und allgemeine Kunstwissenschaft* (Stuttgart, 1906). Ernst Bergmann, *Geschichte der Aesthetik und Kunstphilosophie: Ein Forschungsbericht* (Leipzig, 1914). Frank P. Chambers, *Cycles of Taste* (Cambridge, Mass., 1928); *The History of Taste* (New York, 1932). A Baeumler, *Aesthetik (Handbuch der Philosophie*, I, C, Munich-Berlin, 1934). For poetry and literature: G. Saintsbury, *A History of Criticism and Literary Taste in Europe*, 3 vols. (Edinburgh, 1900–04; extremely weak on the theoretical side). For music: H. Sahlender, *Die Bewertung der Musik im System der Kuenste: Eine historisch-systematische Untersuchung* (thes. Jena, 1929). For the visual arts: A. Dresdner, *Die Kunstkritik: Ihre Geschichte und Theorie*, vol. I (Munich, 1915). Julius Schlosser, *Die Kunstliteratur* (Vienna, 1924). Lionello Venturi, *History of Art Criticism* (New York, 1936); *Storia della critica d'arte* (Rome, 1945). R. Wittkower, "The Artist and the Liberal Arts," *Eidos* I (1950), 11–17. More special studies will be quoted in the course of this paper.

[2] M. Menendez y Pelayo, *Historia de las Ideas estéticas en España* III (Buenos Aires, 1943). E. Cassirer, *Die Philosophie der Aufklärung* (Tübingen, 1932), 368 ff. T. M. Mustoxidi, *Histoire de l'Esthétique française* (Paris, 1920).

[3] L. Venturi, "Per il nome di 'Arte,'" *La Cultura*, N.S. I (1929), 385–88. R. G. Collingwood, *The Principles of Art* (Oxford, 1938), 5–7. See also the books of Parker and McMahon, cited below.

of painting, sculpture, architecture, music and poetry. These five constitute the irreducible nucleus of the modern system of the arts, on which all writers and thinkers seem to agree.[4] On the other hand, certain other arts are sometimes added to the scheme, but with less regularity, depending on the different views and interests of the authors concerned: gardening, engraving and the decorative arts, the dance and the theatre, sometimes the opera, and finally eloquence and prose literature.[5]

The basic notion that the five "major arts" constitute an area all by themselves, clearly separated by common characteristics from the crafts, the sciences and other human activities, has been taken for granted by most writers on aesthetics from Kant to the present day. It is freely employed even by those critics of art and literature who profess not to believe in "aesthetics"; and it is accepted as a matter of course by the general public of amateurs who assign to "Art" with a capital A that ever narrowing area of modern life which is not occupied by science, religion, or practical pursuits.

It is my purpose here to show that this system of the five major arts, which underlies all modern aesthetics and is so familiar to us all, is of comparatively recent origin and did not assume definite shape before the eighteenth century, although it has many ingredients which go back to classical, medieval and Renaissance thought. I shall not try to discuss any metaphysical theories of beauty or any particular theories concerning one or more of the arts, let alone their actual history, but only the systematic grouping together of the five major arts. This question does not directly concern any specific changes or achievements in the various arts, but primarily their relations to each other and their place in the general framework of Western culture. Since the subject has been overlooked by most historians of aesthetics and of literary, musical or artistic theories,[6] it is hoped that a brief and quite tentative study may throw light on some of the problems with which modern aesthetics and its historiography have been concerned.

[4] Theodore M. Greene, *The Arts and the Art of Criticism* (Princeton, 1940), 35 ff. P. Frankl, *Das System der Kunstwissenschaft* (Brünn-Leipzig, 1938), 501 ff.

[5] See the works of Zimmermann and Schasler, cited above, note 1.

[6] I have come across only two authors who saw the problem quite clearly: H. Parker, *The Nature of the Fine Arts* (London, 1885), esp. 1-30. A. Philip McMahon, *Preface to an American Philosophy of Art* (Chicago, 1945). The latter study is better documented but marred by polemical intentions. I hope to add to their material and conclusions.

II

The Greek term for Art (τέχνη) and its Latin equivalent (ars) do not specifically denote the "fine arts" in the modern sense, but were applied to all kinds of human activities which we would call crafts or sciences. Moreover, whereas modern aesthetics stresses the fact that Art cannot be learned, and thus often becomes involved in the curious endeavor to teach the unteachable, the ancients always understood by Art something that can be taught and learned. Ancient statements about Art and the arts have often been read and understood as if they were meant in the modern sense of the fine arts. This may in some cases have led to fruitful errors, but it does not do justice to the original intention of the ancient writers. When the Greek authors began to oppose Art to Nature, they thought of human activity in general. When Hippocrates contrasts Art with Life, he is thinking of medicine, and when his comparison is repeated by Goethe or Schiller with reference to poetry, this merely shows the long way of change which the term Art had traversed by 1800 from its original meaning.[7] Plato puts art above mere routine because it proceeds by rational principles and rules,[8] and Aristotle, who lists Art among the so-called intellectual virtues, characterizes it as a kind of activity based on knowledge, in a definition whose influence was felt through many centuries.[9] The Stoics also defined Art as a system of cognitions,[10] and it was in this sense that they considered moral virtue as an art of living.[11]

The other central concept of modern aesthetics also, beauty, does not appear in ancient thought or literature with its specific modern connotations. The Greek term καλόν and its Latin equivalent (pulchrum) were never neatly or consistently distinguished from the moral good.[12] When Plato discusses beauty in the Sym-

[7] ὁ βίος βραχύς, ἡ δὲ τέχνη μακρή. Hippocrates, Aphorisms, 1. Seneca, De brevitate vitae, 1. Schiller, Wallensteins Lager, Prolog, 138. Goethe, Faust I, Studierzimmer 2, 1787.

[8] Gorgias, 462 b ff.

[9] Nicomachean Ethics, VI 4, 1140 a 10.

[10] Stoicorum Veterum Fragmenta, ed. H. von Arnim, I, p. 21; II, p. 23 and 30; III, p. 51.

[11] Ibid., III, pp. 49 and 148 f.

[12] R. G. Collingwood, "Plato's Philosophy of Art," Mind, N.S. 34 (1925), 154-72, esp. 161 f.

posium and the *Phaedrus,* he is speaking not merely of the physical beauty of human persons, but also of beautiful habits of the
soul and of beautiful cognitions, whereas he fails completely to
mention works of art in this connection.[13] An incidental remark
made in the *Phaedrus*[14] and elaborated by Proclus[15] was certainly
not meant to express the modern triad of Truth, Goodness and
Beauty. When the Stoics in one of their famous statements connected Beauty and Goodness,[16] the context as well as Cicero's
Latin rendering[17] suggest that they meant by "Beauty" nothing
but moral goodness, and in turn understood by "good" nothing
but the useful. Only in later thinkers does the speculation about
"beauty" assume an increasingly "aesthetic" significance, but
without ever leading to a separate system of aesthetics in the
modern sense. Panaetius identifies moral beauty with decorum,[18]
a term he borrows from Aristotle's *Rhetoric*,[19] and consequently
likes to compare the various arts with each other and with the
moral life. His doctrine is known chiefly through Cicero, but it
may also have influenced Horace. Plotinus in his famous treatises
on beauty is concerned primarily with metaphysical and ethical
problems, but he does include in his treatment of sensuous beauty
the visible beauty of works of sculpture and architecture, and the
audible beauty of music.[20] Likewise, in the speculations on beauty
scattered through the works of Augustine there are references to
the various arts, yet the doctrine was not primarily designed for

[13] *Symposium*, 210 a ff. *Phaedrus*, 249 d.

[14] τὸ δὲ θεῖον καλόν, σοφόν, ἀγαθόν, καὶ πᾶν ὅτι τοιοῦτον. 246 d–e.

[15] *Commentary on Plato's Alcibiades* I (ed. Cousin, 356–57). I am indebted
for this reference to Dr. Laurence Rosán. The καλόν does not denote aesthetic
beauty in this passage any more than in Plato, and to interpret the σοφόν as
Truth seems arbitrary. Yet the passage may have influenced its editor, Cousin.

[16] *Stoicorum Veterum Fragmenta* III, p. 9 ff. (μόνον τὸ καλὸν ἀγαθόν).

[17] *Ibid.*, III, p. 10 f., and I, pp. 47 and 84. Cicero, *De finibus* III, 26 (quod
honestum sit id solum bonum).

[18] Cicero, *De officiis* I 27, 93 ff. R. Philippson, "Das Sittlichschoene bei
Panaitios," *Philologus* 85 (N.F. 39, 1930), 357–413. Lotte Labowsky, *Die Ethik
des Panaitios* (Leipzig, 1934).

[19] III 7, 1408 a 10 ff.

[20] *Enn.* V 8, 1. I 6, 1–3. See also I 3, 1. There is no evidence that Plotinus
intended to apply his remarks on music to all the other fine arts, as E.
Krakowski believes (*Une philosophie de l'amour et de la beauté: L'esthétique
de Plotin et son influence* [Paris, 1929], 112 ff.). The triad of Goodness, Truth
and Beauty is made a basis of his interpretation by Dean William R. Inge
(*The Philosophy of Plotinus* II [London, 1918], 74 ff. and 104) but does not
occur in the works of Plotinus.

an interpretation of the "fine arts."[21] Whether we can speak of aesthetics in the case of Plato, Plotinus or Augustine will depend on our definition of that term, but we should certainly realize that in the theory of beauty a consideration of the arts is quite absent in Plato and secondary in Plotinus and Augustine.

Let us now turn to the individual arts and to the manner in which they were evaluated and grouped by the ancients. Poetry was always most highly respected, and the notion that the poet is inspired by the Muses goes back to Homer and Hesiod. The Latin term (*vates*) also suggests an old link between poetry and religious prophecy, and Plato is hence drawing upon an early notion when in the *Phaedrus* he considers poetry one of the forms of divine madness.[22] However, we should also remember that the same conception of poetry is expressed with a certain irony in the *Ion*[23] and the *Apology*,[24] and that even in the *Phaedrus* the divine madness of the poet is compared with that of the lover and of the religious prophet.[25] There is no mention of the "fine arts" in this passage, and it was left to the late sophist Callistratus[26] to transfer Plato's concept of inspiration to the art of sculpture.

Among all the "fine arts" it was certainly poetry about which Plato had most to say, especially in the *Republic,* but the treatment given to it is neither systematic nor friendly, but suspiciously similar to the one he gives to rhetoric in some of his other writings. Aristotle, on the other hand, dedicated a whole treatise to the theory of poetry and deals with it in a thoroughly systematic and constructive fashion. The *Poetics* not only contains a great number of specific ideas which exercised a lasting influence upon later criticism; it also established a permanent place for the theory of poetry in the philosophical encyclopaedia of knowledge. The mutual influence of poetry and eloquence had been a permanent feature of ancient literature ever since the time of the Sophists, and the close relationship between these two branches of literature received a theoretical foundation through the proximity of the *Rhetoric* and the *Poetics* in the corpus of Aristotle's works. Moreover, since the order of the writings in the Aris-

---

[21] K. Svoboda, *L'esthétique de Saint Augustin et ses sources* (Brno, 1933). E. Chapman, *Saint Augustine's Philosophy of Beauty* (New York, 1939). E. Gilson, *Introduction à l'étude de Saint Augustin,* 3rd ed. (Paris, 1949), 279 f.

[22] 245 a.

[23] 533 e ff.

[24] 22 a ff.

[25] 244 a ff.

[26] *Descriptiones,* 2.

totelian Corpus was interpreted as early as the commentators of late antiquity as a scheme of classification for the philosophical disciplines, the place of the *Rhetoric* and the *Poetics* after the logical writings of the *Organon* established a link between logic, rhetoric and poetics that was emphasized by some of the Arabic commentators, the effects of which were felt down to the Renaissance.[27]

Music also held a high place in ancient thought; yet it should be remembered that the Greek term μουσική, which is derived from the Muses, originally comprised much more than we understand by music. Musical education, as we can still see in Plato's *Republic,* included not only music, but also poetry and the dance.[28] Plato and Aristotle, who also employ the term music in the more specific sense familiar to us, do not treat music or the dance as separate arts but rather as elements of certain types of poetry, especially of lyric and dramatic poetry.[29] There is reason to believe that they were thus clinging to an older tradition which was actually disappearing in their own time through the emancipation of instrumental music from poetry. On the other hand, the Pythagorean discovery of the numerical proportions underlying the musical intervals led to a theoretical treatment of music on a mathematical basis, and consequently musical theory entered into an alliance with the mathematical sciences which is already apparent in Plato's *Republic,*[30] and was to last far down into early modern times.

When we consider the visual arts of painting, sculpture and architecture, it appears that their social and intellectual prestige in antiquity was much lower than one might expect from their actual achievements or from occasional enthusiastic remarks which date for the most part from the later centuries.[31] It is true

---

[27] L. Baur, "Die philosophische Einleitungslitteratur bis zum Ende der Scholastik," in: Dominicus Gundissalinus, *De divisione philosophiae*, ed. L. Baur (*Beiträge zur Geschichte der Philosophie des Mittelalters*, IV, 2–3, Muenster, 1903), 316 ff. See also J. Mariétan, *Problème de la classification des sciences d'Aristote à St. Thomas* (thes. Fribourg, 1901).

[28] *Republic* II, 376 e ff.

[29] *Poetics* 1, 1447 a 23 ff. *Laws* II, 669 e f.

[30] VII, 531 a ff.

[31] Dresdner, *l.c.,* 19 ff. E. Zilsel, *Die Entstehung des Geniebegriffs* (Tübingen, 1926), 22 ff. B. Schweitzer, "Der bildende Künstler und der Begriff des Künstlerischen in der Antike," *Neue Heidelberger Jahrbücher*, N.F. (1925), 28–132. Hans Jucker, *Vom Verhältnis der Römer zur bildenden Kunst der Griechen* (Frankfurt, 1950). For ancient art theories in general: Eduard Mueller, *Geschichte der Theorie der Kunst bei den Alten*, 2 vols. (Breslau,

that painting was compared to poetry by Simonides[32] and Plato,[33] by Aristotle[34] and Horace,[35] as it was compared to rhetoric by Cicero,[36] Dionysius of Halicarnassus[37] and other writers.[38] It is also true that architecture was included among the liberal arts by Varro[39] and Vitruvius,[40] and painting by Pliny[41] and Galen,[42] that Dio Chrysostom compared the art of the sculptor with that of the poet,[43] and that Philostratus and Callistratus wrote enthusiastically about painting and sculpture.[44] Yet the place of painting among the liberal arts was explicitly denied by Seneca[45] and ignored by most other writers, and the statement of Lucian that everybody admires the works of the great sculptors but would not want to be a sculptor oneself, seems to reflect the prevalent view among writers and thinkers.[46] The term δημιουργός, commonly applied to painters and sculptors, reflects their low social stand-

---

1834–37). Julius Walter, *Die Geschichte der Aesthetik im Altertum* (Leipzig, 1893). For Plato and Aristotle: G. Finsler, *Platon und die Aristotelische Poetik* (Leipzig, 1900). S. H. Butcher, *Aristotle's Theory of Poetry and Fine Art*, 4th ed. (London, 1911). A. Rostagni, "Aristotele e Aristotelismo nella storia dell'estetica antica," *Studi italiani di filologia classica*, N.S. 2 (1922), 1–147. U. Galli, "La mimesi artistica secondo Aristotele," *ibid.*, N.S. 4 (1927), 281–390. E. Cassirer, "Eidos und Eidolon: Das Problem des Schönen und der Kunst in Platons Dialogen," *Vorträge der Bibliothek Warburg*, II: Vorträge 1922–23, I (Leipzig-Berlin, 1924), 1–27. R. G. Collingwood, "Plato's Philosophy of Art," *Mind*, N.S. 34 (1925), 154–72. E. Bignami, *La Poetica di Aristotele e il concetto dell'arte presso gli antichi* (Florence, 1932). P.-M. Schuhl, *Platon et l'art de son temps* (*Arts plastiques*; Paris, 1933). R. McKeon, "Literary Criticism and the Concept of Imitation in Antiquity," *Modern Philology*, 34 (1936–37), 1–35.

[32] Plutarch, *De gloria Atheniensium* 3, 346 F ff.

[33] *Republic* X, 605 a ff.

[34] *Poetics* 1, 1447 a 19 ff.; 2, 1448 a 4 ff.

[35] *De arte poetica* 1 ff.; 361 ff.

[36] *De inventione* II, 1.

[37] *De veteribus scriptoribus* 1.

[38] Quintilian, *Institutio Oratoria* XII, 10, 3 ff.

[39] F. Ritschl, "De M. Terentii Varronis disciplinarum libris commentarius," in his *Kleine philologische Schriften* III (Leipzig, 1877), 352–402.

[40] Cf. *De architectura* I, 1, 3 ff.

[41] *Natural History* XXXV, 76 f.

[42] *Protrepticus* (*Opera*, ed. C. G. Kuehn, I [Leipzig, 1821], 39).

[43] *Oratio* XII. Cf. S. Ferri, "Il discorso di Fidia in Dione Crisostomo," *Annali della R. Scuola Normale Superiore di Pisa, Lettere, Storia e Filosofia*, Ser. II, vol. V (1936), 237–66.

[44] Philostratus, *Imagines*. Callistratus, *Descriptiones*. Ella Birmelin, "Die kunsttheoretischen Gedanken in Philostrats Apollonios," *Philologus* 88, N.F. 42 (1933), 149–80; 392–414.

[45] *Epistolae Morales* 88, 18.

[46] *Somnium* 14. Cf. Plutarch, *Pericles* 1–2.

ing, which was related to the ancient contempt for manual work. When Plato compares the description of his ideal state to a painting[47] and even calls his world-shaping god a demiurge,[48] he no more enhances the importance of the artist than does Aristotle when he uses the statue as the standard example for a product of human art.[49] When Cicero, probably reflecting Panaetius, speaks of the ideal notions in the mind of the sculptor,[50] and when the Middle Platonists and Plotinus compare the ideas in the mind of God with the concepts of the visual artist they go one step further.[51] Yet no ancient philosopher, as far as I know, wrote a separate systematic treatise on the visual arts or assigned to them a prominent place in his scheme of knowledge.[52]

If we want to find in classical philosophy a link between poetry, music and the fine arts, it is provided primarily by the concept of imitation ($\mu\iota\mu\eta\sigma\iota\varsigma$). Passages have been collected from the writings of Plato and Aristotle from which it appears quite clearly that they considered poetry, music, the dance, painting and sculpture as different forms of imitation.[53] This fact is significant so far as it goes, and it has influenced many later authors, even in the eighteenth century.[54] But aside from the fact that none of the passages has a systematic character or even enumerates all of the "fine arts" together, it should be noted that the scheme excludes

[47] *Republic* V, 472 d. Cf. VI, 501 a ff.

[48] *Timaeus* 29 a.

[49] *Physics* II 3, 194 b 24 f. and 195 a 5 f. *Metaphysics* IV 2, 1013 a 25 f. and b 6 f.

[50] *Orator* 8 f.

[51] W. Theiler, *Die Vorbereitung des Neuplatonismus* (Berlin, 1930), 1 ff. Birmelin, *l.c.*, p. 402 ff. Plotinus, *Enn.* I 6, 3; V 8, 1. E. Panofsky, *Idea* (Leipzig-Berlin, 1924). The ancient comparison of God with the craftsman was reversed by the modern aestheticians who compared the "creative" artist with God. Cf. Milton C. Nahm, "The Theological Background of the Theory of the Artist as Creator," *Journal of the History of Ideas* 8 (1947), 363–72. E. Kris and O. Kurtz, *Die Legende vom Künstler* (Vienna, 1934), 47 ff.

[52] The opinion of S. Haupt ("Die zwei Buecher des Aristoteles περὶ ποιητικῆς τέχνης, *Philologus* 69, N.F. 23 [1910], 252–63) that a lost section of Aristotle's *Poetics* dealt with the visual arts, as well as with lyrical poetry, must be rejected.

[53] See above, note 31. Cf. esp. Plato, *Republic* II, 373 b; X, 595 a ff. *Laws* II, 668 b f. Aristotle, *Poetics* 1, 1447 a 19 ff. *Rhetoric* I 11, 1371 b 6 ff. *Politics* VIII 5, 1340 a 38 f.

[54] It seems clear, at least for Plato (*Republic* X and *Sophist* 234 a ff.) that he arrived at his distinction between the productive and imitative arts without any exclusive concern for the "fine arts," since imitation is for him a basic metaphysical concept which he uses to describe the relation between things and Ideas.

architecture,[55] that music and the dance are treated as parts of poetry and not as separate arts,[56] and that on the other hand the individual branches or subdivisions of poetry and of music seem to be put on a par with painting or sculpture.[57] Finally, imitation is anything but a laudatory category, at least for Plato, and wherever Plato and Aristotle treat the "imitative arts" as a distinct group within the larger class of "arts," this group seems to include, besides the "fine arts" in which we are interested, other activities that are less "fine," such as sophistry,[58] or the use of the mirror,[59] of magic tricks,[60] or the imitation of animal voices.[61] Moreover, Aristotle's distinction between the arts of necessity and the arts of pleasure[62] is quite incidental and does not identify the arts of pleasure with the "fine" or even the imitative arts, and when it is emphasized that he includes music and drawing in his scheme of education in the *Politics*,[63] it should be added that they share this place with grammar (writing) and arithmetic.

The final ancient attempts at a classification of the more important human arts and sciences were made after the time of Plato and Aristotle. They were due partly to the endeavors of rival schools of philosophy and rhetoric to organize secondary or preparatory education into a system of elementary disciplines (τὰ ἐγκύκλια). This system of the so-called "liberal arts" was subject to a number of changes and fluctuations, and its development is not known in all of its earlier phases.[64] Cicero often speaks of the liberal arts and of their mutual connection,[65] though he does not

[55] Perhaps lyrical poetry is also excluded. It is not discussed by Aristotle, except for certain special kinds, and there are passages in Plato's *Republic* (X, 595 a) that imply that only certain kinds of poetry are imitative.

[56] See above, note 29.

[57] Aristotle, *Poetics* 1, 1447 a 24 ff.

[58] Plato, *Sophist* 234 e f.

[59] *Republic* X, 596 d f.

[60] *Ibid.*, 602 d. Cf. *Sophist*, 235 a.

[61] Plato, *Cratylus*, 423 c. Cf. Aristotle, *Poetics* 1, 1447 a 21 (a controversial passage). See also *Rhetoric* III 2, 1404 a 20 ff. for the imitative character of words and language.

[62] *Metaphysics* I 1, 981 b 17 ff.

[63] VIII 3, 1337 b 23 ff.

[64] Moritz Guggenheim, *Die Stellung der liberalen Künste oder encyklischen Wissenschaften in Altertum* (progr. Zürich, 1893). E. Norden, *Die antike Kunstprosa* II, 4th ed. (Leipzig-Berlin, 1923), 670 ff. H.-J. Marrou, *Histoire d l'éducation dans l'antiquité* (Paris, 1948), 244 f. and 523 f.; also *Saint Augustin et la fin de la culture classique* (Paris, 1938), 187 ff. and 211 ff.

[65] *Pro Archia poeta* 1, 2: "etenim omnes artes quae ad humanitatem pertinent habent quoddam commune vinculum."

give a precise list of these arts, but we may be sure that he did not think of the "fine arts" as was so often believed in modern times. The definitive scheme of the seven liberal arts is found only in Martianus Capella: grammar, rhetoric, dialectic, arithmetic, geometry, astronomy, and music. Other schemes which are similar but not quite identical are found in many Greek and Latin authors before Capella. Very close to Capella's scheme, and probably its source, was that of Varro, which included medicine and architecture, in addition to Capella's seven arts.[66] Quite similar also is the scheme underlying the work of Sextus Empiricus. It contains only six arts, omitting logic, which is treated as one of the three parts of philosophy. The Greek author, Sextus, was conscious of the difference between the preliminary disciplines and the parts of philosophy, whereas the Latin authors who had no native tradition of philosophical instruction were ready to disregard that distinction. If we compare Capella's scheme of the seven liberal arts with the modern system of the "fine arts," the differences are obvious. Of the fine arts only music, understood as musical theory, appears among the liberal arts. Poetry is not listed among them, yet we know from other sources that it was closely linked with grammar and rhetoric.[67] The visual arts have no place in the scheme, except for occasional attempts at inserting them, of which we have spoken above. On the other hand, the liberal arts include grammar and logic, mathematics and astronomy, that is, disciplines we should classify as sciences.

The same picture is gained from the distribution of the arts among the nine Muses. It should be noted that the number of the Muses was not fixed before a comparatively late period, and that the attempt to assign particular arts to individual Muses is still later and not at all uniform. However, the arts listed in these late schemes are the various branches of poetry and of music, with eloquence, history, the dance, grammar, geometry and astronomy.[68] In other words, just as in the schemes of the liberal arts, so in the schemes for the Muses poetry and music are grouped with some of the sciences, whereas the visual arts are

[66] See above, note 39.

[67] Charles S. Baldwin, *Ancient Rhetoric and Poetic* (New York, 1924), esp. 1 ff., 63 ff., 226 ff.

[68] J. von Schlosser, "Giusto's Fresken in Padua und die Vorläufer der Stanza della Segnatura," *Jahrbuch der Kunsthistorischen Sammlungen des Allerhöchsten Kaiserhauses* XVII, pt. 1 (1896), 13–100, esp. 36. Pauly-Wissowa, *Real-Encyclopaedie der klassischen Altertumswissenschaft* 16 (1935), 680 ff. esp. 685 f. and 725 ff.

omitted. Antiquity knew no Muse of painting or of sculpture; they had to be invented by the allegorists of the early modern centuries. And the five fine arts which constitute the modern system were not grouped together in antiquity, but kept quite different company: poetry stays usually with grammar and rhetoric; music is as close to mathematics and astronomy as it is to the dance, and poetry;[69] and the visual arts, excluded from the realm of the Muses and of the liberal arts by most authors, must be satisfied with the modest company of the other manual crafts.

Thus classical antiquity left no systems or elaborate concepts of an aesthetic nature,[70] but merely a number of scattered notions and suggestions that exercised a lasting influence down to modern times but had to be carefully selected, taken out of their context, rearranged, reemphasized and reinterpreted or misinterpreted before they could be utilized as building materials for aesthetic systems. We have to admit the conclusion, distasteful to many historians of aesthetics but grudgingly admitted by most of them, that ancient writers and thinkers, though confronted with excellent works of art and quite susceptible to their charm, were neither able nor eager to detach the aesthetic quality of these works of art from their intellectual, moral, religious and practical function or content, or to use such an aesthetic quality as a standard for grouping the fine arts together or for making them the subject of a comprehensive philosophical interpretation.

III

The early Middle Ages inherited from late antiquity the scheme of the seven liberal arts that served not only for a comprehensive classification of human knowledge but also for the curriculum of the monastic and cathedral schools down to the twelfth century.[71] The subdivision of the seven arts into the Trivium (grammar, rhetoric, dialectic) and Quadrivium (arithmetic, geom-

---

[69] Carolus Schmidt, *Quaestiones de musicis scriptoribus Romanis* . . . (thes. Giessen, Darmstadt, 1899).

[70] Schlosser, *Kunstliteratur*, 46 ff.

[71] P. Gabriel Meier, *Die sieben freien Künste im Mittelalter* (progr. Einsiedeln, 1886–87). Norden, *l.c.* A. Appuhn, *Das Trivium und Quadrivium in Theorie und Praxis* (thes. Erlangen, 1900). P. Abelson, *The Seven Liberal Arts* (thes. Columbia University, New York, 1906). For artistic representations of this scheme, see P. d'Ancona, "Le rappresentazioni allegoriche delle arti liberali nel medio evo e nel rinascimento," *L'Arte* 5 (1902), 137–55; 211–28; 269–89; 370–85. E. Mâle, *L'art religieux du XIIIe siècle en France*, 4th ed. (Paris, 1919), 97 ff.

etry, astronomy and music) seems to have been emphasized since Carolingian times.[72] This classification became inadequate after the growth of learning in the twelfth and thirteenth centuries. The classification schemes of the twelfth century reflect different attempts to combine the traditional system of the liberal arts with the threefold division of philosophy (logic, ethics and physics) known through Isidore, and with the divisions of knowledge made by Aristotle or based on the order of his writings, which then began to become known through Latin translations from the Greek and Arabic.[73] The rise of the universities also established philosophy, medicine, jurisprudence and theology as new and distinct subjects outside the liberal arts, and the latter were again reduced from the status of an encyclopaedia of secular knowledge they had held in the earlier Middle Ages to that of preliminary disciplines they had held originally in late antiquity. On the other hand, Hugo of St. Victor was probably the first to formulate a scheme of seven mechanical arts corresponding to the seven liberal arts, and this scheme influenced many important authors of the subsequent period, such as Vincent of Beauvais and Thomas Aquinas. The seven mechanical arts, like the seven liberal arts earlier, also appeared in artistic representations, and they are worth listing: *lanificium, armatura, navigatio, agricultura, venatio, medicina, theatrica*.[74] Architecture as well as various branches of sculpture and of painting are listed, along with several other crafts, as subdivisions of *armatura*, and thus occupy a quite subordinate place even among the mechanical arts.[75] Music appears in all these schemes in the company of the mathematical disciplines,[76] whereas poetry, when mentioned, is closely linked to grammar, rhetoric and logic.[77] The fine arts are not

[72] P. Rajna, "Le denominazioni Trivium e Quadrivium," *Studi Medievali*, N.S. 1 (1928), 4–36.

[73] Besides the works of Baur and Mariétan, cited above (note 27), see M. Grabmann, *Die Geschichte der scholastischen Methode* II (Freiburg, 1911), 28 ff.

[74] Hugonis de Sancto Victore *Didascalicon*, ed. Ch. H. Buttimer (Washington, 1939), bk. II, ch. 20 ff.

[75] *Ibid.*, ch. 22. For the position of the architect in particular, see N. Pevsner, "The Term 'Architect' in the Middle Ages," *Speculum* XVII (1942), 549–62.

[76] Cf. G. Pietzsch, *Die Klassifikation der Musik von Boetius bis Ugolino von Orvieto* (thes. Freiburg, 1929).

[77] Ch. S. Baldwin, *Medieval Rhetoric and Poetic* (New York, 1928). E. Faral, *Les arts poétiques du XIIe et du XIIIe siècle* (Paris, 1924). R. McKeon, "Poetry and Philosophy in the Twelfth Century," *Modern Philology* 43 (1946), 217–34.

grouped together or singled out in any of these schemes, but scattered among various sciences, crafts, and other human activities of a quite disparate nature.[78] Different as are these schemes from each other in detail, they show a persistent general pattern and continued to influence later thought.

If we compare these theoretical systems with the reality of the same period, we find poetry and music among the subjects taught in many schools and universities, whereas the visual arts were confined to the artisans' guilds, in which the painters were sometimes associated with the druggists who prepared their paints, the sculptors with the goldsmiths, and the architects with the masons and carpenters.[79] The treatises also that were written, on poetry and rhetoric, on music, and on some of the arts and crafts, the latter not too numerous, have all a strictly technical and professional character and show no tendency to link any of these arts with the others or with philosophy.

The very concept of "art" retained the same comprehensive meaning it had possessed in antiquity, and the same connotation that it was teachable.[80] And the term *artista* coined in the Middle Ages indicated either the craftsman or the student of the liberal arts.[81] Neither for Dante[82] nor for Aquinas has the term Art the meaning we associate with it, and it has been emphasized or admitted that for Aquinas shoemaking, cooking and juggling, grammar and arithmetic are no less and in no other sense *artes* than painting and sculpture, poetry and music, which latter are never grouped together, not even as imitative arts.[83]

On the other hand, the concept of beauty that is occasionally

---

[78] E. De Bruyne, *Études d'Esthétique médiévale* II (Bruges, 1946), 371 ff., and III, 326 ff.

[79] Schlosser, *Kunstliteratur*, 65. N. Pevsner, *Academies of Art, Past and Present* (Cambridge, 1940), 43 ff. M. Wackernagel, *Der Lebensraum des Künstlers in der Florentinischen Renaissance* (Leipzig, 1938), 306 ff.

[80] De Bruyne, *l. c.*

[81] C. Du Cange, *Glossarium Mediate et Infimae Latinitatis* I (Paris, 1937), 413.

[82] D. Bigongiari, "Notes on the Text of Dante," *Romanic Review* 41 (1950), 81 f.

[83] L. Schuetz, *Thomas-Lexikon*, 2nd ed. (Paderborn, 1908), 65–68. A. Dyroff, "Zur allgemeinen Kunstlehre des hl. Thomas," *Abhandlungen zur Geschichte der Philosophie des Mittelalters, Festgabe Clemens Bäumker . . . (Beiträge zur Geschichte der Philosophie des Mittelalters, Supplementband II, Münster, 1923*), 197–219. De Bruyne, *l.c.*, III, 316 ff. J. Maritain, *Art et Scolastique* (Paris, 1920), 1 f. and 28 f. G. G. Coulton, *Art and the Reformation* (Oxford, 1928), 559 ff.

discussed by Aquinas[84] and somewhat more emphatically by a few other medieval philosophers[85] is not linked with the arts, fine or otherwise, but treated primarily as a metaphysical attribute of God and of his creation, starting from Augustine and from Dionysius the Areopagite. Among the transcendentals or most general attributes of being, *pulchrum* does not appear in thirteenth-century philosophy, although it is considered as a general concept and treated in close connection with *bonum*. The question whether Beauty is one of the transcendentals has become a subject of controversy among Neo-Thomists.[86] This is an interesting sign of their varying attitude toward modern aesthetics, which some of them would like to incorporate in a philosophical system based on Thomist principles. For Aquinas himself, or for other medieval philosophers, the question is meaningless, for even if they had posited *pulchrum* as a transcendental concept, which they did not, its meaning would have been different from the modern notion of artistic beauty in which the Neo-Thomists are interested. Thus it is obvious that there was artistic production as well as artistic appreciation in the Middle Ages,[87] and this could not fail to find occasional expression in literature and philosophy. Yet there is no medieval concept or system of the Fine Arts, and if we want to keep speaking of medieval aesthetics,

[84] M. De Wulf, "Les théories esthétiques propres à Saint Thomas," *Revue Neo-Scolastique* 2 (1895), 188–205; 341–57; 3 (1896), 117–42. M. Grabmann, *Die Kulturphilosophie des Hl. Thomas von Aquin* (Augsburg 1925), 148 ff. I. Chapman, "The Perennial Theme of Beauty," in *Essays in Thomism* (New York, 1942), 333–46 and 417–19. E. Gilson, *Le Thomisme*, 5th ed. (Paris, 1945), 382–83.

[85] M. Grabmann, "Des Ulrich Engelberti von Strassburg O.P. (+1277) Abhandlung De pulchro," *Sitzungsberichte der Bayerischen Akademie der Wissenschaften, Philosophisch-Philologische und Historische Klasse (Jahrgang 1925)*, no. 5. Cf. H. Pouillon, "Le premier Traité des propriétés transcendentales, La Summa de bono du Chancelier Philippe," *Revue Néoscolastique de Philosophie* 42 (1939), 40–77. A. K. Coomaraswamy, "Medieval Aesthetic," *The Art Bulletin* 17 (1935), 31–47; 20 (1938), 66–77 (reprinted in his *Figures of Speech or Figures of Thought* [London, 1946], 44–84. I am indebted for this reference to John Cuddihy). E. Lutz, "Die Ästhetik Bonaventuras," *Studien zur Geschichte der Philosophie Festgabe . . . Clemens Bäumker gewidmet (Beiträge zur Geschichte der Philosophie des Mittelalters, Supplementband*, Münster, 1913), 195–215.

[86] Maritain, *l.c.*, p. 31 ff., esp. 40; Chapman, *l.c.* L. Wencelius, *La philosophie de l'art chez les Néo-Scolastiques de langue française* (Paris, 1932), esp. 93 ff.

[87] M. Schapiro, "On the Aesthetic Attitude in Romanesque Art," in *Art and Thought, Essays in Honor of A. K. Coomaraswamy* (London, 1947), 130–50.

we must admit that its concept and subject matter are, for better or for worse, quite different from the modern philosophical discipline.

IV

The period of the Renaissance brought about many important changes in the social and cultural position of the various arts and thus prepared the ground for the later development of aesthetic theory. But, contrary to a widespread opinion, the Renaissance did not formulate a system of the fine arts or a comprehensive theory of aesthetics.

Early Italian humanism, which in many respects continued the grammatical and rhetorical traditions of the Middle Ages, not merely provided the old Trivium with a new and more ambitious name (*Studia humanitatis*) but also increased its actual scope, content and significance in the curriculum of the schools and universities and in its own extensive literary production. The *Studia humanitatis* excluded logic, but they added to the traditional grammar and rhetoric not only history, Greek and moral philosophy, but also made poetry, once a sequel of grammar and rhetoric, the most important member of the whole group.[88] It is true that in the fourteenth and fifteenth centuries poetry was understood as the ability to write Latin verse and to interpret the ancient poets, and that the poetry which the humanists defended against some of their theological contemporaries or for which they were crowned by popes and emperors was a quite different thing from what we understand by that name.[89] Yet the name poetry, meaning at first Latin poetry, received much honor and glamor through the early humanists, and by the sixteenth century vernacular poetry and prose began to share in the prestige of Latin literature. It was the various branches of Latin and vernacular poetry and literature which constituted the main pursuit of the numerous "Academies" founded in Italy during that period and imitated later in the other European countries.[90] The revival of Platonism also helped to spread the notion of the divine mad-

[88] See my article, "Humanism and Scholasticism in the Italian Renaissance," *Byzantion* 17 (1944–45), 346–74, esp. 364–65. In *Renaissance Thought* (New York, Harper Torchbooks, 1961).

[89] K. Vossler, *Poetische Theorien in der italienischen Frührenaissance* (Berlin, 1900).

[90] M. Maylender, *Storia delle Accademie d'Italia*, 5 vols. (Bologna, 1926–30). See also Pevsner, *l. c.*, 1 ff.

ness of the poet, a notion that by the second half of the sixteenth century began to be extended to the visual arts and became one of the ingredients of the modern concept of genius.[91]

With the second third of the sixteenth century, Aristotle's *Poetics,* along with his *Rhetoric,* began to exercise increasing influence, not only through translations and commentaries, but also through a rising number of treatises on Poetics in which the notions of Aristotle constituted one of the dominant features.[92]

[91] Zilsel, *l. c.,* 293 ff.

[92] J. E. Spingarn, *A History of Literary Criticism in the Renaissance,* 6th ed. (New York, 1930). G. Toffanin, *La fine dell'umanesimo* (Turin, 1920). Donald L. Clark, *Rhetoric and Poetry in the Renaissance* (New York, 1922). Charles S. Baldwin, *Renaissance Literary Theory and Practice* (New York, 1939). Among the commentators, Franciscus Robortellus groups poetry with rhetoric and various parts of logic (*In librum Aristotelis de arte poetica explicationes* [Florence, 1548], p. 1) and takes *Poetics* 1447 a 18 ff. to refer to painting, sculpture and acting (p. 10 f.: "sequitur similitudo quaedam ducta a pictura, sculptura et histrionica"). Vincentius Madius and Bartholomaeus Lombardus also group poetry with logic and rhetoric (*In Aristotelis librum de poetica communes explanationes* [Venice, 1550], p. 8) but interpret the same passage in terms of painting and music (p. 40–41): "aemulantium coloribus et figuris alios, pictores inquam, voce autem alios, phonascos scilicet (music teachers), aemulari, quorum pictores quidem arte, phonasci autem consuetudine tantum imitationem efficiunt." Petrus Victorius states that Aristotle does not list all the imitative arts in the beginning of the *Poetics* (*Commentarii in primum librum Aristotelis de arte poetarum,* 2nd ed. [Florence, 1573], p. 4) and refers the imitation through voice not to music, but to the copying of the song of birds (p. 6: "cum non extet ars ulla qua tradantur praecepta imitandi cantum avis aut aliam rem voce") and of other animals (p. 7). Lodovico Castelvetro repeatedly compares poetry to painting and sculpture as to other imitative arts (*Poetica d'Aristotele volgarizzata et sposta* [Basel, 1576], p. 14 ff.; 581) but recognizes music and the dance as parts of poetry (p. 13: "la poesia di parole, di ballo e di suono"). Significant is his attempt to relate poetry to the realm of the soul as opposed to the body (p. 342: "il dipintore rappresenta la bontà del corpo, cio è la bellezza, e'l poeta rappresenta la bontà dell'animo, cio è i buoni costumi"; cf. H. B. Charlton, *Castelvetro's Theory of Poetry* [Manchester, 1913], 39). Francesco Patrizi, anti-Aristotelian in poetics as well as in philosophy, rejects the principle of imitation altogether and calls it a term with many meanings, unfit to serve as a genus for several arts (*Della Poetica, La Deca disputata* [Ferrara, 1586], p. 63): "Perciò che così in confuso presa (*i.e.,* imitation), non pare potere essere genere univoco nè analogo a Pittori, a Scoltori, a Poeti e ad Istrioni, artefici cotanto tra loro differenti"; p. 68: "essendo adunque la imitazione della favola stata commune a scrittori, istorici, a filosofi, a sofisti, a dialogisti, ad istoriali e a novellatori." Bernardino Daniello (*Della poetica* [Venice, 1536], p. 69 f.) compares the poet not only to the painter but also to the sculptor. Antonius Minturnus compares poets, musicians and painters as imitators (*De poeta* [Venice, 1559], p. 22: "Videbam enim ut pictorum musicorumque ita poetarum esse imitari") but stresses repeatedly that music in ancient times

Poetic imitation is regularly discussed along Aristotelian lines, and some authors also notice and stress the analogies between poetry, painting, sculpture and music as forms of imitation. However, most of them know that music for Aristotle was a part of poetry, and that he knew other forms of imitation outside of the "fine arts," and hardly anyone among them is trying to establish the "imitative arts" as a separate class.

Musical theory retained during the Renaissance its status as one of the liberal arts,[93] and the author of an early treatise on the dance tries to dignify his subject by the claim that his art, being a part of music, must be considered as a liberal art.[94] It seems that the practice of the Improvvisatori as well as the reading of classical sources suggested to some humanists a closer link between music and poetry than had been customary in the preceding period.[95] This tendency received a new impetus by the end of the sixteenth century, when the program of the Camerata and the creation of the opera brought about a reunion of the two arts.

---

was joined to poetry (p. 49; 60; 91: "eosdem poetas ac musicos fuisse"; 391) and compares poetry also with history and other sciences (p. 76; 87 ff.; 440 f.). In another work, the same author, echoing Aristotle's *Poetics*, compares poetry to painting and acting (*L'arte poetica* [Naples, 1725], p. 3: "i pittori con li colori e co' lineamenti la facciano, i parasiti e gl'istrioni con la voce e con gli atti, i poeti . . . con le parole, con l'armonia, con i tempi") and treats music and dance as parts of poetry (*ibid.*). Johannes Antonius Viperanus defines poetry as imitation through verse and thus differentiates it from other forms of imitation. Lucian can be called a poet, "sed ea dumtaxat ratione qua pictores, mimi et imitatores alii propter nominis generalem quandam lateque diffusam signicationem nominari possunt et nominantur etiam poetae" (*De poetica libri tres* [Antwerp, 1579], p. 10). Giovanni Pietro Capriano divides the imitative arts into two classes, the noble and the ignoble. The former appeal to the noble senses of seeing and hearing and have durable products, such as poetry, painting and sculpture, the latter for which no examples are given appeal to the three lower senses and produce no lasting works (*Della vera poetica* [Venice, 1555], fol. A 3–A 3v. Cf. Spingarn, p. 42). Music is treated as a part of poetry (*ibid.*). Other writers on poetics whom I have examined, such as Fracastoro or Scaliger, have nothing to say on the other "fine arts," except for occasional comparisons between poetry and painting. B. Varchi also groups poetry with logic, rhetoric, history and grammar (*Opere*, ed. A. Racheli, II [Trieste, 1859], p. 684). Cf. Spingarn, 25.

[93] A. Pellizzari, *Il Quadrivio nel Rinascimento* (Naples, 1924), 63 ff.

[94] Guglielmo Ebreo Pesarese, *Trattato dell'arte del ballo* (*Scelta di curiosità letterarie*, 131, Bologna, 1873), p. 3 and 6–7.

[95] Raphael Brandolinus, *De musica et poetica opusculum* (ms. Casanatense C V 3, quoted by Adrien de La Fage, *Essais de diphthérographie musicale* . . . [Paris, 1864], 61 ff.).

It would even seem that some of the features of Marinismo and baroque poetry that were so repulsive to classicist critics were due to the fact that this poetry was written with the intention of being set to music and sung.[96]

Still more characteristic of the Renaissance is the steady rise of painting and of the other visual arts that began in Italy with Cimabue and Giotto and reached its climax in the sixteenth century. An early expression of the increasing prestige of the visual arts is found on the Campanile of Florence, where painting, sculpture, and architecture appear as a separate group between the liberal and the mechanical arts.[97] What characterizes the period is not only the quality of the works of art but also the close links that were established between the visual arts, the sciences and literature.[98] The appearance of a distinguished artist who also was a humanist and writer of merit, such as Alberti, was no coincidence in a period in which literary and classical learning began, in addition to religion, to provide the subject matter for painters and sculptors. When a knowledge of perspective, anatomy, and geometrical proportions was considered necessary for the painter and sculptor, it was no wonder that several artists should have made important contributions to the various sciences. On the other hand, ever since Filippo Villani, the humanists, and their journalist successors in the sixteenth century, looked with favor upon the work of contemporary artists and would lend their pen to its praise. From the end of the fourteenth century through the sixteenth the writings of the artists and of authors sympathetic to the visual arts repeat the claim that painting should be considered as one of the liberal, not of the mechanical arts.[99] It has been rightly noted that the classical testimonies in favor of painting, mainly from Pliny, Galen and Philostratus, were not as authoritative and strong as the Renaissance authors who quoted them in support of their claim believed or pretended to believe.

---

[96] Lodovico Zuccolo, *Discorso delle ragioni del numero del verso italiano* (Venice, 1623), 65 ff. ("mentre si addatta non la musica a i versi, ma questi si accommodano a quella contro ogni dovere," p. 65).

[97] Schlosser, "Giusto's Fresken," 70 ff.; *Kunstliteratur*, 66.

[98] Dresdner, 77 ff. L. Olschki, *Geschichte der neusprachlichen wissenschaftlichen Literatur*, I: *Die Literatur der Technik und der angewandten Wissenschaften vom Mittelalter bis zur Renaissance* (Heidelberg, 1919), 31 ff.

[99] Schlosser, *Kunstliteratur*, 50; 79 f.; 98; 136; 138; 385. Anthony Blunt, *Artistic Theory in Italy 1450–1600* (Oxford, 1940), 48 ff. K. Birch-Hirschfeld, *Die Lehre von der Malerei* (thes. Leipzig, 1911), 25. For a French example of 1542, see F. Brunot, *Histoire de la langue française* . . . VI, 1 (1930), 680.

Yet the claim of Renaissance writers on painting to have their art recognized as liberal, however weakly supported by classical authority, was significant as an attempt to enhance the social and cultural position of painting and of the other visual arts, and to obtain for them the same prestige that music, rhetoric, and poetry had long enjoyed. And since it was still apparent that the liberal arts were primarily sciences or teachable knowledge, we may well understand why Leonardo tried to define painting as a science and to emphasize its close relationship with mathematics.[100]

The rising social and cultural claims of the visual arts led in the sixteenth century in Italy to an important new development that occurred in the other European countries somewhat later: the three visual arts, painting, sculpture and architecture, were for the first time clearly separated from the crafts with which they had been associated in the preceding period. The term *Arti del disegno*, upon which "Beaux Arts" was probably based, was coined by Vasari, who used it as the guiding concept for his famous collection of biographies. And this change in theory found its institutional expression in 1563 when in Florence, again under the personal influence of Vasari, the painters, sculptors and architects cut their previous connections with the craftsmen's guilds and formed an Academy of Art (*Accademia del Disegno*), the first of its kind that served as a model for later similar institutions in Italy and other countries.[101] The Art Academies followed the pattern of the literary Academies that had been in existence for some time, and they replaced the older workshop tradition with a regular kind of instruction that included such scientific subjects as geometry and anatomy.[102]

The ambition of painting to share in the traditional prestige of literature also accounts for the popularity of a notion that appears prominently for the first time in the treatises on painting of the sixteenth century and was to retain its appeal down to the eighteenth: the parallel between painting and poetry. Its basis was the *Ut pictura poesis* of Horace, as well as the saying of Simonides reported by Plutarch, along with some other passages in

[100] *The Literary Works of Leonardo da Vinci*, ed. Jean Paul Richter, I, 2nd ed. (London, 1939), 31 ff.

[101] Schlosser, *Kunstliteratur*, 385 ff. Olschki, II (*Bildung und Wissenschaft im Zeitalter der Renaissance in Italien*, Leipzig, 1922), 188 ff. Blunt, 55 ff. Pevsner, 42 ff.

[102] Pevsner, 48.

Plato, Aristotle and Horace. The history of this notion from the sixteenth to the eighteenth century has been carefully studied,[103] and it has been justly pointed out that the use then made of the comparison exceeded anything done or intended by the ancients. Actually, the meaning of the comparison was reversed, since the ancients had compared poetry with painting when they were writing about poetry, whereas the modern authors more often compared painting with poetry while writing about painting. How seriously the comparison was taken we can see from the fact that Horace's *Ars poetica* was taken as a literary model for some treatises on painting and that many poetical theories and concepts were applied to painting by these authors in a more or less artificial manner. The persistent comparison between poetry and painting went a long way, as did the emancipation of the three visual arts from the crafts, to prepare the ground for the later system of the five fine arts, but it obviously does not yet presuppose or constitute such a system. Even the few treatises written in the late sixteenth and early seventeenth century that dealt with both poetry and painting do not seem to have gone beyond more or less external comparisons into an analysis of common principles.[104]

The sixteenth century formulated still other ideas that pointed in the direction of later developments in the field of aesthetics. Just as the period attached great importance to questions of "precedence" at courts and in public ceremonies, so the Academies and educated circles inherited from the medieval schools and

---

[103] Rensselaer W. Lee, "Ut pictura poesis: The Humanistic Theory of Painting," *The Art Bulletin* 22 (1940), 197–269. See also W. G. Howard, "Ut pictura poesis," *Publications of the Modern Language Association* 24 (1909), 40–123. Lessing, *Laokoon*, ed. William G. Howard (New York, 1910), p. L ff. Denis Mahon, *Studies in Seicento Art and Theory* (London, 1947).

[104] *Due dialoghi* di M. Giovanni Andrea Gilio da Fabriano, *Nel primo de' quali si ragiona de le parti morali, e civili appertenenti a Letterati Cortigani, et ad ogni gentil'huomo, e l'utile, che i Prencipi cavano da i Letterati. Nel secondo si cagiona de gli errori de Pittori circa l'historie* . . . (Camerino, 1564). Antonius Possevinus, *De poesi et pictura ethnica humana et fabulosa collata cum vera honesta et sacra* (1595), in his *Bibliotheca selecta de ratione studiorum* II (Cologne, 1607), 407 ff. (this treatise is based on an explicit comparison between the two arts, cf. 470: "quae poeticae eadem picturae conveniunt monita et leges"). Filippo Nuñes, *Arte poetica, e da pintura e symmetria, com principios de perspectiva* (Lisbon, 1615; not seen; the *Arte de pintura* was reprinted separately in 1767; cf. Innocenzo Francisco da Silva, *Diccionario Bibliographico Portuguez* II [Lisbon, 1859], 303–04).

universities the fancy for arguing the relative merits and superiority of the various sciences, arts or other human activities. This type of debate was by no means limited to the arts, as appears from the old rivalry between medicine and jurisprudence,[105] or from the new contest between "arms and letters." Yet this kind of discussion was also applied to the arts and thus helped to strengthen the sense of their affinity The parallel between painting and poetry, in so far as it often leads to a plea for the superiority of painting over poetry, shows the same general pattern.[106] No less popular was the contest between painting and sculpture, on which Benedetto Varchi in 1546 held a regular inquiry among contemporary artists, whose answers are extant and constitute interesting documents for the artistic theories of the time.[107] The question was still of interest to Galileo.[108] The most important text of this type is Leonardo's *Paragone,* which argues for the superiority of painting over poetry, music, and sculpture.[109] In a sense, this tract contains the most complete system of the fine arts that has come down to us from the Renaissance period. However, the text was not composed by Leonardo in its present form, but put together from his scattered notes by one of his pupils, and again rearranged by most of the modern editors. In any case, architecture is omitted, the separation between poetry and music is not consistently maintained, and the comparison seems to be extended to the mathematical disciplines with which painting, as a science, is closely linked for Leonardo.

Another line of thinking which might be called the amateur tradition appears in several writers of the sixteenth and seven-

[105] E. Garin, *La disputa delle Arti nel Quattrocento* (Florence, 1947).

[106] Schlosser, *Kunstliteratur,* 154 ff.

[107] G. G. Bottari, *Raccolta di lettere sulla pittura scultura ed architectura* I (Rome, 1754), 12 ff. Cf. Schlosser, *Kunstliteratur,* 200 ff. See also Varchi's own lecture on this subject (*Opere,* ed. A. Racheli, II [Trieste, 1859], 627 ff.

[108] Letter to Lodovico Cardi da Cigoli (1612), in his *Opere, Edizione Nazionale* XI (Florence, 1901), 340–43. On the authenticity of this letter, see Margherita Margani, "Sull'autenticità di una lettera attribuita a G. Galilei," *Atti della Reale Accademia delle Scienze di Torino* 57 (1921-22), 556–68. I am indebted for this reference to Edward Rosen.

[109] *The Literary Works, l. c. Paragone: A Comparison of the Arts by Leonardo da Vinci,* ed. Irma A. Richter (London, 1949). Lionardo da Vinci, *Das Buch von der Malerei,* ed. H. Ludwig, I (Vienna, 1882). Miss Richter changes the arrangement of the manuscript, which in its turn is not due to Leonardo himself.

teenth centuries, probably first in Castiglione's *Courtier*.[110] The exercise, as well as the appreciation of poetry, music and painting are grouped together as pursuits appropriate for the courtier, the gentleman, or the prince. Again, the occupation with these "fine arts" is not clearly marked off from fencing, horseriding, classical learning, the collecting of coins and medals and of natural curiosities or other equally worthy activities. But there seems to be a sense of the affinity between the various arts in their effect upon the amateur, and by the first half of the seventeenth century, the taste and pleasure produced by painting, music and poetry is felt by several authors to be of a similar nature.[111] It does not seem that Plotinus' view that beauty resides in the objects of sight, hearing, and though exercised any particular influence at that time.[112]

The most explicit comparison between poetry, painting, and music that I have been able to discover in Renaissance literature is the appendix which the Bohemian Jesuit, Jacobus Pontanus, added to the third edition of his treatise on poetics.[113] In stressing

[110] B. Castiglione, *Il Cortegiano*, Bk. I. Giovanni Battista Pigna, *Il Principe* (Venice, 1561), fol. 4 v–5. Peacham's *Compleat Gentleman* (1622), ed. G. S. Gordon (Oxford, 1916), chs. 10–13.

[111] Lodovico Zuccolo (*Discorso delle ragioni del numero del verso Italiano*, Venice, 1623), speaking of our judgment concerning verse and rhythm in poetry, refers for a comparison to painting and music (p. 8: "onde habbiamo in costume di dire, che l'occhio discerne la bellezza della Pittura, e l'orecchio apprende l'armonia della Musica; . . . quel gusto della Pittura e della Musica che sentiamo noi . . ."; cf. B. Croce, *Storia dell'estetica per saggi* [Bari, 1942], 44 f.). A comparison between painting and music is made also by Richard Asheley in the preface of his translation of Louis Le Roy (1594); cf. H. V. S. Ogden, "The Principles of Variety and Contrast in Seventeenth Century Aesthetics and Milton's Poetry," *Journal of the History of Ideas*, 10 (1949), 168.

[112] *Enn*. I 6, 1. Marsilius Ficinus, *Commentarium in Convivium Platonis de amore*, Oratio 5, cap. 2 (*Marsilio Ficino's Commentary on Plato's Symposium*, ed. Sears R. Jayne, *The University of Missouri Studies* XIX, 1 [Columbia, 1944], 65–66). Cf. his *Theologia Platonica*, Bk. XII, chs. 5–7 (*Opera* [Basel, 1576], I, 275 ff.). See also St. Thomas, *Summa Theologiae* II, I, 27, 1.

[113] Jacobi Pontani de Societate Jesu *Poeticarum Institutionum libri III*. Editio tertia cum auctario . . . (Ingolstadt, 1600), 239–50: "Auctarium. Collatio Poetices cum pictura, et musica" (I have used the copy of Georgetown University; the passage is lacking in the first edition of 1594, of which Columbia University has a copy, and in the second edition of 1597 owned by the Newberry Library and kindly examined for me by Hans Baron; my attention was drawn to it by K. Borinski, *Die Antike in Poetik und Kunsttheorie* II [Leipzig, 1924], 37 ff. and 328 ff.

the affinity between the three arts as forms of imitation aiming at pleasure, the author goes beyond his classical sources.[114] He argues for the status of painting as a liberal art, as many others had done before, but also places musical composition (not musical theory) as a separate art on the same plane with poetry and painting. The passage is quite remarkable, and I should like to think that it was influential, since the work was often reprinted, in France also, where much of the later discussion on these topics took place.[115]

Renaissance speculation on beauty was still unrelated to the arts and apparently influenced by ancient models. Nifo's treatise De pulchro, still quoted in the eighteenth century, dealt exclusively with personal beauty.[116] Francesco da Diacceto's main philosophical work, which carries the same title, continues the metaphysical speculations of Plotinus and of his teacher Ficino and does not seem to have exercised any lasting influence.[117]

That the Renaissance, in spite of these notable changes, was still far from establishing the modern system of the fine arts appears most clearly from the classifications of the arts and sciences that were proposed during that period. These schemes continued in part the traditions of the Middle Ages, as is clear in the case of such Thomists as S. Antonino or Savonarola.[118] On the whole,

[114] "Scriptores antiqui Poeticem cum pictura et musica componere soliti, plurimam utique illius cum hisce duabus artibus affinitatem cognationemque magnam et omnino ingenium eius ac proprietatem declarare voluerunt" (239-40). "Omnium insuper commune est delectationem gignere, siquidem ad honestam animi voluptatem potius quam ad singularem aliquam utilitatem repertae . . . videntur. Porro poetica et musica . . . auditum permulcent . . . pictura oculis blanditur" (242). Sculpture is also once brought in: "fas sit sculptores, caelatores, fictores propter similitudinem quandam pictoribus sociare" (244).

[115] A. de Backer and Ch. Sommervogel, Bibliothèque des écrivains de la Compagnie de Jésus, new ed., II (Liége-Lyon, 1872), 2075-81, list several French printings of the work, of which at least one is clearly based on the third edition. See also the catalogue of the Bibliothèque Nationale, which lists a 3rd ed. issued in Avignon, 1600.

[116] Augustinus Niphus, De pulchro, de amore (Lyons, 1549). The work is quoted by J. P. de Crousaz, Traité du Beau, 2nd ed. (Amsterdam, 1724), I, 190. I have not seen Marcus Antonius Natta, De pulcro (Pavia, 1553; cf. Catalogo ragionato dei libri d'arte e d'antichità posseduti dal Conte Cicognara I [Pisa, 1821], 188 f.).

[117] See my article, "Francesco da Diacceto and Florentine Platonism in the Sixteenth Century," Miscellanea Giovanni Mercati IV (Studi e Testi 124, Vatican City, 1946), 260-304, esp. 279 ff.; Studies in Renaissance Thought and Letters (Rome, 1956), 304 ff.

[118] Baur, l. c., 391 ff. Spingarn, 24.

however, there is a greater variety of ideas than in the preceding period, and some of the thinkers concerned were neither backward nor unrepresentative. Vives, Ramus, and Gesner largely follow the old scheme of the liberal arts and the university curriculum of their time.[119] Neither Agrippa of Nettesheim[120] nor Scaliger,[121] nor in the seventeenth century Alsted[122] or Vossius,[123]

[119] Johannes Ludovicus Vives, De disciplinis, in his Opera omnia VI (Valencia, 1785). Petrus Ramus, Collectaneae, Praefationes, Epistolae, Orationes (Marburg, 1599). Conrad Gesner (Bibliotheca Universalis II, Zürich, 1548) places poetry between rhetoric and arithmetic; music between geometry and astronomy; and lists architecture, sculpture and painting scattered among the mechanical arts such as transportation, clothmaking, alchemy, trade, agriculture and the like. Gesner is important as the author of a classification scheme designed for bibliographical purposes. The later history of such schemes has been studied, and it appears that the arts, meaning the visual arts and music, did not attain a distinct place in them before the eighteenth century, whereas up to the present day poetry, for obvious reasons, has never been combined with the other arts in these bibliographical schemes. Cf. Edward Edwards, Memoirs of Libraries (London, 1859), 747 ff. W. C. Berwick Sayers, An Introduction to Library Classification, 7th ed. (London, 1946), 74 ff. My attention was drawn to this material by Prof. Thomas P. Fleming.

[120] Henricus Cornelius Agrippa ab Nettesheim, De incertitudine et vanitate scientiarum (no place, 1537) gives a random list of arts and sciences, in which poetry appears between grammar and history, music between gambling and the dance, painting and sculpture between perspective and glassmaking (specularia), architecture between geography and metal work. In his De occulta philosophia (Opera I [Lyons, s.a.], bk. I, ch. 60; cf. E. Panofsky, Albrecht Dürer I [Princeton, 1943], 168 ff.), Agrippa distinguishes three kinds of melancholy and inspiration which he assigns, respectively, to the manual artists such as painters and architects, to the philosophers, physicians and orators, and to the theologians. It is significant that he has the manual artists share in inspiration, but does not link them with the poets mentioned in the same chapter, and he clearly places them on the lowest of the three levels.

[121] In a rather incidental passage, he groups architecture with cooking and agriculture; singing and the dance with wrestling; speech with navigation (Julius Caesar Scaliger, Poetices libri septem [no place, 1594] bk. III, ch. 1, p. 206). Varchi has several random groupings of the arts and finally gives the prize to medicine and next to architecture (Opere II, 631 ff.). Nizolius classes poetry with grammar, rhetoric and history (Robert Flint, Philosophy as Scientia Scientiarum and a History of Classifications of the Sciences [New York, 1904], 98 f.).

[122] He includes poetry under philology, and music under theoretical philosophy (Ibid., 113-15).

[123] Gerardus Johannes Vossius, De artium et scientiarum natura ac constitutione libri quinque (in his Opera III, Amsterdam, 1697). He lists four groups of arts: The vulgar arts such as tailoring and shoemaking; the four popular arts of reading and writing, of sports, of singing and of painting (this group is borrowed from Aristotle's Politics VIII 3, 1337 b 23 ff.); the seven liberal arts; the main sciences of philosophy (with eloquence), jurisprudence, medicine and theology.

makes any attempt to separate the fine arts from the sciences; they list them scattered among all kinds of sciences and professions, and the same is still true of the eighteenth-century *Cyclopaedia* of E. Chambers.[124] Francis Bacon connects poetry with the faculty of imagination,[125] but does not mention the other arts, and the same is true of Vico,[126] whom Croce considers the founder of modern aesthetics.[127] Bonifacio stresses the link between poetry and painting, but otherwise does not separate the fine arts from the sciences,[128] and the same is true of Tassoni.[129] Even Muratori, who again stresses imagination in poetry and at times compares poetry and painting, when he speaks of the *arti* connected with poetry means eloquence and history, in other words, the *studia humanitatis*.[129a] The modern system of the fine arts does not appear in Italy before the second half of the eighteenth century,

[124] 5th ed. (London, 1741), III (first published in 1727). He classes painting with optics under mixed mathematics, music again under mixed mathematics, architecture and sculpture with the trades also under mixed mathematics, gardening with agriculture, and poetry with rhetoric, grammar and heraldry.

[125] *Of the Advancement of Learning* (*The Philosophical Works of Francis Bacon*, ed. John M. Robertson [London, 1905], 79 and 87 ff.). Cf. F. H. Anderson, *The Philosophy of Francis Bacon* (Chicago, 1948), 149.

[126] Vico's theory of phantasy refers to poetry only. In an incidental passage he lists two groups of arts: the visual arts, and oratory, politics, medicine (*De antiquissima Italorum sapientia*, ch. 2, in *Le orazioni inaugurali . . .*, ed. G. Gentile and F. Nicolini [Bari, 1914], 144).

[127] *Estetica, l. c.,* 243 ff.

[128] Giovanni Bonifacio, *L'Arte de' Cenni . . .* (Vicenza, 1616). He combines painting with poetry on account of their similarity, but places them between rhetoric and history (553 ff.). Music appears between astrology and arithmetic (517 ff.), architecture with sculpture between navigation and woolmaking (614 ff.).

[129] Alessandro Tassoni, *Dieci libri di pensieri diversi*, 4th ed. (Venice, 1627). He places poetry between history and oratory (597 ff.), puts architecture after agriculture and before decoration, sculpture, painting and clothing (609 ff.), whereas music appears between arithmetic and astronomy (657 ff.). Benedetto Accolti, another forerunner of the *Querelle des anciens et modernes* who lived in the fifteenth century, discusses only military art and politics, philosophy, oratory, jurisprudence, poetry, mathematics and theology (*Dialogus de praestantia virorum sui aevi*, in Philippi Villani *liber de civitatis Florentiae famosis civibus*, ed. G. C. Galletti [Florence, 1847], 106–07 and 110–28).

[129a] Lodovico Antonio Muratori, *Della perfetta poesia italiana*, ch. 6: "quelle arti nobili che parlano all'intelletto, come sono la Rettorica, la Storica, la Poetica" (in his *Opere* IX, pt. I [Arezzo, 1769], 56). These three arts are called "figliuole o ministre della filosofia morale" (*ibid.*), and the analogy with painting, based on the concept of imitation, is applied to all three of them (*ibid.*, 59).

when such writers as Bettinelli began to follow the lead of contemporary French, English and German authors.[130]

V

During the seventeenth century the cultural leadership of Europe passed from Italy to France, and many characteristic ideas and tendencies of the Italian Renaissance were continued and transformed by French classicism and the French Enlightenment before they became a part of later European thought and culture. Literary criticism and poetic theory, so prominent in the French classical period, seem to have taken little notice of the other fine arts.[131] Only La Mesnardière in his *Poetics* has an introductory remark on the similarity between poetry, painting and music, a point he calls a commonplace in Latin and Italian treatises on poetics,[132] which is but vaguely reminiscent of such writers as Madius, Minturno, and Zuccolo, but for which we can indicate no specific source unless we assume the author's familiarity with the appendix of Jacobus Pontanus.[133]

[130] *Dell'Entusiasmo delle Belle Arti* (1769). The author lists as Belle Arti: poetry, eloquence, painting, sculpture, architecture, music and the dance (Saverio Bettinelli, *Opere II* [Venice, 1780], 36 ff.). In the preface, apparently added in 1780, he cites the *Encyclopédie*, André, Batteux, Schatfibury (*sic*), Sulzer and others (11).

[131] F. Brunetière, *L'évolution des genres dans l'histoire de la littérature*, 5th ed. (Paris, 1910). A. Soreil, *Introduction à l'histoire de l' Esthétique française: Contribution à l'étude des théories littéraires et plastiques en France de la Pléiade au XVIIIe siècle* (thes. Liége, Brussels, 1930).

[132] "Mais entre les plus agréables (*i.e.*, arts and sciences), dont le principal objet est de plaire à la phantasie, on sçait bien que la peinture, la musique et la poësie sont sa plus douce nourriture" (Jules de la Mesnardière, *La poétique* I [Paris, 1639], 3). "Plusieurs livres sont remplis de la grande conformité qui est entre ces trois Arts. C'est pourquoy, sans m'arrester à des redites importunes, dont les Traittez de Poësie Latins et Italiens ne sont desia que trop chargez . ." (*ibid.*, 4). Cf. Soreil, 48. Helen R. Reese, *La Mesnardière's Poétique* (1639): *Sources and Dramatic Theories* (Baltimore, 1937), 59.

[133] See above, notes 92, 111, 113–15. It is also instructive to compare the subtitles in the Italian and French editions of Cesare Ripa's famous *Iconologia*. In Italian (Padua, 1618): *Opera utile ad Oratori, Predicatori, Poeti, Pittori, Scultori, Disegnatori, e ad ogni studioso, per inventar concetti, emblemi ed imprese, per divisare qualsivoglia apparato Nuttiale, Funerale, Trionfale*. In French (Paris, 1644): *Oeuvre . . . nécessaire à toute sorte d'esprits, et particulièrement à ceux qui aspirent à estre, ou qui sont en effet orateurs, poëtes, sculpteurs, peintres, ingenieurs, autheurs de medailles, de devises, de ballets, et de poëmes dramatiques.*

Yet the *Siècle de Louis XIV* was not limited in its achievements to poetry and literature. Painting and the other visual arts began to flourish, and with Poussin France produced a painter of European fame. Later in the century Lulli, although of Italian birth, developed a distinctive French style in music, and his great success with the Parisian public went a long way to win for his art the same popularity in France it had long possessed in Italy.[134]

This rise of the various arts was accompanied by an institutional development which followed in many respects the earlier Italian model, but was guided by a conscious governmental policy and hence more centralized and consistent than had been the case in Italy.[135] The Académie Française was organized in 1635 by Richelieu for the cultivation of the French language, poetry, and literature after the model of the Accademia della Crusca.[136] Several years later, in 1648, the Académie Royale de Peinture et de Sculpture was founded under Mazarin after the model of the Accademia di S. Luca in Rome, and tended to detach French artists from the artisans' guilds to which they had previously belonged.[137] Many more Academies were founded by Colbert between 1660 and 1680. They included provincial academies of painting and sculpture,[138] the French Academy in Rome, dedicated to the three visual arts,[139] as well as Academies of Architecture,[140] of Music,[141] and of the Dance.[142] However, the system of

[134] J. Écorcheville, *De Lulli à Rameau, 1690–1730: L'Esthétique musicale* (Paris, 1906).

[135] My attention was called to this problem by Dr. Else Hofmann. Cf. Pevsner, 84 ff. *La Grande Encyclopédie* I, 184 ff. *L'Institut de France: Lois, Statuts et Réglements concernant les anciennes Académies et l'Institut, de 1635 à 1889*, ed. L. Aucoc (Paris, 1889). *Lettres, Instructions et Mémoires de Colbert*, ed. P. Clement, V (Paris, 1868), LIII ff. and 444 ff.

[136] Aucoc, p. XXI–XLIII.

[137] Aucoc, p. CIV ff. Pevsner, 84 ff.

[138] Founded in 1676. Aucoc, CXXXVIII ff.

[139] Founded in 1666. *Lettres . . . de Colbert*, p. LVIII ff. and 510 f.

[140] Founded in 1671. Aucoc, CLXVI ff. *Lettres . . . de Colbert*, LXXII.

[141] This Academy, which was nothing else but the Paris Opera, can be traced back to a privilege granted to Pierre Perrin in 1669; cf. *La Grande Encyclopédie* I, 224 f. The Opera was definitely established in 1672 when a similar privilege was granted to Lulli, authorizing him "d'establir une académie royale de musique dans nostre bonne ville de Paris . . . pour faire des représentations devant nous . . . des pièces de musique qui seront composées tant en vers français qu'autres langues estrangères, pareille et semblable aux académies d'Italie" (*Lettres . . . de Colbert*, 535 f.).

[142] Founded in 1661. *La Grande Encyclopédie* I, 227.

the arts that would seem to underly these foundations is more apparent than real. The Academies were founded at different times, and even if we limit ourselves only to the period of Colbert, we should note that there were also the Académie des Sciences[143] and the Académie des Inscriptions et Médailles,[144] which have no relation to the "Fine Arts"; that there was at least a project for an Académie de Spectacles to be devoted to circus performances and other public shows;[145] and that the Académie de Musique and the Académie de Danse, like this projected Académie de Spectacles, were not organizations of distinguished professional artists or scientists, like the other Academies, but merely licensed establishments for the regular preparation of public performances.[146] Moreover, an extant paper from the time of Colbert that proposed to consolidate all Academies in a single institution makes no clear distinction between the arts and the sciences[147] and lends additional though indirect support to the view that Colbert's Academies reflect a comprehensive system of cultural disciplines and professions, but not a clear conception of the Fine Arts in particular.

Along with the founding of the Academies, and partly in close connection with their activities, there developed an important and extensive theoretical and critical literature on the visual arts.[148] The Conférences held at the Académie de Peinture et

[140] Founded in 1666. Aucoc, IV. Lettres . . . de Colbert, LXII ff.

[144] Founded in 1663. It changed its name to Académie Royale des Inscriptions et belles-lettres in 1716. Aucoc, IV and LI ff.

[145] The privilege granted to Henri Guichard in 1674 but not ratified authorizes him "de faire construire des cirques et des amphithéâtres pour y faire des carrousels, des tournois, des courses, des joustes, des luttes, des combats d'animaux, des illuminations, des feux d'artifice et généralement tout ce qui peut imiter les anciens jeux des Grecs et des Romains," and also "d'establir en nostre bonne ville de Paris des cirques et des amphithéâtres pour y faire lesdites représentations, sous le titre de l'Académie Royale de spectacles" (Lettres . . . de Colbert, 551 f.).

[146] This appears clearly from the charters, cited or referred to above.

[147] A note prepared by Charles Perrault for Colbert in 1666 proposes an Académie générale comprising four sections: belles-lettres (grammaire, éloquence, poésie); histoire (histoire, chronologie, géographie); philosophie (chimie, simples, anatomie, physique experimentale); mathématiques (géometrie, astronomie, algèbre). Lettres . . . de Colbert, 512 f. Poetry appears thus among belles-lettres with grammar and eloquence, and the other fine arts are not mentioned.

[148] Lee, l. c. Soreil, l. c. A. Fontaine, Les doctrines d'art en France . . . De Poussin à Diderot (Paris, 1909).

Sculpture are full of interesting critical views,[149] and separate treatises were composed by Du Fresnoy, De Piles, Fréart de Chambray, and Félibien.[150] Du Fresnoy's Latin poem *De arte graphica,* which was translated into French and English and made the subject of notes and commentaries, was in its form a conscious imitation of Horace's *Ars poetica,* and it begins characteristically by quoting Horace's *Ut pictura poesis* and then reversing the comparison.[151] The parallel between painting and poetry, as well as the contest between the two arts, were important to these authors, as to their predecessors in Renaissance Italy, because they were anxious to acquire for painting a standing equal to that of poetry and literature. This notion, which has been fully studied,[152] remained alive until the early eighteenth century,[153] and it is significant that the honor painting derives from its similarity to poetry is sometimes extended, as occasionally in the Italian Renaissance, to sculpture, architecture and even engraving as related arts.[154] Even the term *Beaux Arts,* which seems to have been intended at first for the visual arts alone, corresponding to *Arti del Disegno,* seems sometimes for these authors to include also music or poetry.[155] The comparison between painting and music is also made a few times,[156] and Poussin himself, who lived in Italy, tried to transfer the theory of the Greek musical modes to poetry and especially to painting.[157]

[149] *Conférences de l'Académie Royale de Peinture et de Sculpture,* ed. Félibien (London, 1705). *Conférences de l'Académie Royale de Peinture et de Sculpture,* ed. H. Jouin (Paris, 1883). *Conférences inédites de l'Académie Royale de Peinture et de Sculpture,* ed. A. Fontaine (Paris, n.d.).

[150] Cf. Lee, *l. c.,* and Schlosser, *l. c.*

[151] "Ut pictura poesis erit; similisque poesi sit pictura . . ." (C. A. Du Fresnoy, *De arte graphica* [London, 1695], 2).

[152] Fontaine, *l. c.;* Lee, *l. c.*

[153] P. Marcel, "Un débat entre les Peintres et les Poètes au début du XVIIIe siècle," *Chronique des Arts* (1905), 182–83; 206–07.

[154] Cf. *L'Art de Peinture* de C. A. Du Fresnoy, ed. R. de Piles, 4th ed. (Paris, 1751), 100. Félibien, *Entretiens sur les vies . . .* 4 (Paris, 1685), 155.

[155] *Conférences,* ed. Jouin, 240. R. de Piles, *Abrégé de la vie des Peintres . . .* (Paris, 1699), 23. Cf. Brunot, *Histoire de la langue française,* 6, 1, 681.

[156] *Conférences,* ed. Félibien, preface ("dans la musique et dans la poësie qui conviennent le plus avec la Peinture"). Félibien, *Entretiens sur les vies et sur les ouvrages des plus excellens peintres anciens et modernes,* pt. IV (Paris, 1685), 155. R. de Piles, *Cours de Peinture par principes* (Paris, 1708), 9. *Conférences,* ed. Jouin, 240; 277–78; 328.

[157] N. Poussin, *Traité des modes,* in his *Correspondance,* ed. Ch. Jouanny (Paris, 1911), 370 ff. Cf. *Conférences,* ed. Jouin, 94. Soreil, 27.

One of the great changes that occurred during the seventeenth century was the rise and emancipation of the natural sciences. By the second half of the century, after the work of Galileo and Descartes had been completed and the Académie des Sciences and the Royal Society had begun their activities, this development could not fail to impress the literati and the general public. It has been rightly observed that the famous *Querelle des Anciens et Modernes,* which stirred many scholars in France and also in England during the last quarter of the century, was due largely to the recent discoveries in the natural sciences.[158] The Moderns, conscious of these achievements, definitely shook off the authority of classical antiquity that had weighed on the Renaissance no less than on the Middle Ages, and went a long ways toward formulating the concept of human progress. Yet this is only one side of the Querelle.

The Querelle as it went on had two important consequences which have not been sufficiently appreciated. First, the Moderns broadened the literary controversy into a systematic comparison between the achievements of antiquity and of modern times in the various fields of human endeavor, thus developing a classification of knowledge and culture that was in many respects novel, or more specific than previous systems.[159] Secondly, a point by point examination of the claims of the ancients and moderns in the various fields led to the insight that in certain fields, where everything depends on mathematical calculation and the accumulation of knowledge, the progress of the moderns over the ancients can be clearly demonstrated, whereas in certain other fields, which depend on individual talent and on the taste of the critic, the

---

[158] This aspect has been studied especially by Richard F. Jones (*Ancients and Moderns,* St. Louis, 1936). For a broader treatment of the *Querelle:* H. Rigault, *Histoire de la querelle des Anciens et des Modernes,* in his *Oeuvres complètes I* [Paris, 1859]. H. Gillot, *La Querelle des anciens et des modernes en France* [Paris, 1914]. O. Diede, *Der Streit der Alten und Modernen in der englischen Literaturgeschichte des XVI. und XVII. Jahrhunderts* (thes. Greifswald, 1912). J. Delvaille, *Essai sur l'histoire de l'idée de progrès jusqu'à la fin du XVIIIe siècle* (Paris, 1910), 203 ff. J. B. Bury, *The Idea of Progress* (London, 1920), 78 ff.

[159] Brunetière (120) emphasizes that Perrault extended the discussion from literary criticism toward a general aesthetics, by drawing upon the other arts and even the sciences. The Italian forerunners of the *Querelle* had no system of the arts and sciences comparable to that of Perrault or Wotton, see above, note 128.

relative merits of the ancients and moderns cannot be so clearly established but may be subject to controversy.[160]

Thus the ground is prepared for the first time for a clear distinction between the arts and the sciences, a distinction absent from ancient, medieval or Renaissance discussions of such subjects even though the same words were used. In other words, the separation between the arts and the sciences in the modern sense presupposes not only the actual progress of the sciences in the seventeenth century but also the reflection upon the reasons why some other human intellectual activities which we now call the Fine Arts did not or could not participate in the same kind of progress. To be sure, the writings of the *Querelle* do not yet attain a complete clarity on these points, and this fact in itself definitely confirms our contention that the separation between the arts and the sciences and the modern system of the fine arts were just in the making at that time. Fontenelle, as some scholars have noticed, indicates in an occasional statement of his *Digression* that he was aware of the distinction between the arts and the sciences.[161]

Much more important and explicit is the work of Charles Perrault. His famous *Parallèle des Anciens et des Modernes* discusses the various fields in separate sections which reflect a system: the second dialogue is dedicated to the three visual arts, the third to eloquence, the fourth to poetry, and the fifth to the sciences.[162] The separation of the fine arts from the sciences is almost complete, though not yet entirely, since music is treated in the last book among the sciences, whereas in his poem, *Le Siècle de Louis le Grand,* which gave rise to the whole controversy, Perrault

---

[160] Rigault (323 f.) recognizes this distinction in Wotton, and Bury (104 f. and 121 ff.) attributes it to Fontenelle and Wotton. We shall see that it is also present in Perrault. For Wotton, see below.

[161] Fontenelle (*Digression sur les Anciens et les Modernes,* 1688, in his *Oeuvres* IV [Amsterdam, 1764], 114–31, esp. 120–22) admits the superiority of the ancients in poetry and eloquence, but stresses the superiority of the moderns in physics, medicine and mathematics. Significant is the emphasis on the more rigorous method introduced by Descartes.

[162] Charles Perrault, *Parallèle des Anciens et des Modernes,* 4 vols. (Paris, 1688–96). These are the subjects treated in the fifth dialogue (vol. 4, 1696): astronomie, géographie, navigation, mathématiques (geometry, algebra, and arithmetic), art militaire, philosophie (logique, morale, physique, métaphysique), médecine, musique, jardinage, art de la cuisine, véhicles, imprimerie, artillerie, estampes, feux d'artifice.

seems to connect music with the other arts.[163] Moreover, in his prefaces Perrault states explicitly that at least in the case of poetry and eloquence, where everything depends on talent and taste, progress cannot be asserted with the same confidence as in the case of the sciences which depend on measurement.[164] Equally interesting, though unrelated to the *Querelle,* is another writing of Perrault, *Le Cabinet des Beaux Arts* (1690). This is a description and explanation of eight allegorical paintings found in the studio of a French gentleman to whom the work is dedicated. In the preface, Perrault opposes the concept *Beaux Arts* to the traditional *Arts Libéraux,* which he rejects,[165] and then lists and describes the eight "Fine Arts" which the gentleman had represented

[163] This is the grouping in the poem (*Parallèle,* vol. I (Paris, 1693), 173 ff.): oratory, poetry, painting, sculpture, architecture, gardening, music. In the second dialogue also Perrault compares the visual arts repeatedly with music which he calls a *bel art* (146 and 149). Another work connected with the Querelle, François de Callière's *Histoire poëtique de la guerre nouvellement déclarée entre les anciens et les modernes* (Amsterdam, 1688; first ed., Paris, 1687) deals primarily with poetry and eloquence, but gives one section (Book 11, p. 213 ff.) to painting, sculpture and music. This is brought out in the title of the anonymous English translation: *Characters and Criticisms, upon the Ancient and Modern Orators, Poets, Painters, Musicians, Statuaries, and other Arts and Sciences* (London, 1705). Cf. A. C. Guthkelch, " 'The Tale of a Tub Revers'd' and 'Characters and Criticisms upon the Ancient and Modern Orators, etc.'," *The Library,* 3rd ser., vol. 4 (1913), 270–84.

[164] "Si nous avons un avantage visible dans les Arts dont les secrets se peuvent calculer et mesurer, il n'y a que la seule impossibilité de convaincre les gens dans les choses de goût et de fantaisie, comme sont les beautez de la Poësie et de l'Eloquence qui empesche que nous ne soyons reconnus les maîtres dans ces deux Arts comme dans tous les autres" (*Parallèle* I [Paris, 1693], preface). "Les Peintres, les Sculpteurs, les Chantres, les Poëtes / Tous ces hommes enfin en qui l'on voit regner / Un merveilleux sçavoir qu'on ne peut enseigner" (*Le génie, verse* epistle to Fontenele, *ibid.,* 195 f.). "Si j'avois bien prouvé, comme il est facile de le faire, que dans toutes les Sciences et dans tous les Arts dont les secrets se peuvent mesurer et calculer, nous l'emportons visiblement sur les Anciens; il n'y auroit que l'impossibilité de convaincre les esprits opiniastres dans les choses de goust et de fantaisie, comme sont la plupart des beautez de l'Eloquence et de la Poësie, qui pust empescher que les Modernes ne fussent reconnus les maistres dans ces deux arts comme dans tous les autres" (*ibid.,* 202). Cf. also vol. III, preface. In his general conclusion also (IV, 292 f.) Perrault excepts poetry and eloquence from his proof for the superiority of the Moderns.

[165] "Apres avoir abandonné cette division (of the seven liberal arts), on a choisi entre les Arts qui méritent d'être aimés et cultivés par un honnête homme ceux qui se sont trouvées être davantage du goût et du genie de celui qui les a fait peindre dans son cabinet" (p. 1 f.).

to suit his taste and interests: Éloquence, Poésie, Musique, Architecture, Peinture, Sculpture, Optique, Méchanique.[166] Thus on the threshold of the eighteenth century we are very close to the modern system of the Fine Arts, but we have not yet quite reached it, as the inclusion of Optics and Mechanics clearly shows. The fluctuations of the scheme show how slowly the notion emerged which to us seems so thoroughly obvious.

VI

During the first half of the eighteenth century the interest of amateurs, writers and philosophers in the visual arts and in music increased. The age produced not only critical writings on these arts composed by and for laymen,[167] but also treatises in which the arts were compared with each other and with poetry, and thus finally arrived at the fixation of the modern system of the fine arts.[168] Since this system seems to emerge gradually and after many fluctuations in the writings of authors who were in part of but secondary importance, though influential, it would appear that the notion and system of the fine arts may have grown and crystallized in the conversations and discussions of cultured circles in Paris and in London, and that the formal writings and treatises merely reflect a climate of opinion resulting from such conversations.[169] A further study of letters, diaries and articles in elegant journals may indeed supplement our brief survey, which we must limit to the better known sources.

The treatise on Beauty by J. P. de Crousaz, which first appeared in 1714 and exercised a good deal of influence, is usually considered as the earliest French treatise on aesthetics.[170] It has

[166] Eloquence, poetry, and music are put together in one group, as are the three visual arts (p. 2).

[167] Dresdner, 103 ff.

[168] Fontaine, Les doctrines d'art. Soreil, l. c. W. Folkierski, Entre le classicisme et le romantisme: Étude sur l'esthétique et les l'esthéticiens du XVIIIe siècle (Cracow-Paris, 1925). T. M. Mustoxidi, Histoire de l'Esthétique française, 1700–1900 (Paris, 1920). For music, see also Écorcheville, l. c. Hugo Goldschmidt, Die Musikaesthetik des 18. Jahrhunderts und ihre Beziehungen zu seinem Kunstschaffen (Zürich-Leipzig, 1915). While these scholars discuss most of the relevant sources, none of them focuses on the problem which concerns us.

[169] "Tel livre qui marque une date n'apporte, à vrai dire, rien de nouveau sur le marché des idées, mais dit tout haut et avec ordre ce que beaucoup de gens pensent en détail et disent tout bas, sans s'arrêter à ce qu'ils disent" (Soreil, 146).

[170] Traité du Beau, 2 vols. (Amsterdam, 1724).

indeed something to say on the visual arts and on poetry, and devotes a whole section to music. Moreover, it is an important attempt to give a philosophical analysis of beauty as distinct from goodness, thus restating and developing the notions of ancient and Renaissance Platonists. Yet the author has no system of the arts, and applies his notion of beauty without any marked distinction to the mathematical sciences and to the moral virtues and actions as well as to the arts, and the fluidity of his "aesthetic" thought is shown by the fact that in his second edition he substituted a chapter on the beauty of religion for the one dealing with music.[171]

During the following years, the problem of the arts seems to have dominated the discussions of the Académie des Inscriptions, and several of its lectures which were printed somewhat later and exercised a good deal of influence stress the affinity between poetry, the visual arts and music.[172] These discussions no doubt influenced the important work of the Abbé Dubos that appeared first in 1719 and was reprinted many times in the original and in translations far into the second half of the century.[173] Dubos' merits in the history of aesthetic or artistic thought are generally

[171] "Le dernier chapître où j'avois entrepris d'établir sur mes principes les fondemens de ce que la musique a de beau . . . on y en a substitué un autre. . . . C'est celui de la beauté de la religion" (preface of the second edition). On the treatment of music in the first edition, which I have not seen, cf. H. Goldschmidt, 35–37.

[172] In a lecture given in 1709, Abbé Fraguier describes poetry and painting as arts that have only pleasure for their end (Histoire de l'Académie Royale des Inscriptions et Belles Lettres . . . I (1736), 75 ff.). In a Deffense de la Poësie, presented before 1710, Abbé Massieu distinguishes "ceux [arts] qui tendent à polir l'esprit" (eloquence, poetry, history, grammar); "ceux qui ont pour but un délassement et un plaisir honneste" (painting, sculpture, music, dance); and "ceux qui sont les plus nécessaires à la vie" (agriculture, navigation, architecture) (Mémoires de littérature tirez de l'Académie Royale des Inscriptions II (1736), 185 f.). In a lecture of 1721, Louis Racine links poetry with the other beaux arts (ibid., V, [1729], 326). In a lecture of 1719, Fraguier treats painting, music, and poetry as different forms of imitation (ibid., VI [1729], 265 ff.). There are many more papers on related subjects.

[173] Réflexions critiques sur la poësie et sur la peinture, 4th ed., 3 vols. (Paris, 1740). A. Lombard, L'Abbé Du Bos: Un initiateur de la pensée moderne (1670–1742) (thes. Paris, 1913). Id., La Querelle des anciens et des modernes; l'abbé du Bos (Neuchatel, 1908). Aug. Morel, Étude sur l'Abbé Dubos (Paris, 1850). Marcel Braunschvig, L'Abbé DuBos renovateur de la critique au XVIIIe siècle (thes. Paris, Toulouse, 1904). P. Peteut, Jean-Baptiste Dubos (thes. Bern, 1902). E. Teuber, "Die Kunstphilosophie des Abbé Dubos", Zeitschrift für Aesthetik und allgemeine Kunstwissenschaft 17 (1924), 361–410. H. Trouchon, Romantisme et Préromantisme (Paris, 1930), 128 ff.

recognized. It is apparent that he discusses not only the analogies between poetry and painting but also their differences, and that he is not interested in the superiority of one art over the others, as so many previous authors had been. His work is also significant as an early, though not the first, treatment of painting by an amateur writer, and his claim that the educated public rather than the professional artist is the best judge in matters of painting as well as of poetry is quite characteristic.[174] He did not invent the term *beaux-arts,* nor was he the first to apply it to other than the visual arts, but he certainly popularized the notion that poetry was one of the *beaux-arts.*[175] He also has a fairly clear notion of the difference between the arts that depend on "genius" or talent and the sciences based on accumulated knowledge,[176] and it has been rightly observed that in this he continues the work of the "Moderns" in the *Querelle des Anciens et des Modernes,* especially of Perrault.[177] Significant also is his acquaintance with English authors such as Wotton and Addison.[178] Finally, although the title of his work refers only to poetry and painting, he repeatedly has occasion to speak also of the other visual arts as linked with painting, especially of sculpture and engraving,[179] and he discusses music so frequently[180] that his English translator chose to mention this art in the very title of the book.[181] However, Dubos is as unsystematic in his presentation and arrangement as he is interesting for the variety

[174] II, 323 ff.

[175] I, 4; II, 131.

[176] "Qu'il est des professions où le succès dépend plus du génie que du secours que l'art peut donner, et d'autres où le succès dépend plus du secours qu'on tire de l'art que du génie. On ne doit pas inferer qu'un siècle surpasse un autre siècle dans les professions du premier genre, parce qu'il le surpasse dans les professions du second genre." The ancients are supreme in poetry, history and eloquence, but have been surpassed in the sciences such as physics, botany, geography, and astronomy, anatomy, navigation. Among the fields where progress depends "plus du talent d'inventer et du génie naturel de celui qui les exerce que de l'état de perfection où ces professions se trouvent, lorsque l'homme qui les exerce fournit sa carrière," Dubos lists painting, poetry, military strategy, music, oratory, and medicine (II, 558 ff.).

[177] Lombard, *La querelle. Id.,* L'Abbé Du Bos, 183 ff.

[178] Lombard, *L'Abbé Du Bos,* 189 f. and 212.

[179] I, 393; 481. II, 157 f.; 177; 195, 224, 226; 228 ff.

[180] I, 435 ff.; 451 ("Les premiers principes de la musique sont donc les mêmes que ceux de la poësie et de la peinture. Ainsi que la poësie et la peinture, la musique est une imitation"). The third volume, which deals with the ancient theatre, contains an extensive treatment of music and the dance.

[181] *Critical Reflections on Poetry, Painting and Music,* translated by Thomas Nugent (London, 1748).

of his ideas, and he fails to give anywhere a precise list of the arts other than poetry and painting or to separate them consistently from other fields or professions.[182]

Voltaire also in his *Temple du Goût* (1733) seems to link together several of the fine arts, but in an informal and rather elusive fashion which shows that he was unable or unwilling to present a clear scheme.[183] More important for the history of our problem is the Essay on Beauty of Père André (1741), which exercised a good deal of influence.[184] His Cartesian background is worth noticing, although it is not enough to ascribe an aesthetics to Descartes.[185] The major sections of the work discuss visible beauty, which includes nature and the visual arts, the beauty of morals, the beauty of the works of the spirit, by which he means poetry and eloquence, and finally the beauty of music.[186] André thus moves much closer to the system of the arts than either Crousaz or Dubos had done, but in his treatise the arts are still combined with morality, and subordinated to the problem of beauty in a broader sense.

The decisive step toward a system of the fine arts was taken by the Abbé Batteux in his famous and influential treatise, *Les beaux arts réduits à un même principe* (1746).[187] It is true that many elements of his system were derived from previous authors, but at the same time it should not be overlooked that he was the first to set forth a clearcut system of the fine arts in a treatise devoted exclusively to this subject. This alone may account for his claim to originality as well as for the enormous influence he exercised both in France and abroad, especially in Germany.[188]

[182] Thus he once groups together grammarians, painters, sculptors, poets, historians, orators (II, 235). For another example, see above, note 176.

[183] "Nous trouvâmes un homme entouré de peintres, d'architectes, de sculpteurs, de doreurs, de faux connoisseurs, de flateurs" (Voltaire, *Le temple du goût*, ed. E. Carcassonne [Paris, 1938], 66). "On y passe facilement, / De la musique à la peinture, / De la physique au sentiment, / Du tragique au simple agrément, / De la danse à l'architecture" (*ibid.*, 84).

[184] *Essai sur le Beau* (Amsterdam, 1759; first ed. 1741). Cf. E. Krantz, *Essai sur l'esthétique de Descartes* . . . (Paris, 1882), 311 ff.

[185] Krantz, *l. c.*

[186] "Beau visible; beau dans les moeurs; beau dans les pièces de l'esprit; beau musical" (cf. p. 1).

[187] *Les beaux arts réduits à un même principe*, new ed. (Paris, 1747; first ed., 1746). Cf. M. Schenker, *Charles Batteux und seine Nachahmungstheorie in Deutschland* (Leipzig, 1909). Eberhard Freiherr von Danckelman, *Charles Batteux* (thes. Rostock, 1902).

[188] Trouchon, *l. c.* Schenker, *l. c.* For an English treatise based on Batteux, see below.

Batteux codified the modern system of the fine arts almost in its final form, whereas all previous authors had merely prepared it. He started from the poetic theories of Aristotle and Horace, as he states in his preface, and tried to extend their principles from poetry and painting to the other arts.[189] In his first chapter, Batteux gives a clear division of the arts. He separates the fine arts which have pleasure for their end from the mechanical arts, and lists the fine arts as follows: music, poetry, painting, sculpture and the dance.[190] He adds a third group which combines pleasure and usefulness and puts eloquence and architecture in this category. In the central part of his treatise, Batteux tries to show that the "imitation of beautiful nature" is the principle common to all the arts, and he concludes with a discussion of the theatre as a combination of all the other arts. The German critics of the later eighteenth century, and their recent historians, criticized Batteux for his theory of imitation and often failed to recognize that he formulated the system of the arts which they took for granted and for which they were merely trying to find different principles. They also overlooked the fact that the much maligned principle of imitation was the only one a classicist critic such as Batteux could use when he wanted to group the fine arts together with even an appearance of ancient authority. For the "imitative" arts were the only authentic ancient precedent for the "fine arts," and the principle of imitation could be replaced only after the system of the latter had been so firmly established as no longer to need the ancient principle of imitation to link them together. Diderot's criticism of Batteux has been emphasized too much, for it concerned only the manner in which Batteux defined and applied his principle, but neither the principle itself, nor the system of the arts for which it had been designed.

As a matter of fact, Diderot and the other authors of the *Encyclopédie* not only followed Batteux's system of the fine arts, but also furnished the final touch and thus helped to give it a general currency not only in France but also in the other European countries. Montesquieu in his essay on taste written

---

[189] "Le principe de l'imitation que le philosophe grec (Aristotle) établit pour les beaux arts, m'avoit frappé. J'en avois senti la justesse pour la peinture qui est une poesie muette . . ." (p. VIII). " J'allai plus loin: j'essayai d'appliquer le même principe à la musique et à l'art de geste" (VIII f.). He also quotes Cicero, *Pro Archia,* for the unity of the fine arts (p. X).

[190] "Les autres ont pour objet le plaisir . . . on les appelle les beaux arts par excellence. Tels sont la musique, poésie, la peinture, la sculpture et l'art du geste ou la danse" (p. 6).

for the *Encyclopédie* takes the fine arts for granted.[191] Diderot, whose interests included music and the visual arts and who was also acquainted with such English authors as Shaftesbury, Addison and Hutcheson, criticizes Batteux in his *Lettre sur les Sourds et Muets* (1751), in which he demands a better and more detailed comparison between poetry, painting and music that would take into account the different modes of expression of those arts as they would affect their treatment of even the same subject matter.[192] In the article on the Arts for the *Encyclopédie*, Diderot does not discuss the fine arts, but uses the old distinction between the liberal and mechanical arts and stresses the importance of the latter.[193] Yet in his article on beauty, he does discuss the fine arts, mentions Crousaz and Hutcheson and gives qualified approval to both André and Batteux, calling each of these two good works the best in its category and criticizing Batteux merely for his failure to define his concept of "beautiful nature" more clearly and explicitly.[194]

---

[191] *Essai sur le goût (Oeuvres complètes de Montesquieu*, ed. E. Laboulaye, VII [Paris, 1879], 116): "La poésie, la peinture, la sculpture, l'architecture, la musique, la danse, les différentes sortes de jeux, enfin les ouvrages de la nature et de l'art peuvent lui [to the soul] donner du plaisir . . ." Cf. Edwin P. Dargan, *The Aesthetic Doctrine of Montesquieu* (thes. Johns Hopkins University, Baltimore, 1907), 21.

[192] *Oeuvres complètes de Diderot*, ed. J. Assézat, 1 (1875), 343 ff. The preface is addressed to Batteux (*Lettre à l'auteur des Beaux-arts réduits à un même principe*, 347). Towards the end of his treatise, Diderot summarizes his criticism as follows: "Mais rassembler les beautés communes de la poésie, de la peinture et de la musique; en montrer les analogies; expliquer comment le poète, le peintre et le musicien rendent le même image . . . c'est ce qui reste à faire, et ce que je vous conseille d'ajouter à vos Beaux-arts réduits à un même principe. Ne manquez pas non plus de mettre à la tête de cet ouvrage un chapître sur ce que c'est que la belle nature, car je trouve des gens qui me soutiennent que, faute de l'une de ces choses, votre traité reste sans fondement; et que, faute de l'autre, il manque d'application" (385). On Diderot's aesthetic doctrines, see: Werner Leo, *Diderot als Kunstphilosoph* (thes. Erlangen, 1918). R. Loyalty Cru, *Diderot as a Disciple of English Thought* (New York, 1913), 395 ff.

[193] *Encyclopédie ou Dictionnaire Raisonné des sciences, des arts et des métiers* I (Paris, 1751), 713 ff.

[194] "Son Essai sur le beau [*i.e.*, of Père André] est le système le plus suivi, le plus étendu et le mieux lié que je connaisse. J'oserais assurer qu'il est dans son genre ce que le Traité des Beaux Arts réduits à un seul principe est dans le sien. Ce sont deux bons ouvrages auxquelles il n'a manqué qu'un chapître pour être excellents . . . M. l'abbé Batteux rappelle tous les principes des beaux-arts à l'imitation de la belle nature; mais il ne nous apprend point ce que c'est que la belle nature" (Diderot, *Oeuvres* 10 [1876], 17. *Encyclopédie* 2 [1751], 169 ff.). For the same criticism of Batteux, see also the *Lettre sur les sourds*, above, note 192.

Still more interesting is D'Alembert's famous *Discours préliminaire*. In his division of knowledge, purportedly based on Francis
Bacon, D'Alembert makes a clear distinction between philosophy,
which comprises both the natural sciences and such fields as
grammar, eloquence, and history, and "those cognitions which
consist of imitation," listing among the latter painting, sculpture,
architecture, poetry and music.[195] He criticizes the old distinction
between the liberal and mechanical arts, and then subdivides the
liberal arts into the fine arts which have pleasure for their end,
and the more necessary or useful liberal arts such as grammar,
logic and morals.[196] He concludes with a main division of
knowledge into philosophy, history and the fine arts.[197] This
treatment shows still a few signs of fluctuation and of older
notions, but it sets forth the modern system of the fine arts in
its final form, and at the same time reflects its genesis. The
threefold division of knowledge follows Francis Bacon, but
significantly d'Alembert speaks of the five fine arts where Bacon
had mentioned only poetry. D'Alembert is aware that the new
concept of the fine arts is taking the place of the older concept
of the liberal arts which he criticizes, and he tries to compromise
by treating the fine arts as a subdivision of the liberal arts, thus
leaving a last trace of the liberal arts that was soon to disappear.
Finally, he reveals his dependence on Batteux in certain phrases
and in the principle of imitation, but against Batteux and the
classical tradition he now includes architecture among the
imitative arts, thus removing the last irregularity which had
separated Batteux's system from the modern scheme of the fine
arts. Thus we may conclude that the *Encyclopédie*, and especially
its famous introduction, codified the system of the fine arts
after and beyond Batteux and through its prestige and authority
gave it the widest possible currency all over Europe.

After the middle of the century and after the publication of the

[195] "Des connaissances qui consistent dans l'imitation" (D'Alembert,
Oeuvres [Paris, 1853], 99 f. Cf. *Encyclopédie* I (1751), p. I ff.).

[196] "Parmi les arts libéraux qu'on a réduit à des principes, ceux qui se pro-
posent l'imitation de la nature ont été appelés beaux-arts, parce qu'ils ont
principalement l'agrément pour objet. Mais ce n'est pas la seule chose qui
les distingue des arts libéraux plus nécessaires ou plus utiles, comme la
grammaire, la logique ou la morale" (105).

[197] "La peinture, la sculpture, l'architecture, la poésie, la musique et leurs
différentes divisions composent la troisième distribution générale, qui naît de
l'imagination, et dont les parties sont comprises sous le nom de beaux-arts"
(117).

Encyclopédie, speculation on the fine arts in France does not seem to have undergone any basic changes for some time. The notion was popularized and stabilized through such works as Lacombe's portable dictionary of the Fine Arts, which covered architecture, sculpture, painting, engraving, poetry and music, and through other similar works.[198] The term Beaux Arts, and "Art," in the new sense, found its way into the dictionaries of the French language that had ignored it before. And the Revolution gave the novel term a new institutional expression when it merged several of the older Academies into the Académie des Beaux Arts.[199] Gradually, the further developments of aesthetics in Germany began to affect French philosophy and literature. The second edition of the *Encyclopédie,* published in Switzerland in 1781, has additions by Sulzer, including an article on aesthetics[200] and a section on Fine Arts appended to the article on Art that had not appeared in the first edition.[201] Early in the nineteenth century, the philosopher Victor Cousin, following Kant and the Scottish thinkers of the eighteenth century, as well as what he believed he found in Plato, Proclus and other classical sources, centered his philosophical system on the three concepts of the Good, the True and the Beautiful, understanding

[198] Jacques Lacombe, *Dictionnaire portatif des Beaux-Arts ou Abrégé de ce qui concerne l'architecture, la sculpture, la peinture, la gravure, la poésie et la musique, avec la définition de ces arts, l'explication des termes et des choses qui leur appartiennent,* new ed. (Paris, 1753; first ed. 1752). The preface refers to "Le goût que le public témoigne pour les Beaux-Arts" and to "la nécessité d'un livre qui renferme les Recherches et les Connoissances d'un amateur" (p. III). Pierre Estève, *L'esprit des Beaux Arts,* 2 vols. (Paris, 1753). P.-J.-B. Nougaret, *Anecdotes des Beaux Arts, contenant tout ce que la Peinture, la Sculpture, la Gravure, l'Architecture, la Littérature, la Musique etc. et la vie des artistes offrent de plus curieux et de plus piquant,* 3 vols. (Paris, 1776–80; the work actually covers only the visual arts).

[199] Aucoc, 6–7. The section for literature and the fine arts of the *Institut,* created in 1795, comprised: grammaire, langues anciennes, poésie, antiquité et monuments, peinture, sculpture, architecture, musique, déclamation.

[200] *Encyclopédie* 13 (Berne and Lausanne, 1781), 84–86: "Esthétique . . . terme nouveau, inventé pour désigner une science qui n'a été réduite en forme que depuis peu d'années. C'est la philosophie des beaux-arts." [Aristotle did not have such a theory.] "M. Dubos est, si je ne me trompe, le premier d'entre les modernes qui ait entrepris de déduire d'un principe général la théorie des beaux-arts, et d'en démontrer les règles . . . . Feu M. Baumgarten . . . est le premier qui ait hasardé de créer sur des principes philosophiques la science générale des beaux-arts, à laquelle il a donné le nom d'esthétique."

[201] *Ibid.* 3 (1781), 484 ff.

by the latter the realm of art and aesthetics.[202] Cousin's wide influence in the later nineteenth century went a long ways toward establishing this triad in modern value theory and toward fortifying the place of aesthetics in the system of philosophical disciplines. It also induced many thinkers and historians to interpret in terms of this scheme a number of ancient and medieval notions that resembled it superficially but had in reality a very different meaning and context. Meanwhile, as Cousin's doctrine was spreading among philosophers and historians, French literature and criticism had long been feeling the impact of Romanticism. They were beginning to develop modern problems and theories concerning the arts and their interpretation, no longer related to the discussions of the eighteenth century, and were laying the ground for other, more recent tendencies.

VII

Having followed the French development through the eighteenth century, we must discuss the history of artistic thought in England.[203] The English writers were strongly influenced by the French down to the end of the seventeenth century and later, but during the eighteenth century they made important contributions of their own and in turn influenced continental thought, especially in France and Germany. Interest in the arts other than

[202] V. Cousin, *Du Vrai, du Beau et du Bien*, 29th ed. (Paris, 1904; first ed., 1836, based on lectures delivered in 1817–18). Cf. P. Janet, *Victor Cousin et son oeuvre* (Paris, 1885). E. Krantz (*Essai sur l'esthétique de Descartes* [Paris, 1882], 312 f.) emphasizes that Cousin was the first French thinker who gave a separate place to aesthetics and to beauty in his philosophical system.

[203] James E. Tobin, *Eighteenth Century English Literature and Its Cultural Background: A Bibliography* (New York, 1939), 11–16; 27–33. John W. Draper, *Eighteenth Century English Aesthetics: A Bibliography* (Heidelberg, 1931). B. Sprague Allen, *Tides of English Taste (1619–1800)*, 2 vols. (Cambridge, Mass., 1937). F. Mirabent, *La estética inglesa del siglo XVIII* (Barcelona, 1927). Karl L. F. Thielke, *Literatur- und Kunstkritik in ihren Wechselbeziehungen: Ein Beitrag zur englischen Aesthetik des 18. Jahrhunderts* (Halle, 1935). John W. Draper, "Aristotelian 'Mimesis' in Eighteenth Century England," *PMLA* 36 (1921), 372–400. *Id.*, "Poetry and Music in Eighteenth Century Aesthetics," *Englische Studien* 67 (1932–33), 70–85. J. G. Robertson, *Studies in the Genesis of Romantic Theory in the Eighteenth Century* (Cambridge, 1923), 235 ff. Elizabeth W. Manwaring, *Italian Landscape in Eighteenth Century England* (New York, 1925), 14 ff. Herbert M. Schueller, "Literature and Music as Sister Arts: An Aspect of Aesthetic Theory in Eighteenth-Century Britain," *Philological Quarterly* 26 (1947), 193–205.

poetry began to rise slowly in the English literature of the
seventeenth century. Works of an encyclopedic nature show
little awareness of the separate function of the fine arts,[204]
whereas an author such as Henry Peacham, who continued the
amateur tradition of the Renaissance, would not only write a
treatise on drawing, but also recommend the cultivation of painting, music and poetry, of classical studies and the collecting of
coins and other antiquities and of natural curiosities, for the
education of a perfect gentleman.[205] John Evelyn, who was the
model of a *virtuoso,* combined artistic and scientific interests,[206]
but the work of the *virtuosi* of the Royal Society soon led to a
separation between the arts and the sciences.[207] The *Querelle,*
which was at least partly caused by the emancipation of the
natural sciences in the seventeenth century, spread from France
to England. The most important treatise in England representing
the views of the Moderns, that of Wotton, tried to cover system-
atically all the human arts and activities, just as Perrault had
done, and emphasized like Perrault the fundamental difference
between the sciences that had made progress since antiquity,
and the arts that had not.[208] A translation of one of the French

[204] George Hakewill (*An Apologie or Declaration of the Power and Providence of God in the Government of the World . . . ,* 3rd ed., Oxford, 1635),
who compares the ancients and moderns in the arts and sciences (Bury, 89),
puts poetry between history and the art military (278 ff.), architecture and
painting between philosophy and navigation (303 ff.), whereas sculpture and
music receive no separate treatment in his work.

[205] See above, note 110.

[206] *The Literary Remains of John Evelyn,* ed. W. Upcott (London, 1834).

[207] James A. H. Murray, *A New English Dictionary on Historical Principles,*
vol. 10, pt. 2 (Oxford, 1928), 240 f. Several of the seventeenth-century passages
given for "virtuoso" include a scientific interest. The limitation of the term
to a taste for the arts is clear in Shaftesbury, see below. Cf. Manwaring, *l.c.,*
25.

[208] William Wotton, *Reflections upon Ancient and Modern Learning,* 3rd
ed. (London, 1705). ". . . of these particulars there are two sorts: one, of
those wherein the greatest part of those learned men who have compared
Ancient and Modern Performances, either give up the cause to the Ancients
quite, or think, at least, that the Moderns have not gone beyond them. The
other of those, where the Advocates for the Moderns think the case so clear
on their side, that they wonder how any man can dispute it with them.
Poesie, Oratory, Architecture, Painting, and Statuary, are of the first sort;
Natural History, Physiology, and Mathematics, with all their Dependencies,
are of the second" (p. 18, end of ch. 2). "The generality of the learned have
given the Ancients the preference in those arts and sciences which have
hitherto been considered: but for the precedency in those parts of learning

works related to the *Querelle,* Callière's *History of the War of the Ancients and Moderns,* was published as late as 1705, and reveals in its very title the growing sense of the affinity of the fine arts.[209] Even before the end of the seventeenth century, Dryden had translated Du Fresnoy's poem on painting with De Piles' commentary and had added his famous introduction on the Parallel of Painting and Poetry which popularized the notion in England.[210] This translation was still of interest to Sir Joshua Reynolds, who wrote some notes on it.[211] Early in the eighteenth century, Jonathan Richardson was praising painting as a liberal art,[212] and John Dennis in some of his critical treatises on poetics stressed the affinity between poetry, painting and music.[213]

Of greater importance were the writings of Anthony, Earl of Shaftesbury, one of the most influential thinkers of the eight-

---

which still remain to be enquired into, the Moderns have put in their claim, with great briskness. Among this sort, I reckon mathematical and physical sciences, in their largest extent" (p. 74 f., ch. 7). In the first group, Wotton discusses Moral and Political knowledge, Eloquence and Poesie, grammar, architecture, statuary and painting. The second group includes, besides the sciences, philology and theology, also gardening which is treated with agriculture (ch. 22, p. 272) and music which is placed between optics and medicine (ch. 25, p. 307). The chapter on gardening is lacking in the first edition (London, 1694). Wotton does once compare music with painting ("For, in making a Judgment of Music, it is much the same thing as it is in making a judgment of Pictures," 311), but he treats music as a "physico-mathematical science, built upon fixed rules, and stated proportions" (309 f.), and also in other respects his two groups do not coincide with the modern distinction between fine arts and sciences. Wotton is obviously moving towards that distinction, but I do not see that he goes beyond Perrault in this respect, as stated by Rigault (323 f.) and Bury (121 f.). No distinction between the arts and sciences is made by Sir William Temple, "An Essay upon the Ancient and Modern Learning" (1690), in *Critical Essays of the Seventeenth Century,* ed. J. E. Spingarn, vol. 3 (Oxford, 1909), 32-72.

[209] See above, note 163.

[210] C. A. Du Fresnoy, *De arte graphica,* tr. J. Dryden (London, 1695), p. I-LVIII: "Preface of the Translator, with a Parallel of Poetry and Painting." *The Critical and Miscellaneous Prose of John Dryden,* ed. E. Malone, vol. III (London, 1800), 291 ff.

[211] Sir Joshua Reynolds, *The Literary Works* II (London, 1835), 297-358 (first ed., 1783).

[212] Jonathan Richardson, *The Theory of Painting* (first published in 1715), in his *Works* (London, 1792), 5 ff.

[213] *The Critical Works of John Dennis,* ed. Edward N. Hooker, vol. I (Baltimore, 1939), 201 f. ("The Advancement and Reformation of Modern Poetry," 1701); 336 ("The Ground of Criticism in Poetry," 1704).

eenth century, not only in England but also on the continent.[214]
His interest and taste for literature and the arts are well known,
and his writings are full of references to the various arts and to
the beauty of their works. The ideal of the *virtuoso* which he
embodied and advocated no longer included the sciences, as in
the seventeenth century, but had its center in the arts and in
the moral life.[215] Since Shaftesbury was the first major philosopher
in modern Europe in whose writings the discussion of the arts
occupied a prominent place, there is some reason for considering
him as the founder of modern aesthetics.[216] Yet Shaftesbury was
influenced primarily by Plato and Plotinus, as well as by Cicero,
and he consequently did not make a clear distinction between
artistic and moral beauty.[217] His moral sense still includes both
ethical and aesthetic objects.[218] Moreover, although references
to the particular arts are frequent in his writings, and some of
his works are even entirely devoted to the subjects of painting[219]
or of poetry,[220] the passages in which he mentions poetry, the
visual arts and music together are not too frequent, and do not
contain any more specific notions than may be found in earlier
authors.[221] Poetry, especially, appears still in the company not

[214] His importance is stressed by all historians of aesthetics. See also E.
Cassirer, *Die platonische Renaissance in England und die Schule von Cambridge* (Leipzig, 1932), 115; 138 ff. G. Spicker, *Die Philosophie des Grafen
von Shaftesbury* (Freiburg, 1872), 196 ff. Christian Friedrich Weiser, *Shaftesbury und das deutsche Geistesleben* (Leipzig-Berlin, 1916). L. Stuermer, *Der
Begriff "moral sense" in der Philosophie Shaftesbury's* (thes. Königsberg,
1928).

[215] Anthony, Earl of Shaftesbury, *Characteristics*, ed. John M. Robertson
(London, 1900), vol. I, 214 f.; II, 252 f. *The Life, Unpublished Letters, and
Philosophical Regimen of Anthony, Earl of Shaftesbury*, ed. B. Rand (London, 1900), 249 ("A virtuoso to propose poetry, music, dance, picture, architecture, garden, and so on"); 416 f. ("Had Mr. Locke been a virtuoso, he
would not have philosophized thus"); 478; 484; 496; 506.

[216] See Cassirer, *l.c.*, above, note 214.

[217] *Characteristics* II, 128; 138.

[218] *Characteristics* I, 262; II, 136 f.

[219] Anthony, Earl of Shaftesbury, *Second Characters*, ed. B. Rand (Cambridge, 1914).

[220] *Characteristics* I, 101 ff.

[221] "From music, poetry, rhetoric, down to the simple prose of history,
through all the plastic arts of sculpture, statuary, painting, architecture, and
the rest; everything muse-like, graceful, and exquisite was rewarded with the
highest honours . . ." (*i.e.*, by the Greeks). *Characteristics* II, 242. Cf. *ibid.*,
II, 330, where criticism of poetry is compared to the judgment of music or
painting. I, 94 (beauty in architecture, music, poetry); II, 129; 252 f.

only of eloquence but also of history, thus reflecting the Renaissance tradition of the *Studia humanitatis*.[222] Almost equally influential in England as well as on the continent, at least in literary circles, was Joseph Addison. His famous essays on imagination, which appeared in the *Spectator* in 1712, are remarkable not merely for their early emphasis on that faculty, but also for the manner in which he attributes the pleasures of the imagination to the various arts as well as to natural sights. Without ever giving a definite system, he constantly refers to gardening and architecture, painting and sculpture, poetry and music, and makes it quite clear that the pleasures of the imagination are to be found in their works and products.[223]

The philosophical implications of Shaftesbury's doctrine were further developed by a group of Scottish thinkers. Francis Hutcheson, who considered himself Shaftesbury's pupil, modified his doctrine by distinguishing between the moral sense and the sense of beauty.[224] This distinction, which was adopted by Hume[225] and quoted by Diderot, went a long ways to prepare the separation of ethics and aesthetics, although Hutcheson still

[222] II, 242. There seems to be a tendency in Shaftesbury to associate not only the beauty of the senses with the visual arts and music, but also the beauty of character and virtue, or moral beauty, with poetry. I, 136 ("moral artist"); 216 ("poetical and moral truth, the beauty of sentiments, the sublime of characters . . ."); II, 318 ("to morals, and the knowledge of what is called poetic manners and truth"); 331 f. ("a sense of that moral truth on which . . . poetic truth and beauty must naturally depend"). This is not merely a residue of the old moralistic interpretation of poetry, but an attempt to correlate the emerging system of the fine arts with Plato's ladder of beauty. Cf. the statement of Castelvetro, above, note 92.

[223] Joseph Addison, *Works*, ed. Tickell, II (London, 1804), 354 ff. (*Spectator*, no. 411 ff.). Addison includes architecture, and perhaps gardening, along with natural sights, among the primary pleasures, whereas he lists as secondary pleasures the "arts of mimicry," *i.e.*, "statue, picture, description, or sound" (376). Significant also is a sentence from an earlier essay, published in the *Spectator*, no. 29, on April 3, 1711: "that music, architecture, and painting, as well as poetry and oratory, are to deduce their laws and rules from the general sense and taste of mankind . . ." (*ibid.*, I, 78).

[224] Francis Hutcheson, *An Inquiry into the Original of our Ideas of Beauty and Virtue* (Glasgow, 1772; first ed., 1725), p. XI; 8; 100. Cf. Thomas Fowler, *Shaftesbury and Hutcheson* (New York, 1883). William Robert Scott, *Francis Hutcheson* (Cambridge, 1900). John J. Martin, *Shaftesbury's und Hutcheson's Verhältnis zu Hume* (thes. Halle, 1905).

[225] D. Hume, *An Enquiry concerning the Principles of Morals* (1751), Appendix I: "Concerning Moral Sentiment." Cf. *A Treatise of Human Nature* (1739–40), Book III, Part I, Section II.

assigned the taste of poetry to the moral sense.[226] A later philosopher of the Scottish school, Thomas Reid, introduced common sense as a direct criterion of truth, and although he was no doubt influenced by Aristotle's notion of common sense and the Stoic and modern views on "common notions," it has been suggested that his common sense was conceived as a counterpart to Hutcheson's two senses.[227] Thus the psychology of the Scottish school led the way for the doctrine of the three faculties of the soul, which found its final development in Kant and its application in Cousin.

Other English authors, motivated by critical rather than philosophical interests and probably influenced by French authors, popularized the notion of the affinity between poetry, painting, and music, e.g., Charles Lamotte[228] and Hildebrand Jacobs.[229] More philosophical are the essays of James Harris, who continued Shaftesbury and had some influence on German writers. In the first of his three essays, which are written in an elegant dialogue form but heavily annotated with references to classical authors, Harris expounds the concept of art on the basis of Aristotle and with its older comprehensive meaning. In the second essay, he distinguishes between the necessary arts and

[226] *L.c.*, 239 ("We shall find this sense to be the foundation also of the chief pleasures of poetry"). For the root of this idea in Shaftesbury, see above, note 222.

[227] Thomas Reid, *Works*, 4th ed. (Edinburgh, 1854). Matthias Keppes, *Der Common Sense als Princip der Gewissheit in der Philosophie des Schotten Thomas Reid* (Munich, 1890), 15. Cf. F. Ueberweg, *Grundriss der Geschichte der Philosophie*, III, 12th ed. (Berlin, 1924), 416. O. Robbins, "The Aesthetics of Thomas Reid," *The Journal of Aesthetics and Art Criticism* 5 (1942), 30–41.

[228] Charles Lamotte, *An Essay upon Poetry and Painting . . .* (Dublin, 1745; first ed., 1730).

[229] Hildebrand Jacobs, *Of the Sister Arts; an Essay*, in his *Works* (London, 1735), 379–419 (first ed., 1734). "If it be allow'd with Cicero that all Arts are related, we may safely conclude, that Poetry, Painting, and Music are closely ally'd" (379). "Poetry is much nearer ally'd to Painting, than to Music. Lyric Poetry approaches more to Music than any other Species of it, as Dramatic, and Pastoral Poetry do to Painting" (380). "The same Rules which Aristotle lays down as necessary for the Poets to observe in the Formation of he (*sic*) Manners, or Characters, are equally instructive to the Painters" (401). "That the Ancients were more excellent than we in most Parts of these Arts of Ornament, is as manifest, as that latter Ages have invented many useful Things entirely unknown to them" (412). However, the moderns are said to be superior in music (392). These statements are so explicit and interesting that it would be worth while to explore the influence of this author in France and Germany.

the arts of elegance, putting under the latter category especially music, painting and poetry, and comparing these three arts with each other according to their relative merits. The third essay deals with happiness as the art of human conduct.[230] About the same time, the poet Akenside continued the work of Addison;[231] and before the middle of the century the important French works of Dubos and Batteux were presented to English readers, the former in a translation,[232] the latter in an anonymous version or summary, entitled *The Polite Arts*.[233]

[230] J(ames) H(arris), *Three Treatises, the first concerning art, the second concerning music, painting, and poetry, the third concerning happiness* (London, 1744). "All arts have this in common that they respect human life. Some contribute to its necessities, as medicine and agriculture; others to its elegance, as music, painting, and poetry" (53). These three arts are called mimetic (65; 94).

[231] Mark Akenside, *The Pleasures of Imagination*, in his *Poetical Works*, ed. G. Gilfillan (Edinburgh, 1857), 1 ff. In the preface of 1744, painting and sculpture, music and poetry are listed as imitative arts, and the poem is said to cover "all the various entertainment we meet with, either in poetry, painting, music, or any of the elegant arts" (p. 1). In the general argument added to the edition of 1757, the pleasures of imagination are said to proceed from natural objects or "from works of art, such as a noble edifice, a musical tune, a statue, a picture, a poem," and music, sculpture, painting and poetry are called "elegant arts" (77).

[232] See above, note 181.

[233] *The Polite Arts, or, a Dissertation on Poetry, Painting, Musick, Architecture, and Eloquence* (London, 1749). The work is anonymous, and dedicated to William Cheselden. In the copy of the Yale University Library I have used, a contemporary manuscript note at the end of the preface identifies the author as follows: "Hippesley, son of the player, & bred under Mr. Cheselden & now surgeon abroad to the African company, 1753" (p. IX). This is obviously John Hippisley (d. 1767) son of the actor (d. 1748), to whom the following anonymous writings have been attributed: Dissertation on Comedy . . . (London, 1750); Essays, 1. On the Populousness of Africa, 2. On the Trade at the Forts on the Gold Coast, 3. On the Necessity of erecting a Fort at Cape Appollonia (London, 1764). Cf. *Dictionary of National Biography* IX, 903. The essay on *The Polite Arts* appears to depend closely on Batteux. This is the division of the arts given in ch. 2: "Arts may be divided into three kinds. The first have the Necessities of Mankind for their Object . . . . From this the Mechanick Arts arose. The next kind have Pleasure for their Object . . . They are called Polite Arts by way of Excellency, such are Musick, Poetry, Painting, Sculpture, and the Art of Gesture or Dancing. The third kind are those which have usefulness and Pleasure at the same time for their Object: such are Eloquence and Architecture" (5–6). A close comparison between the anonymous English essay and Batteux's treatise shows that the former follows the latter verbatim for large sections of the text, but alters its model through numerous transpositions, omissions and additions. The most important among the latter are two chapters on Eloquence and Architecture at the end of the English essay.

During the second half of the eighteenth century, English writers continued to discuss the various arts. But they were not so much interested in expounding and developing a system of the fine arts, which they took pretty much for granted, as in discussing general concepts and principles concerning the arts; e.g., Home, Burke, and Gerard; or else the relations between the particular arts; e.g., Daniel Webb or John Brown, to mention only some of the more influential writers.[234] All these English and Scottish writers show a strong preoccupation with psychology, as might be expected from the general trend of English thought in that century. They exercised considerable influence on the continent, especially in Germany, where many of their works appeared in translations. It has been noted that the emphasis of writers and literary critics on the affinity between poetry and painting was followed after the middle of the century by an increasing insistence on the links between poetry and music.[235] One reason for this may have been the public attention which music received in London after the appearance of Handel,[236] just as had been the case in Paris after the success of Lulli. On the other hand, if poetry really tended to exchange the company of painting for that of music, this merely reflects a change in style and taste

[234] Henry Home, Lord Kames, *Elements of Criticism* (New York, 1830; first ed., 1762). He lists poetry, painting, sculpture, music, gardening and architecture as "fine arts" (11). E. Burke, *A Philosophical Enquiry into the Origin of our Ideas of the Sublime and Beautiful* (London, 1770; first ed., 1757). Alexander Gerard, *An Essay on Taste* (London, 1759). He lists as the "finer arts": music, painting, statuary, architecture, poetry and eloquence (189). Daniel Webb, *Observations on the Correspondence between Poetry and Music* (London, 1769; cf. Hans Hecht, *Daniel Webb*, Hamburg, 1920). Dr. (John) Brown, *A Dissertation on the Rise, Union, and Power, the Progressions, Separations, and Corruptions, of Poetry and Musick* (London, 1763; cf. Hermann M. Flasdieck, *John Brown (1715–66) und seine Dissertation on Poetry and Music*, Halle, 1924). Thomas Robertson, *An Inquiry into the Fine Arts* (London, 1784; he quotes Batteux and Bettinelli, and lists as fine arts: music, speech, architecture, painting, sculpture, gardening, dance, eloquence, poetry and also history, cf. 14–17). Sir William Jones, *Essay II. on the Arts, commonly called Imitative*, in his *Poems*, 2nd ed. (London, 1777), 191 ff. (he also quotes Batteux and discusses especially poetry, music and painting). James Beattie, *An Essay on Poetry and Music, as they affect the Mind*, 3rd ed. (London, 1779; written in 1762). Hugh Blair, *Lectures on Rhetoric and Belles Lettres* (London, 1787; first ed., 1783).

[235] John W. Draper, "Poetry and Music in Eighteenth Century Aesthetics," *Englische Studien* 67 (1932–33), 70–85. Herbert M. Schueller, "Literature and Music as Sister Arts . . . ," *Philological Quarterly* 26 (1947), 193–205.

[236] Cf. H. Parker, *The Nature of the Fine Arts* (London, 1885), 18 ff.

from descriptive to emotional poetry that corresponds to the transition from classicism to romanticism. A new epoch in English critical and artistic theory begins toward the very end of the century with Coleridge, who imported from Germany some of the aesthetic notions of Kant and of the early Romanticists. The further developments these ideas received through Coleridge and his English successors in the nineteenth century is beyond the scope of this paper.

VIII

Discussion of the arts does not seem to have occupied many German writers of the seventeenth century, which was on the whole a period of decline.[237] The poet Opitz showed familiarity with the parallel of poetry and painting,[238] but otherwise the Germans did not take part in the development we are trying to describe before the eighteenth century. During the first part of that century interest in literature and literary criticism began to rise, but did not yet lead to a detailed or comparative treatment of the other arts. However, some of the French and English writers we have mentioned were widely read and also translated into German during the course of the century, such as Dubos and Batteux, Shaftesbury and Harris. The critical writings of the Swiss authors, Bodmer and Breitinger, focus from the very beginning on the parallel between painting and poetry, and reflect the influence of Addison and perhaps of

[237] For German aesthetics in the eighteenth century, see, besides the general histories of aesthetics: F. Braitmaier, *Geschichte der poetischen Theorie von den Diskursen der Maler bis auf Lessing*, 2 pts. (Frauenfeld, 1888–89). E. Gurcker, *Histoire des doctrines littéraires et esthétiques en Allemagne*, 2 vols. (Paris, 1883–96). Robert Sommer, *Grundzüge einer Geschichte der deutschen Psychologie und Aesthetik von Wolff-Baumgarten bis Kant-Schiller* (Würzburg, 1892). M. Dessoir, *Geschichte der neueren deutschen Psychologie*, 2nd ed. (Berlin, 1902). H. Goldschmidt, *Die Musikaesthetik des 18. Jahrhunderts* . . . (Zürich and Leipzig, 1915). W. Dilthey, *Das Erlebnis und die Dichtung*, 4th ed. (Leipzig, 1913), 42 ff. E. Cassirer, *Freiheit und Form*, 2nd ed. (Berlin, 1918), 97 ff. Herman Wolf, *Versuch einer Geschichte des Geniebegriffs in der deutschen Aesthetik des 18. Jahrhunderts* (Heidelberg, 1923). K. Bauerhorst, *Der Geniebegriff* . . . (thes. Breslau, 1930). B. Rosenthal, *Der Geniebegriff des Aufklärungszeitalters* (Berlin, 1933).

[238] C. Borinski, *Die Kunstlehre der Renaissance in Opitz' Buch von der deutschen Poeterey* (thes. Munich, 1883), 44 f.

Dubos,[239] Even their classicist opponent, Gottsched, mentions occasionally the affinity between poetry, painting, music, and the other arts,[240] as does Johann Elias Schlegel, who is said to have been influenced by the lectures of Fraguier and other authors published in the Memoirs of the Académie des Inscriptions.[241] His brother Johann Adolf Schlegel, who was one of the translaters of Batteux, added to his version several original essays in which he criticizes the theory of imitation and also presents a modified system of the fine arts.[242] Yet all these writers were primarily interested in poetics and literary criticism and drew upon the other arts only for occasional analogies.

These critical discussions among poets and literati constitute the general background for the important work of the philosopher Alexander Gottlieb Baumgarten and of his pupil Georg Friedrich Meier.[243] Baumgarten is famous for having coined

[239] *Die Discourse der Mahlern* (1721–22), ed. Th. Vetter (Frauenfeld, 1891). The analogy between poetry and painting is stressed in discourse no. 19 (p. 91) and extended to sculpture in discourse no. 20 (97 ff.). The same analogy is stressed in the later works of Bodmer and Breitinger. See Johann Jacob Bodmer, *Critische Betrachtungen ueber die Poetischen Gemälde der Dichter* (Zürich, 1741), 27 ff. Johann Jacob Breitinger, *Critische Dichtkunst* (Zürich, 1740), 3 ff. and 29 ff. (where the comparison with painting is extended to history and eloquence). Cf. R. De Reynold, *Histoire littéraire de la Suisse au XVIIIe siècle*, II (Lausanne, 1912): *Bodmer et l'École Suisse*. R. Verosta, *Der Phantasiebegriff bei den Schweizern Bodmer und Breitinger* (progr. Vienna, 1908). F. Braitmaier, *Die poetische Theorie Gottsched's und der Schweizer* (progr. Tübingen, 1879). F. Servaes, *Die Poetik Gottscheds und der Schweizer* (Strassburg, 1887).

[240] Johann Cristoph Gottsched, *Versuch einer Critischen Dichtkunst*, 3rd ed. (Leipzig, 1742), 98 (where poetry is compared with painting, sculpture, music and dance).

[241] Johann Elias Schlegels *Aesthetische und dramaturgische Schriften*, ed. J. von Antoniewicz (Heilbronn, 1887). In an essay composed in 1745, Schlegel compares poetry with architecture, painting and sculpture (97), in another essay dated 1742–43 with painting, sculpture and music (107 ff.). On his French sources, see the introduction, p. XXXVI ff. and XCV ff.

[242] Herrn Abt Batteux . . . . *Einschränkung der Schönen Künste auf einen einzigen Grundsatz*, tr. Johann Adolf Schlegel, 3rd ed. (Leipzig, 1770; first ed., 1751), II, 155 ff.: "Abhandlung no. 5. Von der Eintheilung der schönen Künste nach ihrer verschiednen Absicht." Schlegel summarizes Batteux but insists that eloquence and architecture should be included among the fine arts (157) and also adds prose poetry as well as drawing and engraving to the list (180–81). Cf. Hugo Bieber, *Johann Adolf Schlegels poetische Theorie in ihrem historischen Zusammenhange untersucht* (Berlin, 1912).

[243] Alexander Gottlieb Baumgarten, *Aesthetica*, ed. B. Croce (Bari, 1936; first ed., 1750–58). This edition also contains (1–45) his *Meditationes Philos-*

the term aesthetics, but opinions differ as to whether he must
be considered the founder of that discipline or what place he occupies in its history and development. The original meaning of
the term aesthetics as coined by Baumgarten, which has been well
nigh forgotten by now, is the theory of sensuous knowledge, as
a counterpart to logic as a theory of intellectual knowledge.[244]
The definitions Baumgarten gives of aesthetics show that he is
concerned with the arts and with beauty as one of their main
attributes, but he still uses the old term liberal arts, and he
considers them as forms of knowledge.[245] The question whether
Baumgarten really gave a theory of all the fine arts, or merely a
poetics and rhetoric with a new name, has been debated but
can be answered easily. In his earlier work, in which he first
coined the term aesthetic, Baumgarten was exclusively concerned

---

ophicae de nonnullis ad poema pertinentibus (1735). B. Poppe, *Alexander
Gottlieb Baumgarten* (thes. Münster, Borna-Leipzig, 1907), who publishes
from a Berlin manuscript the text of Baumgarten's course on Aesthetics,
delivered in German, probably in 1750–51 (65 ff.). Georg Friedrich Meier,
Abbildung eines Kunstrichters (Halle, 1745). Id., *Anfangsgründe aller schönen
Wissenschaften*, 2nd ed. (Halle, 1754–59; first ed., 1748–50). Thomas Abbt,
Alexander Gottlieb Baumgartens Leben und Character (Halle, 1765). Georg
Friedrich Meier, *Alexander Gottlieb Baumgartens Leben* (Halle, 1763). Th.
W. Dannel, *Gottsched und seine Zeit*, 2nd ed. (Leipzig, 1855), 211 ff. Carolus
Raabe, *A. G. Baumgarten aestheticae in disciplinae formam redactae parens
et auctor* (thes. Rostock, 1873). Hans Georg Meyer, *Leibniz und Baumgarten
als Begründer der deutschen Aesthetik* (thes. Halle, 1874). Johannes Schmidt,
Leibnitz und Baumgarten, ein Beitrag zur Geschichte der deutschen Aesthetik
(thes. Halle, 1875). E. Prieger, *Anregung und metaphysische Grundlagen der
Aesthetik von Alexander Gottlieb Baumgarten* (thes. Berlin, 1875). M. Boja-
nowski, *Literarische Einflüsse bei der Entstehung von Baumgartens Aesthetik*
(thes. Breslau, 1910). Ernst Bergmann, *Die Begründung der deutschen Aesthetik durch Alexander Gottlieb Baumgarten und Georg Friedrich Meier*
(Leipzig, 1911). A. Riemann, *Die Aesthetik Alexander Gottlieb Baumgartens*
(Halle, 1928). Hans Georg Peters, *Die Aesthetik Alexander Gottlieb Baumgartens und ihre Beziehungen zum Ethischen* (Berlin, 1934).

[244] "Sint ergo νοητά cognoscenda facultate superiore objectum logices;
αἰσθητά, ἐπιστήμης αἰσθητικῆς sive aestheticae" (*Meditationes, ed. Croce, #116,
p. 44). The distinction is reminiscent of the one made by Speusippus and
related by Sextus Empiricus (*Adversus Mathematicos* VII, 145: Σπεύσιππος δὲ
ἐπεὶ τῶν πραγμάτων τὰ μὲν αἰσθητὰ τὰ δέ νοητά, τῶν μὲν νοητῶν κριτήριον
ἔλεξεν εἶναι τὸν ἐπιστημονικὸν λόγον, τῶν δὲ αἰσθητῶν τὴν ἐπιστημονικὴν αἴσθησιν).
Aesthetica, #1 (ed. Croce, p. 55): "Aesthetica theoria liberalium artium,
gnoseologia inferior, ars pulcre cogitandi . . . est scientia cognitionis
sensitivae."

[245] *Ibid*. See also #3 (p. 55) where the usefulness of aesthetics is thus described: "bona principia studiis omnibus artibusque liberalibus sub-
ministrare."

with poetics and rhetoric.[246] In his later, unfinished work, to which he gave the title *Aesthetica,* Baumgarten states in his introduction that he intends to give a theory of all the arts,[247] and actually makes occasional references to the visual arts and to music.[248] This impression is confirmed by the text of Baumgarten's lectures published only recently,[249] and by the writings of his pupil Meier.[250] On the other hand, it is quite obvious, and was noted by contemporary critics, that Baumgarten and Meier develop their actual theories only in terms of poetry and eloquence and take nearly all their examples from literature.[251] Baumgarten is the founder of aesthetics in so far as he first conceived a general theory of the arts as a separate philosophical discipline with a distinctive and well-defined place in the system of philosophy. He failed to develop his doctrine with reference to the arts other than poetry and eloquence, or even to propose a systematic list and division of these other arts. In this latter respect, he was preceded and surpassed by the French

[246] In the *Meditationes* (#117, ed. Croce, p. 44–45), *rhetorica generalis* and *poetica generalis* are introduced as the main parts of *aesthetica.*

[247] In #5 (ed. Croce, p. 56) he raises this objection against himself: "eam eandem esse cum rhetorica et poetica," and answers thus: "latius patent . . . complectitur has cum aliis artibus ac inter se communia."

[248] #4, p. 55 (musicus); #69, p. 76 (musici); #780, p. 461–62 (music, painting); #83, p. 82–83 (music, the dance, painting, where painting is also assigned to one of the Muses.)

[249] "Die ganze Geschichte der Maler, Bildhäuer, Musikverständigen, Dichter, Redner wird hierher gehören, denn alle diese verschiedenen Teile haben ihre allgemeinen Regeln in der Aesthetik" (ed. Poppe, 67). "Er [Aristotle] teilt seine Philosophie, wodurch die menschliche Kenntnis verbessert werden soll, in die Logik, Rhetorik und Poetik, die er zuerst als Wissenschaften vorträgt. Die Einteilung selbst ist unvollkommen. Wenn ich sinnlich schön denken will, warum soll ich bloss in Prosa oder in Versen denken? Wo bleibt der Maler und Musikus?" (69). ". . . da die Erklärung auch auf Musik und Malerei gehen muss" (71). ". . . alle Künste, die man schön nennt, werden von der Kenntnis dieser Regeln den grössten Nutzen haben" (75). "Die Aesthetik geht viel weiter als die Rhetorik und Poetik" (76). These lectures are also notable for the more frequent references to French and English authors.

[250] "So lange es Maler, Dichter, Redner, Musickverständige und so weiter gegeben hat, so lange ist Aesthetik ausgeübt worden" (*Anfangsgründe,* vol. I, #6, p. 10). He then lists as liberal arts and "fine sciences": "die Redekunst, die Dichtkunst, die Music, die Historie, die Malerkunst und wie sie alle heissen" (#16, p. 27). Cf. p. 21; 581, etc.

[251] "Wir werden in den Exempeln immer bei der Rede stehen bleiben . . ." (Baumgarten, ed. Poppe, #20, p. 82). "Ob nun gleich die Aesthetik auch die Gründe zu den übrigen schönen Künsten enthält, so werde ich doch meine allermeisten Exempel aus den Rednern und Dichtern nehmen" (Meier, *Anfangsgründe,* pt. 1, #19, p. 31).

writers, especially by Batteux and the Encyclopaedists, whereas the latter failed to develop a theory of the arts as part of a philosophical system. It was the result of German thought and criticism during the second half of the eighteenth century that the more concrete French conception of the fine arts was utilized in a philosophical theory of aesthetics for which Baumgarten had formulated the general scope and program.

When Meier tried to answer the critics of his teacher Baumgarten, he stated that Baumgarten and himself had spoken only about literature, since they did not know enough about the other arts.[252] The broadening scope of German aesthetics after Baumgarten, which we must now try to trace, was due not only to the influence of Batteux, of the Encyclopaedists, and of other French and English writers but also to the increasing interest taken by writers, philosophers, and the lay public in the visual arts and in music. Winckelmann's studies of classical art are important for the history of our problem for the enthusiasm which he stimulated among his German readers for ancient sculpture and architecture, but not for any opinion he may have expressed on the relation between the visual arts and literature.[253] Lessing's *Laokoon* (1766), too, has a notable importance, not only for its particular theories on matters of poetry and of the visual arts, but also for the very attention given to the latter by one of the most brilliant and most respected German writers of the time.[254] Yet the place of the *Laokoon* in the history of our problem has been misjudged. To say that the *Laokoon* put an end to the age-old tradition of the parallel between painting and poetry that had its ultimate roots in classical antiquity and found its greatest development in the writers of the sixteenth, seventeenth, and early eighteenth century, and thus freed poetry from the emphasis on description, is to give only one side of the

---

[252] "Und wenn philosophische Köpfe, welche die Music, Malerkunst, und alle übrige schöne Künste ausser der Rede und Dichtkunst, verstehen, die aesthetischen Grundsätze auf dieselben werden anwenden: so wird der einzige Einwurf, der bisher mit Artigkeit und vielem Scheine wider die Aesthetic gemacht worden, gänzlich wegfallen" (*Alexander Gottlieb Baumgartens Leben*, 43 f.).

[253] G. Baumecker, *Winckelmann in seinen Dresdner Schriften* (Berlin, 1933). Henry C. Hatfield, *Winckelmann and his German Critics* (New York, 1943).

[254] Lessings *Laokoon*, ed H. Bluemner, 2nd ed. (Berlin, 1880). *Laokoon*, ed. William G. Howard (New York, 1910). Howard, "Ut pictura poesis," *l. c.* R. Lee, "Ut pictura poesis," *l. c.* Croce, *Estetica*, *l. c.*, 505 ff. K. Leysaht, *Dubos et Lessing* (thes. Rostock, Greifswald, 1874).

picture. It is to forget that the parallel between painting and poetry was one of the most important elements that preceded the formation of the modern system of the fine arts, though it had lost this function as a link between two different arts by the time of Lessing, when the more comprehensive system of the fine arts had been firmly established. In so far as Lessing paid no attention to the broader system of the fine arts, especially to music, his *Laokoon* constituted a detour or a dead end in terms of the development leading to a comprehensive system of the fine arts. It is significant that the *Laokoon* was criticized for this very reason by two prominent contemporary critics, and that Lessing in the posthumous notes for the second part of the work gave some consideration to this criticism, though we have no evidence that he actually planned to extend his analysis to music and to a coherent system of the arts.[255]

The greatest contributions to the history of our problem in the interval between Baumgarten and Kant came from Mendelssohn, Sulzer, and Herder. Mendelssohn, who was well acquainted with French and English writings on the subject, demanded in a famous article that the fine arts (painting, sculpture, music, the dance, and architecture) and belles lettres (poetry and eloquence) should be reduced to some common principle better than imitation,[256] and thus was the first among the Germans to formulate a system of the fine arts. Shortly afterwards, in a book review, he criticized Baumgarten and Meier for not having carried out the program of their new science, aesthetics. They wrote as if they had been thinking exclusively in terms of poetry and literature, whereas aesthetic principles should be formulated in such a way as to apply to the visual arts and to music as well.[257] In his annotations to Lessing's *Laokoon*, published long

[255] Several passages in Lessing's notes for a continuation of the *Laokoon* refer to music and the dance and to their connection with poetry (ed. Bluemner, *l. c.*, 397; 434 ff.).

[256] Moses Mendelssohn, "Betrachtungen über die Quellen und die Verbindungen der schönen Künste und Wissenschaften" (1757), in his *Gesammelte Schriften (Jubiläumsausgabe)* 1 (Berlin, 1929), 165–90. Cf. G. Kannegiesser, *Die Stellung Moses Mendelssohn's in der Geschichte der Aesthetik* (thes. Marburg, 1868). Ludwig Goldstein, *Moses Mendelssohn und die deutsche Aesthetik* (Königsberg, 1904).

[257] Review of G. F. Meier's *Auszug aus den Anfangsgründen aller schönen Künste und Wissenschaften* (1758), in his *Gesammelte Schriften*, vol. 4, pt. 1, Leipzig, 1844, 313–18. "Allein uns dünkt, dass der Erfinder dieser Wissenschaft der Welt nicht alles geliefert habe, was seine Erklärung des Wortes Aesthetik

after his death, Mendelssohn persistently criticizes Lessing for not giving any consideration to music and to the system of the arts as a whole;[258] we have seen how Lessing, in the fragmentary notes for a continuation of the *Laokoon*, tried to meet this criticism. Mendelssohn also formulated a doctrine of the three faculties of the soul corresponding to the three basic realms of goodness, truth and beauty, thus continuing the work of the Scottish philosophers.[259] He did not work out an explicit theory of aesthetics, but under the impact of French and English

verspricht. Die Aesthetik soll eigentlich die Wissenschaft der schönen Erkenntnis überhaupt, die Theorie aller schönen Wissenschaften und Künste enthalten; alle Erklärungen und Lehrsätze müssen daher so allgemein seyn, dass sie ohne Zwang auf jede schöne Kunst insbesondere angewendet werden können. Wenn man z.B. in der allgemeinen Aesthetik erklärt, was erhaben sei, so muss sich die Erklärung sowohl auf die erhabene Schreibart, als auf den erhabenen Contour in der Malerei und Bildhauergunst, auf die erhabenen Gänge in der Musik, und auf die erhabene Bauart anwenden lassen . . ." (314). Baumgarten and Meier give the impression, "als wenn man bei der ganzen Einrichtung des Werks bloss die schönen Wissenschaften, d.i. die Poesie und Beredsamkeit, zum Augenmerk gehabt hätte . . ." (315). "Eine Aesthetik aber, deren Grundsätze bloss entweder a priori geschlossen, oder bloss von der Poesie und Beredsamkeit abstrahirt worden sind, muss in Ansehung dessen, was sie hätte werden können, wenn man die Geheimnisse aller Künste zu Rathe gezogen hätte, ziemlich eingeschränkt und unfruchtbar seyn. Dass aber die Baumgarten'sche Aesthetik wirklich diese eingeschränkte Gränzen hat, ist gar nicht zu läugnen" (316).

[258] *Laokoon*, ed. Bluemner, *l. c.*, 359; 376; 384; 386 (Dichtkunst, Malerey, Baukunst, Musik, Tanzkunst, Farbenkunst, Bildhauerkunst). Mendelssohn, *Gesammelte Schriften* 2 (1931), 231 ff.

[259] "Man pflegt gemeiniglich das Vermögen der Seele in Erkenntnissvermögen und Begehrungsvermögen einzutheilen, und die Empfindung der Lust und Unlust schon mit zum Begehrungsvermögen zu rechnen. Allein mich dünkt, zwischen dem Erkennen und Begehren liege das Billigen, der Beyfall, das Wohlgefallen der Seele, welches noch eigentlich von Begierde weit entfernt ist. Wir betrachten die Schönheit der Natur und der Kunst, ohne die mindeste Regung von Begierde, mit Vergnügen und Wohlgefallen. . . . Ich werde es in der Folge Billigungsvermögen nennen, um es dadurch sowohl von der Erkenntniss der Wahrheit, als von dem Verlangen nach dem Guten abzusondern" (*Morgenstunden*, ch. 7 (Frankfurt-Leipzig, 1786), 118–19 (first ed. 1785). See also the fragment of 1776, *Gesammelte Schriften*, vol. 4, pt. 1 (1844), 122 f. L. Goldstein, *l. c.*, 228–29. A similar distinction appears already in an article of 1763 ("Abhandlung über die Evidenz in den metaphysischen Wissenschaften," *Gesammelte Schriften* 2 (1931), 325; cf. K. F. Wize, *Friedrich Justus Riedel und seine Aesthetik* [Berlin, 1907], 19–20): "Das Gewissen ist eine Fertigkeit, das Gute vom Bösen, und der Wahrheitssinn, eine Fertigkeit, das Wahre vom Falschen durch undeutliche Schlüsse richtig zu unterscheiden. Sie sind in ihrem Bezirke das, was der Geschmack in dem Gebiete des Schönen und Hässlichen ist."

authors he indicated the direction in which German aesthetics was to develop from Baumgarten to Kant.

What Mendelssohn had merely set forth in a general outline and program, the Swiss thinker Sulzer, who was well versed in French literature but spent the greater part of his life in Northern Germany, was able to develop in a more systematic and elaborate fashion. Sulzer began his literary activity with a few short philosophical articles in which his interest for aesthetics was already apparent, and in which he also leaned toward the conception of an aesthetic faculty of the soul separate from the intellectual and moral faculties,[260] a conception in whose development Mendelssohn and the philosopher Tetens also took their part.[261] Some years later, Sulzer was prompted by the example of Lacombe's little dictionary of the fine arts to compile a similar dictionary in German on a much larger scale.[262] This General Theory of the Fine Arts, which appeared in several editions, has been disparaged on account of its pedantic arrangement, but it is clear,

[260] Johann Georg Sulzer, *Vermischte Philosophische Schriften*, 2 vols. (Leipzig, 1773–81). In an article of 1751–52, he distinguishes between *Sinne, Herz, Einbildungskraft* and *Verstand*, relating the second faculty to moral sentiments and the third to the fine arts (vol. 1, pp. 24 and 43; see also vol. 2, p. 113; A. Palme, *J. G. Sulzers Psychologie und die Anfänge der Dreivermögenslehre*, Berlin, 1905). Otherwise, the distinction of the three faculties of the soul does not yet appear clearly or consistently in these early writings, but only in his *Allgemeine Theorie der Schönen Künste*, 2nd ed., II (Leipzig, 1778), 240, art. *Geschmak*). "Der Geschmak ist im Grunde nichts anders, als das Vermögen das Schöne zu empfinden, so wie die Vernunft das Vermögen ist, das Wahre, Vollkommene und Richtige zu erkennen; das sittliche Gefühl, die Fähigkeit, das Gute zu fühlen" (cf. Wize, *l. c.*, 24).

[261] Johann Nicolas Tetens, *Philosophische Versuche ueber die menschliche Natur und ihre Entwickelung*, 2 vols. (Leipzig, 1777). He distinguishes three faculties: *Verstand, Wille*, and *Empfindsamkeit* or *Gefühl* (I, 619 ff.). Cf. J. Lorsch, *Die Lehre vom Gefühl bei Johann Nicolas Tetens* (thes. Giessen, 1906). W. Uebele, *Johann Nicolaus Tetens* (Berlin, 1911), 113 ff. A. Seidel, *Tetens' Einfluss auf die kritische Philosophie Kants* (thes. Leipzig, Würzburg, 1932), 17 ff.

[262] *Allgemeine Theorie der Schönen Künste*, 2nd ed., 4 vols. (Leipzig, 1777–78; first ed., 1771–74, new ed., 4 vols., 1792–99). For his dependence on Lacombe, see his *Vermischte Philosophische Schriften* 2, p. 70 ("In diesem Jahre [1756] erhielt er durch ein französisches Werkchen, das Dictionaire des beaux Arts vom Herrn La Combe, nach des Herrn Hirzel Erzählung, die Veanlassung zu seiner allgemeinen Theorie, oder vielmehr zu seinem Wörterbuch der schönen Künste"). Johannes Leo, *Zur Entstehungsgeschichte der "Allgemeinen Theorie der Schönen Künste" J. G. Sulzers* (thes. Heidelberg, Berlin, 1906), 31 ff. and 57. See also: Ludwig M. Heym, *Darstellung und Kritik der aesthetischen Ansichten Johann Georg Sulzers* (thes. Leipzig, 1894). Karl J. Gross, *Sulzers Allgemeine Theorie der Schönen Künste* (thes. Berlin, 1905).

comprehensive and learned, and had a considerable importance in its time. The work covers all the fine arts, not only poetry and eloquence, but also music and the visual arts, and thus represents the first attempt to carry out on a large scale the program formulated by Baumgarten and Mendelssohn. Thanks to its wide diffusion, Sulzer's work went a long way to acquaint the German public with the idea that all the fine arts are related and connected with each other. Sulzer's influence extended also to France, for when the great *Encyclopédie* was published in Switzerland in a second edition, many additions were based on his General Theory, including the article on aesthetics and the section on the Fine Arts.[263]

In the decades after 1760, the interest in the new field of aesthetics spread rapidly in Germany. Courses on aesthetics were offered at a number of universities after the example set by Baumgarten and Meier, and new tracts and textbooks, partly based on these courses, appeared almost every year.[264] These authors have been listed, but their individual contributions remain to be investigated. The influence of the great *Encyclopédie* is attested by a curious engraving printed in Weimar in 1769 and attached to a famous copy of the *Encyclopédie*.[265] It represents the tree of the arts and sciences as given in the text of D'Alembert's *Discours*, putting the visual arts, poetry and music with their subdivisions under the general branch of imagination. Among the minor aesthetic writers of this period, Riedel has attracted some scholarly attention, probably because he was the target of Herder's criticism.[266] In his treatise on aesthetics, based on university lectures, Riedel gives a full discussion

[263] See above, note 200–201.

[264] Sulzer, *Allgemeine Theorie*, new ed., I (1792), 47 ff. I. Koller, *Entwurf zur Geschichte und Literatur der Aesthetik . . .* (Regensburg, 1799). E. Bergmann, *Geschichte der Aesthetik und Kunstphilosophie* (Leipzig, 1914), 15 ff.

[265] This copy was exhibited in New York by the Services Culturels de l'Ambassade de France in January, 1951. The engraving has the title: "Essai d'une distribution généalogique des sciences et des arts principaux. Selon l'explication détaillée du Système des connoissances humaines dans le Discours préliminaire des Éditeurs de l'encyclopédie, publiée par M. Diderot et M. d'Alembert, à Paris en 1751. Reduit en cette forme pour découvrir la connaissance humaine d'un coup d'oeuil. Par Chrétien Guillaume Roth. À Weimar, 1769." The section corresponding to imagination contains poetry, painting, engraving, sculpture, music and architecture with their respective subdivisions.

[266] Friedrich Just Riedel, *Theorie der schönen Künste und Wissenschaften* (Jena, 1767). Kasimir Filip Wize, *Friedrich Justus Riedel und seine Aesthetik* (thes. Leipzig, Berlin, 1907). Richard Wilhelm, *Friedrich Justus Riedel und die Aesthetik der Aufklärung* (Heidelberg, 1933).

of all the fine arts, and also sets out with a general division of philosophical subjects into the True, the Good and the Beautiful.[267]

It is interesting to note the reaction to this aesthetic literature of the leaders of the younger generation, especially of Goethe and of Herder. Goethe in his early years published a review of Sulzer which was quite unfavorable. Noticing the French background of Sulzer's conception, Goethe ridicules the grouping together of all the arts which are so different from each other in their aims and means of expression, a system which reminds him of the old-fashioned system of the seven liberal arts, and adds that this system may be useful to the amateur but certainly not to the artist.[268] This reaction shows that the system of the fine arts was something novel and not yet firmly established, and that Goethe, just like Lessing, did not take an active part in developing the notion that was to become generally accepted. Toward the very end of his life, in the *Wanderjahre*, Goethe shows that he had by then accepted the system of the fine arts, for he assigns

[267] "Der Mensch hat dreyerley Endzwecke, die seiner geistigen Vollkommenheit untergeordnet sind, das Wahre, das Gute und das Schöne; für jeden hat ihm die Natur eine besondere Grundkraft verliehen: für das Wahre den sensus communis, für das Gute das Gewissen, und für das Schöne den Geschmack . . . " (*Theorie*, 6). Johann Georg Heinrich Feder in his *Oratio de sensu interno* (1768) quotes Riedel and lists: veritas, pulchritudo (bonitas idealis), honestas (pulchritudo moralis); sensus veri sensusque communis, sensus pulchri sive gustus, sensus iusti et honesti seu conscientiae moralis (Wize, 21–22). On Platner's unpublished aesthetics of 1777–78, see E. Bergmann, *Ernst Platner und die Kunstphilosophie des 18. Jahrhunderts* (Leipzig, 1913).

[268] J. W. Goethe, review of Sulzer's *Die schönen Künste in ihrem Ursprung* (1772). "Sehr bequem in's Französische zu übersetzen, könnte auch wohl aus dem Französischen übersetzt sein." "Hier sei für niemanden nichts gethan als für den Schüler, der Elemente sucht, und für den ganz leichten Dilettanten nach der Mode." "Dar sind sie denn (the fine arts) . . . wieder alle beisammen, verwandt oder nicht. Was steht im Lexikon nicht alles hintereinander? Was lässt sich durch solche Philosophie nicht verbinden? Mahlerei und Tanzkunst, Beredsamkeit und Baukunst, Dichtkunst und Bildhauerei, alle aus einem Loche, durch das magische Licht eines philosophischen Lämpchens auf die weisse Wand gezaubert. . . ." "Dass einer, der ziemlich schlecht räsonnierte, sich einfallen liess, gewisse Beschäftigungen und Freuden der Menschen, die bei ungenialischen gezwungenen Nachahmern Arbeit und Mühseligkeit wurden, liessen sich unter die Rubrik Künste, schöne Künste, klassifizieren zum Behuf theoretischer Gaukelei, das ist denn der Bequemlichkeit wegen Leitfaden geblieben zur Philosophie darüber, da sie doch nicht verwandter sind, als septem artes liberales der alten Pfaffenschulen." "Denn um den Künstler allein ist es zu thun. . . . Am gaffenden Publikum, ob das, wenn's ausgegafft hat, sich Rechenschaft geben kann, warum es gaffte oder nicht, was liegt an dem?" (*Goethes Werke, Sophien-Ausgabe*, 37 [Weimar, 1896], 206 ff.).

a place to each of them in his pedagogical province.[269] Yet his awareness of the older meaning of art is apparent when in a group of aphorisms originally appended to the same work he defines art as knowledge and concludes that poetry, being based on genius, should not be called an art.[270]

Herder, on the other hand, took an active part in the development of the system of the fine arts and used the weight of his literary authority to have it generally accepted. In an early but important critical work (*Kritische Waelder, 1769*), he dedicates the entire first section to a critique of Lessing's *Laokoon*. Lessing shows merely, he argues, what poetry is not, by comparing it with painting. In order to see what its essence is, we should compare it with all its sister arts, such as music, the dance, and eloquence. Quoting Aristotle and Harris, Herder stresses the comparison between poetry and music, and concludes that this problem would require another Lessing.[271] In the fourth section, he quotes Mendelssohn as well as the more important English and French authors, and presents his own system of the fine arts, which includes all the essential elements though it differs from previous authors in some detail.[272] Herder's later contributions to aesthetics are beyond the scope of this paper.

I should like to conclude this survey with Kant, since he was the first major philosopher who included aesthetics and the

[269] *Wilhelm Meisters Wanderjahre*, Bk II, ch. 8 (*Sophien-Ausgabe*, 25 [1895], 1 ff.) where music, poetry and the visual arts are treated as sisters. See also Bk. III, ch. 12 (*ibid.*, 216 ff.).

[270] "Künste und Wissenschaften erreicht man durch Denken, Poesie nicht: denn diese ist Eingebung. . . . Man sollte sie weder Kunst noch Wissenschaft nennen, sondern Genius" (*Aus Makariens Archiv*, in *Goethe's Werke, Vollständige Ausgabe letzter Hand*, vol. 23 [Stuttgart-Tübingen, 1829], 277–78. *Sophien-Ausgabe*, 42, pt. 2 [1907], 200).

[271] "Hr.L. zeigt, was die Dichtkunst gegen Malerei gehalten nicht sey; um aber zu sehen, was sie denn an sich in ihrem ganzen Wesen völlig sey, müsste sie mit allen schwesterlichen Künsten und Wissenschaften, z.E. Musik, Tanzkunst und Redekunst verglichen, und philosophisch unterschieden werden" (*Herders Sämmtliche Werke*, ed. B. Suphan, 3 [Berlin, 1878], 133). "Hier (on the distinction of poetry and music) wünsche ich der Dichtkunst noch einen Lessing" (161). David Bloch, *Herder als Aesthetiker* (thes. Würzburg, Berlin, 1896). Guenther Jacoby, *Herders und Kants Aesthetik* (Leipzig, 1907). Kurt May, *Lessings und Herders kunsttheoretische Gedanken in ihrem Zusammenhang* (Berlin, 1923). Emilie Lutz, *Herders Anschauungen vom Wesen des Dichters und der Dichtkunst in der ersten Hälfte seines Schaffens* (thes. Erlangen, 1925). Wolgang Nufer, *Herders Ideen zur Verbindung von Poesie, Musik und Tanz* (Berlin, 1929).

[272] *Sämmtliche Werke*, ed. Suphan, 4 (1878), 3 ff. Malcolm H. Dewey, *Herder's Relation to the Aesthetic Theory of his Time* (thes. Chicago, 1920).

philosophical theory of the arts as an integral part of his system. Kant's interest in aesthetic problems appears already in his early writing on the beautiful and sublime, which was influenced in its general conception by Burke.[273] He also had occasion to discuss aesthetic problems in several of his courses. Notes based on these courses extant in manuscript have not been published, but have been utilized by a student of Kant's aesthetics. It appears that Kant cited in these lectures many authors he does not mention in his published works, and that he was thoroughly familiar with most of the French, English and German writers on aesthetics.[274] At the time when he published the *Critique of Pure Reason*, he still used the term aesthetics in a sense different from the common one, and explains in an interesting footnote, that he does not follow Baumgarten's terminology since he does not believe in the possibility of a philosophical theory of the arts.[275] In the following years, however, he changed his view, and in his *Critique of Judgment*, which constitutes the third and concluding part of his philosophical system, the larger of its two major divisions is dedicated to aesthetics, whereas the other section deals with teleology. The system of the three *Critiques* as presented in this last volume is based on a threefold division of the faculties of the mind, which adds the faculty of judgment, aesthetic and teleological, to pure and practical reason. Aesthetics, as the philosophical theory of beauty and the arts, acquires equal standing with the theory of truth (metaphysics or epistemology) and the theory of goodness (ethics).[276]

[273] *Beobachtungen über das Gefühl des Schönen und Erhabenen* (1764), in *Immanuel Kants Werke*, ed. E. Cassirer, 2 (Berlin, 1922), 243–300.

[274] O. Schlapp, *Kants Lehre vom Genie und die Entstehung der Kritik der Urteilskraft* (Göttingen, 1901).

[275] "Die Deutschen sind die einzigen, welche sich jetzt des Worts Aesthetik bedienen, um dadurch das zu bezeichnen, was andere Kritik des Geschmacks heissen. Es liegt hier eine verfehlte Hoffnung zum Grunde, die der vortreffliche Analyst Baumgarten fasste, die kritische Beurtheilung des Schönen unter Vernunftprincipien zu bringen, und die Regeln derselben zur Wissenschaft zu erheben. Allein diese Bemühung ist vergeblich." He then states that he will use the term aesthetics for the critical analysis of perception (*Kritik der Reinen Vernunft, Transszendentale Aesthetik* #1, ed. Cassirer, 3 [1923], 56 f.).

[276] *Kritik der Urteilskraft* (1790). Juergen Bona Meyer, *Kant's Psychologie* (Berlin, 1870). Carl Theodor Michaelis, *Zur Entstehung von Kants Kritik der Urteilskraft* (progr. Berlin, 1892). A. Apitzsch, *Die psychologischen Voraussetzungen der Erkenntniskritik Kants* (thes. Halle, 1897). A. Bäumler, *Kants Kritik der Urteilskraft* (Halle, 1923). W. Bröcker, *Kants Kritik der aesthetischen Urteilskraft* (thes. Marburg, 1928). H. W. Cassirer, *A Commentary on Kant's Critique of Judgment* (London, 1938), 97 ff.

In the tradition of systematic philosophy this was an important innovation, for neither Descartes nor Spinoza nor Leibniz nor any of their ancient or medieval predecessors had found a separate or independent place in their system for the theory of the arts and of beauty, though they had expressed occasional opinions on these subjects. If Kant took this decisive step after some hesitation, he was obviously influenced by the example of Baumgarten and by the rich French, English, and German literature on the arts his century had produced, with which he was well acquainted. In his critique of aesthetic judgment, Kant discusses also the concepts of the sublime and of natural beauty, but his major emphasis is on beauty in the arts, and he discusses many concepts and principles common to all the arts. In section 51 he also gives a division of the fine arts: speaking arts (poetry, eloquence); plastic arts (sculpture, architecture, painting, and gardening); arts of the beautiful play of sentiments (music, and the art of color).[277] This scheme contains a few ephemeral details that were not retained by Kant's successors.[278] However, since Kant aesthetics has occupied a permanent place among the major philosophical disciplines, and the core of the system of the fine arts fixed in the eighteenth century has been generally accepted as a matter of course by most later writers on the subject, except for variations of detail or of explanation.

IX

We shall not attempt to discuss the later history of our problem after Kant, but shall rather draw a few general conclusions from the development so far as we have been able to follow it. The grouping together of the visual arts with poetry and music into the system of the fine arts with which we are familiar did not exist in classical antiquity, in the Middle Ages or in the Renaissance. However, the ancients contributed to the modern system the comparison between poetry and painting, and the theory of imitation that established a kind of link be-

[277] #51. "Von der Einteilung der schönen Künste" (ed. Cassirer, 5 [1922], 395 ff.).
[278] The *Farbenkunst*, mentioned also by Herder and by Mendelssohn in his notes on Lessing's *Laokoon* (ed. Bluemner, 386) refers to the color piano invented by Abbé Castel, which was expected to produce a new art of color combinations. Cf. Bluemner, *l. c.*, 596–97. L. Goldstein, *Moses Mendelssohn*, 92–93. The commentators of the *Critique of Judgment* (J. H. v. Kirchmann, J. C. Meredith, J. H. Bernard, H. W. Cassirer) fail to explain this detail.

tween painting and sculpture, poetry and music. The Renaissance
brought about the emancipation of the three major visual arts
from the crafts, it multiplied the comparisons between the various
arts, especially between painting and poetry, and it laid the
ground for an amateur interest in the different arts that tended
to bring them together from the point of view of the reader,
spectator and listener rather than of the artist. The seventeenth
century witnessed the emancipation of the natural sciences and
thus prepared the way for a clearer separation between the arts
and the sciences. Only the early eighteenth century, especially in
England and France, produced elaborate treatises written by and
for amateurs in which the various fine arts were grouped together,
compared with each other and combined in a systematic scheme
based on common principles. The second half of the century,
especially in Germany, took the additional step of incorporating
the comparative and theoretical treatment of the fine arts as a
separate discipline into the system of philosophy. The modern
system of the fine arts is thus pre-romantic in its origin, although
all romantic as well as later aesthetics takes this system as its
necessary basis.

It is not easy to indicate the causes for the genesis of the system in the eighteenth century. The rise of painting and of music
since the Renaissance, not so much in their actual achievements
as in their prestige and appeal, the rise of literary and art criticism, and above all the rise of an amateur public to which art
collections and exhibitions, concerts as well as opera and theatre
performances were addressed, must be considered as important
factors. The fact that the affinity between the various fine arts
is more plausible to the amateur, who feels a comparable kind
of enjoyment, than to the artist himself, who is concerned with
the peculiar aims and techniques of his art, is obvious in itself
and is confirmed by Goethe's reaction. The origin of modern
aesthetics in amateur criticism would go a long way to explain
why works of art have until recently been analyzed by aestheticians from the point of view of the spectator, reader and listener
rather than of the producing artist.

The development we have been trying to understand also
provides an interesting object lesson for the historian of philosophy and of ideas in general. We are accustomed to the process
by which notions first formulated by great and influential thinkers
are gradually diffused among secondary writers and finally become the common property of the general public. Such seems to

have been the development of aesthetics from Kant to the present. Its history before Kant is of a very different kind. The basic questions and conceptions underlying modern aesthetics seem to have originated quite apart from the traditions of systematic philosophy or from the writings of important original authors. They had their inconspicuous beginnings in secondary authors, now almost forgotten though influential in their own time, and perhaps in the discussions and conversations of educated laymen reflected in their writings. These notions had a tendency to fluctuate and to grow slowly, but only after they had crystallized into a pattern that seemed generally plausible did they find acceptance among the greater authors and the systematic philosophers. Baumgarten's aesthetics was but a program, and Kant's aesthetics the philosophical elaboration of a body of ideas that had had almost a century of informal and non-philosophical growth. If the absence of the scheme of the fine arts before the eighteenth century and its fluctuations in that century have escaped the attention of most historians, this merely proves how thoroughly and irresistibly plausible the scheme has become to modern thinkers and writers.

Another observation seems to impose itself as a result of our study. The various arts are certainly as old as human civilization, but the manner in which we are accustomed to group them and to assign them a place in our scheme of life and of culture is comparatively recent. This fact is not as strange as may appear on the surface. In the course of history, the various arts change not only their content and style, but also their relations to each other, and their place in the general system of culture, as do religion, philosophy or science. Our familiar system of the five fine arts did not merely originate in the eighteenth century, but it also reflects the particular cultural and social conditions of that time. If we consider other times and places, the status of the various arts, their associations and their subdivisions appear very different. There were important periods in cultural history when the novel, instrumental music, or canvas painting did not exist or have any importance. On the other hand, the sonnet and the epic poem, stained glass and mosaic, fresco painting and book illumination, vase painting and tapestry, bas relief and pottery have all been "major" arts at various times and in a way they no longer are now. Gardening has lost its standing as a fine art since the eighteenth century. On the other hand, the moving picture is a good example of how new techniques may lead to modes of artistic expression for which the aestheticians of the eighteenth and nineteenth century had no place in their systems. The branches of the arts all have their rise and decline, and even their birth and death, and the distinction between "major" arts and their subdivisions is arbitrary and subject to change. There is hardly any ground but critical tradition or philosophical preference for deciding whether engraving is a separate art (as most of the eighteenth-century authors believed) or a subdivision of painting, or whether poetry and prose, dramatic and epic poetry, instrumental and vocal music are separate arts or subdivisions of one major art.

As a result of such changes, both in modern artistic production and in the study of other phases of cultural history, the traditional system of the fine arts begins to show signs of disintegration. Since the latter part of the nineteenth century, painting has moved further away from literature than at any previous time, whereas music has at times moved closer to it, and the crafts have taken great strides to recover their earlier standing as decorative arts. A greater awareness of the different techniques of the various arts has produced dissatisfaction among artists and critics with the conventions of an aesthetic system based on a situation no longer existing, an aesthetics that is trying in vain to hide the fact that its underlying system of the fine arts is hardly more than a postulate and that most of its theories are abstracted from particular arts, usually poetry, and more or less inapplicable to the others. The excesses of aestheticism have led to a healthy reaction which is yet far from universal. The tendency among some contemporary philosophers to consider Art and the aesthetic realm as a pervasive aspect of human experience rather than as the specific domain of the conventional fine arts also goes a long way to weaken the latter notion in its traditional form.[279] All these ideas are still fluid and ill defined, and it is difficult to see how far they will go in modifying or undermining the traditional status of the fine arts and of aesthetics. In any case, these contemporary changes may help to open our eyes to an understanding of the historical origins and limitations of the modern system of the fine arts. Conversely, such historical understanding might help to free us from certain conventional preconceptions and to clarify our ideas on the present status and future prospects of the arts and of aesthetics.

[279] John Dewey, *Art as Experience* (New York, 1934).

X

Rhetoric in Medieval
and Renaissance Culture*

THE TERM *rhetoric*, long despised, has become once more respectable in recent years, but its precise meaning, whether applied to antiquity or the Middle Ages, to the Renaissance or modern times, seems far from clear. Rhetoric has been defined or understood as the art of persuasion, of the probable argument, of prose style and composition, or of literary criticism; and each of these different, though related, definitions has come to the fore in a different period or context. The art of composition has at times emphasized the speech, orally delivered and heard by an audience, and at other times the letter or the essay, silently written and read. Apart from its own intrinsic meaning, rhetoric has had changing associations with other subjects and disciplines that have significantly affected the way rhetoric itself has been understood: rhetoric has been associated with grammar and logic, with poetics, with ethics and politics, to mention only some of its more significant connections. The place of rhetoric in the classifications of the arts and sciences and in the curriculum of schools and universities has also undergone many changes over the centuries. I cannot hope to do justice to all these aspects in a brief essay but shall concentrate on Renaissance rhetoric, its medieval antecedents and its place in Renaissance culture. I shall also attempt to indicate some of the many problems that in my opinion need further investigation.[1]

* Reprinted by permission from *Renaissance Eloquence*, ed. James J. Murphy (Berkeley, University of California, 1983), pp. 1–19.
[1] For supplementary information and bibliography, see Paul Oskar Kristeller, *Renaissance Thought and Its Sources* (New York, 1979), esp. the section titled "Philosophy and Rhetoric from Antiquity to the Renaissance" (pp. 211–59, 312–27). Also see George A. Kennedy, *Classical Rhetoric and Its Christian and Secular Tra-*

It has been stated more than once in recent years that rhetoric holds the key to Renaissance humanism and to Renaissance thought and civilization in general.[2] Because of an article I published well over thirty years ago, I am often counted among the supporters of that view.[3] I may be forgiven if I use this occasion to clarify my position on this important subject. I do believe that Renaissance rhetoric is much more important, in need of much more study and attention, than most scholars of the past few generations were willing to admit. However, I never meant to say and I still do not believe that Renaissance humanism, let alone Renaissance thought and learning in general, is reducible to rhetoric alone. Rhetoric was only one of the five *studia humanitatis* cultivated by the humanists, whose work as grammarians (and classical scholars), historians, poets, and moralists cannot be derived from their rhetoric, although this work may often seem inseparable from it. Moreover, as I have kept insisting (although many historians have refused to listen to me), humanism constitutes only one aspect, though an important one, of Renaissance thought and learning; furthermore, the history of theology and jurisprudence, of the sciences and of philosophy, in the Renaissance is not limited to Renaissance humanism, let alone to humanist rhetoric, though this history was in many ways affected by rhetoric.[4] I should like to keep these distinctions firmly in mind when I try to discuss, without exaggerated claims, some aspects of Renaissance rhetoric and its impact on the other areas of humanist and nonhumanist learning in the Renaissance. As usual, I shall focus my attention on Italy since I am acquainted with the history of that country and since in the history of

---

dition from Ancient to Modern Times (Chapel Hill, N.C., 1980), and Ernesto Grassi, Rhetoric as Philosophy: The Humanist Tradition (University Park, Pa., 1980).

[2] Hannah H. Gray, "Renaissance Humanism: The Pursuit of Eloquence," Journal of the History of Ideas 24 (1963), 497–514; Jerrold E. Seigel, Rhetoric and Philosophy in Renaissance Humanism (Princeton, N.J., 1968); Hannah H. Gray, "History and Rhetoric in Quattrocento Humanism" (Ph.D. diss., Harvard University, 1956); and Nancy Struever, The Language of History in the Renaissance (Princeton, N.J., 1970).

[3] Paul Oskar Kristeller, "Humanism and Scholasticism in the Renaissance," Byzantion 17 (1944–1945), 346–74, rpt. in his Studies in Renaissance Thought and Letters (Rome, 1956), pp. 553–83, and in his Renaissance Thought (New York, 1961), pp. 92–119, 153–66.

[4] Paul Oskar Kristeller, "The Impact of Early Italian Humanism on Thought and Learning," in Developments in the Early Renaissance, ed. Bernard S. Levy (Albany, N.Y., 1972), pp. 120–57.

rhetoric, during the Renaissance as well as during the Middle Ages, the leading role of the Italians is generally recognized.

For a proper understanding of Renaissance rhetoric, as of many other Renaissance developments, we must begin with the ancient sources. For general rhetorical theory, Cicero's *De inventione* and the pseudo-Ciceronian *Rhetorica ad Herennium* were the basic sources throughout the Middle Ages. As standard textbooks, they generated numerous commentaries, especially during the twelfth and fourteenth centuries, and these commentaries have received much attention in recent years.[5] The fifteenth century added the more mature rhetorical works of Cicero, especially the *Orator* and the *De oratore*. They exercised a very great influence on Renaissance literature and thought, an influence that has been noticed in many instances but should be explored in a more comprehensive way. Quintilian, whose work had been known to the Middle Ages only in a truncated version, was also rediscovered in his complete text and widely studied in the fifteenth century. His influence has not yet been fully explored, but it is significant that Lorenzo Valla attributed to him a greater authority than even to Cicero himself.[6] Cicero's orations, some of them long known and others newly discovered, were widely admired and imitated; in fact, the newly found introductions of Asconius to some of Cicero's orations inspired Antonio Loschi and Sicco Polenton to try doing the same for some of Cicero's other speeches. For the composition of letters, those of Seneca and Pliny and, above all, the newly found letters of Cicero provided the chief sources and models.

The expansion of ancient source material during the Renaissance, in rhetoric as in other areas, becomes much more apparent when we pass from the Latin to the Greek sources. The Greek rhetorical sources known to the later Middle Ages were very few indeed: Aristotle's *Rhetoric* and the pseudo-Aristotelian *Rhetorica ad Alexandrum*, the treatise *De elocutione* attributed to Demetrius of Phaleron, and the speech *Ad Demonicum* attributed to Isocrates. The last three texts had a very limited circulation;[7] and since Aristotle's

[5] John O. Ward, "*Artificiosa Eloquentia in the Middle Ages*" (Ph.D. diss., University of Toronto, 1972); Ward, "From Antiquity to the Renaissance: Glosses and Commentaries on Cicero's *Rhetorica*," in *Medieval Eloquence*, ed. James J. Murphy (Berkeley and Los Angeles, 1978), pp. 25–67.

[6] Lorenzo Valla, *Dialecticae Disputationes* 2.20–23; 3.15 (*Opera omnia*, Basel, 1540, rpt. Turin, 1962), pp. 719–31 and 752–56; *Repastinatio Dialectice et Philosophie*, ed. G. Zippel, Padua, 1982, vol. I, pp. 244–275; 334–345; II, pp. 501–524; 578–587.

[7] Paul Oskar Kristeller, *Renaissance Thought and Its Sources*, p. 322, notes 50–53.

Rhetoric, though widely known, was studied by the scholastic philosophers as a part of moral philosophy,[8] but not by the professional rhetoricians, we may safely assert that medieval rhetoric was not affected by any Greek theories or writings except through the intermediary of the ancient Roman rhetorical writers.

During the Renaissance, the entire body of Greek rhetorical literature became accessible to the West, both through the original texts and through Latin and vernacular translations. The humanists came to know not only Hermogenes and Aphthonius, who had dominated the rhetorical tradition among the Greeks in late antiquity and during the Byzantine period, but also pseudo-Longinus, Dionysius of Halicarnassus, Menander, and other minor Greek writers on rhetoric.[9] The *Rhetorica ad Alexandrum* and pseudo-Demetrius became more widely known,[10] and, most important, Aristotle's *Rhetoric* was recognized and widely studied as a work on rhetoric rather than on moral philosophy. When Aldus Manutius published the first Greek edition of Aristotle's collected writings (1495–1498), he significantly omitted the *Rhetoric* (and the newly acquired *Poetics*) and included it instead in the corpus of Greek rhetorical writings he published a few years later (1508).[11] In the sixteenth century, Aristotle's *Rhetoric* had many commentators, all of them humanists and rhetoricians rather than moral philosophers.[12] This whole body of commentaries on the *Rhetoric* should be examined for its contributions to rhetorical and literary theory with the same careful attention that the commentaries on the *Poetics*, some of them by the same authors, have recently received.[13] To the theoretical treatises on rhetoric we must add the actual products of ancient Greek oratory. The Attic orators, especially Lysias, Isocra-

[8] The medieval commentators of Aristotle's *Rhetoric* include Giles of Rome, Guido Vernani, John Buridan, and John of Jandun.

[9] For Hermogenes, see Annabel M. Patterson, *Hermogenes in the Renaissance* (Princeton, N.J., 1970); and John Monfasani, *George of Trebizond* (Leyden, 1976).

[10] For Demetrius, see Bernard B. Weinberg in *Catalogus Translationum et Commentariorum*, vol. 2, eds. Paul Oskar Kristeller and F. Edward Cranz (Washington, 1971), pp. 27–41. Latin translation of the *Rhetoric ad Alexandrum* by Francesco Filelfo was widely diffused.

[11] Lorenzo Minio-Paluello, "Attività filosofico-editoriale dell' umanesimo," in his *Opuscula* (Amsterdam, 1972), pp. 483–500.

[12] The sixteenth-century commentators on the *Rhetoric* include Daniel Barbarus, Petrus Victorius, M. A. Maioragius, Franciscus Portus, and Antonius Riccobonus. See F. Edward Cranz, *A Bibliography of Aristotle Editions 1501–1600* (Baden-Baden, 1971), pp. 162–63.

[13] Bernard B. Weinberg, *A History of Literary Criticism in the Italian Renaissance*, 2 vols. (Chicago, 1961).

tes, and Demosthenes, were all translated, read, and imitated; so were some of the later Greek orators, such as Dio of Prusa, Aristides, and Libanius. We may add the speeches found in the works of Thucydides, Dio Cassius, and other historians, speeches sometimes translated and studied as separate pieces.[14] The vast body of Greek letters, most of them late and apocryphal, and hence neglected by modern classical scholars, were enormously popular among Renaissance humanists. The letters attributed to Phalaris, Diogenes the Cynic, Brutus, and others were among the most widely read works of ancient literature, to judge from the number of extant translations, manuscripts, and editions; the letters of Libanius, moreover, were nearly doubled in the fifteenth century by the Latin forgeries of Francesco Zambeccari.[15] Much of this material is still awaiting further bibliographical scrutiny, textual study, and exploration of its influence. The somewhat rough and hasty outline I have been trying to draw will eventually have to be corrected and completed accordingly.

Independent treatises on general rhetorical theory were produced rather rarely, if at all, during the later Middle Ages, and their number was still quite limited during the fifteenth century. This fact may be due to the authority of the ancient textbooks, which humanist teachers were more inclined to gloss than to rival. The early examples known to me include several popular treatises by Gasparino Barzizza and Agostino Dati, a systematic and very influential treatise by George of Trebisond,[16] a work by Guillaume Fichet that attempts to introduce an interesting new terminology,[17] treatises by Giorgio Valla[18] and Philippus Callimachus,[19] and probably a few more. In the sixteenth century, the literature of rhetorical textbooks was quite extensive, but even the bibliographical description of this literature is far from complete.[20] To my knowledge

[14] For manuscripts containing them, see Paul Oskar Kristeller, *Iter Italicum*, 4 vols. (Leiden, 1963–1989), and other catalogues.

[15] R. Foerster, *Francesco Zambeccari und die Briefe des Libanios* (Stuttgart, 1878).

[16] Monfasani, *George of Trebizond.*

[17] Paul Oskar Kristeller, "An Unknown Humanist Sermon on St. Stephen by Guillaume Fichet," in *Mélanges Eugène Tisserant*, Studi e Testi 236 (Vatican City, 1964), pp. 459–97.

[18] Gray, "History and Rhetoric."

[19] Philippus Callimachus, *Rhetorica*, ed. K. F. Kumaniecki (Warsaw, 1950).

[20] Donald L. Clark, *Rhetoric and Poetry in the Renaissance* (New York, 1922, rpt. 1963); Charles S. Baldwin, *Renaissance Literary Theory and Practice* (New York, 1939, rpt. 1959); O. B. Hardison, *The Enduring Monument* (Chapel Hill, N.C.,

there are no detailed studies of Renaissance rhetoric comparable to those dealing with the treatises on grammar, logic, or poetics of the same period.[21] I may be imperfectly informed, but I should not know where to turn for precise information on the individual doctrines of specific authors and on their differences from the doctrines of other ancient or contemporary writers. The same is true for the history of individual concepts, topics, or theories, with the possible exception of the figures of speech, which have interested the historians of poetics and of literary criticism. Peter Ramus's reform of logic also involved rhetoric, since he changed the traditional division between the two disciplines, and thus his rhetoric, or rather that of his friend Talaeus, has received attention from recent historians of Ramism.[22]

One specific problem that was important to theorists and writers in the Renaissance, as it had been in late antiquity, was the imitation of ancient models. The humanists all agreed that some kind of imitation was necessary, but there was a lively discussion between the Ciceronians, who recognized only Cicero as their model in prose style and vocabulary, and their opponents, who advocated a more eclectic and in a way a more original prose style. The debate, which found Barzizza, Paolo Cortesi, and Bembo, among the Ciceronians, and Lorenzo Valla, Poliziano, Gianfrancesco Pico, Erasmus, and Lipsius, among their opponents, has been the subject of some scholarly discussion.[23] But it deserves further detailed and comprehensive investigation, as do many other specific concepts and doctrines of rhetorical theory. We may add that the extensive medieval and Renaissance literature on memory, which has recently received

---

1962); W. S. Howell, *Logic and Rhetoric in England, 1500–1700* (Princeton, 1956); F. Buisson, *Répertoire des ouvrages pédagogiques du XVIe siècle* (Paris, 1886, rpt. Nieuwkoop, 1962); and Susan Gallick, "The Continuity of the Rhetorical Tradition: Manuscript to Incunabulum," *Manuscripta* 23 (1979), 31–47.

[21] G. Arthur Padley, *Grammatical Theory in Western Europe 1500–1700* (Cambridge, 1976); W. Risse, *Bibliographia Logica* (Hildesheim, 1965); and Weinberg, *A History of Literary Criticism*.

[22] Walter J. Ong, *Ramus: Method and the Decay of Dialogue* (Cambridge, Mass., 1958) and *Ramus and Talon Inventory* (Cambridge, Mass., 1958); Neal W. Gilbert, *Ranaissance Concepts of Method* (New York, 1960).

[23] R. Sabbadini, *Storia del Ciceronianismo* (Turin, 1885); Izora Scott, *Controversies Over the Imitation of Cicero as a Model for Style* (New York, 1910); *Le Epistole "De imitatione" di Giovanfrancesco Pico della Mirandola e di Pietro Bembo*, ed. G. Santangelo (Florence, 1954); Erasmus, *Il Ciceroniano*, ed. A. Gambaro (Brescia, 1965); Erasmus, *Dialogus Ciceronianus*, ed. P. Mesnard, in *Opera omnia*, ordo 1, tomus 2 (Amsterdam, 1971), pp. 581–710.

some scholarly attention,[24] may be considered to some extent a part of rhetoric. For according to ancient theory, memory was one of the five parts of rhetoric, and some of the earliest treatises on memory are actually commentaries on the section of the *Rhetorica ad Herennium* that deals with memory.[25] New fields of investigation have often originated as monographic treatments of what used to be one chapter in a broader traditional discipline.

Much more extensive than the literature on rhetoric in general or on specific topics such as imitation seems to be the literature on the various genres of prose literature, and especially that on the letter, the speech, and the sermon; this fact may be considered a medieval inheritance. The treatise, the dialogue, and the essay, though much cultivated by Renaissance humanists and other writers, did not receive much theoretical attention, though there were a few sixteenth-century treatises on the dialogue.[26]

The theory of the letter as a main genre of prose literature appears rather late and seldom in classical rhetoric, whereas it came to acquire a central place in the Middle Ages.[27] The composition of documents and letters was a legal and administrative necessity throughout the early Middle Ages. In an age of widespread illiteracy, the popes and other church officials, the princes, and later the cities depended on the services of notaries, chancellors, and secretaries properly trained for their tasks. This training was based on formularies and collections of models and probably also on oral instruction. The earliest extant treatise that deals specifically with the art of writing letters, or *ars dictandi*, was composed by Alberic of Montecassino in the late eleventh century. It appears from his work

[24] Helga Hajdu, *Das Mnemotechnische Schrifttum des Mittelalters* (Vienna, 1936); and Frances Yates, *The Art of Memory* (London and Chicago, 1966).

[25] *Ad Herennium* III. 16, 24–28, 40.

[26] Rudolf Hirzel, *Der Dialog*, 2 vols. (Leipzig, 1895, rpt. Hildesheim, 1963).

[27] James J. Murphy, *Rhetoric in the Middle Ages* (Berkeley and Los Angeles, 1974); Murphy, *Medieval Rhetoric: A Select Bibliography* (Toronto, 1971); Giles Constable, *Letters and Letter-Collections* (Turnhout, 1976); Kristeller, *Renaissance Thought and Its Sources*, pp. 317–19; Kennedy, *Classical Rhetoric*, pp. 173–94; H. M. Schaller, "Dichtungslehren und Briefsteller," in *Die Renaissance der Wissenschaften im 12. Jahrhundert*, ed. P. Weimar (Zurich and Munich, 1981), pp. 249–71; id., "Ars dictaminis, ars dictandi," in *Lexikon des Mittelalters* (Zurich and Munich, 1980), coll. 1034–39. It appears that the ancient Egyptians treated the letter as a literary genre. There are formal letters from the third millennium B.C. and manuals of letter-writing and collections of form letters from the second millennium. See G. Posener, "Les malheurs d'un prêtre égyptien," *Journal des Savants* (1979), pp. 199–205, esp. pp. 199–201.

and from the introductions of later works that the *ars dictandi* originated as a part of the larger field of rhetoric and eventually received special treatment because of the great practical and professional importance of its subject. The twelfth century produced a very large number of works on *dictamen* that included both theoretical treatises and collections of form letters, many of them anonymous. Most of the authors who have been identified for the early twelfth century were active at Bologna, whereas later in the same century Orléans and other French centers became important and developed a style of their own. During the thirteenth century, the school of Bologna retained its importance and produced some of its most famous masters, such as Boncompagno, Guido Faba, Giovanni di Bonandrea, and Lawrence of Aquileia. Their influence, as we may see from the diffusion of their manuscripts, extended throughout Europe; during the fourteenth century, if not earlier, we find a number of *dictatores* active outside Italy, not only in France but also in England, Spain, Germany, and Bohemia. In Italy, we also find treatises on *dictamen* from the fourteenth and even from the fifteenth century, but characteristically their authors are known as prehumanists and humanists.[28] This fact would seem to confirm my theory, first presented in 1945, that there is a direct link between the medieval *ars dictaminis* and humanist epistolography (I never meant to suggest that humanism as a whole was derived from the *ars dictaminis*).

In their formal aspects, not in their style or specific content, or even in their titles, the humanist treatises on letter-writing and their collections of form letters are the direct continuation of the medieval *artes dictandi*; moreover, in their activity as chancellors and secretaries, with attendant administrative and political functions, the humanists were the direct successors of the medieval *dictatores*, who included such figures as Petrus de Vineis and Rolandino Passeggeri. Many humanists, including Salutati, had notarial training or even the rudiments of legal training. The humanist *ars epistolandi*, which took the place of the medieval *ars dictandi*, inherited certain features from it, such as the emphasis on and the separate treatment of the address (*salutatio*) and the introduction (*exordium*), the

[28] Paul Oskar Kristeller, "Un 'ars dictaminis' di Giovanni del Virgilio," *Italia Medioevale e Umanistica* 4, 1961, 181–200. Dictamen treatises by Francesco da Buti and Dominicus Bandinus appear in several manuscripts. Also see Paul F. Gehl, "Vat. Ottobonianus Lat. 1854: Apropos of Catalogue Notices and the History of Grammatical Pedagogy," *Revue d'Histoire des Textes* 8 (1978), 303–7 (on Alberic of Montecassino).

theory of punctuation and that of the parts of the letter. The humanists rejected the medieval doctrine of the *cursus* and returned in theory and practice to the ancient theory of the metrical *clausula* known from Cicero. Above all, they cultivated a different style and followed different models, especially Cicero and their own humanist predecessors. Erasmus's and Vives's treatises on letter-writing have attracted some recent attention, but Mario Filelfo's large collection of form letters has been largely ignored. For the other treatises and model collections of the fifteenth and sixteenth centuries, even the bibliographical spadework remains to be done.[29]

Much more numerous than the treatises and collections of form letters are the extant collections of actual letters, public or private, original or edited. The vast body of extant material has thus far defied any attempt to achieve bibliographical control or a comprehensive study and interpretation based on the actual sources. Some of the state letters of Salutati were published in the eighteenth century,[30] but the state letters of Bruni and other prominent humanist chancellors are awaiting scholarly attention in the archives not only of Florence but also of other Italian and northern centers.[31] Historians, mainly interested in political events, have often been satisfied with calendars and regests. The humanist influence on the chanceries affected the style of handwriting, which has received some re-

[29] Giles Constable, *Letters and Letter-Collections*; Cecil H. Clough, "The Cult of Antiquity: Letters and Letter Collections," in *Cultural Aspects of the Italian Renaissance*, ed. Cecil H. Clough (Manchester and New York, 1976), pp. 33–67; Alois Gerlo, "The *Opus de conscribendis epistolis* of Erasmus and the Tradition of Ars Epistolica," in *Classical Influences on European Culture A.D. 500–1500*, ed. R. R. Bolgar (Cambridge, 1971), pp. 103–14; Erasmus, *De conscribendis epistolis*, ed. J. C. Margolin, *Opera omnia*, ordo I, tomus 2 (Amsterdam, 1971), pp. 153–579. For the numerous incunabula containing Johannes Marius Philelphus, *Novum Epistolarium*, see Hain 12968–80 and Copinger 4744–45. The first edition (Hain 12968) was printed in Paris, 1481, according to Reichling.

[30] Coluccio Salutati, *Epistolae*, ed. Josephus Rigaccius, 2 vols. (Florence, 1741–1742). See Ronald G. Witt, *Coluccio Salutati and His Public Letters* (Geneva, 1976); Paul M. Kendall and V. Ilardi, *Dispatches with Selected Documents of Milanese Ambassadors in France and Burgundy*, vol. 1 (1450–1460) (Athens, Ohio, 1970); and Lorenzo de' Medici, *Lettere*, ed. N. Rubinstein and R. Fubini, vols. 1–4 (Florence, 1977–81); H. Langkabel, *Die Staatsbriefe Coluccio Salutatis* (Cologne, 1981); Ronald Witt, "Medieval 'Ars Dictaminis' and the beginnings of Humanism," *Renaissance Quarterly* 35, 1982, 1–35.

[31] Peter Herde, "Die Schrift der Florentiner Behoerden in der Fruehrenaissance," *Archiv für Diplomatik* 17 (1971), 301–35; Thomas Frenz, "Das Eindringen humanistischer Schriftformen in die Urkunden und Akten der paepstlichen Kurie im 15. Jahrhundert," *Archiv für Diplomatik* 19 (1973), 287–418, and 20 (1974), 384–506.

cent attention, but above all it influenced the style of composition and the terminology used in addressing popes and princes and in rendering their titles and prerogatives in a humanist Latin that sometimes offended traditional legal or court practice. I once came across a curious episode involving Bartolomeo Scala, whose wording of the credentials for some Florentine ambassadors was challenged by no less a person than Pope Paul II.[32] Now that the text of the credentials has been found, the controversy can be understood and interpreted in greater detail.[33] We actually need a listing of humanist state letters as they are found in archives and libraries, and a study of their style and terminology, especially where it departs from previous practice. A complete edition of these letters is hardly possible and perhaps not even worthwhile, but certainly some well-selected specimens should be edited as a starting point for further study. To illustrate the medieval connection also in this area, I may mention that we have a small group of manuscripts that contain together the state letters of both Petrus de Vineis and Coluccio Salutati, preceded by a letter from a fifteenth-century father to his student son, who was evidently supposed to study and imitate these medieval and humanist letters combined in this single volume.[34]

The private letters of the Renaissance humanists constitute another vast body of uncharted material. They are much more numerous than the comparable letters from the Middle Ages and hardly less extensive than the extant body of state letters from the fifteenth and sixteenth centuries. These private letters, however, have received greater scholarly attention, and a somewhat larger part of them has been printed, both in early and modern editions. In the case of Petrarch, Ficino, and other authors, it has been rightly observed that these letters were usually collected and edited by their authors. This fact can be checked and confirmed when the original letters or copies deriving from the recipient rather than from the sender have been preserved.[35] These private letters are of

[32] Paul Oskar Kristeller, "An Unknown Correspondence of Alessandro Braccesi . . . ," in *Classical Mediaeval and Renaissance Studies in Honor of Berthold Louis Ullman*, ed. Charles Henderson, vol. 2 (Rome, 1964), pp. 311–64, esp. 334–41; Alison Brown, *Bartolomeo Scala* (Princeton, N.J., 1979), pp. 135–92.

[33] I have recently found the text of these credentials in Florence, Biblioteca Nazionale, ms. Pal. 1133, f. 19ᵛ–20ᵛ.

[34] Kristeller, *Studies in Renaissance Thought and Letters*, p. 565, note 28. For one of the mss., Naples V F 37, see Kristeller, *Iter Italicum* 1.420.

[35] Francesco Petrarca, *Le familiari*, ed. V. Rossi and U. Bosco, 4 vols. (Florence, 1933–1942). For the problem, see the studies by Constable and Clough, cited above (note 29), and my article on Braccesi (above, note 32). For Marsilio Ficino,

great interest, not only for their style but also for their content. They are an invaluable record of the life, thought, and scholarship of their authors, and of the literary and political history of their time. We now have good critical editions of some of the letters of Petrarch and Bruni, of the correspondence of Salutati and Guarino, Ermolao Barbaro, Erasmus and other similar editions for Poggio, Filelfo, Ficino, Pico, Poliziano, and others are now being prepared or should be undertaken.[36] When a critical edition is not necessary or feasible, at least critical lists with regests and selected texts should be published. Special attention should also be paid to certain genres of letters of which medieval and humanist theorists were aware, genres that correspond to the permanent needs of human life and society and that are still with us in the twentieth century: letters of sympathy and of congratulation, letters of recommendation, love letters and invectives, and several more.

The second important genre of Renaissance prose literature we have to discuss is the speech or oration. In classical antiquity, the oration was the very center of rhetorical theory and practice, though among the three types of speech—deliberative, judiciary, and epideictic—the last was to become the most important in the later centuries of antiquity. During the Middle Ages, the secular public speech and the political and social institutions supporting it disappeared more or less completely. The statement, often repeated by historians, that medieval rhetoric was exclusively concerned with the letter and with the sermon, since public oratory was

---

see Kristeller, *Supplementum Ficinianum*, 2 vols. (Florence, 1937, rpt. 1973); the same, *Marsilio Ficino and his Work after Five Hundred Years* (Florence, 1987), pp. 18–33.

[36] Petrarca, *Le familiari*. Leonardo Bruni Aretino, *Humanistisch-Philosophische Schriften*, ed. H. Baron (Leipzig and Berlin, 1928). The study of F. P. Luiso on Bruni's letters, printed many decades ago but never published, has now been edited by Lucia Gualdo Rosa (*Studi su l'episiolario di Leonardo Bruni* [Rome, 1980]). Coluccio Salutati, *Epistolario*, ed. F. Novati, 4 vols. in 5 (Rome, 1891–1911). Guarino, *Epistolario*, ed. R. Sabbadini, 3 vols. (Venice, 1915–1919). Ermolao Barbaro, *Epistolae, Orationes et Carmina*, ed. V. Branca, 2 vols. (Florence, 1943). Erasmus, *Opus Epistolarum*, ed. P. S. Allen, 12 vols. (Oxford, 1906–1958). Erasmus, *Correspondence*, tr. R.A.B. Mynors and D.F.S. Thomson, vols. 1–9 (Toronto, 1974–1989). Thomas More, *The Correspondence*, ed. Elizabeth F. Rogers (Princeton, N.J., 1947, rpt. Freeport, N.Y., 1970); Laurentius Valla, *Epistole*, ed. O. Besomi and M. Regoliosi (Padua, 1984); Poggio Bracciolini, *Epistolae*, ed. H. Harth (vols. 1–3, Florence (1984–87). An edition of Francesco Filelfo is being prepared by Vito Giustiniani, and of Ficino by Sebastiano Gentile.

unknown during those centuries, is correct up to a certain point. It is, however, not entirely correct. In Italy, the rise of the city-states and their new institutions brought about a revival of secular, public oratory; and the practice was followed by instruction and theory, and by the composition of treatises and form speeches.[37] The earliest testimonies of the practice of secular oratory date from the twelfth century. From the thirteenth century, well within the accepted area of the medieval period, we have not only testimonies but speeches actually delivered, form speeches, and theoretical treatises. The *ars arengandi*, as it was called, became an accepted counterpart of the *ars dictandi*, and it was taught and treated by the same authors.

As early as the thirteenth century, the secular speech was frequently composed, delivered, and recorded in the vernacular; and the same also is true for the public and private letter, although later. Secular speeches are mentioned by the historians of the thirteenth century, and a few such speeches have actually been preserved. The handbooks written for the podestà, the city official called in from the outside, contain form speeches for funerals and other occasions.[38] Boncompagno's *Rhetorica novissima* is not a handbook of *dictamen*, as widely believed, but a handbook for lawyers that includes models of judiciary speeches.[39] We have collections of vernacular speeches of all kinds from the same century.[40] The epideictic genre tends to prevail, and we encounter some of the same types of speeches that were to dominate the oratory of the humanist period: funeral and wedding speeches, ambassador's speeches, welcoming speeches for entering officials or distinguished visitors, university speeches delivered at the beginning of the academic year or upon the graduation of successful candidates, and several more. As in the case of the *ars dictaminis*, we have before us again a fully developed medieval pattern, and again I am prompted to repeat what I stated many years ago, namely, that there is an express link between the Italian *ars arengandi* of the late Middle Ages and the oratory of the humanists (again, I never meant to claim that hu-

[37] Alfredo Galletti, *L'eloquenza dalle origini al XVI secolo* (Milan, 1904–1938). Kristeller, *Renaissance Thought and Its Sources*, pp. 320–21.

[38] Fritz Hertter, *Die Podestaliteratur Italiens im 12 und 13. Jahrhundert* (Leipzig and Berlin, 1910).

[39] Boncompagnus, *Rhetorica novissima*, ed. A. Gaudenzi in *Bibliotheca Juridica Medii Aevi*, vol. 2 (Bologna, 1892), pp. 249–97.

[40] Guido Faba, *Parlamenti ed epistole*, in A. Gaudenzi, *I suomi, le forme e le parole dell' odierno dialetto della città di Bologna* (Turin, 1889). Matteo dei Libri, *Arringhe*, ed. Eleonora Vincenti (Milan and Naples, 1974).

manism as a whole was derived from the *ars arengandi*). This link consists in the formal and institutional pattern of the speeches, not in their specific literary style or content.

The extant literature of humanist speeches is very large indeed, although perhaps less so than the letters from the same period. It consists not only of individual speeches but also of collections of speeches by one or more authors, and also of collections of speech models, many of them anonymous. The speeches of the humanists have been less studied and edited than their letters and treatises,[41] and they need much more research and investigation. We should have a bibliography of humanist orations, manuscript and printed, by known and anonymous authors, in Latin and in the vernacular, with incipits to permit identification—all arranged by genres as well as by authors and dates. The use of a computer might be considered, and this might attract the necessary funds and manpower. In addition to the genres we have mentioned, which are found in medieval specimens as well, we also have orations to congratulate a new pope, bishop, prince, or other official upon his accession; orations delivered at the opening of church councils or synods, of chapters of a religious order, of public disputations (a genre to which Pico's famous oration belongs); orations by a professor given at the beginning of his course, usually in praise of his subject; orations in praise of Saint Jerome, Saint Augustine, Saint Thomas Aquinas, or others, delivered on specific occasions; orations addressed to newly elected public officials or judges, usually in praise of justice (a practice that seems worth reviving).[42] These speeches follow certain patterns that should be examined. They are not as empty as is usually asserted, for they are often written in good Latin (which can be appreciated by those who know Latin), and they are full of interesting details, biographical and historical as well as literary or scholarly and even philosophical and theological. The speeches of the humanists deserve much further study, not only as

[41] K. Muellner, *Reden und Briefe italienischer Humanisten* (Vienna, 1899).

[42] Charles Trinkaus, "A Humanist's Image of Humanism: The Inaugural Orations of Bartolommeo della Fonte," *Studies in the Renaissance* 7 (1960), 90–147. For orations on Saint Jerome, see Eugene F. Rice, *St. Jerome in the Renaissance* (Baltimore, 1985). For orations on Thomas Aquinas, see Kristeller, *Medieval Aspects of Renaissance Learning*, ed. and tr. Edward P. Mahoney (Durham, N.C., 1974), pp. 60–62. John W. O'Malley, "Some Renaissance Panegyrics of Aquinas," *Renaissance Quarterly* 27 (1974), 174–93. For public speeches in fifteenth-century Florence, see E. Santini, *Firenze e i suoi "Oratori" nel Quattrocento* (Milan, 1922), Santini, "La *Protestatio de iustitia* nella Firenze medicea del sec. XV," *Rinascimento* 10 (1959), 33–106; and John M. Mcmanamon, *Funeral Oratory and the Cultural Ideals of Italian Humanism* (Chapel Hill, 1989).

a distinct literary genre but also in conjunction with the other writings and activities of their authors.

The third genre of rhetorical prose we must briefly consider, besides the letter and the speech, is the sermon. Like the letter, and much more so than the oration, the sermon of the Renaissance was heavily dependent on a strong and prolific medieval tradition. The enormous literature of medieval sermons has but recently become the subject of a critical bibliography.[43] Apparently it was customary during the Carolingian era and beyond to recite in church the homilies of the Church Fathers. The composition of new sermons received a fresh impulse with the Cistercians in the twelfth century and with the mendicant orders in the thirteenth. These sermons were composed in a new pattern that involved a verse from Scripture as a theme, a division of this verse into several parts, and a development of these parts through logical arguments and illustrative stories, or *exempla*. The practice of preaching was accompanied in the twelfth and thirteenth centuries by voluminous treatises on the *ars praedicandi*. They have been carefully listed and studied by modern historians.[44]

Preaching in the fourteenth and fifteenth centuries, in Italy as elsewhere, seems to have followed in many ways the practice and theory of the preceding centuries; some curious examples show that even the newly developing art of secular eloquence followed for a while certain patterns of the sermon.[45] But as we go further along in time, the reverse influence of secular eloquence upon its sacred counterpart becomes more and more apparent. Preachers such as Remigio de'Girolami began to deliver sermons not only on holidays and on saint's days, as had been the prevailing custom, but also on the same occasions that were favored by secular orators, such as funerals, weddings, or public events.[46] The famous preachers of fifteenth-century Italy, from Saint Bernardino of Siena to Roberto da Lecce and Girolamo Savonarola, followed to some extent the medieval pattern, but the wide emotional appeal of their

[43] J. P. Schneyer, *Repertorium der lateinischen Sermones des Mittelalters für die Zeit von 1150–1350*, Beiträge zur Geschichte der Philosophie des Mittelalters 43, 7 vols. (Münster, 1969–1976).

[44] Harry Caplan, *Mediaeval Artes Praedicandi*, 2 vols. (Ithaca, N.Y., 1934–1936); Thomas M. Charland, *Artes Praedicandi* (Ottawa, 1936).

[45] Petrus de Vineis gave a speech in Padua, taking for his theme a verse from Ovid (Rolandinus Patavinus, *Cronica*, book 4, chap. 10, ed. A. Bernardi, Città di Castello, 1905–1908, p. 64). Petrarch took for the speech given at his coronation as a poet in 1341 a theme from Vergil (Attilio Hortis, *Scritti inediti di Francesco Petrarca*, Trieste, 1874, p. 311).

[46] For Remigio Girolami as a public orator, see Galletti, pp. 166–68, 503–6.

sermons must have been due to other factors that to my knowledge have not yet been sufficiently clarified. Alberto da Sarteano, often associated as a preacher with Saint Bernardino, exchanged at the same time elegant letters with contemporary humanists,[47] and we may wonder how these different interests were reflected in his preaching.

The practice of lay preaching, which may be traced back to the early thirteenth century (Albertano da Brescia is the earliest example that comes to mind), and the increasing influence of humanist scholarship and rhetoric, also among the members of the clergy and of the religious orders, may explain the fact that after the middle of the fifteenth century, especially in Italy, sacred eloquence was influenced increasingly by secular, that is, by humanist oratory. The theme from Scripture is supplemented or even replaced by a regular introduction, and the logical argument makes room for a freer flow of religious considerations and admonitions in a style that conforms to the rhetorical taste of the period. Luther and Erasmus felt offended by this style. Modern historians have echoed these feelings and have often dismissed with contempt the entire area of humanist preaching. They do not seem to notice that they are in fact condemning in literature the same phenomenon that they profess to admire in the art of the same period, namely, a combination of religious content and classical form. More recently, at least some aspects of this literature, such as the sermons delivered before the popes on certain holidays, the funeral sermons for some popes of the period, and the sermons in praise of Saint Thomas Aquinas, have received a fair and competent treatment.[48] It is to be hoped that the same kind of study will be applied to other types of humanist sermons delivered in various cities and on diverse occasions. An especially interesting group, mostly in the vernacular, consists of the sermons delivered by young laymen, many of them later humanists, before the religious guilds of fifteenth-century Florence.[49]

[47] S. Albertus a Sarthiano, *Vita et opera*, ed. F. Haroldus (Rome, 1688).

[48] John W. O'Malley, "Preaching for the Popes," in *The Pursuit of Holiness in Late Medieval and Renaissance Religion*, ed. Charles Trinkaus and Heiko A. Oberman (Leiden, 1974), pp. 408–40; John M. McManamon, "The Ideal Renaissance Pope: Funerary Oratory from the Papal Court," *Archivum Historiae Pontificiae* 14 (1976), 9–70; and "Renaissance Preaching: Theory and Practice, A Holy Thursday Sermon of Aurelio Brandolini," *Viator* 10 (1979), 355–79. See also O'Malley. And now see also O'Malley, *Praise and Blame in Renaissance Rome* (Durham, N.C., 1979).

[49] Collections of such sermons are found in Florence, Biblioteca Nazionale, ms. Magl. XXXV 211, and in Biblioteca Riccardiana, ms. 2204. Kristeller, *Studies in Renaissance Thought and Letters*, p. 105, note 17; Kristeller, *Iter Italicum* 1.141–

After this very brief survey of Renaissance rhetoric, its major genres and their medieval antecedents, I should like to mention even more briefly the impact of Renaissance rhetoric on the other areas of Renaissance civilization. The other *studia humanitatis* were of direct concern to the humanists and were cultivated by them along with rhetoric. Grammar, the first of these *studia*, was considered more elementary than rhetoric, but the borderline between grammar and rhetoric was not always clearly marked. Grammar included not only orthography and metrics but also phraseology, which we may consider a part of composition or stylistics and hence of rhetoric. Valla's *Elegantiae* was by the standards of its time a work of advanced grammar, but it also served for many centuries as a handbook of style and good writing. Rhetoric and poetics were considered sisters by the humanists, for they were thought to provide the rules for writing well in prose and in verse, respectively. This view omitted several important dimensions of both rhetoric and poetics that were well understood in classical Greece, but it accorded with ideas that had been widespread in late antiquity and during the Middle Ages. Long before the term *humanista* had been coined, the humanists called themselves poets and orators, as did their contemporaries. Thus there was in the Renaissance, as for some time before, a close parallelism between rhetorical and poetical theory, and a good deal of mutual influence between the two areas. The historians of rhetoric will do well to study and emphasize these influences, especially since the historians of poetics, under the spell of romantic preconceptions, have ignored or deplored them and have not attempted to understand them.

The relation between rhetoric and history is of a different type. As a chief genre of prose literature, historiography ever since classical antiquity was thought to be subject to the rules of rhetorical theory. The Greek and Roman historians were among the chief prose authors read and interpreted in humanist courses. The introduction to a course that dealt with an ancient historian often included a discussion of the goals and merits of historiography.[50] When the theory of the art of history became the subject of separate treatises in the late sixteenth century, it was considered a counterpart of rhetoric and poetics and was in many ways influenced by

---

42, 216–17. A third manuscript, formerly owned by the Principe Ginori Conti (*Iter* 1.228) is now in the Stanford University Library.

[50] Beatrice Reynolds, "Shifting Currents in Historical Criticism," *Journal of the History of Ideas* 14 (1953), 471–92, rpt. in *Renaissance Essays*, ed. Paul Oskar Kristeller and P. P. Wiener (New York, 1968), pp. 115–36.

the older traditions of rhetorical (and poetical) literature.[51] In a more specific way, the impact of rhetoric on historiography is apparent in the speeches, fictitious at least in their wording, that formed an integral part of historical literature in the Renaissance as well as in antiquity and the Middle Ages. These speeches were composed according to the rhetorical taste of the time. This practice of following the taste of the times is not necessarily bad merely because it has been abandoned in this century, and there is no good reason for blaming the humanists any more than their ancient and medieval predecessors. Conversely, the charge often made that the rhetorical, that is, the literary style of the humanists diminishes their trustworthiness as critical historians, does not stand scrutiny any better. We may dislike the style of the humanists, but their literary ambitions do not stand in the way of their critical judgment or their use of historical evidence any more than is the case with ancient or modern historians. They vary among each other in the quality of both their style and their reliability, and each of them has to be examined and judged according to his own merits or demerits. We surely do not wish to imply that a historian must write badly to deserve our confidence.

The last area of humanist learning and literature that we must consider is that of moral philosophy, which according to the humanists' view included ethics and politics as well as several other subjects. The moral literature of the humanists is influenced by their rhetoric and grammar in more than one way. They revive the classical genres of the treatise and the dialogue in accordance with such favorite ancient models as Plato, Cicero, and Plutarch. They like to restate the doctrines found in the works of ancient writers and to cite these writers as authorities in support of their own opinions. *Auctoritas* is in fact an ancient rhetorical category, one by no means peculiar to medieval theology or jurisprudence, as many historians seem to believe. The humanists cultivate in their treatises and dialogues an elegant, classicizing, and often Ciceronian style, avoiding the tight arguments of the scholastic philosophers and also their precise terminology. Thus they often lose in conceptual clarity what they gain in literary elegance. As professional rhetoricians, they attribute the highest value to eloquence and claim that they achieve in their moral treatises a combination of eloquence and wisdom that had escaped their scholastic predecessors. A leading humanist such as Lorenzo Valla even places rhetoric above or in the place of philosophy.[52] The combination of wisdom and eloquence

[51] G. Cotroneo, *I trattati dell' "Ars historica"* (Naples, 1971).

[52] Hanna-Barbara Gerl, *Rhetorik als Philosophie: Lorenzo Valla* (Munich, 1974).

sounds like a very appealing program, but we cannot help feeling that wisdom is often sacrificed to eloquence or understood in a rather trivial sense. Our feeling is confirmed by a Renaissance thinker like Pico, certainly not unaffected by humanist rhetoric, who defends the scholastic philosophers against Ermolao Barbaro because they subordinate form to content, as befits a philosopher concerned with the discovery of truth.[53]

If we pass from the *studia humanitatis* to the other learned disciplines that were taught at the Renaissance universities and rooted in the late medieval tradition, we must note that Renaissance rhetoric had a special and strong, though perhaps only temporary, influence on logic. A number of humanists, from Lorenzo Valla to Ramus and Nizolius, tried to reform logic by subordinating it to rhetoric, and this development, which affected not only Italy and France but also many other countries including early America, has received a good deal of recent scholarly attention.[54] The humanist influence in the other learned disciplines, such as theology and jurisprudence, natural philosophy and metaphysics, mathematics and medicine, is pervasive but less specific. It appears in the use of literary genres such as the dialogue or the monographic treatise as against the commentary and the question, in the use and imitation of classical sources and authorities, and above all in the elegant literary style that avoids the tight argument and often also the precise terminology developed by the scholastics, often from Greek sources, but alien to the ancient Roman authors.[55] In recent studies, interesting attempts have also been made to link the theory and practice of the visual arts and music with classical and humanist rhetoric, but I do not feel competent to pursue this subject further.[56]

Although I have dealt with a broad and complex problem in a rather summary and superficial manner, I hope it has become ap-

See also J. Lindhardt, *Rhetor, Poeta, Historicus: Studien über rhetorische Erkenntniss und Lebensanschauung im italienischen Renaissancehumanismus* (Leiden, 1979) (deals with Salutati).

[53] Quirinus Breen, "Giovanni Pico della Mirandola on the Conflict of Philosophy and Rhetoric," *Journal of the History of Ideas* 13 (1952), 384–426, rpt. in his *Christianity and Humanism*, ed. Nelson Peter Ross (Grand Rapids, Mich., 1968), pp. 1–68.

[54] See above, note 22. Juan Luis Vives, *Against the Pseudodialecticians*, ed. and tr. Rita Guerlac (Dordrecht and Boston, 1979).

[55] For humanism and jurisprudence, D. Maffei, *Gli inizi dell'umanesimo giuridico* (Milan, 1956); G. Kisch, *Humanismus and Jurisprudenz* (Basel, 1955); and Donald R. Kelley, *Foundations of Modern Historical Scholarship* (New York, 1970).

[56] Warren Kirkendale, "Ciceronians versus Aristotelians on the Ricercar as

parent that Renaissance rhetoric, though indebted in many ways to ancient and medieval antecedents, had a physiognomy of its own. It occupied an important place in the civilization of its period, thanks to its own role in theory and practice, in education and literature, but also because of its impact on other areas of humanist learning and on other sectors of learning and civilization that were outside the proper domain of the humanists. Renaissance rhetoric is a large area that is still insufficiently explored by modern scholarship and badly in need of much further investigation. We need a correct and complete listing of the manuscript and printed sources, as far as that is possible, an analysis of their content, and critical editions of the more important texts. We need monographs on the more important writers who should also help us understand the links between their contributions to rhetoric and their other works and activities. We should try to understand, in this area as in others, the differences that distinguish the various stages within the Renaissance and the various countries, regions, and cities that played a role in the general development. Special attention should also be paid to the differences between Latin and vernacular rhetoric in both theory and practice, and to their mutual influence where pertinent. What we ultimately need, but cannot hope to achieve at this time, is a comprehensive history of Renaissance rhetoric that will be based on a detailed study of the sources and that will describe not only the internal history of rhetorical theory and practice but also its impact on all other areas of Renaissance civilization.

Exordium, from Bembo to Bach," *Journal of the American Musicological Society* 32 (1979), 1–44.

Afterword

"Creativity" and "Tradition"*

THE TERM "CREATIVITY" has been much used and misused in recent literary and popular discussion, but it is vague and ill defined, and has poor philosophical and historical credentials. As a professional philosopher I should feel prompted to define such a word or term as creativity, and as a historian I am interested in its history. Although I am not an "ordinary language" philosopher, I am often inclined to start from a definition supplied by a standard dictionary. When I tried to do that in this case, I was greatly surprised to discover that the word "creativity" does not appear in the *Oxford English Dictionary*[1] or in the fifth edition of *Webster's Collegiate Dictionary*.[2] If I were a linguistic analyst, especially of the British school, I should have stopped after I failed to find the word in the first dictionaries I consulted, and concluded my discourse with the remark that since the word does not exist it must be dismissed as meaningless. Fortunately, I am not a linguistic analyst but an intellectual historian, and hence quite willing to admit that ordinary language is subject to continuing change, and that thinkers and writers as well as other people are perfectly free to coin new words and phrases to express new objects and thoughts. It is a relief, however, to find our

* Reprinted by permission from the *Journal of the History of Ideas*, vol. XLIV (1983), pp. 105–113.

[1] Compact edition, 1971.

[2] Springfield, Mass., 1939, based on the second edition of the *New International Dictionary* (1934).

word at least in the *Seventh New Collegiate Dictionary*.[3] Here "creativity" is defined as the ability to create. The definition is satisfactory, but we are led to infer that the word became an accepted part of the standard English vocabulary only between 1934 and 1961. We may even go back a few more years. The great philosopher, Alfred North Whitehead used "creativity" in his *Religion in the Making* (1927) and in his major work, *Process and Reality* (1929), and in view of the great influence of this last work, we may very well conjecture that he either coined the term or at least gave it wide currency.

Whereas the word "creativity" is apparently of recent vintage, it is derived from other words such as "creative" and "to create" that have a much earlier origin and history and that enable us to trace with much greater precision the origin and history of the ideas expressed or implied in these terms. In trying to indicate the main features of this important development, I shall make much use of a recent book by a leading historian of aesthetics, the late Władysław Tatarkiewicz.[4]

The word "to create" and its equivalents and derivatives have been used in Western thought in three different contexts which we might roughly describe as theological, artistic, and broadly human. For most of the history of Western thought, the ability to create was attributed exclusively or primarily to God, and to human makers or artists only in a restricted or metaphorical sense. Only after the latter part of the eighteenth century, that is, with the first stirrings of the Romantic movement, did poets and artists come to be considered as creators *par excellence*, and this notion has run strong through the entire nineteenth century down to the twentieth. A further change occurred in the present century when it has become a widespread belief that the ability to create is not limited to artists or writers but extends to many more, and perhaps to all, areas of human activity and endeavor: we speak of the scientist, of the statesman, and of many others as creative, and I for one should wish to defend the view that the philosopher and the scholar also are or may be creative in the pursuit of their work.

[3] Springfield, Mass., 1972, based on the *Third New International Dictionary* of 1961.

[4] W. Tatarkiewicz, *A History of Six Ideas* (Warsaw and The Hague, 1980), chap. 8, 244–65. See also Milton C. Nahm, "Creativity in Art," *Dictionary of the History of Ideas*, ed. Philip P. Wiener (New York, 1972), I, 577–89, and Nahm, *The Artist as Creator* (Baltimore, 1956). It should be noted that Tatarkiewicz and Nahm use "creativity" as a heading of their recent articles, but that the term does not occur in the sources they quote except for the most recent ones.

Before inquiring into the conceptual problems involved in our understanding of creativity, we need to pursue the history of the terms "to create" and "creative" somewhat further. As always in such investigations, we have to begin with the Greek language and with ancient Greek philosophy which is certainly the ultimate source of our philosophical method and terminology, although we do not deny the fact that later and modern trends of thought have in many ways transformed and outgrown the limits of ancient thought. The Greek language has only a single word for making and creating (poiein), and since the Greek word for poet (poietes), which is still our word, means maker, it is no wonder that the poets were often considered "creative" and inspired. On the other hand, the divine powers that Plato and other later philosophers considered as creators of the world were not thought to have created the world out of nothing, but rather to have given shape to a formless matter that preceded their action, and for this very reason the divine creators or makers were often compared to human artisans, architects, or sculptors. The analogy was sometimes reversed, and the human artist was thought to have shaped his work out of his material just as the divine artisan shaped the universe out of matter. Since for Plato and his Neoplatonic successors the divine artist conveyed form to matter by taking immaterial and intelligible forms for his models, it was sometimes claimed, or at least implied, that the perfect human work of art was also a material copy of some immaterial model to which the artist in his mind had direct access.

When we pass from Greek pagan philosophy to Latin Christian and medieval thought, two noteworthy changes took place. The Latin language, unlike Greek, had two separate words for creating and making, *creare* and *facere*, which suggested a significant difference between the divine and the human maker. Moreover, on the basis of the account of divine creation in the Old Testament, St. Augustine developed the doctrine, followed by all later Christian theologians, that God created the world not out of a preexisting matter but out of nothing. Creation out of nothing was the exclusive prerogative of God, and a human artist who produced a work out of material given to him could not be remotely compared with the divine creator, even less so than in Greek antiquity. The outlook began to change with the Renaissance when the achievement of the artist and the poet began to be more widely admired and when the attribute "divine" was associated with Dante and Michelangelo. But the cases where a poet (let alone an artist) was said to create remained rare and exceptional. I take it that it is in the aftermath of

the theological tradition, though in a naturalistic context and less
rigid sense, that Bergson speaks of "creative evolution" in the world
of living organisms, and that Whitehead uses creativity as the universal principle of cosmic innovation which belongs to God (who
not only precedes the world but also pervades and follows it) and
to all astronomical, biological, and social units within the world (I
hope I correctly understand the thought of this great but obscure
thinker).

The real turning point in Western thinking on what we now call
"creativity" came in the eighteenth century. Poetry, music, and the
visual arts were for the first time grouped together as fine arts[5]
which became the subject of a new separate discipline, aesthetics or
the philosophy of art, and the Romantic movement exalted the artist above all other human beings. For the first time, the term "creative" was applied not only to God but also to the human artist, and
a whole new vocabulary was developed to characterize the artist and
his activity although there were some partial or scattered precedents to be found in ancient and Renaissance thought. The artist
was guided no longer by reason or by rules but by feeling and sentiment, intuition and imagination; he produced what was novel and
original, and at the point of his highest achievement he was a genius. In the nineteenth century, this attitude became pervasive, and
we might note with surprise that an age that found it difficult to
believe that God created the world out of nothing apparently had
no difficulty in believing that the human artist would create his
work out of nothing. It is a part of the broader movement to free
modern man (and woman) completely from all rules, restrictions,
and traditions. In the arts it led in many cases to the disappearance
of traditional forms and contents, and led either to other entirely
new forms and contents or to complete anarchy.

If we wish to add a social factor (as it nowadays seems mandatory
to many people, even where it is quite irrelevant to the problem
under discussion), we may say that the social position of the artist
underwent a profound change after the middle of the eighteenth
century. He gradually lost the patronage of the Church and the
state, of the aristocracy and patriciate that had sustained him for
centuries, and found himself confronted with an anonymous,
amorphous, and frequently uneducated public which he often despised and which he would either flatter with a bad conscience or

[5] P. O. Kristeller, "The Modern System of the Arts," *JHI*, XII (1951), 496–
527; XIII (1953), 17–46; see above, pp. 163–227.

openly defy, claiming that it was the public's duty to approve and support the artist even when it could not understand or appreciate the products of the artist's unbridled self expression. The examples of geniuses unrecognized in their time (something rarley heard of before the nineteenth century) finally gave the public and the critics such a bad conscience that by now almost anything has become acceptable. The artist no longer has to face or to fear any outside criticism, and only if he is serious his self-criticism and that of his friends may suffice to guide him. The excessive cult of the genius was exposed and ridiculed by the late Edgar Zilsel half a century ago in two incisive books,[6] but this telling critique of Neo-romantic excesses has had no lasting effect. Perhaps the concept of genius has been less widely used in recent decades since it is definitely an "elitist" notion, whereas in an egalitarian age such as ours it is claimed and believed that everybody, not only some gifted and talented artists, is original and creative.

Egalitarianism, if not outright envy, is also the source of the more recent tendency, increasingly common during the last few decades, to apply the concepts of originality and creativity to other human activities besides the arts. Any person who is original in his field and who produces something novel has a right to be called creative. The term has been applied especially to scientists and to statesmen and reformers who obviously try to bring about something that is novel, but it is sporadically also extended to technicians, managers, editors, gourmet cooks, and fashion designers. I do not intend to deny the claims of these useful and respectable activities and professions, and merely wish to add the humble plea that not only philosophers and scholars but also humorists and punners should be admitted as stockholders in this flourishing creativity business. If present trends continue, and creativity will take the place of competence and intelligence as an educational and professional standard, we may look forward to methods of measuring and testing creativity, and if the term continues to defy precise definition, we may end up with the profound claim advanced some time ago by the testers of intelligence, namely, that creativity is what is tested by a creativity test.

To approach our problem in a more serious vein, we may start from the definition of creativity as the ability to produce something "novel."[7] The most obvious way in which this ability may be attrib-

[6] Edgar Zilsel, *Die Geniereligion* (Vienna and Leipzig, 1918); *Die Entstehung des Geniebegriffs* (Tuebingen, 1926).

[7] It is amusing to remember that Erasmus in his *Encomium Moriae* introduced Folly as the daughter of Wealth and Novelty (*Neotes*).

uted to a human being is usually not mentioned in recent discussions, although Aristotle often refers to it: the ability to beget another human being. The current discussion of creativity is still largely dominated by the romantic notion of artistic creativity in spite of the recent tendency to apply the term to other areas of human activity. Creativity in this sense is a legitimate subject of psychological inquiry, and although there are evidently great differences in the extent and quality of artistic and other human products, it is quite possible to admit that every human being is creative to a greater or lesser extent, at least potentially. It is also plausible, so far as education is concerned, that creativity may be encouraged and developed mainly by removing such obstacles as timidity, rigidity, or inertia. Yet it definitely cannot be taught, and the occasional tendency to use creativity as an excuse for not teaching anything at all is sheer nonsense.

It is often believed that the test of creativity and originality is the feeling which the artist himself experiences before or in producing his work. This feeling is hard for an external observer to ascertain, and it may even be doubted that the intensity of this subjective feeling corresponds precisely to the originality and novelty, let alone to the artistic quality, of the work of art produced by the artist. There are instances in which artists who spoke with great emphasis of their originality and vocation did not have much to show for their effort, and vice versa, many authors of widely admired works have been rather reticent or humble about their feelings and efforts. We might even say that in the detached judgment of posterity the periods in which critics spoke most loudly about the artist and his creativity were not always those that produced the greatest works of art, and vice versa. It is evidently not very original or creative to speak about originality and creativity (just as the talk about an important subject is not always important[8]), nor does the talk about a thing necessarily produce the thing. Perhaps we are inclined to talk most emphatically about the very things which we should like to have but do not have, at least not to the extent to which we should wish to have them.

The best way to judge the creativity and originality of artists is to examine the novelty and originality of their works and to infer from them the creativity of their authors, just as in the old days the

[8] We are reminded of Galileo's statement that the nobility of a science depends on the certainty of its method and not on the dignity of its subject matter; see *Opere*, Edizione Nazionale, ed. A. Favaro, VI (1896), 237 and VII (1897), 246. For the historical context of this statement, see P. O. Kristeller, *Renaissance Thought and Its Sources* (New York, 1979), 286, n. 76.

perfection of the universe was used as one of the arguments to prove the existence and perfection of its divine creator. A close survey of the large treasures of art, music, and literature that have been preserved for us from many different times and places suggests that irrespective of quality there is not a single work of art that is completely novel or original, and hardly a single product that is altogether unoriginal. What we have are different degrees of novelty and originality, and we are, of course, inclined to give a higher rating to those works and artists which show a higher degree of originality. Even the most original work of art is likely to be a new attempt within a well established genre—a novel, a play, a poem, a building, a painting, a composition for the piano or orchestra—and will have a greater or smaller number of traits in common with other specimens of the same genre. It is likely to retain at least residual traces of the patterns and vocabularies associated with its respective genre. Conversely, a copy of an original work will always be distinct from the model and its other copies, intentionally or not, and if one master makes a copy of the work of another master, Rubens of Titian, Manet of Goya, Van Gogh of Hiroshige, the copy will have its own originality and value without ceasing to be a copy. The same master may paint several works that have the same style or general content or that are outright replicas of the same composition, but each of them is an original work that any gallery will be happy to own since it cannot have all the others at the same time. Their subtle differences will be recognized only when they can be displayed side by side in an exhibition. The interpretation of a work of art also has this double aspect. A musical or theatrical performance is not original in relation to the work of the composer or writer, but it may also be considered original insofar as it transforms the work into another more complete reality and is an interpretation different from other interpretations of the same work. The same is true of a critic or scholar who tries to understand a work of literature or of abstract thought; it is true also of a translator who tries to render a work of literature or of abstract thought in another language and may succeed in giving to it a new and impressive appearance. Even a verbatim quotation of one author by another may show the subtle transformation of an insight from one context to another.

In other words, originality and novelty, if we take them as descriptive terms, are never completely present or absent in any work of art but are always mixed with different degrees of unoriginality and of imitation. If we wish to set up originality as the main criterion of artistic quality and excellence, we must accept the consequence that a higher degree of originality will indicate a higher degree of excellence, unless we wish to reject as "elitism" all degrees of excellence (and of originality) and prefer to recognize even a product of minimum originality as a welcome expression of human creativity. This latter tendency is apparent in the applause that has been given to "action painting" and to the work of children and the insane.

Within the tradition of creativity (I do not hesitate to use this apparently paradoxical phrase) originality, as we have seen, is not only a descriptive term but also a highly praised value. I do not deny that a work of art may owe some of its excellence to its originality, but even if it were granted that originality is a *necessary* condition for artistic excellence (which I think it is not), I should argue very strongly that it is not a *sufficient* condition (a distinction that is all too often forgotten in many current discussions of this and similar problems). Originality as such does not assure the excellence of a work of art, or for that matter, of any human product. In the field of the arts, there are many works that are quite original but not especially good, and there are works of limited originality that attain a high degree of artistic quality. There are other criteria than originality that may be used to judge the excellence of a work of art, and in the critical and philosophical literature on the arts prior to Romanticism, these criteria were often set forth and emphasized: we may mention beauty, form, style, imitation of nature and of previous works of art, or of intelligible essences, good taste, human relevance, emotional power, truthfulness, moral and social consciousness, playfulness, usefulness, entertainment, craftsmanship, and many other features. I cannot now go into the precise meaning or validity of these criteria or into the question of whether and how they may be combined with each other or with originality. Yet I hope it has become apparent that on philosophical and historical grounds we are forced to admit that originality is not the only or even the main factor in determining artistic quality. The matter becomes even worse when we enter the areas of theoretical or moral creativity. In the fields of the sciences, scholarship, and philosophy no original idea is of any worth that does not also claim to be true. Velikowski's theory of worlds in collision may be original, but it is in conflict with the available astronomical, archaeological, and historical evidence, and hence it belongs to the realm of science fiction. Hitler's theory of National Socialism was certainly original, but hardly anybody would take that as an excuse for its violation of moral, legal, and political principles which are widely if not universally recognized.

I also do not think that the artist creates out of nothing. He obviously must have talent, from God or nature or chance, and the amount of talent is unequally, and if you wish, unjustly distributed among human beings. The artist must be trained in those skills and techniques that can be taught and that are pertinent to his craft. He should be exposed to those rules that have been considered useful by his predecessors, without being obliged to follow them blindly and uncritically, and to some of the masterpieces of the recent and distant past from which he may derive a standard of artistic quality, without trying to imitate the details that no longer fit his time and his own character. We do not know exactly how he works, although we have learned from drawings and sketchbooks how a painter arrived at his final work. He will draw on his memory and on the store of his knowledge, and must make an effort and take a risk that cannot be anticipated by planning. Mere intentions are not enough if the completed work does not embody them, and no artist should be judged by his intentions rather than by his actual work. The empty sheet or canvas breeds a *horror vacui*, and not a good idea. I like the story of the Japanese artist who promised a painting to the emperor. When the emperor became impatient, visited the artist in his study, and found no sketches or drawings, he blamed the painter for not having done any work. The painter grew angry, explained that he had been thinking about the work for months, went to his easel and started and completed his painting in a few minutes before the eyes of the emperor. I find this story more plausible than most other things I have heard or read about artistic creativity.

In other words, originality is not the main factor in a work of art, and it should not be the major goal of the artist. His goal should be to do a good piece of work, and if he succeeds, he will also turn out to be original.

In facing now the second part of our topic, tradition (and its relation to creativity), we are confronted with even greater difficulties and complexities. In an obvious sense, tradition does not form a simple contrast with creativity; it is only the advocates of creativity who have set tradition up as a straw man and claim that in their pursuit of novelty they free themselves and their contemporaries from the dead weight of tradition. It is clear that tradition means the preservation of extant ideas and possessions that are considered valuable, but when we talk about tradition it is not clear what the content of this tradition is, and whether there is, even in any given instance, one single tradition, or rather a multiplicity of traditions. Moreover, there have not been, at least in the areas that interest us and in recent times, any vocal or influential defenders of tradition, as there have been of novelty and creativity. When people talk about traditional scholarship or traditional philosophy, they usually do so with a negative and derogatory overtone, and one has to be rather careful and defensive in expressing even a qualified approval of both. The highly respected periodical *Traditio* represents traditional scholarship in the fields of ancient and medieval studies, but it has hardly been noticed by any except specialists of the subject. I must try briefly to clarify and to correct some of the current views on tradition. Since the defenders of creativity have been so much opposed to tradition, the temptation will be great to counter one exaggeration with another and to overemphasize the value of tradition. I shall try to avoid this temptation, to give a qualified defense of tradition, and to maintain that the excellence of works of art and of other human endeavors is usually not due to creativity alone but to a combination of originality and tradition.

We should realize from the beginning that a completely stable or rigid tradition that never admits change is humanly impossible and has never existed. Even those primitive societies that are most traditional and that oddly enough are held up as models by many anthropologists are stable only in a relative sense and subject to more or less subtle changes. The view often assumed by social scientists that human societies are stable by nature and that we must introduce special categories, ideological or otherwise, in order to account for change, strikes me as naive, because it is contradicted by the fact that these societies are made up of individuals that are constantly being born, grow up, engage in various activities, and finally die, to be replaced by others. The problem should be formulated the other way around: change is the general condition of nature, of societies, and even of individuals, and it requires a special effort to preserve continuity and, if you wish, tradition in the midst of change. A human individual does not easily maintain his style and identity from youth to old age when hardly a single part of the body and mind remain the same, and a family, a social group, a tribe, or a nation would constantly change and even disintegrate unless it created special institutions and traditions in order to maintain at least some of its identity. For any young member of a society it is necessary to learn and acquire the knowledge and skills needed for the functioning of that society. This has been known and practiced in all primitive societies, and if a highly complex society such as ours, that believes itself to be very advanced, neglects to teach its young the basic knowledge and skills needed for even a modest role in that society, it prepares its own destruction whatever the high

sounding slogans used to justify or excuse this neglect. A writer has
to know his language and its literature, if not other languages and
literatures, before he can adequately begin to write; he must be familiar with the patterns and rules of the genres he wishes to employ, whether he wants to write novels or plays, poems or essays;
and he must know some of the best specimens of previous literature
in order to emulate their quality if not to imitate their external features. The same is true of the musician, the painter, and other artists, and an analogous rule applies to all areas of human activity. An
architect must also learn the mechanical rules that will prevent his
building from collapsing, and know the practical functions for
which his building is intended, whether it is a home or office building, a factory, a museum, or a church. He may also have original
ideas and express himself, but originality and self-expression will
not excuse him when his building collapses or proves unsuitable for
the purpose for which it was built.

Within each branch of the arts there are also traditions concerning the subject matter as well as the form of the work of art. Greek
tragedy treated the same old myths for generations, and medieval
and Renaissance painting treated the same religious subjects for
centuries, yet we do not think that Euripides in his *Electra* lacks
originality because the theme had been treated by Aeschylus and
Sophocles before him, or that a particular Madonna or Adoration
lacks originality or distinctive merit because the same subjects were
treated by many painters of the same time or other times. The same
is true of landscapes and still lifes that allow of a great variety in
detail and quality among numerous works of similar content. The
artist evidently does not lose his originality when he adopts a theme
previously treated by others, and the fact that the theme is generally known to his public and understood by it provides a challenge
to treat the same subject in a novel way and to concentrate on fine
details and nuances while the rough outline of the theme is given
beforehand and cannot be changed. Variations on a theme are
among the best compositions in music and also in other arts,
whereas the invention of a new plot does not assure excellence or
even originality because in many cases the plot is old and only the
names of the characters have been altered.

However, in stressing the value of tradition in the arts and elsewhere, we must also emphasize that tradition as such is not always
valuable. Within the multiplicity of traditions and traditional elements that have been handed down to us, there are many which are
not valuable, or which have lost their value with changing conditions, and which hence do not deserve to be retained or revived.

The appeal to tradition is valid only for those elements of a tradition which are considered to be valuable. Thus a tradition can be kept alive only by retaining what is valuable in it, by discarding what is bad or antiquated, and by replacing the discarded elements with novel features derived from other sources or from the originality of new carriers of the tradition. I have found this to be the only way to understand and interpret Platonism, one of the most respectable traditions in Western philosophy. However, traditional elements are also important in another way. Ideas, styles, and motifs of the past may lose their appeal in a certain period or climate of opinion, but this must not be final, for they may regain their validity at another time and under different conditions. It is therefore important to preserve in libraries and museums the monuments of past thought and productive activity. They should always be studied by specialists, for antiquarian purposes, if you wish, but they may also regain their life and relevance, as it were, at any time, and what was dead or unknown to one generation may suddenly and unexpectedly become important for the next. I may be permitted to cite the example of the period to which I have devoted much work for many years, the Italian Renaissance. In that period, the remnants of classical civilization, its literature, philosophy, and art, though not completely forgotten during the Middle Ages, suddenly regained an actuality and importance they had not had before, and the study, reinterpretation, and sometimes misinterpretation of classical models led to a period in the arts, literature, the sciences, and philosophy that impresses us, if for any reason, by its productivity and originality. I cite the Renaissance as evidence that creativity is not always stifled by tradition and must not always assert itself by denying the value of all tradition, but may very well combine with a selective use of valuable traditional elements to bring about quite excellent works of art, of literature, and of abstract thought. In the world of the intellect, that is, of the sciences, of philosophy, and of scholarship, new ideas and insights will constantly come forth but will have to be examined and tested for their compatibility with available empirical and rational evidence, whereas in private and public life, all actions, taken with or without precedents, should be tested and judged according to their conformity with valid and accepted principles and standards of ethics, law, and politics. In all these domains any laudable achievement requires originality and talent, but it must also conform to the rules of the game as well as to the standards of the past which we may or may not wish to call "tradition."[9]

[9] I am indebted to Paul Kuntz for suggestions and information.

Index

259